Lecture Notes in Computer Science   11243

Commenced Publication in 1973
Founding and Former Series Editors:
Gerhard Goos, Juris Hartmanis, and Jan van Leeuwen

More information about this series at http://www.springer.com/series/7409

Stefan Göbel · Augusto Garcia-Agundez
Thomas Tregel · Minhua Ma
Jannicke Baalsrud Hauge · Manuel Oliveira
Tim Marsh · Polona Caserman (Eds.)

Serious Games

4th Joint International Conference, JCSG 2018
Darmstadt, Germany, November 7–8, 2018
Proceedings

 Springer

Editors
Stefan Göbel
Technische Universität Darmstadt
Darmstadt, Germany

Augusto Garcia-Agundez
Technische Universität Darmstadt
Darmstadt, Germany

Thomas Tregel
Technische Universität Darmstadt
Darmstadt, Germany

Minhua Ma (iD)
Staffordshire University
Stoke on Trent, UK

Jannicke Baalsrud Hauge (iD)
University of Bremen
Bremen, Germany

Manuel Oliveira
SINTEF Technology and Society
Trondheim, Norway

Tim Marsh
Griffith University
Brisbane, QLD, Australia

Polona Caserman
Technische Universität Darmstadt
Darmstadt, Germany

ISSN 0302-9743   ISSN 1611-3349   (electronic)
Lecture Notes in Computer Science
ISBN 978-3-030-02761-2   ISBN 978-3-030-02762-9   (eBook)
https://doi.org/10.1007/978-3-030-02762-9

Library of Congress Control Number: 2018958465

LNCS Sublibrary: SL3 – Information Systems and Applications, incl. Internet/Web, and HCI

This Springer imprint is published by the registered company Springer Nature Switzerland AG
The registered company address is: Gewerbestrasse 11, 6330 Cham, Switzerland

Preface

The 4th International Joint Conference on Serious Games (JCSG 2018) was held in Darmstadt, Germany, and hosted by the Serious Games group at the Multimedia Communications Lab – KOM – at TU Darmstadt and httc e.V. Since 2015, JCSG has been bringing together the two conferences Serious Games Development and Applications (SGDA) and GameDays International Conference on Serious Games (GameDays Conference), both fully dedicated to serious games. Previous JCSG conferences were held in Huddersfield, UK (2015), Brisbane, Australia (2016) and Valencia, Spain (2017).

Following the tradition of JCSG, the principal aim of JCSG 2018 was to bring together academia and industry in the broad, interdisciplinary field of serious games and to discuss the current trends, grand challenges, and potentials of serious games. The main topics of JCSG 2018 included serious games studies and serious games development covering the game design and the use of particular emerging technologies for serious games. From an application perspective, the focus was set on educational games (game-based learning and teaching) and games for health (personalized exergames, prevention, and rehabilitation).

We received 40 submissions from which 15 were selected as full papers and 12 as short/demo papers. All papers submitted to JCSG 2018 were peer-reviewed on a single-blind basis by three independent reviewers, and several contributions were reviewed by four reviewers. The reviewers' comments were communicated to the authors, who incorporated the recommendations in their revised versions of the manuscripts. The papers were presented in the form of traditional talks and presentations; additionally, some authors brought their latest demos/posters and presented them within the exhibition area of the conference.

During the opening, Stefan Göbel from TU Darmstadt provided an overview of the status quo of serious games and introduced the Serious Games Information Center as a classic information system for serious games, based on the DIN SPEC 91380 Serious Games Metadata Format as standard for the description and retrieval of serious games. André Czauderna from TH Cologne complemented the status quo update with an overview of existing education and qualification programs for serious games/serious games design in Europe and abroad. Remco Polman from Queensland University of Technology in Australia gave a keynote talk about personalized exergames with direct links to physical training and nutrition as well as exergames and E-Sports. Wim van der Vegt, Enkhbold Nyamsuren, and Wim Westera from the Open University of The Netherlands described the European flagship project RAGE (Realizing an Applied Gaming Ecosystem) and gave a practical workshop/tutorial how to build serious games with RAGE software components.

The Steering Committee of JCSG 2018 would like to thank all 48 Program Committee (PC) members for their tremendous work and all the institutions, associations, and companies for supporting the JCSG 2018 conference: Technische Universität

Darmstadt (Multimedia Communications Lab – KOM; Forum for Interdisciplinary Research – FIF; and research area Internet and Digitalization – InDi), httc (Hessian Telemedia Technology Competence Center), digitales hessen (action line for digitization of the state of Hesse), the German Association of Computer Science, the German Chapter of the ACM, game (German game association), Darmstadt Marketing, and Springer.

Further information about JCSG 2018 and the overall conference series is available at http://jointconference-on-seriousgames.org/.

November 2018   Stefan Göbel
Augusto Garcia-Agundez
Thomas Tregel
Minhua Ma
Jannicke Baalsrud Hauge
Manuel Oliveira
Tim Marsh
Polona Caserman

Organization

Conference Chairs

General Chair

Stefan Göbel — TU Darmstadt, Germany

Publication Chairs

Augusto Garcia-Agundez — TU Darmstadt, Germany
Thomas Tregel — TU Darmstadt, Germany

Technical Chair

Polona Caserman — TU Darmstadt, Germany

Steering Committee

Mariano Alcañiz — Universitat Politècnica de València, Spain
Jannicke Baalsrud Hauge — University of Bremen, Germany
Stefan Göbel — TU Darmstadt, Germany
Minhua Ma — Staffordshire University, UK
Tim Marsh — Griffith University, Australia
Manuel Fradinho Oliveira — SINTEF Technology and Society, Norway
Josef Wiemeyer — TU Darmstadt, Germany

Program Committee

Mohamed Abbadi — Università Cà Foscari, Italy
Mariano Alcañiz — Universitat Politècnica de València, Spain
Jannicke Baalsrud Hauge — University of Bremen, Germany
Per Backlund — University of Skövde, Sweden
Tom Baranowski — Baylor College of Medicine, Houston, USA
Michael Brach — University of Münster, Germany
Licia Calvi — Breda University of Applied Sciences, The Netherlands
Maiga Chang — Athabasca University, Canada
Michael Christel — Carnegie Mellon University, USA
Karin Coninx — Hasselt University, Belgium
Owen Conlan — Trinity College Dublin, Ireland
Ann de Smet — Ghent University, Belgium

Ralf Dörner	RheinMain University of Applied Sciences, Germany
Wolfgang Effelsberg	University of Mannheim, Germany
Kai Erenli	University of Applied Sciences Vienna, Austria
Baltasar Fernandez-Manjon	Universidad Complutense de Madrid, Spain
Augusto Garcia-Agundez	TU Darmstadt, Germany
Tom Gedeon	Australian National University, Australia
Stefan Göbel	TU Darmstadt, Germany
Maads Haahr	Trinity College, Dublin, Ireland
Matthias Hemmje	Fernuniversität Hagen, Germany
Peter Henning	PH Weingarten, Germany
Helmut Hlavacs	University of Vienna, Austria
Shamim Hossain	King Saud University, Saudi Arabia
Jun Hu	Eindhoven University of Technology, The Netherlands
Fares Kayali	Vienna University of Technology, Austria
Michael Kickmeier-Rust	PH St. Gallen, Switzerland
Robert Konrad	TU Darmstadt, Germany
Effie Lai-Chong	University of Leicester, UK
Fotis Liarokapis	Masaryk University, Czech Republic
Minhua Eunice Ma	Staffordshire University, UK
Rainer Malaka	University of Bremen, UK
Tim Marsh	Griffith University, Australia
Alke Martens	University of Rostock, Germany
Anna Lisa Martin	Zurich University of the Arts, Switzerland
André Miede	HTW Saar, Germany
Wolfgang Mueller	University of Education Weingarten, Germany
Frank Nack	University of Amsterdam, The Netherlands
Manuel Fradinho Oliveira	SINTEF Technology and Society, Norway
Johanna Pirker	Graz University of Technology, Austria
Alenka Poplin	Iowa State University, USA
Ulrike Spierling	RheinMain University of Applied Sciences, Germany
Alexander Streicher	Fraunhofer IOSB, Karlsruhe, Germany
Heinrich Söbke	Bauhaus University, Germany
Thomas Tregel	TU Darmstadt, Germany
Alf Inge Wang	Norwegian University of Science and Technology, Norway
Josef Wiemeyer	TU Darmstadt, Germany
Kevin Wong	Murdoch University, Australia

Contents

Serious Games for Health

Invited Talks and Workshops

eSport: Friend or Foe?

Remco Polman[1]([✉]), Michael Trotter[1,2], Dylan Poulus[1,2],
and Erika Borkoles[3]

[1] School of Exercise and Nutrition Sciences,
Queensland University of Technology, Brisbane, Australia
remco.polman@qut.edu.au
[2] Queensland University of Technology, eSport Centre, Brisbane, Australia
[3] School of Public Health and Social Work,
Queensland University of Technology, Brisbane, Australia

Abstract. eSport is a growing industry in terms of its players, spectators and economic value and will be included in the 2024 Paris Olympics. Although interest initially in eSport was mainly associated with younger males, eSport has the potential to bring about health behaviour change across the wider population of users. This paper discusses the potential of eSport to influence health outcomes across the lifespan and address some of the major barriers that will help individuals to change their physical activity behaviours. Considering the exponential growth in eSport, it is important for academics and policy makers to recognise and seize the opportunities arising from eSport.

Keywords: eSport · Public health · Behavioural change · Implementation

1 Introduction

Dating back to a 1999 press release by the Online Gamers Association [1] the term eSport (also referred to as electronic sports; competitive video gaming; cyber sports) is used to describe the competitive and organised playing of video games [2]. This rapidly growing industry sector has the potential to influence and reach millions of (younger) individuals. For example, it is anticipated that by 2020 this industry's worth will exceed 23.5 billion USD [3]. Currently, around 385 million people watch eSport (either online or in stadiums) worldwide and this is predicted to grow to 589 million by 2020 [4]. Its popularity is also indexed by its inclusion in the 2024 Paris Olympics and by the significant increases in prize money on offer for participants [4].

Whether eSport is a 'sport' and its players 'athletes' is still equivocal. There is also no generally accepted definition of eSport. However, this is not pertinent to the current paper. In contrast to eSport, video gaming has received significant attention from the scientific community, whereas eSport research is still in its infancy. eSport research to date has mainly concentrated on the economic and game developmental aspects. For example, a recently launched eSport academic programme at Staffordshire University in the UK is mainly focussed on event management of eSport.

© Springer Nature Switzerland AG 2018
S. Göbel et al. (Eds.): JCSG 2018, LNCS 11243, pp. 3–8, 2018.
https://doi.org/10.1007/978-3-030-02762-9_1

2   Video Gaming vs eSport Research

Contrary Serious Gaming, video gaming research has mainly focussed on the potential negative consequences of excessive playing of video games, its association with video game addiction, and the potential negative consequences of violence. In fact, video game addictions and its associated behavioural consequences are now included in the 5th edition of the Diagnostic and Statistical Manual of Mental Disorders under the umbrella term of "Internet Gaming Disorders" [5] as an area for further research.

The association between video game addiction, mental, physical, and social health as well as academic/cognitive functioning is still equivocal, as is the research on violence. A meta-analysis by Ferguson et al. [6] provided some evidence that video game addiction has the strongest negative effect on social functioning of gamers. Although associations have also been found between video game addiction and lower mental (stress, anxiety, depression, suicidal ideation) and physical (physical inactivity, BMI, sleep) health. Most of this work, however, is cross-sectional, not allowing to establish cause and effect, and many of such research are methodologically flawed as they did not control for potential confounding factors (e.g., playing time). Importantly, most research did not distinguish between (intense) engagement and addiction [7]. The former is likely to have no negative consequences but a curiosity and prioritisation of gaming as a hobby or lifestyle choice [8].

The limited research in eSport, on the other hand, has focussed on differences and similarities between eSport and traditional sport [2, 9]. In particular, psychological similarities could indicate that sports psychology practices and interventions would also be applicable to eSport. For example, Himmelstein and colleagues [10] interviewed eSport athletes (League of Legends) to examine the mental skills they currently utilise and the mental obstacles or barriers they encounter. Our own research is also aligned with the more traditional sport research, which examines psychosocial factors that determine success in eSport. This is an important 'paradigm shift' and has the potential to enhance the focus on the prospective benefits of eSport rather than highlighting the presumed negative consequences.

3   eSport for Public Health?

Whereas Serious Games are generally developed with altruistic and humane motives to, for example, help with the rehabilitation of stroke patients or improve the learning of children with cerebral palsy, eSports have been developed to gain commercial success. Serious Gaming is often aimed at improving public health outcomes for specific populations, but so far improvements are limited, probably due the relatively small number of individuals making use of the games and the difficulty of its implementation across settings.

Considering the significant number of individuals playing and watching eSport there is a real opportunity to influence health behaviours. Although eSports appeal currently more to certain segments of the population (younger and male) this is, like traditional sport, likely to change over time. An important question, which arises from this is how eSport manufactures and organisations can work together with, for example, behaviour change specialists, to tackle important public health issues using eSport as a vehicle?

Change in physical activity and sedentary behaviour are two topics which comes to mind when considering the wider implications of eSport participation. Lack of physical activity and sitting too much is a worldwide problem [11] and has been shown to have detrimental physical, psychosocial and cognitive consequences and is one of the most important public health concerns with increasing individual, societal and economic cost [12]. A lack of physical activity is for example, associated with obesity in children and adolescents [13]. Childhood obesity predicts development of chronic conditions in adulthood and is associated with poor fundamental motor skills. Obesity, low physical fitness and poor fundamental movement skills during childhood and adolescence are all associated with poor cognitive development (e.g. language) and academic performance [14]. Obese children are also more likely to place higher demands on educational, social, health and criminal justice systems during this time of development, which again often carries over into adulthood [15].

Of course the idea that physical and cognitive development should go hand in hand is not new. As Socrates stated (400 BC): For in everything men do the body is useful, and in all uses of the body it is of great importance to be in as high a state of physical efficiency as possible. Why, even in the process of thinking, in which the use of the body seems to be reduced to a minimum, it is a matter of common knowledge that grave mistakes may often be traced to bad health. Such a view opposes the pervasive Decartian dualism viewpoint, which has been prevalent across western societies. In contrast, psychology suggest that a holistic development of a sound body will enhance the development and functioning of the mind [16].

Being a competent mover is an important determinant of physical activity and play behaviour in young people [17]. A physically active lifestyle, in turn, builds resilience to mental, social, and physical ill health. Through eSports, and making use of immersive environments and sensor technology, it might be possible to assist children and adolescents to develop these fundamental movement skills [18]. Mastering a range of motor skills through playing eSport could help overweight children to gain confidence in their movement skills when participating in a wide variety of physical activities in multiple environments, which will ultimately contribute to the healthy development of the whole person.

Video game and eSport developers have been consistently applying psychological principles to their designs in order to 'hook' players to their games. These or other strategies (e.g., priming) could also be used to initiate and maintain health behaviour change when designing eSport games in the future. Because of the design of video games and eSport games are divergent, researchers need to understand how to apply behaviour change techniques to motivate the wider population to engage with health behaviours and movement skills learning through eSport.

Similar to traditional sport, to excel at the highest level in eSport it is likely to be associated with being fit and healthy (something we currently exploring in our research). If this is the case, strategies might be developed to help aspiring eSport athletes to develop 'eSport fitness'. It is probable that eSport athletes' fitness will vary during its development and increase with eSport's professionalization. Such a development would be similar to what happened historically in golf. The significance of physical training and fitness in professional golf has only emerged from the 1990s when Tiger Woods started to pay attention to being physically fit and athletic. Most golfers now have a physical trainer and spend significant amount of their training in the gym. Playing eSport at the elite level requires the ability to sustain high levels of attention, respond as quickly as possible to stimuli, and make numerous important decisions under time pressure. In addition, with the development of more immersive environments various physical skills might also become important to success. Therefore, current and future skill requirements in eSport will necessitate players (or athletes) to be fit, healthy and movement competent in order to perform at the highest level of competition, just like in the physical environment during the Olympics.

Currently, it is unknown how individuals perceive the difference of creating a professional high sporting performance in the virtual versus physical environments. Our research team is investigating such differences, including the transitioning from virtual to physical, which is the crucial element of playing eSport and its transference to physical health. We hypothesise that initially, playing eSport might be the most beneficial for the development of cognitive skills. In the study by Himmelstein and colleagues [10], players reported to develop self-regulatory skills and a growth mindset. Such skills are not only important for optimal eSport performance, but are also transferable to other domains and highly sought after in the world of work [19].

4   eSport and Implementation Science

While the potential for using eSport to bring about health behaviour change is apparent, the way this might be approached needs some careful consideration. There are many factors that influence the transfer of an evidence based research into daily practice and ultimately to population health. There needs to be a careful consideration and research into the adoption and uptake of eSport for health benefits both from the users' and the designers' perspectives. From the outset of the planning of using eSport for changing physical activity behaviours in children/adolescents an implementation logic model will need to be designed to aid the understanding of the underlying processes of adoption and maintenance of learned skills.

5   Roadblocks in Doing eSport Research

Like all new endeavours conducting research in eSport or using eSport to implement public health strategies will not be without obstacles. To date we have identified 3 categories of potential problems: Commercial protectionism, research weariness, and ethical issues.

Commercial protectionism: It is understandable that the makers of the different eSport games try to protect their brand. However, like traditional sports, there will be a need to be more open and transparent in its governance. Despite many traditional sports not being structured and managed according to best practice principles, ultimately, traditional sport has become part of the political landscape. For example, the Australian Government recently presented their Sport 2030 plan [20]. This has resulted in national or local governments across many countries providing significant support to traditional sport in terms of building infrastructure or organising major events. In addition, traditional sport is now increasingly being used to promote health behaviour change. Despite eSport being recognised in some countries (e.g., Korea and Denmark) if it wants to become 'mainstream', it will also need to develop an independent and autonomous administration for one or multiple eSports internationally [21]. This also requires compliance with international sport regulations on aspects like doping and betting whilst at the same time enhancing legitimacy and augment its potential for sponsorship and governmental support [21].

Research weariness: Within the computer gaming community there has been a weariness to research potentially because of its emphasis on the negative consequences in terms of excessive play and/or violence. Over the years, we have found more difficulties with participant recruitment either during events or at relevant online forums. Some of the responses to attempted recruitment, online or in person, have been hostile to say the least. As such we are developing alternative strategies to engage the eSport community to participate in research. For example, team owners have been supportive of our work and we are trialling other online methods (e.g., through Youtube channels) to interest and involve the eSport community.

Ethics: eSport is an important activity for many adolescents. Their preferred way of communication, and thus future data collection, is through online or electronic means. This, however, creates a number of ethical barriers. For example, in Australia the age at which adolescents can consent is normally 18 years. This makes it extremely challenging to involve younger eSport players in our studies. This is not a request to abandon consent from either participants or their guardians. However, we have to think creatively to involve as many individuals as possible to reap future benefits. In addition to this, many eSports collect significant amounts of data of their players, with virtually every move and keystroke being recorded. This also raises questions of who owns the data and how we can use this future research purposes?

6   Conclusion

In this paper, we have provided a case to use eSport as a potential vehicle to influence health behaviours. We acknowledge that there are significant obstacles which we have to overcome. However, the accelerated growth of eSport in terms of its participants, spectators, and economic value makes it a domain which cannot be ignored by researchers, public servants and politicians. In addition, it has the potential to reach groups in society which to date have been hard to influence. Most of our interventions to make children and adolescents more active have failed. We are optimistic and believe that eSport is our friend and an important vehicle to stop that trend.

References

1. Wagner, M.G.: On the scientific relevance of eSports. In: Symposium conducted at 2006 International Conference on Internet Computing & Conference on Computer Games Development, Las Vegas, Nevada (2006)
2. Jenny, S.E., Manning, R.D., Keiper, M.C., Olrich, T.W.: Virtual(ly) athletes: where eSports fit within the definition of 'sport'. Quest 69(1), 1–18 (2017)
3. Holden, J.T., Rodenberg, R.M., Kaburakis, A.: ESports corruption: Gambling, doping and global governance. Md. J. Int. Law 32(1), 236–273 (2017)
4. Newzoo: 2017 Global eSports market report: trends, revenues, and audience toward 2020 (2017)
5. American Psychiatric Association.: Diagnostic and Statistical Manual of Mental Disorders, 5th edn. APA, Washington (2013)
6. Ferguson, C.J., Coulson, M., Barnett, J.: A meta-analysis of pathological gaming prevalence and comorbidity with mental health, academic and social problems. J. Psychiatr. Res. 45(12), 1573–1578 (2011)
7. Charlton, J.P., Danforth, I.D.: Distinguishing addiction and high engagement in the context of online game playing. Comput. Hum. Behav. 23(3), 1531–1548 (2007)
8. Seok, S., DaCosta, B.: Distinguishing addiction from high engagement: an investigation into the social lives of adolescent and young adult massively multiplayer online game players. Games Cult. 9(4), 227–254 (2014)
9. Schaeperkoetter, C.C., et al.: The 'new' student-athlete: An exploratory examination of scholarship eSport players. J. Intercoll. Sport. 10, 1–21 (2017)
10. Himmelstein, D., Liu, Y., Shapiro, J.L.: An exploration of mental skills among competitive league of legend players. Int. J. Gaming Comput.-Mediat. Simul. 9(2), 1–21 (2017)
11. Guthold, R., Stevens, G.A., Riley, L.M., Bull, F.C.: Worldwide trends in insufficient physical activity from 2001 to 2016: a pooled analysis of 358 population based surveys with 1.9 million participants. Lancet Global Health (available ahead of print) (2018)
12. Ding, D., et al.: The economic burden of physical inactivity: a global analysis of major non-communicable diseases. Lancet 388, 1311–1324 (2016)
13. Hills, A.P., Andersen, L.B., Byrne, N.M.: Physical activity and obesity in children. Br. J. Sport. Med. 45(11), 866–870 (2011)
14. Kantomaa, M.T., et al.: Physical activity and obesity mediate the association between childhood motor function and adolescent academic achievement. PNAS 110(5), 1917–1922 (2013)
15. McDaid, D.: Making the long-term economic case for investing in mental health to contribute to sustainability. EU, Brussels (2011)
16. Forstmann, M., Burgmer, P., Mussweiler, T.: The mind is willing, but the flesh is weak: the effects of mind-body dualism on health behaviour. Psychol. Sci. 23(10), 1239–1245 (2012)
17. Rudd, J., Barnett, L., Farrow, D., Berry, J., Borkoles, E., Polman, R.C.J.: Effectiveness of a 16 week gymnastic curriculum at developing movement competence in children. J. Sci. Med. Sport. 20(2), 164–169 (2017)
18. Bisi, M.C., Panebionco, P., Polman, R., Stagni, R.: Objective assessment of movement competence in children using wearable sensors: an instrumented version of the TGMD-2 locomotor subset. Gait Posture 56, 42–48 (2017)
19. Bloomberg next.: Building tomorrow's talent: Collaboration can close emerging skill gap. The Bureau of National Affairs Inc (2018)
20. Sport Australia: Sport 2030: Participation, Performance, Integrity, Industry. Australian Government, Canberra (2018)
21. Jonasson, K., Thiborg, J.: Electronic sport and its impact on future sport. Sport. Soc. 13(2), 287–299 (2010)

Academic Game Design Education:
A Comparative Perspective

André Czauderna^(✉)

TH Köln, Schanzenstr. 28, 51063 Köln, Germany
andre.czauderna@th-koeln.de

Abstract. This paper outlines a model of game design education that considers not only the creative and technological design and development of digital games, but also their broader aesthetic, historical and cultural contexts and implications. The model is derived from a comparative analysis of several undergraduate programs in Australia, Germany, Great Britain and the United States which was presented by the author at JCSG 2018.

Keywords: Digital games · Game design · Game design education
Higher education

1 Introduction

More and more universities offer undergraduate and postgraduate programs in game design and/or game development. The expansion of academic game design and game development education is a global trend which can be observed across Western countries. On the one hand, universities exchange curricular and didactic approaches beyond institutional and national borders. On the other hand, the field can be characterized by a diversity of approaches and local particularities. According to a 2014 study by the Higher Education Video Game Alliance, classes offered in game design and game development programs "span more than 240 subjects ranging from Advanced Drawing and 3D Modeling to Artificial Intelligence and Computer Programming in C++ to Marketing Principles and Business Law" [1].

This paper, as well as my talk at JCSG 2018, focuses on Bachelor of (Fine) Arts and Design programs, rather than their Bachelor of Science counterparts or postgraduate programs. My presentation at JCSG 2018 compared concepts from programs in Australia, Germany, Great Britain and the United States: the Bachelor of Design (Games) at RMIT University in Melbourne; the Digital Games BA at TH Köln; the Game Design BA at the University of the Arts London; and the Game Design BFA at New York University (NYU).

This comparative analysis reconstructs a common model of academic game design education that does not only aim at short-term employability, but also provides sustainable preparation for the labor market of the 21st century, in and beyond the gaming industry. This model also facilitates students' intellectual and creative abilities, which hold value beyond the workplace.

© Springer Nature Switzerland AG 2018
S. Göbel et al. (Eds.): JCSG 2018, LNCS 11243, pp. 9–12, 2018.
https://doi.org/10.1007/978-3-030-02762-9_2

2 A Model of Academic Game Design Education

In the following, the model of academic game design education, derived from my comparative analysis delivered at JCSG 2018, will be outlined along the following criteria: generalist and specialist education, variety of contents, design over technology, student body diversity, variety of games, learning in collaborative projects and general education. A more comprehensive account of this model as well as a similar comparative analysis can be found in an earlier article [2]. In "Games studieren – was, wie, wo? Staatliche Studienangebote im Bereich digitaler Spiele," a book on German game design and development education, I published the results of a broader comparative analysis including Bachelor of Science as well as graduate programs [3].

Generalist and Specialist Education: The programs featured in this paper pursue an approach to game design education that aims to educate its students as both generalists and specialists. The curricula of all programs imply the assumption that academically educated game professionals should own: (a) a basic understanding of the work done in all departments involved in game development as well as its media-theoretical contexts and economic conditions, and (b) a specialization in one of the departments, such as Game Design, Game Arts, Game Programming or Game Producing—though the depth and degree of formality of specialization strongly varies between study programs. An individual student's specialization might include a further, more in depth specialization in a certain sub-field, which is especially true in the domain of Game Arts, where some students specialize as Character Designer, Environment Artist, 2D or 3D Animator, or 3D Modeler at an early stage. At the end of their studies, graduates are either generalists with an informal specialization in one of the departments involved in game development (e.g., NYU) or specialists in one of these departments with a solid understanding of the other departments (e.g., TH Köln).

Variety of Contents: In their generalist philosophy, all programs offer an enormous variety of classes, ranging from Figure Drawing to Artificial Intelligence to Publishing. Overall, courses can be classified to the following five core areas of study: Game Design (understood as the design of gameplay, mechanics and narration); Game Arts (including CG Art, Animation, Sound Design, etc.); Game Programming & Engineering; Game Economics & Producing; and Media & Game Studies (including approaches from the humanities as well as social sciences).

Design over Technology: Above all, the described programs target the education of designers who create gameplay, mechanics and narration (Game Designers); interface, characters and environments (Game Artists); or source code (Game Programmers). In this sense, technology is primarily seen as a means to an end. In the case that programs are concerned with the education of programmers, they do not aim to educate computer scientists, but creatively trained programmers who work at the intersection of design, arts and technology—as gameplay programmers, for instance.

Student Body Diversity: The observed programs set diversity as a central goal. This certainly includes the integration of female students, though this mission is more broadly concerned with the inclusion of those who are typically excluded from the core target group of AAA games. This trend towards a diversified student body fits to broader developments such as a changing market of digital games and the opening of the gaming industry to new target groups. Programs assume that a diverse student body —accompanied by the inclusion of new perspectives—helps to think outside the box of traditional game development and contributes to the diversification of game concepts (concerning aesthetics, mechanics and narration). An increase in diversity of digital games (including new innovative forms of games and play), in turn, allows for greater reach to new broad and diverse audiences.

Variety of Games: In accordance with the above-mentioned trend towards the diversification of the student body, the programs described in my presentation at JCSG 2018 not only encourage students to deal with long-established genres (based on well-known aesthetics, mechanics and narrative forms; sold by the AAA industry to the former core audience of digital games), but also support engagement with new genres and game forms, as well as those that often go overlooked, such as virtual reality games, experimental games, art games and serious games. Overall, programs intend to promote a broad game literacy based on the engagement with a variety of genres and game forms.

Learning in Collaborative Projects: When it comes to didactics, the programs exhibit an art school style project orientation. This implies the notion that learning in game school should not be based on ex-cathedra teaching and top-down instruction. Instead, it relies on constructivist theories of learning, on learning-by-doing and peer-to-peer learning, among other things. Learning in projects, as applied in the respective programs, usually rests up-on a collaboration of individuals in interdisciplinary teams.

General Education: Although the examined programs work with the gaming industry and usually consider its needs in curriculum development, they pursue an approach that goes beyond the short-term tailor-made creation of specialists for the gaming industry. Their model of game design education can be clearly differentiated from solely vocational approaches. Programs' curricula usually entail a set of classes from the humanities, social sciences and in some cases natural sciences. Theoretical perspectives are valued through the comprehensive inclusion of respective professorships and a high ratio of theory classes. The NYU program is part of the tradition of liberal arts education and thus includes a broad choice of classes (from anthropology to neuroscience) that are not necessarily linked to game development in an obvious way. In all cases, programs aim at academic education in general: the facilitation of a broad store of reference knowledge as well as analytical and critical thinking skills; the broadening of students' horizons; and the support of an intellectual and creative mindset, among other things—all of which are assessed as valuable for game development as well as personality and identity development.

3 Conclusion

All four programs considered in my presentation at JCSG 2018 combine a vocational higher education and a broader academic education including contents from the humanities and social sciences. On the one hand programs teach a range of necessary generalist and specialist skills for immediate employability in the gaming industry. On the other hand programs take into account that "if the fit [to the current industry] is too narrow and the program too short-sighted in serving the immediate hiring needs, its graduates might find their skills losing value when the needs of the industry shift in response to new technologies" [4]. Thus, programs aim to impart enduring and transferable 21st century knowledge and skills including communication and collaboration competencies as well as an academic and creative mindset and habitus—valuable for a constantly changing work life, but also a fulfilling creative and intellectual life beyond the workplace.

In general, programs are highly concerned with the short- and long-term employability of their graduates as well as the short- and long-term needs of the gaming industry. Different from pure vocational programs, they pursue an approach of game design education that forms their students as both specialists and generalists—assuming that a combination of specialism and generalism based on an interdisciplinary practical and theoretical game design education will improve employability in general, but even more so in the long run. In contrast to programs in traditional academic disciplines, there is a strong focus on interdisciplinary collaborative practices, as they are required in the gaming industry. Finally, programs are keen on facilitating students' entrepreneurial spirit and competencies.

To sum up, it can be said that the programs' shared model of academic game design education focuses on the interdisciplinary and collaborative design and development of digital games as well as a reflection of their wider aesthetic, historical and cultural contexts and implications. In doing so, the model intends to educate well-rounded game designers who have even more to offer than their comprehensive specialized artistic and technical skills.

References

1. Steinkuehler, C., Fullerton, T., Phelps, A., Davidson, D., Isbister, K.: Our state of play: higher education video game alliance survey 2014–15, Washington, DC (2015). https://hevga.org/wp-content/themes/hevga2wp/assets/our-state-of-play-2014-15%20.pdf. Accessed 24 Aug 2018
2. Czauderna, A.: International game design education: six examples from five countries. In: Freyermuth, G.S.: Games|Game Design|Game Studies: An Introduction, pp. 241–256. Transcript, Bielefeld (2015)
3. Czauderna, A.: Games-Studium im Ausland. Ein vergleichender Blick auf Angebote in Westeuropa, Nordamerika und Australien. In: Bartholdy, B., Breitlauch, L., Czauderna, A., Freyermuth, G.S. (eds.) Games studieren – was, wie, wo? Staatliche Studienangebote im Bereich digitaler Spiele. Transcript, Bielefeld (2018)
4. Murray, J., Bogost, I., Mateas, M., Nitsche, M.: Game design education: integrating computation and culture. Computer 39(6), 43–51 (2006)

Making Serious Games with Reusable Software Components

Wim van der Vegt$^{(\boxtimes)}$, Enkhbold Nyamsuren, and Wim Westera

Open University of the Netherlands, Valkenburgerweg 177, 6419 AT Heerlen,
The Netherlands
{wim.vandervegt, enkhbold.nyamsuren, wim.westera}@ou.nl

Abstract. This paper explains the RAGE project, which proposes a component-based software architecture to accommodate and amplify serious game development. The RAGE project (rageproject.eu) is a serious gaming flagship project funded by the Horizon 2020 Programme of the European Commission. Compliancy with the component-based architecture preserves the portability of software to different platforms and programming languages and its easy integration in wide variety of game engines. RAGE has developed up to 40 cutting edge reusable software components (all free, open source software) and has made these available on its market place portal at gamecomponents.eu.

Keywords: Serious games · Software components · Game development
Reuse · Cross-platform · Portability · Game engines

1 Introduction

Serious gaming is a priority area of the European Commission, having recognised the potential of games for e.g. teaching and training, social inclusion, heath, the digital transformation and other societal purposes. Although scholars and teachers have shown great interest in serious games for quite some years, the uptake of games in schools and business has been quite limited [1, 2]. While the leisure game industry has become a well-established industry dominated by major hardware vendors, publishers, and a fine-grained network of development studios, distributors and retailers, the serious game industry still displays many features of an emerging, immature branch of business, which is characterised by weak interconnectedness, limited knowledge exchange, and absence of harmonising standards [3]. Notably, progress is hampered by the wide variety of programming languages, game development systems and delivery platforms that game studios have in use, all of which go with specific technical constraints and incompatibilities that pose severe barriers to growth. Moreover, the small game studios often do not have access to emerging media technologies that could be incorporated in serious game projects, such as novel adaptation algorithms, artificial intelligence kernels, or natural language processing methods, while the alternative of in-company development of such technologies is not feasible, either because of required investments or because of lacking know-how.

© Springer Nature Switzerland AG 2018
S. Göbel et al. (Eds.): JCSG 2018, LNCS 11243, pp. 13–16, 2018.
https://doi.org/10.1007/978-3-030-02762-9_3

This paper provides a brief summary of the work in RAGE in order to provide a starting point for the technical workshop arranged by RAGE at the Joint Conference of Serious Games 2018.

2 The RAGE Component-Based Software Architecture (RCSA)

The RAGE component-based software architecture (RCSA) was devised to accommodate the development of software components that can be easily reused and integrated in serious game projects across a wide variety of prevailing technology platforms. The RCSA [4, 5] distinguishes between server-side components and client-side components. While remote communications of server-side components with centralised applications can be easily achieved with web services using the HTTP-protocol (e.g., REST), client-side components need to be integrated into client-machine applications (viz. game engines), which is often problematic. With respect to client-side components, the RCSA is based on a limited set of established coding practices and software patterns (API, Bridge, Publish/Subscribe, Web Services), generally aiming at the abstraction of operations in order to accommodate reuse in different technical environments. Components based on the RCSA avoid dependencies on external software frameworks and minimise code that may hinder integration with game engine code. They do not access or do not make assumptions about the underlying operating system, do not directly interfere with the game code, and consequently, do not access the game's user interface, thus leaving all functional and creative decisions about screen layout style, look and feel in the hands of the game designers and developers. Technical proofs of concept of the RCSA portability have been established for C#, C++, Java and JavaScript/TypeScript, which are among the predominant programming languages used in game development [6]. Also, RCSA-compliant components have been successfully integrated in various game engines, including e.g. Unity3D, MonoGame, Cocos2D, Xamarin and Emergo, and have been deployed at the most popular desktop and mobile delivery platforms [5].

3 Game Software Components at Gamecomponents.eu

An initial set of game components can be accessed through the RAGE marketplace portal at gamecomponents.eu (Fig. 1). The exposed components offer a variety of cutting-edge functionalities of potential relevance for serious games, ranging from adaptation and personalisation, to language-based sentiment analysis, facial emotion recognition, sensor-based arousal detection, social gamification, affective computing and other topics. All components are compliant with the RCSA, which guarantees the seamless integration into a variety of game engines or other software environments. The collection of components includes both server-side components and client-side components, as well as hybrids. To maximize the reuse of software, all components use the Apache 2.0 license (white label software), which allows for reuse by third parties both for commercial and non-commercial purposes, either under open source or closed source conditions.

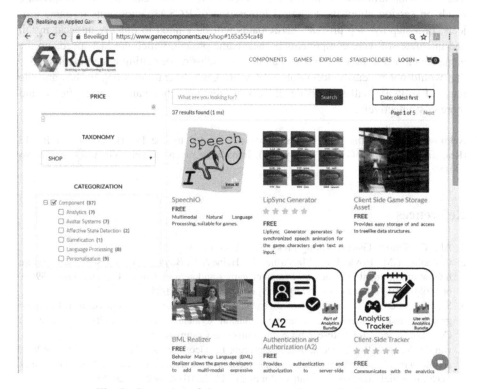

Fig. 1. Screenshot of the gamecomponents.eu marketplace.

All software exposed at the portal are enriched with user guides, manuals, instructional materials, integration templates, demonstrators, and proof cases. For the purpose of practical validation a set of seven serious games based on the various software components was developed, which were then tested and evaluated in real end-user pilots. The games focus on various social and entrepreneurial skills and address diverse educational contexts. Overall, over 1500 participants were involved in the game pilots. The gamecomponents.eu marketplace portal differs from existing portals by its platform independency: the compliancy with the RCSA preserves the easy integration of components across a variety of different software environments. In contrast, existing platforms such as the Unity Asset Store and the Unreal Marketplace, are inherently platform bound, and thereby lead to vendor lock-in. Moreover, existing marketplaces are mostly dominated by media objects (e.g. terrains, audio, buildings, weapons, user-interface objects, and templates) rather than software, which reduce the efforts required for content creation, but still preserve the programming load.

4 The Component Integration Workshop

The workshop arranged at the Joint Conference on Serious Games 2018 comprises a hands-on session about the technical integration of RCSA components in game projects. In a step-by-step process, participants will be guided to quickly unpack, install and integrate software components in their game project, which not just speeds up the game development process, but also allows the inclusion of cutting-edge functionalities that would not be easily accessible otherwise. Component-based approaches and the reuse of software will support developers at creating better games easier, faster, and more cost-effectively.

Acknowledgment. This work has been partially funded by the EC H2020 project RAGE (Realising an Applied Gaming Ecosystem); http://www.rageproject.eu/; Grant agreement No 644187.

References

1. Abt, C.: Serious Games. Viking Press, New York (1970)
2. Connolly, T.M., Boyle, E.A., MacArthur, E., Hainey, T., Boyle, J.M.: A systematic literature review of empirical evidence on computer games and serious games. Comput. Educ. **59**(2), 661–686 (2013). https://doi.org/10.1016/j.compedu.2012.03.004
3. Stewart, J., et al.: The potential of digital games for empowerment and social inclusion of groups at risk of social and economic exclusion: evidence and opportunity for policy. In: Centeno, C. (ed.) Joint Research Centre, European Commission (2013)
4. van der Vegt, G.W., Westera, W., Nyamsuren, E., Georgiev, A., Martinez Ortiz, I.: RAGE architecture for reusable serious gaming technology components. Int. J. Comput. Games Technol. Article ID 5680526. https://doi.org/10.1155/2016/5680526 (2016)
5. van der Vegt, W., Nyamsuren, E., Westera, W.: RAGE reusable game software components and their integration into serious game engines. In: Kapitsaki, G.M., Santana de Almeida, E. (eds.) ICSR 2016. LNCS, vol. 9679, pp. 165–180. Springer, Cham (2016). https://doi.org/10.1007/978-3-319-35122-3_12
6. RedMonk: The RedMonk programming languages rankings: January 2015. http://redmonk.com/sogrady/2015/01/14/language-rankings-1-15/. Accessed 5 Sept 2018

Serious Games Studies

The Development of the Serious Game "Composites Cup on Tortuga" with the Support of "Kraken"

Marietta Menner[✉], Klaus Bredl, Stefan Büttner, Lukas Rust, and Simon Flutura

University Augsburg, Universitätsstr. 1a, 86159 Augsburg, Germany
marietta.menner@amu.uni-augsburg.de

Abstract. In the course of a research project, a serious game on the subject of fiber composite materials was developed and tested in cooperation with students, teachers and academic experts of different disciplines. The concept process was evaluated formatively. In the process, different evaluation instruments were used. This paper will introduce and describe the instrument "Kraken", as well as illustrate which role it played in the development of the serious game "Composites Cup on Tortuga".

Keywords: Serious game · Composites · Design-based research

1 Introduction

While developing the serious game "Composites Cup on Tortuga" the target group (students of the 8th grade and teachers of general public schools) was taken into account. The development was formatively evaluated. During the evaluation process, different qualitative and quantitative methods were used. The game testers received questionnaires to give feedback to the respective stage of the development of the game. A so-called "World Café" format [1] was carried out, where students could discuss their experience with the game. Expert interviews and feedback discussions were held with teachers and the so-called "Kraken" was used. This client-server-application can test to see if the information collected through common instruments really matches the actual usage of the game. In this paper, the experience with this evaluation instrument is illustrated in detail. The serious game was designed for the school student laboratory [2]. With the support of this game, students should playfully learn about fiber composite materials independently. Until now, the school lab visitors went through learning circles about fiber composites to receive an introduction to the topic, but the learning circle was rather high maintenance regarding the supervision of the student.

Disclaimer. Please note that some terms in this paper are in German. The serious game "Composites Cup on Tortuga" was created in the German language and is not available in English; therefore, the following screenshots of the game have to remain German. In some cases, terms are translated in parentheses behind the respective term.

S. Göbel et al. (Eds.): JCSG 2018, LNCS 11243, pp. 19–29, 2018.
https://doi.org/10.1007/978-3-030-02762-9_4

Furthermore, students were only able to look at the individual materials (fiber and matrix) and then again at the finished fiber composites. In addition, changing characteristics, which caused the merging of these different materials, could not be visualized clearly. Such serious games can be assigned as homework in school, which was another aspect taken into consideration for the development of such a digital medium. Therefore, students would have more time on the practical work during their school laboratory unit. So far, class material that could replace this introductory tool was missing in German schools.

The focus on fiber composites was not only chosen because there is a school laboratory tool for students available at the University of Augsburg, but because lightweight material, which consist of fiber composites, in the course of the sustainable use of resources, will play a big role in the future. Nowadays, there is no aircraft, which does not contain fiber composite materials [3]. In the production of electronic automobiles, lightweight materials are also primarily utilized [4].

In the serious games composites cup on Tortuga, the focus lies on the most commonly fiber composites used for industry and every day applications (sport and leisure) with glass fiber reinforced plastic (GRP) and carbon reinforced/carbon dioxide reinforced plastic (CFK) [5]. The plastic is called matrix in a technical jargon [6]. In the game, the students should get to know the characteristics of fiber composites and apply the acquired knowledge in transfer tasks (for example the creation of a diving board).

2   Design Based Development of the Serious Game "Composites Cup on Tortuga"

The serious game "Composites Cup on Tortuga" was designed in an interdisciplinary cooperation of prospective informatics (students, who programmed the game), an educator, who created the content of the game and evaluated the development, as well as academic experts (teachers, composites experts and usability students).

Technically, the game was put together in the development environment Unity. In order for the game to be usable beyond the school laboratory, two versions, one for iPad application and one for desktop application, were created. The development process was evaluated with the design-based research approach taken into account. Design-based research normally goes through phases of problem definition, the development of a didactic design, the cyclical design implementation as well as the evaluation and reflection in tight cooperation of science and practice. Additionally, the goal is to address the development of practically relevant interventions and the advancement of scientific theories [7].

For the description of the serious game "Composites Cup on Tortuga", the model of research and development cycles within the design-oriented research of Euler was used [8]. The sequence "design-test-analysis-redesign-test" was repeated multiple times (after every test with the target group).

Description of the Serious Game "Composite Cup on Tortuga"

The main information on the serious game is listed in the following Table 1. The description is based on the game description of the Serious Games Information Center (SG-IC) and oriented on the DIN SPEC 91380 [9].

Table 1. Description of the serious game according to SG-IC

Title	Composites cup on tortuga
Objective	Increased learning in the area fiber composites
Summary	Educational game: student need to get to know the characteristics of fiber composites materials and fiber composites
Keywords	Composites, fiber composites materials, new materials, nature and technology
Genre	Racing games, logic and puzzle games
Game mode	Single player
Game time	45 min
Status	Complete
Application area	Education, schools
Target group	Players – Students Players – private individuals Age: 13–15 year olds
Language	German
Learning resources type	Introduction, exercise
Scope	Student laboratory, school, at home
Level of difficulty	Moderate
Typical learning time	45 min
Replayability	Yes
Progress indicators	Advancing to the next level, stars for solved tasks, feedback from game characters
Needed previous knowledge	None
Fees	None

For the setting of the game, a pirate scenario was chosen, since the background story was compatible with this context. There are many possible applications to integrate fiber composite materials in such a setting. Furthermore, the game aims to address adolescence as of 13 years old, who were questioned about the setting.

The game is divided into four levels, which are called "Harpooning" ("Harpunieren"), "Prosthesis Run" ("Prothesenrennen"), "Plank Jumping" ("Plankenspringen") and "Cannonball Trick Shooting" ("Kanonenkunstschießen") in the game. Within these levels, there are consecutive tasks and quiz questions to deepen the newly acquired knowledge.

Description of the Learning Objective

The following learning contents are to be transported over the individual levels:

Harpooning: In the first level, the players have to solve four tasks about the topic fiber types and their characteristics. Following characteristics are addressed: load capacity, current conductivity, diameter, resilience and costs of the fibers.

Prosthesis Run: In the second level, the matrix is introduced and the tasks address the characteristics of fiber composites. It is visualized through a pirate with an artificial leg, which consists of fiber composite materials, who has to solve three challenges.

Plank Jumping: The third level is the hardest. The players have to apply the knowledge they previously gained in three tasks for the creation of a fiber composite. Mechanical characteristics of the materials as well as the fiber direction, the bending strength and the interaction of these characteristics have to be taken into account.

Cannonball trick shooting: The cannonball trick shooting is all about the thermal resistance of fiber composite materials. There are two tasks, in which the player has to choose the most heat-resistant matrix material.

The limitations of the fiber composite materials are addressed in all levels. Therefore, the costs of fiber composite materials out of CFK and GRP are pointed out and it is shown that not all fiber composites are suitable for all application areas. In a timely and content related restricted game like this one, this can only be addressed in a limited fashion.

The following example describes the design of a task. In the beginning of each task, the gamers receive an introductory text in the form of an inserted panel. See Fig. 1 for an example.

Fig. 1. Example of an introductory text before a task

The aim of the level is visualized through a short dialogue with speech bubbles. These also refer to new user-interface-element (UI-elements in the following) and describe the user interface in the beginning of the game. The UI-elements are marked with a red circle or underlined with red. The player cannot continue unless all UI-elements have been clicked. Figure 2 shows the structure of the user interface using the example of the first task of the "Harpooning" levels.

Fig. 2. Structure of the user interface (Color figure online)

Information texts support the solution of the individual tasks, which are accessible in every task. To change the characteristics of the tool, the player can choose either dropdown menus or sliders. Each change made influences the tools in the tool bar on the right hand side of the game. Only tool characteristics that are hard to visualize in the mini-game are shown in the tool bar, such as weight, costs and durability of the tools.

Parameter Search Space of the Levels

To find an ideal material combination is comprehended as an optimization of the parameter space. They can have the following dimensions: fiber material, diameter, matrix material, fiber direction and wall thickness.

The players receive direct feedback in the game, if they did not choose a fitting material combination, for example. See Fig. 3 on the following page.

When the players successfully solve a task, their performance is rated with one to three stars. They therefore receive another direct feedback from the game to see how well they managed to solve the task.

Quizlevel

The integrated quiz tasks in the individual levels were implemented to ensure the results [10] in the game. The students have to answer two to four questions with a maximum of four answer possibilities. If they chose the wrong answer, a short hint pops up to inform them as to why the answer was wrong. If too many questions are not answered correctly, the quiz has to be repeated.

Fig. 3. Direct feedback in the game

3 Description of the Evaluation

The complete gradually evaluation of the game was conducted with N = 185 students (37% female, 58% male, 4% did not wish to enclose their gender). See Fig. 4 on the following page. The examinees were in different grades and from different types of schools. All participating individuals were able to choose whether they wanted to play the game as well as if they wanted to give feedback to the game. The traditional introduction via the learning circle was also a selectable option. The majority of the students happily participated in testing the game. The feedback was queried through different tools. These include questionnaires to give a feedback to the perspective phase of the game; a so-called "World Café" format was conducted, in which the students could discuss their experience in the game and expert interviews and feedback discussions were held with teachers. Furthermore, the so-called "Kraken" was utilized. All responses were anonymous. There was no assignment made, which test person played with which iPad.

The target group was deliberately chosen from different types of schools and different grades, as the student school laboratory can be booked just as individually. The focus target group however were eighth graders. The reason for this was that fiber composite materials are part of the curriculum "LehrplanPlus" (Curriculum Plus) of the Bavarian secondary schools as of the school year 20/21 [11] and is expected to increase user traffic at this age level. In the following, a survey instrument of the evaluation, the client-server-application "Kraken" is to be described.

Description of the Evaluation Tool "Kraken" (Game Event Logging)
In the last third of the evaluation, a module called "Kraken" was developed for the automated, anonymous player data collection. Its data supports the other feedback tools

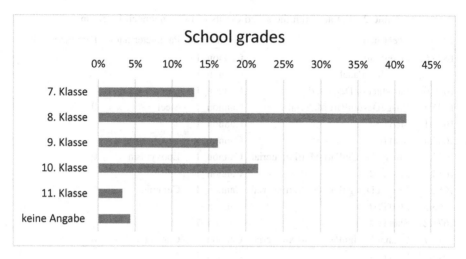

Fig. 4. Distribution of the participants according to their grade

used in the process. These technical evaluation tools, which support the analysis and the understanding of the player behavior, provide an important contribution for the conception of serious games [12]. The acquired data can support the improvement and correction of possible design issues in a timely manner [13]. This way, the effectiveness of the serous games can be improved.

The data collection functions via a, for this purpose developed, client-server-application called "Kraken". It consists of three parts:

- Unity Plugin [14]: The Unity Plugin records, collects and sends events, if there is enough data, via Web-Request to the server. Since not all rooms in the school student laboratory have access to internet, the data is buffered in a file and sent, as soon as the server connection is restored.
- "Kraken" Server: the server consists of a web interface and a MongoDB-database, which saves incoming events. Table 2 (on page 9) shows an extract of the saved events for one run-through of the first task in the cannonball trick shooting level.
- "Kraken" Client: For all data, there is a python-library available, which can read the "Kraken" server and is available for the evaluation. Figure 5 shows a diagram of the system

The Event Format
The event format consists of seven parameters, which are explained in the following. With the GUID (globally unique identifier), the game structure can distinctively be identified. It is generated anew with each start of the game and restricts conclusions of personal data of the test person. The Session Number increases with each new start of the game and is continued from the previous memory state. Together with the parameter Time, which indicates the start of the game, the time used by the students for each program section can be measured. These two data sets do not provide any possibility to restore the exact time of events.

Table 2. Extract from the saved events of the cannonball level run.

Time	Event name	Level name	Parameter name	Parameter value
1623.65	LevelStart	Cannon_1		
1624.53	CloseInfoPanel	Cannon_1		
1629.6	IntroductionDelivered	Cannon_1		
1634.5	ChageDesignPart.Material	Cannon_1	Steel	0
1635.17	StartTest	Cannon_1		
1644.4	StartTest	Cannon_1		
1652.37	ChangeDesignPart-Matrixmaterial	Cannon_1	Epoxyrasin	0
1654.44	StartTest	Cannon_1		
1662.7	ChangeDesignPart-Matrixmaterial	Cannon_1	Ceramic	0
1663.3	StartTest	Cannon_1		
1671.27	StartTest	Cannon_1		
1677.7	ChangeDesignPart-Matrixmaterial	Cannon_1	Cement	0
1678.44	StartTest	Cannon_1		
1683.14	ChangeDesignPart-Matrixmaterial	Cannon_1	Ceramic	0
1685.24	ChangeDesignPart-Fibertype	Cannon_1	Glass	0
1685.84	StartTest	Cannon_1		
1690.07	ChangeDesignPart-Fibertype	Cannon_1	Carbon	0
1696.97	StartTest	Cannon_1		
1712.37	HomeButton	Cannon_1		

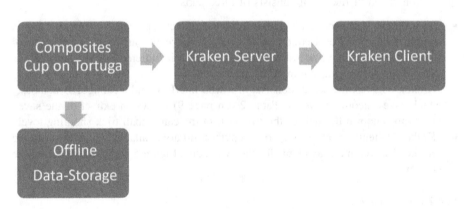

Fig. 5. Visual presentation of the "Kraken" system

The Level Name indicates the currently played level, once the event is recorded. The event name has to be set to indicate the name of the event. It can optionally be expanded by a string parameter name and float parameter value. The "Kraken" Unity Plugin automatically fills in the parameters GUID, Session Number, Time and Level Name.

Table 2 additionally shows a short example for the events, which are recorded in each level. When choosing such events, the possibility of the failure to record in all levels was taken into consideration. It can be noticed in the Log that, after the introduction (IntroductionDelivered), experiments with different material types (ChangeDesignPart.Material/ChangeDesignPart.Matrixmaterial) were made.

Additionally to the Logging of the gameplay, the recording of the results of the quiz level are also part of the range of functions of the Loggers.

In the following, it is shown how the tool "Kraken" was implemented during the evaluation of the serious game "Composites Cup on Tortuga" with an example.

Practical Usage of the Evaluation Tool "Kraken"

Example: Jumping mechanism in the "Plank Jumping" levels

Design: In the initial implementation of the jumping mechanism in the "Plank Jumping" levels, the players had to tap for each individual jump. In doing so, the game character (male or female pirate) would exercise a downward aimed force on the plank as long as the click is held, in order to strain it. Letting go of the click gave the game character an upward impulse. Clicking or rather, tapping at the right time and for the right duration can make the plank swing sufficiently for the character to jump high enough. See Fig. 3 to see how the level is visualized. During the design of the individual tasks it was taken into consideration that it should not be demanded too little of the players, whereas they should not be overstrained either. To boost learning processes and motivate the players, a serious game should be a challenge, yet at the same time should be adapted to the capabilities of the learners and therefore not overstrain them. The optimal degree of severity can therefore be describes as pleasantly frustrating. Thus, it is based slightly above the learners' competences, but is still manageable [15].

Result of the testing: The mechanism was strongly demotivating for most testers, since they not only had to choose the right material, but also needed a good jumping technique. It was frustrating for them, as they might have chosen the right material, yet the jump was not satisfying. Some players started doubting their choice of material and changed it again. This process became more frustrating the longer it went on.

Analysis: Problems with this jumping mechanism were identified during the observation of a player and the evaluation of the "Kraken" data. For these levels, the "Kraken" evaluation showed a significantly longer playing time. Thus, as can be seen in Fig. 5, more than half of the players of the old version needed a lot longer for the second and third "Plank Jumping" task.

Redesign: The first steps were to change the jumping characteristics of the materials. Therefore, the players were able to make the plank swing easier and it was not as hard to jump the needed height. However, some testers were still frustrated with the levels. Since optimizing one's jumping technique made it much harder to find the optimal jumping board parameters and distracted the players from the main task, a much simpler jump mechanism was chosen, which greatly simplified the optimization of the jump technique without completely renouncing an additional small playful component. In the final version, the players merely have to choose the right starting point of the jumping process by one tap and the pirate then jumps on its own.

Result of the Redesign: The reduction of the level of severity in the "Plank Jumping" level had two outcomes. The time spent until success reduced significantly, as can be seen in Fig. 6. However, by reducing the level of severity, the replayability of the levels sank as well. The players did not have to test and try as much to be successful. Yet, the answers to the quiz level questions improved. This allows for the conclusion that the students had an easier time learning the intended teaching content with the easier jumping mechanism.

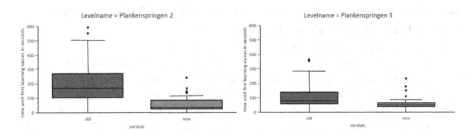

Fig. 6. "Kraken" evaluation of task 2 and 3 of "Plank Jumping" ("Plankenspringen")

4   Conclusion

During the usability engineering, information from the current application is levied by the Logging, to enable the examination of the interaction between system and user behavior. Time periods can be measured together with the interaction points in the software, to identify problem areas with a statistical evaluation. This is of particular advantage in games, because many interactions cannot be broken down to generally standardized methods, such as buttons. An example is the use of a plank with the game character, where there is a variety of possible interaction methods that should be compared in terms of their usability, as explained in this paper. Such analyses provide objective data about the behavior of the players in relation to the design elements and the learning through games. The visualization of the learning behavior enables a comparison between educational intents and the actual player behavior during the serious game [16].

In conclusion, the use of different qualitative and quantitative evaluation tools proves itself. The use of the technical evaluation instrument "Kraken" provided the significant impulses. On the one hand, this data collection tool could exclude the phenomenon of social desirability [17], because one person does not instruct the tested students and the evaluation runs in the background. The data was generated so the individual player is able to solve the task. However, one has to note that the development of the "Kraken" system, the effort to put on the server and to evaluate the event data, is related to a considerable amount of time. From the point of view of the development team, it only makes sense to use this technical evaluation tool if information should specifically be collected for a specific game sequence.

References

1. Brown, J., Isaacs, D.: Das World Café. Kreative Zukunftsgestaltung in Organisationen und Gesellschaft, Heidelberg, pp. 19–20 (2007)
2. MINT_Bildung AMU Universität Augsburg (2018). https://www.amu.uni-augsburg.de/mint_bildung/school_lab-a3/programmbausteine/faserverbund/
3. Jäger, H., Hauke T.: Carbonfasern und ihre Verbundwerkstoffe. Herstellungsprozesse, Anwendungen und Marktentwicklung, Die Bibliothek der Technik, 326, München, p. 4f (2010)
4. Pank, B.: Schlüsseltechnologie Leichtbau: Die branchenübergeifende Querschnittstechnologie. Leichtbau. Neue Werkstoffe und Herstellungsprozesse machen die Fertigung immer leichterer Bauteile in nie da gewesener Qualität möglich. In: Media Planet Leben und Technik (2015). http://www.zukunftstechnologien.info/technik-und-wirtschaft/leichtbau/schluesseltechnologie-leichtbau. zuletzt geprüft am 2 Aug 2018
5. Carbon Composites e.V: Entwicklung und Fertigung von CFK-Bauteilen. Theoretische Grundlagen, p. 7 (2017)
6. Seidel, W., Hahn, F.: Werkstofftechnik. Werkstoffe - Eigenschaften - Prüfung – Anwendung, 10. Aufl. München (Lernbücher der Technik), p. 334 (2014)
7. Brahm, T., Jenert, T.: Wissenschafts-Praxis-Kooperation in desginbasierter Forschung: Im Spannungsfeld zwischen wissenschaftlicher Gültigkeit und praktischer Relevanz. In: Euler, D., Sloane, P.F.E. (Hg.) Design-Based Research. 1. Aufl. s.l.: Franz Steiner Verlag, ZBW Zeitschrift für Berufs- und Wirtschaftspädagogik (27), pp. 45–61 (2014)
8. Euler, D.: Design research - a paradigm under development. In: Euler, D., Sloane, P.F.E. (Hg.) Design-Based Research. 1. Aufl. s.l.: Franz Steiner Verlag, 2014, ZBW Zeitschrift für Berufs- und Wirtschaftspädagogik (27), p. 20 (2014)
9. DIN Deutsches Institut für Normung e.V. (Hg.): DIN SPEC 91380. Serious Games Metadata Format. Beuth Verlag GmbH, Berlin (2018). https://www.beuth.de/de/technische-regel/din-spec-91380/289947896 und SG-IC Serious Games Information Center https://seriousgames-portal.org/
10. Kron, F.W., Sofos, A.: Mediendidaktik. Neue Medien in Lehr- und Lernprozessen, München, p. 134 (2003)
11. Staatsinstitut für Schulqualität und Bildungsforschung München: Realschule, Jahrgangsstufe 8, Werken, Fachlehrpläne. We8 Lernbereich 3: Arbeiten mit dem Werkstoff Kunststoff. München (2017). www.lehrplanplus.bayern.de/fachlehrplan/realschule/8/werken
12. Loh, C.S., Sheng, Y., Ifenthaler, D.: Serious games analytics: theoretical framework. In: Loh, C.S., Sheng, Y., Ifenthaler, D. (eds.) Serious Games Analytics. AGL, pp. 3–29. Springer, Cham (2015). https://doi.org/10.1007/978-3-319-05834-4_1
13. Moura, D., Seif el-Nasr, M., Shaw, C.D.: Visualizing and Understanding Players' Behavior in Video Games: Discovering Patterns and Supporting Aggregation and Comparison. Vancouver, British Columbia, Canada (2011). https://dl.acm.org/citation.cfm?id=2018559
14. https://docs.unity3d.com/Manual/Plugins.html
15. Gee, J.P.: Good Video Games and Good Learning (2005). http://www.academiccolab.org/resources/documents/Good_Learning.pdf. zuletzt geprüft am 5 Aug 2018
16. Smith, S.P., Hickmott, D., Southgate, E., Bille, R., Stephens, L.: Exploring play-learners' analytics in a serious game for literacy improvement. In: Marsh, T., Ma, M., Oliveira, M.F., Baalsrud Hauge, J., Göbel, S. (eds.) JCSG 2016. LNCS, vol. 9894, pp. 13–24. Springer, Cham (2016). https://doi.org/10.1007/978-3-319-45841-0_2
17. Bortz, J., Döring, N.: Forschungsmethoden und Evaluation für Human- und Sozialwissenschaftler, 4th edn. Springer, Heidelberg (2006). https://doi.org/10.1007/978-3-540-33306-7. p. 232f

Evaluating the Adoption of the Physical Board Game Ludo for Automated Assessments of Cognitive Abilities

Fabian Schmitt, Seethu M. Christopher, Kirill Tumanov,
Gerhard Weiss, and Rico Möckel[(✉)]

DKE SwarmLab, Department of Data Science and Knowledge Engineering,
Maastricht University, Maastricht, Netherlands
rico.mockel@maastrichtuniversity.nl

Abstract. Serious games present a valuable tool for continuous cognitive assessments especially in the case of elderly, where there is a lack of cognitive tools to continuously assess the transitory conditions that occur between normal cognition and cognitive failure. However, designing games for elderly poses distinctive challenges since one has to take into account the limited experience of today's elderly with digital gameplay interfaces like touch screens that are second-nature to younger players. In this paper we present an initial user study with young and healthy subjects where we evaluate a computer-vision based digitalization process that is necessary to turn a physical version of the board game "Ludo" into an automated assessment tool. We further evaluate to which extend this tool presents a valid alternative to assess the strategic cognitive capabilities of a person. We have chosen Ludo in its physical form after careful consideration together with elderly and caregivers since many elderlies know this game from their childhood and thus do not need to learn new game rules or to adapt to digital environment.

Keywords: Serious games · Cognitive assessment · Evaluation
Board game · Ludo

1 Introduction

In many countries around the world the relative number of people aged 65 or older is increasing [1, 2]. As a consequence, the capacities for elderly care are predicted to get sparser. The European Union is trying to dampen the effects of such shortcomings by investing in research fields, such as Ambient Assisted Living (AAL) and Serious Games for Health [3, 4]. When Clark Abt first coined the term of Serious Games (SG) in 1970, he described it as a game that is "not intended to be played primarily for amusement." [5]. Overviews of the research field of SG by Susi et al. [6] and Djaouti et al. [7] show the diversity of use cases, ranging from the American military to educational classrooms and from role-play to video games. In the subfield of Health-care Games a similar diversity can be found, ranging from exercise games to train the physical condition, to ones that focus on the mental abilities [8]. Michael and Chen indicate that Serious Games are a combination of learning and assessment [8].

© Springer Nature Switzerland AG 2018
S. Göbel et al. (Eds.): JCSG 2018, LNCS 11243, pp. 30–42, 2018.
https://doi.org/10.1007/978-3-030-02762-9_5

Moreover, Bellotti et al. highlight that in-game assessment provides the opportunity to take advantage of the medium itself and employ alternative, less intrusive and less obvious forms of assessment [9]. Yet, it may provide more detailed and reliable information about the test subject [10]. Shute further mentions the benefits of stealth assessment, an assessment method which is seemingly woven into the game and unobtrusive to the player, which might prove beneficial in the case of elderly [11].

But there are two inherent problems with regards to using SG in elderly care. Firstly, much of the research focus on SG is based on digital games, using computers or tablets as input method [12]. As a result, it requires the elderly to learn technology. This creates a barrier of entrance and leads to the fact that digital SG often assesses in the first place the ability of the elderly to learn new games rules, a new game environment, and how to use a new technology [13, 14] – not necessarily what should be assessed from a caregivers point of view: the ability to remember rules and their strategic abilities. In contrast, many digital SG are meant to teach a certain new objective, and are therefore designed from scratch with these objectives in mind. In elderly care this might overburden the elderly, cause disinterest, and distract the elderly from the assessment objective of the game [14].

To overcome these barriers we propose to study cognitive abilities (1) using a board game that is well-known to elderly from their childhood (2) not in a digital but in its physical form. As a result, elderly do not have to learn new rules or get acquainted with a new technology. Since the game is used in its physical form, elderly can play the way they are used to since their childhood by moving physical pawns on the physical game board. After careful consultations with elderly, caregivers, and experts from social care, together we decided to evaluate the game 'Ludo' which is very popular in Germany under the name "*Mensch ärgere dich nicht*" and in the Netherlands under the name "*Mens erger je niet*". There are only a couple of scientific publications concerning the game, Ludo. The first one uses Ludo as an exemplary game to present the ease of use of some GUI framework [15]. The second publication presents solutions to the AGTIVE 2007 Tool Contest, which required the participants to create and implement a deterministic version of the game [16, 17]. Cujzek and Vranic studied the use of a computerized version of Ludo as a training device for cognitive abilities of elderly [18]. To the best of our knowledge we are the first to study the application of Ludo as an assessment for cognitive abilities.

The study documented in this paper serves two purposes: (1) We explore the required effort to turn the physical board game into an assessment device allowing for continuous and automated assessments. Although digital game devices for serious games pose a barrier for elderly, they come with much comfort for the experimenters since the entire game state can be continuously documented in an automated way with little effort. Using a physical version of the game, we first have to digitize the entire game state, before we can hope to automate the assessment process. (2) We evaluate whether the game Ludo can be used to assess cognitive abilities of players. This question becomes important since the game uses dice to determine the possible moves of a player and thus incorporates a strong element of luck. We explore three key features of game playing:

- To evaluate if the game still can be influenced by the strategic abilities of the players we compare the distribution of the number of moves of human players with the distribution of a gameplay generated by a computer program that plays according to the rule but chooses randomly whenever confronted with a strategic choice.
- To evaluate if players simply follow a strict game policy or if they vary their approach, we evaluate if players familiar with the game of Ludo always choose to kick their opponents' pawn whenever possible.
- Furthermore, we evaluate if players that are expected to possess full cognitive capabilities play the game without making any mistakes with regard to the game rules.

In this paper we present test results from participants with an age in the range of 20 to 28. We explicitly chose to test first with healthy young subjects that are expected to have full cognitive capabilities to reduce the effect of cognitive capabilities on the initial test results and because for ethical reasons we found it important to test only with elderly when the setup is confirmed to work effectively.

2   Methods

2.1   Game Rules of Ludo and Experimental Setup

Figure 1(a) illustrates the board layout. The different shapes in Fig. 1(b) indicate the types of fields. We use a simplified version of the game for elderly where each player plays with 2 pawns (instead of 4 as it is typically the case) of one color (red, green, blue or yellow). The players take turns rolling a die and moving the own pawns by the count of the die. At the beginning, all pawns are placed in their corresponding home fields. The goal of the game is to move all pawns to their target fields of the same color. When a six is rolled, the player has the obligation to place one of its pawns from the home on the start field. On the next die roll this pawn has to be moved along the path of intermediate fields in clockwise direction according to the count shown by the die. An exception is the case, where a six is rolled but the start field is still occupied by a player's own pawn. When this happens, the pawn occupying the start field is moved by the die count. Every field can only be occupied by one pawn at a time. If a player's pawn moves onto a field being occupied by an opponent's pawn, the opponent's pawn has to return to its home field forcing the opponent to start over. Once a pawn has circled the entire board, it can enter the target fields, where it is safe.

The physical board of length 50 cm was placed under a stand (see Fig. 1(c)). A webcam was mounted to the stand at a height of 70 cm, filming the board from the bird's-eye perspective. For the experiments a Logitech C525 webcam was used with a resolution of 720p (1280px × 720px) and the RGB color profile. The video was recorded with 30 frames per second (FPS). However, the algorithm, described in the following used only 3 FPS, which ensured a stable frame rate for online processing of the game state.

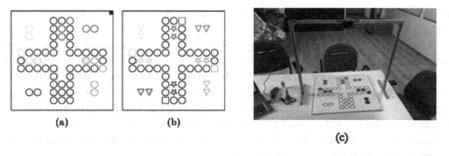

Fig. 1. (a) shows the final layout of the board used for experiments. The different shapes in (b) indicate the types of fields. Triangles: home fields, stars: target fields, squares start fields. (c) Experimental Setup. (Color figure online)

2.2 Digitization of Board Game

The analysis of the game state was performed through computer vision for autonomous detection of the physical game board, its game fields, and the placements of the pawns. Our approach was chosen to enable an assessment tool that could run autonomously and continuously in the background without affecting the players in their natural game play. The detection algorithm was implemented using Python 2.7 and the wrapper for the OpenCV library. The algorithm was designed to be sufficiently light-weight to run online on a standard computer so that we would be able in the future to provide feedback to users during the game. All images were recorded in form of a video file for careful offline analysis.

Our software continuously detects the black boundary of the physical game board by using the Canny edge detection algorithm [19]. From the binary image with detected edges, the largest contour is found using an algorithm first described by Suzuki [20]. The contour's area is then compared to the area of the largest four-sided approximation. If the areas do not differ by more than 2%, the four-sided approximation is used for a perspective transformation to square the edges and cut the image, such that only the board remains. Comparing the contour against a four-sided approximation is done to ensure that no hand is possibly obstructing the image of the board, in which case the contour would have more corners. Circles in the board representing the game fields are detected in the image using the 2-1 Hough Transform [21, 22]. Detected circles are matched up with the closest circles in the theoretical model of Fig. 1(a). A perspective transformation is applied using the homograph from a least squares fit. The fit is computed between detected circles and the expected circles from the model, if more than two circles are detected.

Before a game starts we run a calibration procedure to detect the correct RGB values of all pawns. It was decided to use the RGB color space rather than a more common color detection alternative such as HSV, since the red and yellow pawns used during the experiments had relatively similar hue values and a small change in the lighting situation would cause false detections. We could have used more distinctive colors that are easier to detect. However, after consultations with caregivers and elderly we decided to stay with the colors that are well-known and do not represent a distraction to the elderly.

Once calibrated during game play, game fields being occupied by pawns are automatically detected by finding those circles that are filled with non-white color. This is accomplished by using a threshold that discriminates white empty fields from fields that have other color. To avoid being influenced by the border of the circle, the algorithm only checks the largest square fitting inside the circular field, (see Fig. 2). Furthermore, the algorithm checks whether the number of non-white circles is equal to the total number of pawns. If this is not the case, it is assumed that the board is in an intermediate state where pawns were moved.

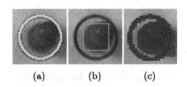

(a)   (b)   (c)

Fig. 2. (a) shows a detected circle, (b) shows the largest square inside the circle used for occupancy detection and (c) shows the circles split in small patches used for color detection. (Color figure online)

For the circles that are detected as non-white, the color is determined (Fig. 2). For this, a majority voting scheme, as described by Molla and Lepetit [23], is deployed. The smallest square encompassing the circle is, therefore, split in 196 patches. Each of the non-white patches determines its color by computing the smallest Euclidean distance to the calibrated colors. Afterwards, the color with the most votes is determined to be the color of the pawn on the field. By using this majority vote system, it is ensured that the color of the pawn is more important than the color of the field. If a red pawn is placed on a field with a green circle, this system will be able to detect the red pawn since it has considerably more votes.

2.3   Data Collection and User Study

We collected data of 15 participants playing in total 12 games in 4 rounds. Testing larger numbers of participants would have been logistically challenging since as part of the validation process of the digitalization approach we had to examine each game play situation by comparing the results from the automated digitalization with the observations that could be derived by a human from the taken video material. This required watching, pausing, and replaying all games of all participants several times and led to several days of work even with only 15 participants. The final digitalization technique simplifies the assessments but its verification that is presented here is very work intensive. One participant (ID = 1 and 16) participated twice. In each game 4 players participated at the same time. Each player played the game three times consecutively always against the same opponents in order to allow the players to adapt to the rules, to reduce the element of chance, and to be able to observe some trends in play behavior.

After playing three times, the players were asked to fill in a questionnaire, reflecting on their game play abilities and emotions. Our questionnaire was developed by adopting questionnaires for assessing technology acceptance of elderly [24, 25] and assesses emotions including stress, comfort, confidence, and excitement on a 5-level Likert scale.

All participants were enrolled students at Maastricht University in the age range of 20 to 28. Only two participants indicated that they had never played the game before. We recorded six female and nine male participants. From the recordings we stored (1) the position of all pawns on the board before a move, (2) the ID of the current player who was in turn to move, (3) the time between the last player finished a move and when the current player rolled the die, (4) the die count, and (5) the position of all pawns after the move of the current player. Invalid moves by players were not prevented during game play but accepted and manually checked against the video file to confirm them.

3   Results on Robustness of Game Board and Game State Detection

We first tested if an automation of the game board detection could be done reliably under real game situations to understand if testing elderly in the future could be reliably automated with the current setup. For each of the four experimental rounds with participants, the first game was used as a reference for testing the robustness of the board detection with varying lightning conditions. The first experimental round was indirectly lit with large windows on two sides of the board. The second and third rounds were in the same environment with a fluorescent light tube at the ceiling and a small window on one side of the board. However, during the third round there was no light coming through the window. Both rounds with fluorescent light show flickering in the video. The last setup was lit indirectly through two windows from one side of the board. During the test games, each frame from the video input was classified as either "board detected" if the contours of the board have been successfully detected or "board not detected" purely based on the detected contours of the game board. Each automatic classification was checked manually for validity and then counted, which resulted in the false positive and false negative rate shown in Table 1.

Table 1 show that round 3 has the lowest false negative rate and round 1 the lowest false positive rate. Furthermore, it shows that the last round has the highest false negative and false positive rate.

We found that once the board contour is detected, finding the circles of the game field is done with a success rate of at least 96%. Despite the fact that the board contour detection shows the aforementioned error rates, misdetections of an overall game state occurred only twice during all experiments when players covered the board with their hands during the entire change of game state.

Table 1. Detection of the board in different scenarios.

Round	1	2	3	4
Scenario	2 windows (2 sides)	1 window & fluorescent tube	Fluorescent tube only	2 windows (1 side)
Total # frames	3330	3401	2699	4581
Total # negative (no board)	1451	686	489	1802
False negative rate	32.80%	9.77%	5.52%	47.84%
Total # positive (board found)	1879	2715	2210	2779
False positive rate	7.24%	8.62%	24.93%	25.84%

4 Results on Ludo as an Assessment Tool for Cognitive Capabilities

In the following we evaluate how much influence players can have on the game of Ludo and if the game is suited as an assessment tool for cognitive abilities.

4.1 Effect by Reduction of Pawns

Based on the advice of caregivers and elderly we had reduced the number of pawns per player from 4 to 2. This was done to reduce the time of a single game and thus the time elderly players have to concentrate continuously. To quantify the effect of the reduction of pawns, 20000 simulations with random strategies were executed. The simulations ran for the original version, as well as the reduced version with 10000 iterations. The results were compared with regards to the average number of moves per player, as well as the percentage of moves in which the player had more than one choice. The reduced version has a decrease by more than 300% to a mean of 48.3 (for 2 pawns) from 207.5 (4 pawns) average moves per player per game. Furthermore, the percentage of choices has reduced to a mean of 39.0% (2 pawns) from 65.1% (4 pawns). This shows that despite the fact that the movement possibilities are partially controlled through a die, a player is still confronted with choices for which of the own pawns should be moved.

4.2 Do Human Players Play Randomly?

During games with human players we found that in the 2-pawn version players on average had to make 42.56 moves with a standard deviation of 5.96 (minimum number of moves: 31, maximum number of moves: 54). Figure 3 shows a comparison of the distribution of the number of moves gained from the human players, against those retrieved from a computer simulation using a random strategy. The Anderson-Darling test clearly rejects the null-hypothesis of an equal distribution ($p < 0.01$) indicating that human players do not play randomly but might follow a strategy.

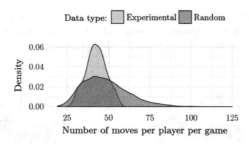

Fig. 3. Histogram comparing the distributions of the number of moves per player per game in the experiments from human players vs the simulation making purely random decisions.

4.3 Rule Conformity

Next we checked the participants' conformity to the game rules. Figure 4 shows those results, where each color represents the participant's ID and the different shapes highlight which game iteration the measurement originates from. Figure 4 shows an approximately equal distribution between participants that did not make any mistakes and those that made at least one mistake. This result rejects the hypothesis that healthy young participants would play the game without making any mistakes. Furthermore, all participants of the second experimental round, participants 5 to 8, have made mistakes in two or more games. However, there is no consistent trend over all participants of this experimental round: one can see a consistent improvement in the game of participant 7, while participant 8 has decreasing rule conformity.

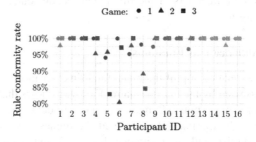

Fig. 4. The plot shows each participant's percentage of valid moves for the three consecutively played games. A rule conformity rate of 100% means that a participant always followed the rules. The data points were colored to better discriminate between participants.

4.4 Strategies

A main strategic decision offered to a player in Ludo is to either move a pawn to the safe target location as quickly as possible or to keep the available pawns close to each other in order to improve the chance of kicking opponents' pawns. Figure 5(a) shows that there is variance between the different participant's strategies, with individuals at either extreme of the scale. However, from the presented data a comparison of the consistency of a particular player's strategy is not possible without obtaining substantially more data since during the recordings several participants had too few active choices: different participants encountered a large variance of choices to decide on this strategy, ranging from 0 to 22 per participant and game.

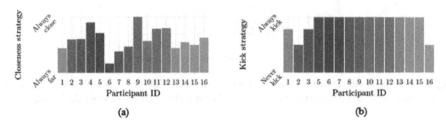

(a)   (b)

Fig. 5. (a) Bar diagram for each participant showing how often they decided to keep their pawns close to each other, when they had the opportunity. (b) Bar diagram for each participant showing how often they decided to kick an opponent out, when they had the choice. No data is available for participant 4.

One of the key elements of Ludo is to kick opponents' pawns out to force them to start over again from their home, causing the opponent to reset some of his/her progress. Figure 5(b) shows the percentage in which the participants decided to kick out one of their opponents whenever they had the opportunity to do so. It is clearly visible that twelve out of 16 participants decided to always kick. As far as the four participants who did not always kick are concerned, we found that all players have reached their lowest percentage in the third game. Moreover, three-quarters of the participants that did not always kick were members of the first experimental round, hinting towards a possible common reason.

4.5 Effect of Confidence and Emotions

Figure 6(a) shows the relationship of the mean total time per move per participant and the excitement, as assessed by the questionnaire. Firstly, it shows that there was a wide variance of excitement levels (min = 2, max = 5, standard deviation = 0.95) across the participants. The second experimental round had the highest diversity. Experimental round 4 contains an outlier, with an excitement level of 2, indicating little excitement, and a mean total time of more than 14 s. Apart from this outlier, a positive trend was detected, suggesting an increase in needed time with increasing excitement. However, testing the slope of a linear regression against 0 does not prove significant at the 5% level.

The relationship between a participant's conformity to the rules and the reflected confidence is displayed in Fig. 6(b). Rather than showing a lower confidence for those participants with a less accurate gameplay, Fig. 6(b) shows no trend. There are two outliers with high confidence and a low conformity. Furthermore, the plot shows that participants of the same experiment have similar confidence levels. The only exception is one member of Experiment 3 who indicates a confidence level of 5 rather than 3.

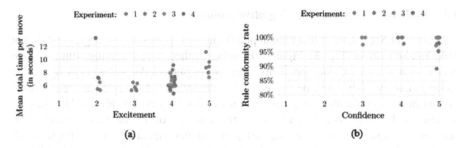

Fig. 6. (a) The average time needed per move with regards to the excitement level of each participant. The color discriminates between the experimental round the player participated in. (b) Relationship between confidence, where a higher number indicates a higher confidence level, and the percentage of valid moves over all games of a certain participant. Colors highlight the experimental round the participant joined.

Data indicates that this trend and clustering do not translate to other emotions, such as excitement.

5 Discussion

5.1 Robustness of Game State Detection

A robust detection of the game states is an essential precondition for using the physical version of the game for automated continuous assessments. When purely looking at the detection of the game board from its contours, the data from Sect. 3 indicates an expected strong dependency of the false and true negative detection rates on the light conditions. A high false negative rate is especially problematic since it could prevent the detection of a new game state. Game board and state detection is further problematic since human players can partially occlude the board with their hands when moving pawns. However, despite the fact that the game board contour detection by itself turned out to be problematic under challenging light conditions, the overall algorithm proved to provide satisfying results: Misdetections of a game state occurred only twice during all experiments when players covered the board with their hands during the entire change of game state. We believe that the robustness of the game state recognition comes from three features: (1) We can compare the digitized game with its known structure; (2) The detection of pawns based on their color is very robust after calibration if light conditions are not changed drastically during the game; (3) Most importantly, human players play at a relatively low speed that allows taking and analyzing many images in between game state changes. We found that players on average use 7.3 s to change the game state with a standard deviation of 4.36. So even for the scenario with the most challenging light conditions (Table 1) where no board contours have been detected in 43.5% of the images taken from the game board, given a frame rate of 3 frames per second, for each game move on average 21.9 images have been taken and the board contour has been detected and could be automatically analyzed about 14 times per change of game state.

5.2   Ludo as Assessment for Cognitive Abilities

The results of Sect. 4 show that human players indeed apply some strategies and do not make random moves (Fig. 3). Figure 5(b) indicates that players familiar with the game decide to always kick out opponents. Yet, some players did not always apply the kicking strategy. This could be caused by less awareness of the rules and game-flow. Furthermore, it could also be assumed that players who do not always kick have a tendency to become more "aggressive" over the course of the three experiments. The decrease in "aggressiveness" in the last game of participants 1 to 3, who were all members of the first experimental round, indicates a possible agreement in kicking strategy. During the game the experimenter observed that players lost interest in the game and stopped kicking opponents to force the game to be shorter. In particular, the closeness strategy of a player's pawns did show a lot of variation between participants (see Fig. 5(a)). However, the large variance of scenarios in which players had to act on this strategy did cause this study to not be able to determine clear strategies for participants with regards to their decision of keeping pawns close to each other on the field. The significance of the results of this strategy might be increased by playing more games per participant or using more pawns per player in the future.

Interestingly, our assumption of participants with lower confidence making more mistakes was not supported (see Fig. 6(b)). Rather, Fig. 6(b) shows a clustering of confidence between the different experimental groups. Whether this clustering was caused by grouping similar players or assimilation within the group is unknown. Yet, it might have influences on the performance and is worthwhile investigating further. In addition, it is worth mentioning that manually logging the die roll, which required the players to state the number of their roll, might have caused an increased awareness for an opponent's move. Future research should explore these open issues.

In any case our experiments indicate that even young healthy participants make mistakes during the game (see Fig. 4) – despite the relatively simple game rules. Since there seems to be no correlation between making mistakes and self-reflection on confidence in the game rules as being assessed by the questionnaire (Fig. 6(b)), human players seem not aware of their mistakes in applying game rules. Following our results and after discussions with experts from social care we decided to use rule conformity as key indicator of cognitive abilities for further studies with elderly.

6   Conclusion

In this paper we study if the board game Ludo can be transformed into a tool for continuous automated assessment of cognitive abilities by recording and analyzing movements and positions of pawns on the physical game board. To the best of our knowledge we are the first to study the application of Ludo as assessment for cognitive abilities. We presented a computer vision algorithm to transform a video recording of the game into a digital representation resulting in only two game state detection errors in 12 games. Overall, the results presented in this paper show that Ludo in its physical form is suitable for assessing automatically and continuously cognitive abilities including reaction times, rule conformity, and strategic game decision of players and they encourage a study with the demographic target group.

Acknowledgement. We thank Ms. Rosel Cleef-Lind from Seniorenzentrum Breberen GmbH (Heinrichs Gruppe), and Ms. Kathrin Polfers, Familienzentrum Lindenbaum e.V., for advice regarding the game and its layout to make the game suitable for elderly and children.

References

1. EU: People in the EU – population projections (2018)
2. U.S. Bureau: FFF: Older Americans Month: May 2017 (2018)
3. EGDF: European Games Developer Federation (2018)
4. Aal: Objectives | Active and assisted living programme (2018)
5. Abt, C.C.: Serious games. University Press of America (1987)
6. Susi, T., Johannesson, M., Backlund, P.: Serious games: an overview. Institutionen för kommunikation och information (2007)
7. Djaouti, D., Alvarez, J., Jessel, J.-P., Rampnoux, O.: Origins of serious games. In: Ma, M., Oikonomou, A., Jain, L. (eds.) Serious Games and Edutainment Applications, pp. 25–43. Springer, London (2011). https://doi.org/10.1007/978-1-4471-2161-9_3
8. Michael, D.R., Chen, S.L.: Serious Games: Games that Educate, Train, and Inform. Muska & Lipman/Premier-Trade (2005)
9. Bente, G., Breuer, J.: Making the implicit explicit. In: Serious Games: Mechanisms and Effects, pp. 322–343 (2009)
10. Bellotti, F., Kapralos, B., Lee, K., Moreno-Ger, P., Berta, R.: Assessment in and of serious games: an overview. In: Advances in Human-Computer Interaction, vol. 2013, p. 1 (2013)
11. Shute, V.J.: Stealth assessment in computer-based games to support learning. Comput. Games Instr. **55**(2), 503–524 (2011)
12. Lemus-Zúñiga, L.-G., Navarro-Pardo, E., Moret-Tatay, C., Pocinho, R.: Serious games for elderly continuous monitoring. In: Fernández-Llatas, C., García-Gómez, J.M. (eds.) Data Mining in Clinical Medicine. MMB, vol. 1246, pp. 259–267. Springer, New York (2015). https://doi.org/10.1007/978-1-4939-1985-7_16
13. Tong, T., et al.: Rapid deployment and evaluation of mobile serious games: a cognitive assessment case study. Procedia Comput. Sci. **69**, 96–103 (2015)
14. Wittland, J., Brauner, P., Ziefle, M.: Serious games for cognitive training in ambient assisted living environments – a technology acceptance perspective. In: Abascal, J., Barbosa, S., Fetter, M., Gross, T., Palanque, P., Winckler, M. (eds.) INTERACT 2015. LNCS, vol. 9296, pp. 453–471. Springer, Cham (2015). https://doi.org/10.1007/978-3-319-22701-6_34
15. Diethelm, I., Jubeh, R., Koch, A., Zündorf, A.: Whitesocks-a simple GUI framework for Fujaba. Volume Editors, p. 30 (2007)
16. Kroll, M., Geiß, R.: A Ludo Board Game for the AGTIVE 2007 Tool Contest (2007). http://gtcases.cs.utwente.nl/wiki/uploads/ludokarlsruhe.pdf
17. Rensink, A., et al.: Ludo: a case study for graph transformation tools. In: Schürr, A., Nagl, M., Zündorf, A. (eds.) AGTIVE 2007. LNCS, vol. 5088, pp. 493–513. Springer, Heidelberg (2008). https://doi.org/10.1007/978-3-540-89020-1_34
18. Cujzek, M., Vranic, A.: Computerized tabletop games as a form of a video game training for old-old. Aging Neuropsychol. Cogn. **24**(6), 631–648 (2017)
19. Canny, J.: A computational approach to edge detection. In: Readings in Computer Vision, pp. 184–203. Elsevier (1987)

20. Suzuki, S.: Topological structural analysis of digitized binary images by border following. Comput. Vis. Graph. Image Process. **30**(1), 32–46 (1985)
21. Davies, E.: A modified hough scheme for general circle location. Pattern Recogn. Lett. **7**(1), 37–43 (1988)
22. Illingworth, J., Kittler, J.: The adaptive hough transform. IEEE Trans. Pattern Anal. Mach. Intell. **5**, 690–698 (1987)
23. Molla, E., Lepetit, V.: Augmented reality for board games. In: ISMAR, pp. 253–254. IEEE (2010)
24. Heerink, M., Krose, B., Evers, V., Wielinga, B.: Studying the acceptance of a robotic agent by elderly users. Int. J. Assistive Robot. Mechatron. **7**(3), 33–43 (2006)
25. Heerink, M., Krose, B., Evers, V., Wielinga, B.: Measuring acceptance of an assistive social robot: a suggested toolkit. In: RO-MAN 2009 - The 18th IEEE International Symposium on Robot and Human Interactive Communication, pp. 528–533 (2009)

Two Decades of Traffic System Education Using the Simulation Game MOBILITY

Heinrich Söbke$^{(\boxtimes)}$ ⓘ, Raimo Harder, and Uwe Planck-Wiedenbeck

Bauhaus-Institute for Infrastructure Solutions (b.is),
Bauhaus-Universität Weimar, Weimar, Germany
{heinrich.soebke, raimo.harder, uwe.
plank-wiedenbeck}@uni-weimar.de

Abstract. MOBILITY is a digital simulation game about traffic system planning, which has been designed as a serious game with the purpose of education and awareness raising. Since the year 2000 it has been used more than a million times in both educational and entertainment contexts. The production of digital serious games, such as MOBILITY, requires a lot of effort. Therefore, serious games are valuable investments that are expected to be of high benefit during their technical lifetime. Much has been written about the effectiveness of the use of serious games and efficiency of game production, however later phases of serious games' lifecycles are comparatively unknown. Based on a lifecycle description of MOBILITY, a categorization of lifetime-determining factors called *game aging* is developed. The categorization is intended to serve as methodological framework to guide lifecycle management of serious games, such as assessing the status of a serious game regarding the categories of game aging. Game aging distinguishes three categories: technology, domain knowledge and user experience. For each of these categories the specific characteristics of MOBILITY are described and discussed. Regarding methodology, the evaluations are based on expert interviews, questionnaires and guided interviews. In summary, after two decades of application MOBILITY is still an effective educational tool for traffic system planning, although each of the examined categories shows signs of game aging. Further research is needed to systematize the framework of game aging.

Keywords: Game aging · Software lifecycle · Serious game
Technical lifetime

1 Introduction

The production of attractive and effective serious games requires a lot of effort. Therefore, there is an interest in being able to use serious games as long as possible. Conversely, a long technical lifetime, along with a high number of users and a high impact, is one of the reasons that can justify large development budgets required for the production of attractive and effective serious games. However, the field of interactive media as a subfield of information technology is very fast-moving. This characteristic is diametrically opposed to long technical lifetimes.

© Springer Nature Switzerland AG 2018
S. Göbel et al. (Eds.): JCSG 2018, LNCS 11243, pp. 43–53, 2018.
https://doi.org/10.1007/978-3-030-02762-9_6

The simulation game MOBILITY can be considered an example of an attractive and effective serious game. It was released in 2000 and has been used more than a million times since then, e.g., it has been successfully used in university courses on traffic system planning. At the same time, it is known from previous work that the simulation game SimCity IV has also been used as an effective serious game for many years. By now, a lot of effort is necessary to provide executable instances of SimCity IV for teaching [1]. The question arises as to how long the technical lifetime of serious games is. Therefore, the determining factors of the technical lifetime of a serious game are also to be investigated.

Profound work on the preservation of computer games, i.e. the possibility to preserve computer games as cultural artifacts for posterity, can be found in the literature, e.g., [2, 3]. In contrast, this paper is not concerned with the problem of making computer games available at all, but rather with problems that arise when games are run in their original application contexts with special regard to affordable effort. It appears that technical lifetime and the later phases of the lifecycle of serious games and factors determining the technical lifetime are not current research topics. Therefore, an initial categorization of factors limiting the technical lifetime of serious games, named game aging, is developed and discussed in this paper using the example of MOBILITY.

The paper is structured as follows: the next section presents MOBILITY, the design of the study and results related to the didactical context. The categories of game aging are then introduced and discussed using the MOBILITY example. Section 4 discusses the results, followed by a summary and conclusions in Sect. 5.

2 MOBILITY

2.1 Lifecycle

This section describes the lifecycle of MOBILITY [4], a simulation game about traffic system planning, as it has proceeded so far. Although the lifecycle is individual, it contains typical characteristics common to other serious games.

Funding and Development. MOBILITY has been developed within a research project funded by the German Federal Ministry of Education and Research (BMBF) [5]. It was released in the year 2000. MOBILITY is based on a monolithic simulation model consisting of 116 variables and 160 causal relations between variables. The development of the simulation model was based on scientifically proven findings. From a technical point of view, MOBILITY is written in C++, without the use of any game engine or other framework. The software company Glamus GmbH was in charge of the development. MOBILITY runs on Microsoft Windows personal computers (PC).

Internationalization. Mobility is available in German and English. Later, Italian was added.

Distribution. At first, 70,000 data carriers with MOBILITY were sold at cost price. Afterwards MOBILITY was distributed via download. Currently, MOBILITY is still available on its homepage [4]. Altogether, the number of short or longtime players is estimated with more than 1 million.

Reception. Mobility has received mostly very positive reviews and has been awarded multiple times. A positive reception in the review of a relevant German computer magazine spurred its proliferation [6]. MOBILITY has been played as an entertainment game without any educational purpose and has been compared to the genre-shaping simulation game SimCity [7]. Thus, in terms of gaming enjoyment MOBILITY was able to compete with SimCity.

Further Development and Maintenance. Shortly after the game's initial release, the necessity to establish a maintenance process became obvious. Shareware fees finance the maintenance process. The functionality of MOBILITY has not been extended since its initial release. However, in 2007 a specific educational package for primary and secondary schools was released based on MOBILITY. It contained localized gaming scenarios (e.g. featuring the German cities of Hanover and Weimar) and supplementary educational resources [8]. An Italian language version was added and MOBILITY was ported to Linux.

Some of the presented characteristics can be considered typical for serious games. Like most serious games, MOBILITY was developed backed by public funding. It is distributed as shareware, which seems to be the currently common business model for serious games. Although a software company manages the distribution of MOBILITY this business model is not sustainable as it does not allow the development of a successor game. At least the maintenance of the game is ensured, which does not seem to be common for serious games. Furthermore, another uncommon serious game feature is the high level of gaming enjoyment that MOBILITY achieves. Altogether, MOBILITY can be seen as a comparatively successful serious game. However, considering the advancing age of MOBILITY and the resulting limitations, the question arises as to at what point of time in its lifecycle MOBILITY will stop working in its application contexts. Thus, in Sect. 3 various aspects of the advancing aging process are analyzed. The analyses are based on a study that is described in the next section.

2.2 Study Design

MOBILITY has been used for more than 10 years in the *Transport Systems Theory* course of the Bachelor's programme in *Environmental Engineering*. *Transport Systems Theory* is concerned with the planning of infrastructure for individual transport, such as streets, and public transport systems, such as bus routes, in urban contexts. In the didactical scenario, students are given a MOBILITY scenario of a city with a dysfunctional public transport system. The task is to analyze the scenario, to collect key performance indicators and to design a public transport system that solves the traffic-related problems of the city. Finally, each student has to submit their resulting MOBILITY scenario including documentation about the solution strategy and achieved values of key performance indicators. The students are prepared in lecture by discussing information about typical problems and appropriate measures (briefing).

The study was carried out as a pilot study on the appropriateness and reception of the chosen design for the didactical scenario. A further research question was concerned with the determination of possible effects attributable to the advanced age of the game software. Table 1 describes the measurements applied in this study. Participation in the questionnaires decreased from questionnaire to questionnaire due to course dropouts and decreasing willingness to participate after completion of the task. The guided interviews were conducted only with students who were available for an interview upon e-mail request.

Table 1. Description of the study's measurements

Measurement	Description	N = ...
Questionnaire 1	• Expectancy – value model [9] to assess the general motivation of the students • Pretest to assess the current knowledge before using MOBILITY	9
Questionnaire 2	• EGameFlow [10] to assess the gaming enjoyment directly after playing MOBILITY	6
Questionnaire 3	• Delayed posttest to assess the current knowledge after using MOBILITY • Students' personal estimation of the didactical scenario and its effects	4
Guided interviews	• Interview with students especially about aspects of game aging	5
Expert interview	• Interview with the lecturer about the didactical scenario and MOBILITY	1

2.3 Evaluation of the Didactical Scenario

The evaluation of the didactical scenario was one of the research questions of the study. In the following, the results are presented according to each measurement method.

Guided Interviews. In the conducted guided interviews, participants assessed the overall study task as interesting and motivating in comparison to other study tasks of the course and of the study programme. In particular, however, the relatively short working time required for the study task was highlighted as positive by the majority of participants. Only two participants mentioned gaming experience as motivating. The good introduction to the study task (briefing) was also repeatedly reported as positive in the conducted interviews. The thorough briefing included short training periods that helped participants become accustomed to MOBILITY. Together with the required simulation time of approximately two hours, the average time required to complete the study task was three hours. Interviewees noted critically that the relation between measures and results had to be observed, as is usual for games, instead of being stated explicitly, as in books. Observations, however, take time. Yet, all interviewees were able to remember experiences of learning, e.g., the surprising ineffectiveness of the suburban railway or the necessity to assign the required number of buses to each bus line. This can be seen as an indication of successful learning processes.

Further potential for improvement resulted from the report of one interviewee who stated that due to her strategy game experience she had taken the necessary measures during the first 15 min of the gaming time. Thereafter, she assured herself that the game scenario was also economically balanced and then she left MOBILITY to itself for the rest of the necessary simulation time. In the end, the results required for the study task were achieved and only had to be briefly documented.

Questionnaires. Although questionnaire items identified a high level of social interaction, the didactical scenario could possibly be improved in this regard. The task can be done individually, which does not lead to social interactions that are considered important for learning processes (e.g. [11]).

Pre- and Posttest. Pre- and posttest consisted of five multiple choice questions consisting of a total of 33 options. While the pretest was completed with an average of 60% of correct answers, participants reached an average of 71% in the posttest. The increase of correctness has to be rated as a positive result. However, it is not representative due to the low sample size and the decreased number of participants in the posttest.

Possible Further Developments of the Didactical Scenario. Identified weaknesses of the didactical scenario were the fact that the students played alone, the difficulties in observing cause-effect relationships, and the possibility of being able to reduce the time spent working on the study task and thus to reduce the possible learning time. In order to remedy this situation, it is recommended that the tasks are solved in groups, that players are asked to produce specific extreme effects in MOBILITY, and that a scenario is provided that requires continuous control. In comparison to other tasks of the study programme, the MOBILITY study task could be extended in terms of working time to provide further learning opportunities.

3 Game Aging

The phenomenon of *software aging* has been described by Parnas [12]. He refers to software aging as a phenomenon similar to human aging: *"Old software has begun to cripple its once-proud owners; many products are now viewed as a burden-some legacy from the past. A steadily increasing amount of effort is going into the support of these older products."* He identifies mainly two types of causes for software aging. The first type, the external cause, refers to changing requirements for the software, which are not met by respective changes of the software. Thus, the software may become unusable from the user's point of view. The second type of cause, the internal cause, is connected to the internal structure of the software: inherently to the maintenance process, it becomes more and more difficult to apply changes to the software. At a certain point in the lifecycle, the software may become unmaintainable from the developer's point of view. This can also make the software unusable, as required changes do not become effective. As the impact of software increases in daily life, measures to slow down or limit the impact of software aging become increasingly important. Parnas focuses on the developer's point of view and thus on the internal causes in the description of possible measures and answers the question of how to sustain the maintainability of software.

Digital games are a specialized kind of software. Therefore, they are also subject to the phenomenon of software aging. However, in the case of digital games – and especially digital serious games – external causes of software aging can be considered as having a greater impact. Externals causes of software aging can be seen mainly as changing requirements that are not met by the software. In the case of digital games, rising standards of computer graphics could be a reason for characterizing a game as old. As digital games rely on aesthetics as one mechanism to elicit enjoyment in the player, the requirement for impressive computer graphics is higher for computer games than for general application software. Furthermore, in the context of a serious game, changes in the domain knowledge to be conveyed by the serious game can make the game obsolete. This requirement hardly exists for digital games serving solely entertainment purposes. Both examples demonstrate that software aging may have further aspects in the context of serious games. A previous work [1] identified more systematically three categories of external software aging (technology, domain knowledge and user experience). As these categories are especially important for games, they are subsumed under the term *game aging*. In the following sections, these categories are described and illustrated using the study of MOBILITY.

3.1   Category: Technology

Description. *Technical game aging* occurs because of the changing environment of **hard- and software**. For example, from time to time new types of game consoles are released that outdate previous console types, e.g., in terms of performance. With regard to PC games, such as MOBILITY, the release of the operating system is a crucial requirement. For example, SimCity IV requires Microsoft Windows XP, which is neither sold nor supported by the producer. Virtual machines solve the problem of **operating systems** that are no longer available [1]. The field of videogame preservation provides further strategies to keep digital games available as cultural artifacts [2, 3]. However, in the context of serious games, it is important that the employed preservation strategy is not only feasible in terms of technology, but that the necessary effort is affordable. Legal issues are another potential source of aging, e.g., expiration of temporal licenses.

Study. The study, especially the guided interviews, revealed no severe technical challenges. This result was to be expected, as each semester students had been able to deliver solutions for the MOBILITY study task. Due to the ongoing maintenance by the supplier of MOBILITY, the game software runs on current Microsoft Windows systems. The only pitfall, mentioned by an interviewee, is the correct configuration of the compatibility settings. License issues have not occurred, as there is a specific agreement of permanent and unlimited educational use of MOBILITY.

3.2   Category: Domain Knowledge

Description. Many serious games, especially educational serious games, have to convey domain knowledge, e.g. about water infrastructure [13] or infrastructure management [1]. In general, each game is based on a model. This model, however, may be subject to changes over time. For example, a game encouraging physical exercises relies on a model of the effects of physical exercises on the human body [14]. If the underlying knowledge of effects of physical exercises changed due to further insights, the game would become outdated. The divergence between reality and the implemented model of the reality that happens over time is a common issue of serious games.

Study. *Expert Interview.* MOBILITY was designed twenty years ago. Although its domain of traffic system planning can be regarded as comparatively stable, the expert interview revealed changes in domain knowledge that are not yet implemented in MOBILITY. The most important of these is the current increase in e-mobility. MOBILITY does not contain any form of e-mobility, which is a major weakness when teaching the knowledge of modern means of transport. In addition to the complete lack of e-mobility means of transport, changes in the distribution of means of transport can also be observed. For example, car sharing was not as popular twenty years ago as it is nowadays. Unfortunately, MOBILITY cannot be adapted to this change of priorities. *Guided Interviews.* The participants of the guided interviews acknowledged that MOBILITY is consistent with reality to a high degree. Only one participant named designated bikeways as a missing element in the game. Thus, most players do not perceive MOBILITY as outdated regarding domain knowledge.

3.3   Category: User Experience

Description. Games should elicit gaming enjoyment. However, when the use of games is mandatory playing becomes work to some extent [15] and the intrinsic motivation arising from gaming enjoyment is reduced. Similarly, outdated user interfaces, such as game graphics, may further reduce gaming enjoyment. Aesthetics is an essential part of gaming experiences. Thus, in general, user experience is considered to be subject to the aging process.

Study. *General Motivation.* Gaming experiences might have been influenced by a low motivation caused by the mandatory character of the game playing as part of the study task. To determine the general motivation of students regarding the study task indicators of motivation were measured using the expectancy value model of Wigfield and Eccles [9]. The model measures motivation by means of the categories of interest, usefulness and importance. Results (see Fig. 1) show that the interest in MOBILITY is higher than perceived usefulness and importance. Two items of comparative data [16, 17] show an inverse relationship. Overall, the values of all of the three categories can be rated as good, but they are consistently below the values of the comparative data. *Gaming Enjoyment.* A key differentiator that distinguishes serious games from other interactive media is gaming enjoyment. Thus, gaming enjoyment has been measured using the EGameFlow questionnaire by Fu et al. [10] in a German translation provided by Eckardt et al. [18]. The results show very typical game characteristics (see Fig. 2) such as high immersion and high challenge. Although MOBILITY is a single-player game, it reached higher values in the category of social interaction than the comparative data [17, 18].

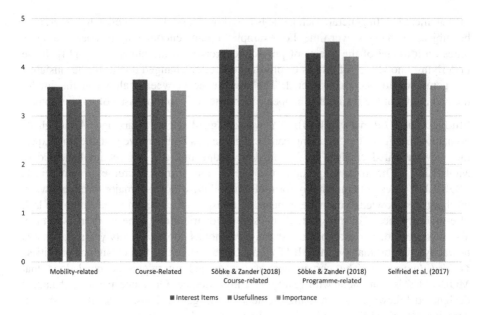

Fig. 1. Expectancy-value-model ([9, 19], compared to results in [16, 17] (5-point Likert scale))

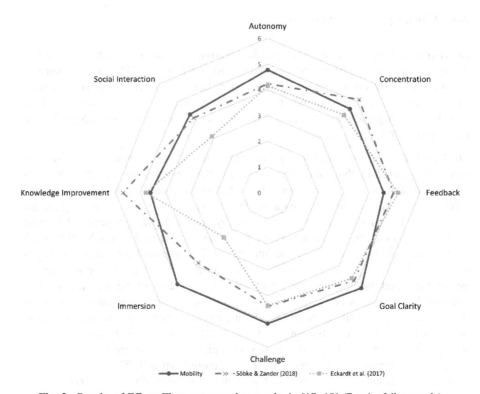

Fig. 2. Results of EGameFlow, compared to results in [17, 18] (7-point Likert scale)

Guided Interviews. The interviewed students assessed MOBILITY rather matter-of-factly. Most praised the short average working time of only two hours, but did not attribute much importance to the **gaming enjoyment**. Gaming enjoyment was severely limited by the mandatory character of the game playing. However, interviewees pointed out that they preferred the MOBILITY study task to other non-lecture tasks, such as those provided in the course on Structural Mechanics. Some interviewees criticized the simple game mechanics: compared to contemporary games, such as Cities: Skylines [20], the game lacks appealing comments on player actions. Randomly interspersed game events that make the game interesting and unpredictable and that tease the player in phases of inactivity are missing as well. At this point, the **game mechanics**, which contribute to the user experience, were identified as being aged. The user interface was explicitly named as outdated due to its low-resolution graphics and its partly aged interaction patterns, such as arrow navigation in a map. However, two interviewees acknowledged the particular charm of the user interface and all but one interviewee rated the user interface as easy and intuitive to use.

4 Discussion

MOBILITY can be regarded as a comparatively successful serious game. Based on a sufficient development budget, an attractive game has been provided, that has also reached a long lifetime. MOBILITY has benefited from an accompanying maintenance process that could be financed via shareware fees, which are still generating revenues. The native development in C++ was another advantage for the maintenance process. As a result, the game did not depend on the lifecycle of game engines, which can be discontinued or also be subject to aspects of software aging. Similar technical dependencies would arise through the use of effort-reducing authoring environments, such as StoryTec [21] or frameworks in general [22]. On the other hand, the game retains its "retro charm" through graphics and interaction patterns, which can be regarded as both motivating and demotivating. The monolithic simulation model of MOBILITY has proved to be disadvantageous. The simulation model makes it very difficult to integrate newer developments, such as e-mobility, into the game [23]. MOBILITY is an example for a serious game, which is still characterized by greater technical detailedness than contemporary commercial urban planning games with strengths in traffic system planning, such as in particular Cities: Skylines [20]. Another reason for still using MOBILITY is certainly the effort required to create a didactic scenario using a commercial urban planning game.

The findings of this study may be of limited applicability, as many serious games are research-oriented prototypes without the intention of a long lifetime. There may be further reasons not to aim at long lifetimes of serious games, such as volatile technical areas covered by serious games. A major problem of serious game development is its unsustainable financing. Often, serious games are developed in time-restricted projects funded by public donors. Frequently, the maintenance phase is not financially backed, which leads to games being discontinued [24]. Up to now, funding for serious games has mostly been provided by public donors. However, if the investments can be spread over such a long lifetime, it is at least more likely that other sources would also be able to contribute to the financing of serious games. Admittedly, the study is not representative due to the small size of the sample and due to the limited period of time covered by measurements. More experiences on complete lifecycles of serious games including all stakeholders are required.

5 Summary and Conclusions

The development of serious games is a complex process that requires high investments. The benefit gained from the investment increases with a longer lifetime of a serious game. However, the lifetime of serious games has hardly been systematically researched to date. Therefore, in this paper the simulation game MOBILITY was presented as an example of a serious game that has existed for almost two decades. Using the example of MOBILITY, the concept of game aging has been introduced as a categorization of possible lifetime-limiting factors. The categories of technology, domain knowledge and user experience are used. Indications of aging of MOBILITY were found in all categories. The same study, however, revealed that MOBILITY is still being used successfully as a valuable learning tool. The evaluation of the didactical scenario also showed potential for improvement. The systematic analysis of causes of game aging could support the creation of an evaluation scheme for assessing the aging status of any serious game. In addition to the causes, systematic analyses of impacts and consequences of game aging is to be done. Such analyses would allow determining the remaining usability of a serious game and support lifecycle management of a serious game. Further, the systematic analyses can be used as a basis to systematically define constructive measures, such as policies and technical remedies, to extend the lifetime of serious games. Moreover, research regarding the validity and completeness of the proposed game aging categories is necessary.

References

1. Arnold, U., Söbke, H., Reichelt, M., Haupt, T.: Simulationsfall Nohra: SimCity als etabliertes Lehrmedium in der universitären Hochschulausbildung [Simulation case Nohra: SimCity as an established teaching medium in university education]. In: Igel, C., Ullrich, C., Wessner, M. (eds.) Bildungsräume DeLFI 2017 vom 5. bis 8. September 2017 Chemnitz Proceedings, pp. 303–308. Gesellschaft für Informatik, Bonn (2017)
2. Guttenbrunner, M., Becker, C., Rauber, A.: Keeping the game alive: evaluating strategies for the preservation of console video games. Int. J. Digit. Curation 5, 64–90 (2010)
3. Brown, S., Lowrance, S., Whited, C.: Preservation Practices of Videogames in Archives. https://ssrn.com/abstract=3174157
4. Glamus GmbH: Mobility - A city in motion! http://www.mobility-online.de
5. Brannolte, U., Griesbach, W., Harder, R., Kraus, T.: Aktualisierung und Erweiterung von Planspielansätzen im Verkehrswesen im Hinblick auf die Erstellung von Mobilitätsspielen [Updating and extending business game approaches in the transport sector with regard to the creation of mobility games.]. Project report, Weimar (2000)
6. Schmitz, P.: CD-ROM-Kritik: Mobility [CD-ROM Review: Mobility]. c't Mag. für Comput. 252 (2000)
7. Wright, W.: SimCity. www.simcity.com
8. Glamus GmbH: dein|t|o|w|n. http://www.deintown.de/

9. Wigfield, A., Eccles, J.S.: Expectancy – value theory of achievement motivation. Contemp. Educ. Psychol. **25**, 68–81 (2000)
10. Fu, F.L., Su, R.C., Yu, S.C.: EGameFlow: a scale to measure learners' enjoyment of e-learning games. Comput. Educ. **52**, 101–112 (2009)
11. Lave, J., Wenger, E.: Situated Learning: Legitimate Peripheral Participation. Cambridge University Press, Cambridge (1991)
12. Parnas, D.L.: Software aging. In: Proceedings of the 16th International Conference on Software Engineering, pp. 279–287. IEEE Computer Society Press (1994)
13. D'Artista, B.R., Hellweger, F.L.: Urban hydrology in a computer game? Environ. Model Softw. **22**, 1679–1684 (2007)
14. Hoffmann, K., Wiemeyer, J., Hardy, S., Göbel, S.: Personalized adaptive control of training load in exergames from a sport-scientific perspective. In: Göbel, S., Wiemeyer, J. (eds.) GameDays 2014. LNCS, vol. 8395, pp. 129–140. Springer, Cham (2014). https://doi.org/10.1007/978-3-319-05972-3_14
15. Rockwell, G.M., Kee, K.: Game studies - the leisure of serious games: a dialogue. Game Stud. - Int. J. Comput. Game Res. **11**(2) (2011). http://gamestudies.org/1102/articles/geoffrey_rockwell_kevin_kee. ISSN: 1604-7982
16. Seifried, E., Kriegbaum, K., Spinath, B.: Veränderung der veranstaltungsbezogenen Motivation über ein Semester und die Rolle von veranstaltungsbezogenen Erwartungen [Change in course-related motivation over a semester and the role of course-related expectations]. In: Seifried, E., Spinath, B. (eds.) PAEPSY 2017 - Gemeinsame Tagung der Fachgruppen Entwicklungspsychologie und Pädagogische Psychologie 11. - 14. 9. in Münster - Arbeitsgruppe Motivation im Hochschulkontext: Entwicklung und beeinflussende Faktoren (2017)
17. Söbke, H., Zander, S.: Motivationsdesign durch Verschränkung von Gamifikation und didaktischem Kontext: Eine Quiz-App in einem ingenieurtechnischen Studiengang [Motivation design by combining gamification and didactic context: a quiz app in an engineering course of study]. In: Krömker, D., Schroeder, U. (eds.) DeLFI 2018 - Die 16. E-Learning Fachtagung Informatik, pp. 141–152. Gesellschaft für Informatik, Bonn, Frankfurt (2018)
18. Eckardt, L., Pilak, A., Löhr, M., van Treel, P., Rau, J., Robra-Bissantz, S.: Empirische Untersuchung des EGameFlow eines Serious Games zur Verbesserung des Lernerfolgs [Empirical study of the EGameFlow of a serious game to improve learning success]. In: Bildungsräume 2017, pp. 285–296. Gesellschaft für Informatik, Bonn (2017)
19. Eccles, J.S., Adler, T.F., Futterman, R., Goff, S.B., Kaczala, C.M., Meece, J.L., et al.: Expectancies, values, and academic behaviors. In: Spence, J.T. (ed.) Achievement and Achievement Motives, pp. 75–146. Freeman, San Francisco (1983)
20. Collossal Order: Cities: Skylines (2015). http://www.citiesskylines.com
21. Göbel, S., Salvatore, L., Konrad, R.: StoryTec: a digital storytelling platform for the authoring and experiencing of interactive and non-linear stories. In: International Conference on Automated Solutions for Cross Media Content and Multi-channel Distribution, AXMEDIS 2008, pp. 103–110 (2008)
22. Söbke, H., Streicher, A.: Serious games architectures and engines. In: Dörner, R., Göbel, S., Kickmeier-Rust, M., Masuch, M., Zweig, K. (eds.) Entertainment Computing and Serious Games. LNCS, vol. 9970, pp. 148–173. Springer, Cham (2016). https://doi.org/10.1007/978-3-319-46152-6_7
23. Schneider, D.: Potentiale für eine Weiterentwicklung des Simulationsspiels Mobility im Bereich der Elektromobilität [Potentials for further development of the simulation game Mobility in the field of electric mobility]. Bachelor thesis, Bauhaus-Universität Weimar (2013)
24. Söbke, H., Schwarz, D.: Serious Games vermitteln technisches Systemwissen [Serious Games convey technical system knowledge]. Wasser und Abfall **18**, 24–28 (2016)

See Me Roar: On the Over-Positive, Cross-Cultural Response on an AR Game for Math Learning

Jingya Li[✉], Erik van der Spek, Jun Hu, and Loe Feijs

Department of Industrial Design, Eindhoven University of Technology, Den Dolech 2, 5612 AZ Eindhoven, The Netherlands
{ji.li,e.d.v.d.spek,j.hu,l.m.g.feijs}@tue.nl

Abstract. Today's children spend a lot of time playing digital games, but may be less interested in their schoolwork, especially for subjects they find difficult and are subsequently not willing to spend much time on it, such as mathematics. Serious games can be an effective method to improve the motivation and learning performance of children in math learning. However, current serious games have limitations in classroom applicability. Augmented Reality provides the opportunity for children to immediately visualize the assignment and can be designed to create a fantasy environment that can engage children to delve deeper into the subject. However, it is less well studied how children from different cultures react to the game design of AR learning games. Therefore, in this study, we have designed the base prototype of an AR game, called See Me Roar, aiming to improve children's learning experience. To investigate the effect of our current base game on children's learning motivation compared to the effect of a more traditional paper exercise, two user studies were conducted, one in China and one in an international school in the Netherlands. The results have shown that compared to a traditional paper exercise, the AR game significantly improved a number of motivational correlates, i.e. likability, enjoyment, the desire to do the exercise in free time, recommendation to others, and in general making math more fun. Both Chinese and international children prefer the game over the paper exercise. Insights regarding Self-Determination theory for the development of future versions of the game are subsequently discussed.

Keywords: Augmented reality · Serious game · Motivation · Mathematics Cross-cultural

1 Introduction

1.1 Serious Games for Mathematics Learning

Children nowadays are born in a world that shows the rapid growth of various multimedia technologies, enjoying and spending more time playing digital games than their previous generations [10]. Therefore, digital games with learning purposes, known as serious games, have become an increasingly important educational method to keep children motivated [10, 31]. Compared to traditional instructional material, such as textbooks, serious games are hypothesized to have great advantages for children in

S. Göbel et al. (Eds.): JCSG 2018, LNCS 11243, pp. 54–65, 2018.
https://doi.org/10.1007/978-3-030-02762-9_7

terms of more motivation [5, 12, 32], greater learning achievements [5, 14, 29, 31], providing engaging and entertaining experiences [3, 12, 32], and customization to different learning abilities [14, 15]. Children express that they are more willing to spend time learning with games, which have been part of their daily life since a young age and are more enjoyable to engage with than traditional instruction [10].

Mathematics learning has been a primary concern in the educational system around the world, as children frequently experience mathematics as a difficult subject during their primary school years [28]. Learning motivation and interests are suggested to play an important role in children's mathematics performance at school [1], where low feelings of competence and engagement for mathematics predict poorer mathematics performance [1, 8]. What's more, children have different abilities in learning mathematics and need to prioritize their goals according to their abilities that best match their personal needs [1]. Therefore, recently some serious games for mathematics learning have emerged and reported to effectively enhance the motivation and enjoyment of children in mathematics learning [17, 19, 30].

1.2 Augmented Reality Games for Learning

Although the above serious games were effective for motivating students in learning and improving their learning performance, overall there is little evidence that serious games are considered more motivating than traditional instruction [31]. Therefore, more research needs to be done on how serious games should be designed to be engaging. In addition, problems have been reported with successfully integrating serious games in the classroom. The computers to play the game on are regularly located in another room and games are not designed to fit into standard classroom hours, leading to scheduling problems [27]. This physical separation also makes it more difficult to integrate games with existing instructional materials such as textbooks and blackboards, even though games are more stressful in reaching their learning goals when they supplement existing instruction [31], and they are more likely to be adopted by teachers when they blend into the curriculum [6]. Lastly, the tangibility, possession, feeling of turning pages, and better information comprehension of the physical textbook [11, 13, 33] are often preferred by students.

Augmented reality (AR) technology is able to combine the advantages of serious games and physical objects, allowing children to interact with and explore virtual objects on the top of real-world objects, completing tasks, learning concepts, and practicing knowledge in both the real and virtual world [15]. To be more specific, AR technology can improve the immersion of children in the learning content [24]. The appearing of AR elements in the real world, such as 3D objects or animations, can put children inside the magic circle and fostering an illusion of being inside the game world, where they will concentrate and engage more at a constant level [24]. Secondly, AR integrates both the sight of virtual objects and the feeling of physical objects, so children can view the previously static images from different perspectives and interact with the virtual content and physical objects more naturally and directly [2, 24]. In addition, one important feature of AR is that it emphasizes the contextual relationships between real and virtual objects [2], offerings meaningful and rich information to help construct an elaborate network of learning content [24]. Last but not least, AR technology can facilitate collaborative learning among children, allowing them to collaborate with classmates, receive support from teachers, and communicate with their parents [7, 16].

1.3 Self-Determination Theory

Self-Determination Theory (SDT) explains why people are motivated to engage and put effort in an activity for pleasure [18]. SDT has been applied to educational research and can improve children's interests in learning and their confidence in their own abilities [18]. Due to the difficulty of mathematics and the higher effort demand required from children, it requires a strong degree of motivation, positive attitudes, and interest towards mathematics to achieve high performance [14]. It has been suggested that the potential of games to satisfy basic psychologic needs for competence, autonomy, and relatedness can lead to increased enjoyment [18, 20, 23, 25], desire for future play [18, 20, 23], recommendation to others [18, 20], and more positive ratings of the game [18]. Therefore, we are designing a textbook-based AR learning game for primary school children, called See Me Roar [16], which aims to provide children a motivating learning environment in doing mathematics exercises. Hypothesis 1 is proposed:

> **H1:** See Me Roar will improve children's (a) enjoyment, (b) desire to do the exercise in free time, (c) recommendation to others, (d) perceived fun of doing math, (e) likability of the experience over a paper exercise.

2 Schoolwork in Different Cultural Background

Cultural issues are important and complex in the design of AR games for learning, especially for mathematics schoolwork in primary school. Children often complain about schoolwork taking away their time for more enjoyable activities [26]. The learning environment is different between different cultures. In countries like China, students get used to having a lot of homework after school. According to a report [4], Chinese students from primary and secondary school spend three hours on average on homework every day, which is three times as much time or even more compared with their counterparts in other countries [4]. What's more, mathematics is also considered as the most difficult subject by students, with 71.9% stating that they spend the most of time on mathematics homework [4]. The overwhelming homework can make students feel frustrated and stressed, resulting in the negative attitudes towards homework as well as the learning experience [4]. In addition, in the home environment in China, parents are highly involved and controlling in children's schoolwork. Parents are asked by teachers to supervise their children in finishing their homework. According to the same report [4], over 80% of the parents feel exhausted from the homework of their children. While children from Western cultures spend fewer hours in school and devote less time after school to academic activities compared to Chinese children [9]. Hypothesis 2 is proposed:

H2: There are measurable differences in perceiving See Me Roar in (a) enjoyment, (b) desire to do the exercise in free time, (c) recommendation to others, (d) perceived fun of doing math, (e) likability of the experience over a paper exercise between children in China and children in the Netherlands.

3 Concept Design of See Me Roar

Based on SDT, we are designing an AR game for primary school students called See Me Roar. The current version of See Me Roar is the base game with basic functions, aiming to provide children a motivating learning environment in doing their math exercises. The game concepts were designed and developed together with two Dutch primary school students.

In the beginning of the gameplay, children are told that there are animals in their textbook waiting for their help to solve math problems. Then, children start to scan the textbook and find animals. When the animal shows up (Fig. 1 up-left), children can interact with the animal by touch-input, leading to a number of different actions, such as lying down, jumping, or flying. Children can control animals to move around (round button in Fig. 1). A relationship bar with the animal shows up on the right corner of the screen (See Fig. 1), starting from 0 point. Children have to find ways to build a relationship with the animal. They can open their bag that contains some food for the animals (Fig. 1 up-middle). For each food item there is a description of animal preferences (Fig. 1 up-right). Children can feed the animals based on their own choice. Once the relationship bar achieves 100 points, an exercise interface will appear and children can write their answer to the displayed exercise (Fig. 1 down-left) (the exercises match their learning progress in their textbook). Upon completion, children will get immediate feedback showing right or wrong answered questions accompanied by either a gift as reward from the animal (Fig. 1 down-middle), or an encouraging message for them to keep on going (Fig. 1 down-right). Different animals carry exercises with different difficulty levels based on the rarity of encountering them.

4 Method

4.1 Participants

Two user studies have been done, including 38 children in total from China and an international school in the Netherlands.

China. 20 Chinese participants (10 Males and 10 Females; M = 8.2 years, SD = 0.62 years) were randomly selected from grade 3 of an average-level primary school. 3 out of the participants reported having used AR before. The most popular games was *Minecraft*, with 13 participants naming this as their most played game.

The Netherlands. In the Netherlands, 18 participants (10 Males and 8 Females; M = 7.1 years, SD = 0.32 years) took part in the user study. They were students from one class in grade 3 in the international school who can speak English in the

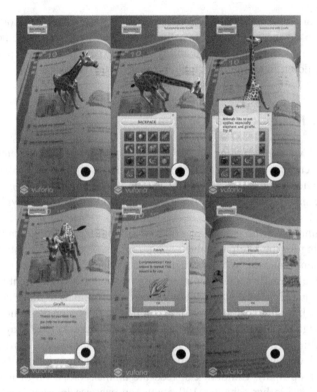

Fig. 1. Screenshot of See Me Roar (up-left: animal shows up; up-middle: interact with animal; up-right: description of food; down-left: exercise interface; down-middle: reward; down-right: encouraging message).

Netherlands. Among them, 3 out of 18 participants claimed that they have experience with AR technology before. Like the Chinese participants, 11 participants in the Netherlands said that *Minecraft* was their most played game.

4.2 Apparatus

The mobile devices used in the study were Galaxy S8 with the Android operating system. We used Unity 3D as the game engine to build the game, with the Vuforia plugin for AR features. The current 3D models of the animals and food items were purchased from the Unity Asset Store.

4.3 Procedure

China. With the help of the teachers, we randomly assigned the 20 participants into two equal groups (Group A and B). We used a within-subject design for the study, where each group experienced the AR game and the paper exercise in different orders: group A played the game first and did the paper exercise, group B did the paper exercise first and then played the game. All participants individually performed 10 mathematics exercises each time with roughly the same difficulty level, on paper or AR game and vice versa. The exercises were chosen and modified from the math textbook of grade 3 by the teacher. The paper exercises contained the same animals and assignments as the AR game, so that purely the interactive AR aspects were tested instead of the fantasy narrative of anthropomorphic animals. Participants were told that there was no time limit and they could finish the exercises at their own speed. After the paper and the AR game, participants were asked to complete a questionnaire independently. At the end of the study, participants were interviewed regarding their preference between the paper exercise and the AR game.

The Netherlands. Due to time constraints, the 18 participants were randomly divided into two groups in the study in the international school in the Netherlands (Group C and D). Participants did the experiment in groups of 9. Same as the user study in China, each group experienced the AR game and the paper exercise in different orders. The paper exercises featured the same animals and exercises with roughly the same difficulty level as the AR game. After both paper and the AR game, participants were asked to complete the questionnaire. An extra PENS questionnaire [23] was filled in by children after playing the AR game. In the end of the study, participants were interviewed in group with questions regarding their preference between the paper and the AR game, other possibilities in the game, other types of animals in the game, and the difficulties of the exercise in the game.

4.4   Measurements

The experiment followed a within-subjects design with counter-balancing to avoid carry-over effects. Enjoyment was measured adapting the Intrinsic Motivation Inventory [22], assessing the participants' enjoyment while experiencing the AR game and the paper exercise. The questions for assessing the desire to do the exercise in free time were adapted from [18, 22], including "Given the chance I would do this activity in my free time". The recommendation to others was assessed by "I would recommend this experience to my friends" [18]. Self-made questions were developed to measure the likability of the AR game and the paper exercise, and to what extent did the game or paper exercise make math more fun, using the statement, "I like playing this game" or "I like doing this exercise", "This game makes math more fun" or "This exercise makes math more fun". The Smileyometer designed for children was used to elicit children's opinion on the AR game and the paper exercise, which is a 5-point Likert scale and uses 5 smileys [21]. The answers of Smileyometer were re-coded to 1 (strongly disagree) to 5 (strongly agree). The PENS questionnaire [23] was used for reflecting the perceived autonomy, competence, and relatedness when playing the AR game. A 7-point Likert scale was used (1 = strongly disagree, 7 = strongly agree). An open-ended interview was conducted after finishing all the exercises and questionnaires, aiming to collect more in-depth feedback and suggestions from children for the future development of the AR game.

5 Results

5.1 Mathematics Performance Test

A paired sample t-test was conducted to examine the final scores for the AR game and the paper exercise in China. There was no significant difference in the scores of the paper exercises (M = 8.40, SD = 1.603) and the game exercises (M = 8.25, SD = 1.585); t (19) = −0.429, p = 0.673. The result shows that the AR game does not have negative influence on children's performance in doing mathematics exercise.

In the Netherlands, participants performed the study in groups of 9. Therefore, we were unable to record the scores of each participant in the AR game. Thus, we didn't compare the performance between the AR game and the paper exercise for the international students.

5.2 Motivation Test

China. When we compare the experience of the AR game with that of the paper exercises, significant differences were found in their likability of the experience (AR game: M = 4.6, SD = 0.598; paper: M = 4.1, SD = 0.788; t (19) = 3.249, p = 0.004), desire to do it in free time (AR game: M = 4.45, SD = 0.686; paper: M = 3.6, SD = 1.142; t (19) = 3.101, p = 0.006), perceived fun of doing math (AR game: M = 4.55, SD = 0.135; paper: M = 4.00 SD = 0.192; t (19) = 2.979, p = 0.008), recommendation of the experience to others (AR game: M = 4.55, SD = 0.686; paper: M = 4.1, SD = 0.912; t (19) = 2.651, p = 0.016), and enjoyment (AR game: M = 4.51, SD = 0.798; paper: M = 4.03, SD = 0.593; t (19) = 4.174, p = 0.001).

The Netherlands. Whereas the children in China already evaluated the AR game very positively, the international school children in the Netherlands rated it even higher, leading to a strong negative skew and ceiling effect for many of the motivational correlates of the AR game (likability: M = 5.0, SD = 0; desire to do the exercise in free time: M = 4.67, SD = 0.97, skewness = −3.58; perceived fun of doing math: M = 4.78, SD = 0.94, skweness = −4.24; recommendation to others: M = 4.72, SD = 0.96, skewness = −3.89; enjoyment: M = 4.71, SD = 0.51, skewness = −1.82). Therefore, we decided to perform Wilcoxon signed rank tests.

The professed desire to continue playing the AR math exercises in the free time was significantly higher than the desire to continue doing the paper exercises (resp. M = 4.67, SD = 0.97 vs. M = 4.18, SD = 1.33; Z = -2.03, p = 0.042). After playing the AR game, the students were also more inclined to recommend it to others than the paper exercises (resp. M = 4.72, SD = 0.96 vs. M = 4.18, SD = 1.24; Z = −2.41, p = 0.016). All other tests n.s.

The Interview Results. The interview results provided more positive and in-depth feedback for playing See Me Roar. We first asked children about their preference between See Me Roar and the paper exercise. In China, 18 out of 20 participants reported that they preferred See Me Roar more than the paper exercise, as the typical positive comments obtained by the participants reporting See Me Roar as more realistic, fun, and vivid. In the international school in the Netherlands, 17 participants out of 18 said that they preferred See Me Roar more than the paper exercise, especially the animated 3D animals were appreciated, as indicated by children that See Me Roar was *"more fun and cool to play"*, *"giving opportunities to learn while playing"*, *"offering different options and multiple interesting stuffs to do"*, *"making it possible to see 3D animals which look real or are hardly to see in real life"*, and *"making learning more fun"*. Conversely, one Chinese participant expressed negative feeling on the scanning of AR animals and another stated that she found no difference between the AR game and the paper exercise. One participant from the international school in the Netherlands complained about the difficulty to find out the AR animals in the game.

5.3 Cultural Differences

Regarding the likability of the experience, desire to do the exercise in free time, perceived fun of doing math, recommendation to others, and enjoyment, there was only one significant difference between the two cultures: the international children significantly like the See Me Roar more than Chinese children ($F (1, 35) = 9.108, p = 0.005$). See Fig. 2. There were also no interaction effects between culture and the likability of the game compared with the paper.

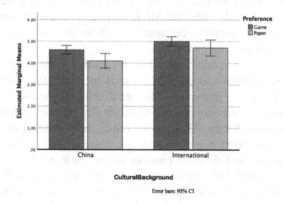

Fig. 2. Comparison on the likability of the experience of the AR game and the paper exercise between the Chinese and the international children.

5.4 PENS Questionnaire

The result of the PENS questionnaire was considered as unreliable in this study since most participants (15 out of 17) chose *strongly agree* for each statement using the 7-point Likert scale, including negatively coded statements.

Although participants rated the game highly in the PENS questionnaire, the interview results revealed deeper insights. When asked about other possibilities in the game, participants expressed their different needs for the game story and game control, such as the movement of the animals, reactions of the animals (such as sound), and let animals have babies. They were also looking for more types of the animals in the game, including the sea creatures, ancient animals they have never seen before, wild animals, and fantasy animals such as unicorns. Participants reported different preferences regarding the difficulties of the math exercises, some expressed that they would like harder exercises in order to practice their skills to learn better and faster, and to feel more challenging. Conversely, some participants would like to start with easy exercises because they were not willing to deal with tricky exercises. It was also observed that during the gameplay, participants shared their screens and communicated with others a lot.

6 Discussion

6.1 Discussion of Results

From the result we can see, H1 is confirmed: that compared to the paper exercise, See Me Roar increased the likability of the experience, enjoyment, desire to do the exercises in their free time, recommendation to others, and perceived fun of doing math. While children from the international school in the Netherlands only significantly increased the desire to do the exercises in their free time and the recommendation of the experience to others by performing See Me Roar than paper exercise. Regarding to H2, no significant difference exists between Chinese children and the international children in the Netherlands, except for the likability of the game and the paper, where international children significantly liked See Me Roar more than the Chinese children. No significant difference was found in the number of items that were answered correctly between the game and the paper exercises.

The interview results provided interesting feedback for the study. Children were attracted by the AR animals and the rich interactions within the game. Feeding and helping animals while doing mathematics helped to immerse themselves into the game world and improved their learning process. Children also provided various ideas related to other possible options for the AR game related to the psychological needs in SDT, namely autonomy, competence, and relatedness. More types of animals, richer reactions from the animals, and different controls of the game were all expected by the children. In addition, the difficulty levels of the exercises were different based on children's own abilities and skills. During the gameplay, it was observed that children tended to share their experience and help each other to play the game, while they also compared with each other in getting rewards and with the finishing speed.

6.2 Limitation and Future Research

Limitations remain in this study. First of all, the study procedure was introduced by the teacher in both China and the Netherlands, which might influence the choice of the children. Secondly, due to the condition limitations in the Netherlands, the exercise score was not recorded, and children were doing the study in groups, which could lead to different results compared to the individual study in China. Thirdly, the Smiley-ometer used in the study was designed for children aged from 10. Younger children around 7 to 8 years old tended to choose the most positive score.

What was especially noteworthy and came as a surprise to us, is just how much the students liked the AR game. So much in fact that it makes us a bit incredulous as to the veracity of the results. To our estimation, the game is barebones and lacks a lot of engaging game mechanics and design features. It is not yet designed to really stimulate competence, autonomy and relatedness, and the learning content is not well integrated with the game mechanics. For all intents and purposes, it should score worse than many other serious games which fail to be motivating [31]. It's tempting to think the design of AR animals walking over one's textbook is indeed by itself incredibly motivating for children of primary school age. However, it is also likely that this statistic is at least partially influenced by both novelty and Hawthorne effects. Regarding the PENS questionnaire, even though a literature search indicated that Likert-scales and the Smileyometer were suitable for children, we noticed a large number of children rating both positive and negatively worded statements with "fully agree". This means that in their enthusiasm or desire to please the experimenter they did not read all the questions correctly. For the future, both quantitative and qualitative measures that tease out more useful or constructive critical reflections should be devised.

This study is the first step in our research, proving the positive motivating effect of the working prototype of the AR game for children from different cultures. Our future work will focus on the design of more specific features in the AR game based on SDT and game mechanics, developing different game features and measuring how these game design decisions influence motivation with the game.

7 Conclusion

To conclude, the presented study suggests that See Me Roar significantly improves the learning experience of children. The results of the study indicate that in general, See Me Roar received very good evaluations for enjoyment, desire to do in free time, perceived fun of doing math, likability, as well as recommendation to others. The game version achieved significantly higher ratings on these subjects by the participants over the paper version. It could be used to help children to do mathematics schoolwork in a more playful and fun way. The study indicates that an AR game with animals walking over ones' textbook is globally accepted by both children from the Eastern and Western cultures. In the future, we will develop the game based on SDT, modifying the based prototype to include game mechanics to stimulate feelings of autonomy, competence, and relatedness. Through the design and implementation process, we will seek to chart the design space of AR games for learning, investigate the magic circle in AR settings and tease out the effects of game mechanics related to SDT on stimulating motivation and learning performance.

References

1. Aunola, K., Leskinen, E., Nurmi, J.E.: Developmental dynamics between mathematical performance, task motivation, and teachers' goals during the transition to primary school. Br. J. Educ. Psychol. **76**(1), 21–40 (2006)

2. Billinghurst, M., Duenser, A.: Augmented reality in the classroom. Computer **45**(7), 56–63 (2012)
3. Boot, W.R., Kramer, A.F., Simons, D.J., Fabiani, M., Gratton, G.: The effects of video game playing on attention, memory, and executive control. Acta Physiol. **120**, 387–398 (2008)
4. China Daily. http://www.chinadaily.com.cn/china/2015-1/26/content_22520832.htm. Accessed 14 June 2018
5. Connolly, T.M., Boyle, E.A., MacArthur, E., Hainey, T., Boyle, J.M.: Systematic literature review of empirical evidence on computer games and serious games. Comput. Educ. **59**(2), 661–686 (2012)
6. De Grove, F., Bourgonjon, J., Looy, J.V.: Digital games in the classroom? A contextual approach to teachers' adoption of digital games in formal education. Comput. Hum. Behav. **28**, 2023–2033 (2012)
7. Durlak, J.A., Weissberg, R.P., Dymnicki, A.B., Taylor, R.D.: The impact of enhancing students' social and emotional learning: a meta-analysis of school-based universal interventions. Child Dev. **82**(1), 405–432 (2011)
8. Frenzel, A.C., Pekrun, R., Goetz, T.: Girls and mathematics—a "hopeless" issue? A control-value approach to gender differences in emotions towards mathematics. Eur. J. Psychol. Educ. **22**(4), 497–514 (2007)
9. Fuligni, A.J., Stevenson, H.W.: Time-use and mathematics achievement among Chinese, Japanese, and American high school students. Child Dev. **66**, 830–842 (1995)
10. Girard, C., Ecalle, J., Magnan, A.: Serious games as new educational tools: how effective are they? A meta-analysis of recent studies. J. Comput. Assist. Learn. **29**, 207–219 (2013)
11. Gregory, C.L.: "But I want a real book": an investigation of undergraduates' usage and attitudes toward electronic books. Ref. User Serv. Q. **47**(3), 266–273 (2008)
12. Hainey, T., Connolly, T., Stansfield, M., Boyle, E.A.: Evaluation of a game to teach requirements collection and analysis in software engineering at tertiary education level. Comput. Educ. **56**, 21–35 (2011)
13. Jeong, H.: A comparison of the influence of electronic books and paper books on reading comprehension, eye fatigue, and perception. Electron. Libr. **30**(3), 390–408 (2012)
14. Kebritchi, M., Hirumi, A., Bai, H.: The effects of modern mathematics computer games on mathematics achievement and class motivation. Comput. Educ. **55**, 427–443 (2010)
15. Kirner, T., Reis, F., Kirner, C.: Development of an interactive book with augmented reality for teaching and learning geometric shapes. In: 2012 7th Iberian Conference on Information Systems and Technologies (CISTI), pp. 1–6 (2012)
16. Li, J., van der Spek, E.D., Hu, J., Feijs, L.: SEE ME ROAR: self-determination enhanced engagement for math education relying on augmented reality. In: CHI PLAY 2017 Extended Abstracts Extended Abstracts Publication of the Annual Symposium on Computer-Human Interaction in Play, pp. 345–351. ACM, New York (2017)
17. McLaren, B.M., Adams, D.M., Mayer, R.E., Forlizzi, J.: A computer-based game that promotes mathematics learning more than a conventional approach. Int. J. Game-Based Learn. (IJGBL) **7**(1), 36–56 (2017)
18. Peng, W., Lin, J.H., Pfeiffer, K.A., Winn, B.: Need satisfaction supportive game features as motivational determinants: an experimental study of a self-determination theory guided exergame. Media Psychol. **15**, 175–196 (2012)
19. Plass, J.L., et al.: The impact of individual, competitive, and collaborative mathematics game play on learning, performance, and motivation. J. Educ. Psychol. **105**(4), 1050–1066 (2013)
20. Przybylski, A.K., Rigby, C.S., Ryan, R.M.: A motivational model of video game engagement. Rev. Gen. Psychol. **14**, 154–166 (2010)

21. Read, J., MacFarlane, S., Casey, C.: Endurability, engagement and expectations: measuring children's fun. In: Proceedings of the International Workshop on 'Interaction Design and Children', pp. 189–198. Shaker Publishing, Eindhoven (2002)

22. Ryan, R.M.: Control and information in the intrapersonal sphere: an extension of cognitive evaluation theory. J. Pers. Soc. Psychol. **43**, 450–461 (1982)

23. Ryan, R.M., Rigby, C.S., Przybylski, A.: The motivational pull of video games: a self-determination theory approach. Motiv. Emot. **30**, 347–363 (2006)

24. Santos, M.E.C., Chen, A., Taketomi, T., Yamamoto, G., Miyazaki, J., Kato, H.: Augmented reality learning experiences: survey of prototype design and evaluation. IEEE Trans. Learn. **7**(1), 38–56 (2014)

25. Tamborini, R., Bowman, N.D., Eden, A., Grizzard, M., Organ, A.: Defining media enjoyment as the satisfaction of intrinsic needs. J. Commun. **60**, 758–777 (2010)

26. Trautwein, U.: The homework–achievement relation reconsidered: differentiating homework time, homework frequency, and homework effort. Learn. Instr. **17**, 372–388 (2007)

27. Tuzun, H.: Blending video games with learning: Issues and challenges with classroom implementations in the Turkish context. Br. J. Edu. Technol. **38**(3), 465–477 (2007)

28. van Steenbrugge, H., Valcke, M., Desoete, A.: Mathematics learning difficulties in primary education: teachers' professional knowledge and the use of commercially available learning packages. Educ. Stud. **36**, 1–13 (2010)

29. Westera, W., Nadolski, R., Hummer, H., Wopereir, I.: Serious games for higher education: a framework for reducing design complexity. Comput. Educ. **56**, 466–474 (2008)

30. Wijers, M., Jonker, V., Kerstens, K.: MobileMath: the phone, the game and the math. In: Proceedings of the 2nd European Conference on Games-Based Learning (ECGBL), Barcelona, Spain, 16–17 October 2008 (2008)

31. Wouters, P., van Nimwegen, C., van Oostendorp, H., van der Spek, E.D.: A meta-analysis of the cognitive and motivational effects of serious games. J. Educ. Psychol. **105**, 249–265 (2013)

32. Wrzesien, M., Raya, M.A.: Learning in serious virtual worlds: evaluation of learning effectiveness and appeal to students in the E-Junior project. Comput. Educ. **55**, 178–187 (2010)

33. Zhou, Z., Cheok, A.D., Tedjokusumo, J., Omer, G.S.: wIzQubesTM-a novel tangible interface for interactive storytelling in mixed reality. Int. J. Virtual Reality **7**(4), 9–15 (2008)

GAP: A Game for Improving Awareness About Passwords

Harshal Tupsamudre[1]([✉]), Rahul Wasnik[2], Shubhankar Biswas[2],
Sankalp Pandit[1], Sukanya Vaddepalli[1], Aishwarya Shinde[1], C. J. Gokul[1],
Vijayanand Banahatti[1], and Sachin Lodha[1]

[1] TCS Research, Pune, India
{harshal.tupsamudre,pandit.sankalp1,sukanya.vaddepalli,
aishwarya.ashinde,gokul.cj,vijayanand.banahatti,sachin.lodha}@tcs.com
[2] IIT Bombay, Mumbai, India
{rahulwasnik,shubhankarbiswas}@iitb.ac.in

Abstract. Text-based password is the most popular method for authenticating users on the internet. However, despite decades of security research, users continue to choose easy-to-guess passwords to protect their important online accounts. In this paper, we explore the potential of serious games to educate users about various features that negatively impact password security. Specifically, we designed a web-based casual game called *GAP* and assessed its impact by conducting a comparative user study with 119 participants. The study results show that participants who played *GAP* demonstrated improved performance in recognizing insecure password features than participants who did not play *GAP*. Besides having educational value, most of the participants also found *GAP* fun to play.

Keywords: Serious games · Passwords · Security · Human factors

1 Introduction

Security studies show that users choose predictable passwords to protect even their important accounts [10,16]. Majority of passwords are either short or composed using dictionary words, lowercase letters and digits *e.g.*, *princess*, *password* and *123456*. As a result, many websites including banking and social-networking services mandate users to include capital (uppercase) letters, symbol and digits in their password for improved security. However, users respond to this requirement by placing capital letters, digits and symbols at predictable positions, mostly at the beginning or at the end of the password, thus affecting the password security [7,25,28]. We refer to passwords resulting from such popular strategies as "insecure passwords".

Several studies in the past have shown that serious games can be effective tools for training and encouraging behaviour change. For instance, Sheng *et*

S. Göbel et al. (Eds.): JCSG 2018, LNCS 11243, pp. 66–78, 2018.
https://doi.org/10.1007/978-3-030-02762-9_8

al. [26] designed an online game called *Anti-Phishing Phil* to teach users to recognize phishing websites while Denning *et al.* [8] designed a card game called *Control-Alt-Hack* to raise awareness about computer security concepts. An evaluation of both these games indicate that educational games are not only more effective in terms of learning, but they are also more engaging and fun as compared to traditional approaches such as reading training materials.

Playing computer games is linked to a range of perceptual, cognitive, behavioural, affective and motivational impacts and outcomes [6]. Games provide situated experiences where players are immersed in complex, problem solving tasks [27]. Games are more engaging as they incorporate a number of strategies and tactics in gameplay [9]. Games facilitate procedural learning by providing the player appropriate and immediate feedback through game elements such as game points, progress bar and messages [24]. Further, games seem to have an advantage when it comes to retention of newly gained information as compared to conventional methods [30].

The use of games as a security training tool is an emerging idea not only in academia but also in the industry [13]. In fact there are commercial games developed by Wombat [21], NPS [19] and others to educate users about various security threats including virus, Trojan horse and phishing. However, relatively less work has been done in the context of passwords. In this work, we explore the use of serious games to educate users about insecure passwords. Since what characteristics constitute a secure password is not fully agreed upon [4], we focus only on educating users about insecure password creation strategies. We designed a web-based casual password awareness game called *GAP* and gauged its effectiveness by conducting a study with 119 participants. The study results indicate that participants who played *GAP* performed much better in identifying insecure password practices than those who did not play the game.

The organization of this paper is as follows. First, we describe the design and mechanics of the *GAP* game. Subsequently, we explain our study methodology and survey results. Finally, we conclude the paper by proposing an extensible and modular game framework for creating educational games for passwords.

2   GAP: A Password Awareness Game

In this section, we describe the design and rationale of *GAP*, a game to educate users about insecure password creation strategies. First, we explain how we derived the educational content for the game. Next, we illustrate the gameplay followed by the justification for choosing the casual game genre. Later, we describe the design principles and technology used to develop the *GAP* game.

2.1   Game Content

Previous password studies show that users place capital letters, symbols and digits at predictable positions in the password. For instance, a study [25] that surveyed university students, faculty and staff found that 55.8% of the users place symbol at the last position, 74.2% of the users place capital letter at the first position and 34.9% users place digit at the last position of their password. Similarly, another study [7] that surveyed users at different universities to understand their password composition found that 44% of the users place capital letters at the beginning, 44% users place symbol at the end, 13% users place symbol at the beginning, 54% users place digits at the end, and 16% users place digit at the beginning of the password. Typical examples of such passwords are *football!*, **football*, *basketball1* and *2basketball.*

To emphasize the fact that composing passwords using a single character class does not provide enough security, we consider an additional insecure strategy where all letters of a password are capital, *e.g.*, BASEBALL. Therefore, in the current version of the game, we focus on educating users about the following six insecure password creation strategies.

1. *use of capital letters at the beginning of the password*
2. *use of only capital letters in the password*
3. *use of digits at the beginning of the password*
4. *use of digits at the end of the password*
5. *use of symbols at the beginning of the password*
6. *use of symbols at the end of the password*

We analysed publicly available password databases [3] to learn about the popular symbol and digit that users add at the beginning and at the end of the password. Our analysis revealed that '!' is the most popular symbol used at the end and '*' is the most popular symbol used at the beginning of the password. Further, '1' is the most popular digit that is used at the beginning as well as at the end of the password. Since the passwords in the RockYou dataset were not created using any composition policy, we estimate the popularity of each of these operations by referring to the findings of a real-world password study [25].

2.2 Game Mechanics

The game world of *GAP* consists of a tank and barriers interspersed on the maze as shown in Fig. 1. Each barrier is labelled with an insecure password obtained by modifying the baseword *princess* with operations listed in Table 1. Presently, the game world consists of six barriers, one corresponding to each insecure operation. The goal of the player is to exit the maze by destroying all six barriers (insecure passwords) along the path.

The controls used in the game are simple (Fig. 2). The movement of the tank is controlled using left and right arrow keys and the movement of the turret is controlled using the mouse. The player rotates the turret to aim at the barrier and clicks the left-button of the mouse to release the ammunition. There are three types of ammunitions out of which the player has to choose the right one depending on the password label of the barrier. For instance, to destroy the barrier labelled with a password that starts or ends with a digit, the right ammunition is loaded by pressing letter **D** on the keyboard. If a wrong

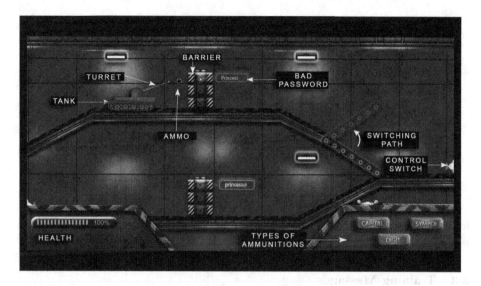

Fig. 1. The interface of GAP, a web-based game to educate players about insecure password creation strategies. The labels in this image are not part of the game and are for understanding purposes only.

ammunition is fired, the health of the tank decreases and the barrier remains unaffected. To make the game more challenging, the maze consists of switching paths that can be re-positioned using a control switch. The player is required to open a new path for navigating the tank through the maze by hitting the control switch with the tank. The information about the rules and controls is provided to the player before the start of the game.

Controls	Action Performed
→	Move the tank Right
←	Move the tank Left
C key	Select Capital Ammunition
S key	Select Symbol Ammunition
D key	Select Digit Ammunition
☜	To Aim the at the Barrier
🖑	To Shoot the Barrier

Fig. 2. Controls for navigating tank and selecting ammunition in the *GAP* game.

In short, the game requires the player to look at the password label (*princess1*), identify insecure operation (digit at the end) and choose the right ammunition (key D) to destroy the barrier. Shooting barriers labelled with

Table 1. The list of insecure operations and corresponding examples along with the correct key for loading ammunition.

Insecure operation	Example	Ammunition
Capital at start	Princess	**C** key
Capitals only	PRINCESS	**C** key
Symbol at end	princess!	**S** key
Symbol at start	*princess	**S** key
Digit at end	princess1	**D** key
Digit at start	2princess	**D** key

insecure passwords signify to the player that such passwords should never be used to protect their online accounts.

2.3 Training Messages

When the player destroys the barrier with the right ammunition, we display certain facts about the insecure password with which the barrier was labelled (Figs. 3 and 4). The purpose of the facts is to make the player aware of how insecure the particular operation is. For instance, if the barrier is labelled with a password that begins with a capital letter (*e.g.*, *Princess*), we display the fact: "More than 70% of the users keep a capital letter in the first position of their password. Hence, it is an insecure practice" and if the barrier is labelled with a password that ends with a symbol (*e.g.*, *princess@*), we display the fact: "More than 50% of the users keep symbol in the last position of their password. Hence, it is an insecure practice." For the current version of the game, we borrowed these facts from the findings of a real-world password study performed by CMU researchers [25].

Fig. 3. Fact presented when barrier labelled with insecure password *princess* is shooted.

Fig. 4. Fact shown when barrier labelled with insecure password *princess@* is shooted.

2.4 Game Genre

As passwords are created by users with diverse backgrounds, making a suitable choice of game genre that teaches users about insecure passwords is critical. We wanted the game to be simple, yet capable of teaching the concept in an impactful manner. Therefore, we designed *GAP* to be a slow-paced casual game that simulates an "escape situation", where the player controls a tank and the objective is to navigate the tank through the maze by demolishing barriers (labelled with insecure passwords) placed along the way. The *GAP* game is web-based (can be played using a web browser), uses simple game controls, has a short gameplay time (less than five minutes) and does not assume any prior experience in gaming.

Casual games are one of the fastest growing segments within the industry [1, 17]. These games are characterized by less complex game controls, faster rewards and shorter gameplay time [15]. As casual games are easy to learn and simple to play, they appeal to users with different age-groups [5]. Further, according to one report, 50% of the casual game players are females [18]. Casual games are mostly available in web-based or mobile-based versions and come in a wide range of genres. Typical examples of casual genre are Pacman, Tetris, Solitaire and Candy Crush. Casual games have been successfully explored in the healthcare domain [11,12]. In this work, we explore the potential of casual games in the security domain.

GAP also exhibits certain characteristics of escape-the-room genre, as the goal of the player is to escape the maze by overcoming obstacles placed along the path. Research shows that escape rooms (maze) are experiential, encourage players to think creatively and engage in critical thinking. The escape-the-room games often consist of puzzles that run in a simple game loop [29]. In the case of *GAP*, the loop consists of the following three steps:

1. Challenge (shooting barrier labelled with insecure password using right ammunition)
2. Solution (a feedback message indicating the potential risk of using insecure password)

3. Reward (the ability to move forward thereby closing in towards the end of the maze)

Escape-the-room genre games make use of (horror) elements to add a sense of urgency to escape. On the contrary, we designed *GAP* to be slow paced where players have a chance to stop and reflect on the new knowledge they have learned.

2.5 Design Principles

We applied two principles from the learning sciences theory to design the *GAP* game: reflection and contextual-procedural.

- *Reflection Principle.* According to this principle [2], learning increases if the learners are given an opportunity to stop and think about what they are learning. This principle is employed in the *GAP* game as we display appropriate factual training messages to the player after destroying the barrier and also after the end of the game.
- *Conceptual-Procedural Principle.* According to this principle [23], conceptual and procedural knowledge influence one another in mutually supportive and integrated ways. This principle is employed in our game since we label each barrier with distinct example (*e.g.*, *princess1*) to teach players about the concept of insecure passwords. To destroy the barrier, the player has to identify the insecure operation (*e.g.*, digit at end) and choose the right ammunition (*e.g.*, **D**) as shown in Table 1. To reinforce the learned concept, we also provide clear procedural tips to the player (*e.g.*, "adding digits at the end of the password is an insecure practice") after the barrier is destroyed.

2.6 Technology Used

We created static images and sprite sheets for the *GAP* game using Adobe Photoshop. The two popular options for creating web-based games are Flash and HTML5. However, Flash is a proprietary software, it is not supported on all devices (e.g., iPhones and iPads) and it has potential security issues. On the other hand, HTML5 and javascript are open standards and supported by all browsers and devices [22]. Therefore, the entire game was developed using HTML5, CSS3 and Phaser javascript library [20]. All the images, libraries and assets required for playing *GAP* were fetched from the server only once before the start of the game to give an uninterrupted gameplay experience to the players. The survey responses of participants were captured using J2EE application server and stored in PostgreSQL database.

3   User Study

To assess the impact of the *GAP* game, we designed a survey questionnaire which consists of the following two parts.

1. In *part 1* of the survey, we asked participants questions related to demographic characteristics *i.e.*, gender, age, education and specialization.
2. In *part 2* of the survey, we asked participants to identify *insecure positions* for adding a symbol, a digit and a capital letter in the password. These questions are listed below.
   (a) *When adding a capital letter to the password, which of the following is/are insecure practices? (Check all that apply)*
      - *Adding a capital letter at the beginning*
      - *Adding a capital letter at the end*
      - *Adding a capital letter in the middle*
      - *Using only capital letters*
      - *Other*
   (b) *When adding a symbol to the password, which of the following is/are insecure practices? (Check all that apply)*
      - *Adding a symbol at the beginning*
      - *Adding a symbol at the end*
      - *Adding a symbol in the middle*
      - *Other*
   (c) *When adding a digit to the password, which of the following is/are insecurepractices? (Check all that apply)*
      - *Adding a digit at the beginning*
      - *Adding a digit at the end*
      - *Adding a digit in the middle*
      - *Other*

3.1   Experiment Groups

We conducted a comparative user study to evaluate the impact of *GAP* on the performance of its users. All participants were randomly assigned to either of the two experimental groups: *control group* or *game group*.

1. *Control group.* In this group, participants were asked to answer the survey questionnaire without being exposed to any kind of training.
2. *Game group.* In this group, participants were asked to answer the survey questionnaire after playing the *GAP* game. In addition to the *part 1* and *part 2* of the survey, participants in the game group were also asked the following open-ended questions regarding the game.
   - *How much fun was the game?*
   - *Did you have any trouble or difficulties while playing the game?*
   - *Are there any possible improvements in the game?*

We measure the impact of *GAP* by comparing the survey responses of participants in the control group and game group. As described earlier, the *part 2* of the survey asks participants to identify insecure positions for adding a digit, a symbol and capital letter in a password. Participants in the game group, responded to the *part 2* of the survey after playing the *GAP* game whereas participants in the control group responded to the *part 2* without playing the game. Therefore, we can observe whether the training messages embedded in the game improved the performance of participants in identifying insecure password practices.

Table 2. Participant demographics in the control group and game group.

	Control	Game
Gender		
Male	65.57%	70.69%
Female	34.43%	29.31%
Age		
18–24	75.41%	75.86%
25–34	24.59%	24.14%
Education		
Bachelors	54.10%	51.72%
Masters	40.98%	44.83%
Doctorate	4.92%	3.45%
Major		
CS	49.18%	51.72%
Non-CS	50.82%	48.28%
#Participants	61	58

3.2 Demographics

We recruited 119 participants within our organization through the use of internal mailing lists. They were assigned randomly to either control group or game group. Table 2 summarises the demographics of participants in each group. Most participants were young and had a bachelor's degree. We found no significant difference in gender, age or education between the control group and game group.

4   Results

After analysing survey responses, we found that participants who played the *GAP* game performed better in correctly identifying insecure password practices than participants in the control group. In particular, participants in the game group performed much better in correctly recognizing that adding a capital letter in the beginning, using only capital letters, adding a symbol at the end and adding a digit at the end are insecure practices. In the remaining cases, participants in the game group performed at least as good as participants in the control group.

To determine whether the difference between the performance of participants in the control group and game group is significant, we perform a two-tailed Fischer's Exact Test (FET). In this case, the variable of interest is whether participants correctly recognized insecure password operations or not. We claim the result to be statistically significant if $p < 0.01$ and we indicate possible significant interest if $p < 0.10$. The results of statistical tests are summarized

Table 3. Proportion of participants who correctly identified insecure password creation practices. The results of statistical tests (FET) are also given.

Question	Control	Game	p-value
Capital - adding at beginning	57.38%	93.10%	<0.0001*
Capital - only capital letters	62.30%	82.76%	0.0147**
Symbol - adding at beginning	70.49%	81.03%	0.2051
Symbol - adding at end	63.93%	79.31%	0.0711**
Digit - adding at beginning	55.74%	68.97%	0.1855
Digit - adding at end	54.10%	87.93%	<0.0001*

in Table 3. We marked the entry with value $p < 0.01$ in the table using (*) and $p < 0.10$ using (**).

We found highly significant difference between the performance of control group and game group participants in recognizing two insecure operations, adding a capital letter at the beginning and adding a digit at the end ($p < 0.0001$). Further, we found significant interest in the performance of control group and game group participants in recognizing two other insecure operations, adding a symbol at the end and using only capital letters ($p < 0.10$). We note that adding capital letter at the beginning and adding digit (or symbol) at the end are the most popular operations [7, 25, 28]. The difference in performance between the two groups in recognizing these insecure operations was either statistically significant ($p << 0.01$) or had significant interest ($p < 0.10$). There was no statistical difference between the performance of the two groups in recognizing remaining two insecure operations, adding a symbol at the beginning or adding a digit at the beginning ($p \geq 0.10$), but the proportion of participants who answered correctly is higher in the game group as compared to the control group.

4.1   Game Feedback

The average time required to complete the *GAP* game was about 3.5 min. The analysis of the game feedback revealed that 81.03% of the participants found the game to be fun while 6.90% of the participants felt otherwise. The remaining 12.07% of the participants remained neutral. When it comes to difficulty, 77.59% of the participants felt that the game was not difficult to play while 18.97% participants reported difficulty in playing the game. Of these 18.97% participants, 12.07% participants reported difficulty in understanding the game instructions and 6.90% participants reported difficulty in understanding the game controls. The rest 3.45% of the participants remained neutral (Table 4).

Overall, we got positive response from the participants for using the game as a training tool. One participant remarked, *"The idea of educating people with the help of game was a very good idea."* Another participant remarked, *"An interesting way to teach what is important and what is not"*. We also received few

Table 4. Feedback about the *GAP* game.

Question	Yes	No	Neutral
Game is fun	81.03%	6.90%	12.07%
Game is difficult	18.97%	77.59%	3.45%

suggestions from participants for improving the *GAP* game. These suggestions mainly include replacing text instructions with a demo video and adding more challenging tasks to the game.

5   Conclusion and Future Work

In this paper, we developed a web-based casual game called *GAP* with an objective of educating users about various insecure password practices. We also assessed its impact by conducting a user study with 119 participants. Our study results show that participants who played *GAP* showed improved awareness of the insecure password practices. Specifically, about 93% of the participants who played the game correctly identified that adding capital letter at the beginning of the password is an insecure practice, about 81% of the participants correctly identified that adding symbol at the beginning is an insecure practice and about 88% of the participants correctly identified that adding digit at the end is an insecure practice. Further, most participants found the game to be fun and completed the gameplay within a short duration of time (less than four minutes).

Currently, the educational content used in the game is derived from external sources (mostly from password research studies [7,25]). Another possibility is to tap into real-world publicly available password sources [3,14] to learn about emerging popular passwords and patterns, and extend *GAP* with more insecure operations. However, the *GAP* game in its current state require changes to the code to support new insecure operations. We plan to make our game code more modular and flexible so that it can be extended to support other insecure operations with minimum effort. This would particularly benefit organizations that may want to customize the *GAP* game to train their employees.

Many organizations enforce stringent password expiry policies mandating employees to change their password after few months. Employees typically circumvent such policies by appending the current month (01–12) to their password. Consequently, the organization wishes to educate their employees about the negative consequences of using month in their password through the *GAP* game. To support a new insecure operation, the code of the *GAP* game needs to be altered with an example of insecure password, training message, new type of ammunition and new control key, this can be restrictive. We envision a separate data module which can be configured with an insecure password (*e.g.,* *Princess07*), appropriate training message, ammunition (*e.g.,* MONTH) and control key (*e.g.,* **M**) before playing the game. Instead of using the same baseword *princess* everytime, the data module can also choose a new baseword at random from the list of breached lowercase alphabetic passwords. Upon initialization, the *GAP* game accesses the data module, reads the game content and configures the gameplay accordingly. We aim to explore this framework further in our future studies.

References

1. Casual Games Association: Casual Games Sector Report. http://cdn2.hubspot. net/hubfs/700740/Newzoo_Games_Industry_Growth_Towards_2017.pdf. Accessed 10 August 2018
2. National Research Council, et al.: How People Learn: Bridging Research and Practice. National Academies Press, Washington, D.C. (1999)
3. Bowes, R.: Passwords. https://wiki.skullsecurity.org/Passwords. Accessed 10 August 2018
4. de Carné de Carnavalet, X., Mannan, M.: From very weak to very strong: analyzing password-strength meters. In: NDSS 2014. Internet Society (2014)
5. Chesham, A., Wyss, P., Müri, R.M., Mosimann, U.P., Nef, T.: What older people like to play: genre preferences and acceptance of casual games. JMIR Serious Games **5**(2), e8 (2017)
6. Connolly, T.M., Boyle, E.A., MacArthur, E., Hainey, T., Boyle, J.M.: A systematic literature review of empirical evidence on computer games and serious games. Comput. Educ. **59**(2), 661–686 (2012)
7. Das, A., Bonneau, J., Caesar, M., Borisov, N., Wang, X.: The tangled web of password reuse. In: NDSS 2014, pp. 23–26. Internet Society (2014)
8. Denning, T., Lerner, A., Shostack, A., Kohno, T.: Control-Alt-Hack: the design and evaluation of a card game for computer security awareness and education. In: CCS 2013, pp. 915–928 (2013)
9. Dickey, M.D.: Engaging by design: how engagement strategies in popular computer and video games can inform instructional design. Educ. Technol. Res. Dev. **53**(2), 67–83 (2005)
10. Florencio, D., Herley, C.: A large-scale study of web password habits. In: WWW 2007, pp. 657–666 (2007)
11. Gerling, K., Fuchslocher, A., Schmidt, R., Krämer, N., Masuch, M.: Designing and evaluating casual health games for children and teenagers with cancer. In: Anacleto, J.C., Fels, S., Graham, N., Kapralos, B., Saif El-Nasr, M., Stanley, K. (eds.) ICEC 2011. LNCS, vol. 6972, pp. 198–209. Springer, Heidelberg (2011). https://doi.org/ 10.1007/978-3-642-24500-8_21
12. Grimes, A., Kantroo, V., Grinter, R.E.: Let's play! Mobile health games for adults. In: Ubicomp 2010, pp. 241–250. ACM (2010)
13. Hendrix, M., Al-Sherbaz, A., Victoria, B.: Game based cyber security training: are serious games suitable for cyber security training? IJSG **3**(1), 53–61 (2016)
14. Hunt, T.: Pwned passwords. https://haveibeenpwned.com/Passwords. Accessed 10 August 2018
15. Kuittinen, J., Kultima, A., Niemelä, J., Paavilainen, J.: Casual games discussion. In: Proceedings of the 2007 Conference on Future Play, pp. 105–112. ACM (2007)
16. Mazurek, M.L., et al.: Measuring password guessability for an entire university. In: CCS 2013, pp. 173–186. ACM (2013)
17. Morrison, C.: Casual Gaming Worth $2.25 Billion, and Growing Fast. https:// venturebeat.com/2007/10/29/casual-gaming-worth-225-billion-and-growing-fast/. Accessed 10 August 2018

18. NPD: The NPD Group: 37 Percent of U.S. Population Age 9 and Older Currently Plays PC Games. https://www.npd.com/wps/portal/npd/us/news/press-releases/37-percent-of-us-population-age-9-and-older-currently-plays-pc-games/. Accessed 10 August 2018
19. NPS: Cyberciege (2004). http://my.nps.edu/web/cisr/cyberciege. Accessed 10 August 2018
20. Phaser: Desktop and Mobile HTML5 Game Framework. https://phaser.io. Accessed 10 August 2018
21. ProofPoint: Wombat Security Technologies. https://www.wombatsecurity.com/. Accessed 10 August 2018
22. Reimers, S., Stewart, N.: Presentation and response timing accuracy in Adobe Flash and HTML5/JavaScript web experiments. Behav. Res. Methods 47(2), 309–327 (2015)
23. Rittle-Johnson, B., Koedinger, K.R.: Comparing instructional strategies for integrating conceptual and procedural knowledge (2002)
24. Schroth, M.L.: The effects of delay of feedback on a delayed concept formation transfer task. Contemp. Educ. Psychol. 17(1), 78–82 (1992)
25. Shay, R., et al.: Encountering stronger password requirements: user attitudes and behaviors. In: SOUPS 2010, pp. 2:1–2:20 (2010)
26. Sheng, S., et al.: Anti-Phishing Phil: the design and evaluation of a game that teaches people not to fall for phish. In: SOUPS 2007, pp. 88–99 (2007)
27. Squire, K.D.: Video game-based learning: an emerging paradigm for instruction. Perform. Improv. Q. 21(2), 7–36 (2008)
28. Ur, B., et al.: "I added '!' at the end to make it secure": observing password creation in the lab. In: SOUPS 2015, pp. 123–140. USENIX Association (2015)
29. Wiemker, M., Elumir, E., Clare, A.: Escape room games. Game Based Learn. (2015)
30. Wouters, P., Van Nimwegen, C., Van Oostendorp, H., Van Der Spek, E.D.: A meta-analysis of the cognitive and motivational effects of serious games. J. Educ. Psychol. 105(2), 249 (2013)

MiniColon; Teaching Kids Computational Thinking Using an Interactive Serious Game

Reham Ayman$^{(\boxtimes)}$, Nada Sharaf, Ghada Ahmed, and Slim Abdennadher

Department of Computer Science, Faculty of Media Engineering and Technology,
German University in Cairo, Cairo, Egypt
reham.saad@student.guc.edu.eg,
{nada.hamed,ghada.bahaeldin,slim.abdennadher}@guc.edu.eg

Abstract. Computer science is about learning how to think. It is applicable to everything. Most industries in the 21st century are directed towards digitized processes using up-to-date technologies. This increases the need for students to know how these technologies work, especially with the availability of smart and handy devices. As a preliminary step to learning programming, students should learn basics of logical and computational thinking. Computational thinking compromises the skills, concepts, and behaviors used to solve problems. Some visual platforms, such as Scratch and Alice [6,17], were introduced to teach children programming. The platform introduced in this paper aims at teaching young children (in the age range of 8–9 years old) the preliminary concepts of programming including *sequential blocks*, *conditional blocks*, and *iterative blocks*. This is achieved through an interactive, gesture-based game, where the Kinect Sensor device is used to control the gameplay instead of playing it using a normal PC. The game was tested using a between-group experimental model with two subgroups; an experimental group and a control group. The experimental group used the game whereas the control group was taught using a traditional educational method. The results showed a significant difference between the two groups with a P-value of < 0.05 for both the learning gain and the engagement level.

Keywords: Serious games · Programming · Computational thinking
Interactive · Children · Kinect

1 Introduction

Computational thinking is increasingly becoming a needed skill [5]. It helps individuals identify a problem and the steps needed to solve it. With the widespread of computers and web applications, a lot of opportunities have been added to the worldwide job market. This encouraged a lot of individuals to try to learn to program.

In addition, there has been an increasing trend recently to introduce programming to children in their early stages [13]. Many schools started to offer

© Springer Nature Switzerland AG 2018
S. Göbel et al. (Eds.): JCSG 2018, LNCS 11243, pp. 79–90, 2018.
https://doi.org/10.1007/978-3-030-02762-9_9

introductory courses to teach programming and computational thinking. These courses help the students to have a better way of thinking and enhance their problem-solving skills.

Some platforms were designed for introducing computational thinking and programming basics to children such as Scratch and Alice [6,14]. These platforms provide a visual programming language to eliminate the need for learning any syntax or understanding complex code structures. In addition, serious games were also employed to introduce programming concepts [2,19]. However, most of these serious games that were played on computers or mobile devices, were missing the interactivity factor. Studies showed that adding the factor of interactivity motivates the students to learn more about programming [1]. The aim of the introduced platform is to add to the existing games the factor of interactivity. Therefore, Kinect [16] is used to capture the movement of the child and incorporate it into the game.

The paper is organized as follows: Sect. 2 provides previous work related to the education of computational thinking through serious games. Section 3 discusses the methodology and explains how the levels of MiniColon are designed. Section 4 explains the experimental model used. Section 5 shows the tests conducted and the results. Finally, Sect. 6 concludes the work and describes directions for future work.

2   Related Work

Various methods of teaching were applied to teach children programming. Visual programming environments were used to enable children to build programs through simple interfaces [9]. Such platforms include Scratch [17] and Alice [6]. According to Armoin et al. [3], teachers reported that using Scratch increased the learning efficiency. Students also reported that they were encouraged to learn more about computer science.

"Program your robot" [11] is a serious game developed for teaching programming and computational thinking. The game aimed at integrating the game-play with the programming concepts and computational thinking skills. The game was evaluated using 25 students. The students enjoyed the game and reported that this type of games can improve their problem-solving skills.

Another example of an educational game for programming used tangible electronic building blocks instead of visual programming is presented in [27]. The Tangible electronic blocks are divided into sensors and sources for these sensors. The child can build a structured block that does a function by connecting the blocks together. The older children were able to debug their structure in case of a problem or undesired function. The results showed that young aged children did not realize the concepts of programming using the Electronic Blocks. Therefore, this way was not effective enough for the young children.

There are other technologies that are used, such as motion-based touchless and virtual reality. Motion-based touchless technology is a new trend in the

field of human-computer interaction[1]. These types of interactive games motivate the students to learn more using game-based technologies [1]. Participating
in Kinect-based learning activities encourage students to brainstorm and active
discussions participation in the classroom. This was proved by [1] that included
Scratch, Microsoft Kinect, and Kinect2Scratch. Microsoft Kinect is a sensor that
tracks body motion and gestures. Kinect2Scratch allows data from a Microsoft
Kinect controller to be sent to Scratch. According to the result of this study,
students showed more interest and learning skills regarding their computational
thinking skills and social skills, during and after the experiment. According to
[20], students who participated in the experiment of VR-based game liked it a
lot. Virtual Reality technology is about immersing the player in a virtual world
that they can interact with. The game was controlled using VR and Kinect technologies. The Kinect sensor was used to make the player move freely without the
need to hold the physical controller of the VR set. Students had to design a dance
choreography using coding blocks. Then the character in the VR environment
performed the dance in front of the player.

Kinect was also used for game-based learning in different fields. It was used
to teach hearing impairments students the American sign language [10]. In this
application, motions were captured using Kinect one, then they were encoded.
Afterwards, a game was developed using Unity and Kinect one. The game was
tested against a face-to-face learning method. The result showed a significant
effect of the game compared to the traditional method with a (P-value < 0.05).
Kinect was also used for teaching the spatial visualization skills [25]. The participants in this work agreed that the interactive learning system made them aware
of various things and increased their interest.

3   Methodology

Serious games have proven to be effective in teaching children, as they enjoy the
game while learning the concept subconsciously. Our aim is to teach children an
introduction to logical thinking and programming. This is achieved through an
interactive serious game that has an enjoyable theme and storyboard. Having
a story makes the game more enjoyable and playable [4]. The storyboard is
designed to be simple and yet attractive to the target age group. The main
idea of "MiniColon" is that the main character is trapped on an island. The
character has to collect some fruits and supplies to escape from the island. The
main character is a carrot and it is moving forward all the time during the
gameplay. The player controls the motion of the carrot in order to achieve the
goal of each level. The interaction with the game was intended to be engaging and
yet seamless so that the player remains focused on the main concept. Kinect was
used to detect the interactions of the player with the game. Kinect is a hands-free
motion control device which implied that the players will not hold any controller
in their hands.

---

[1] A field of study focusing on the design of computer technology and, in particular,
the interaction between humans (the users) and computers.

Motivation is the key to learning as it helps the students to fully engage in learning [26]. Thus, after finishing the level a sound referring to winning is played as well as a congratulation message is displayed. In level 3 and 4, a sound is played on opening the chests to indicate the chest is opened. Also, the objects to be collected in the scene bounce regularly to be more visible and attract the student attention. Moreover, throughout all the game levels, a motivational background music is played.

3.1 Game Structure

MiniColon aims at teaching children the preliminary steps of programming and logical thinking which are *sequential blocks*, *conditional blocks*, and *iterative blocks*. Each concept has a group of levels that the player has to pass. The last level of every asks the player to trace a code snippet. Teaching the student the skill of code tracing is important as it helps in improving code writing skills later on [12]. The code snippets are written in Python language as it is close to pseudocode [24].

Sequential Levels. An algorithm is a set of instructions used to achieve a certain task where the order of the steps is crucial [8]. Delivering this concept to children can be done by describing the instructions for a certain activity in the correct order to reach their target. The consequences of missing a step or changing the order of the instructions have to be demonstrated to the player. The sequence concept is introduced in the game by showing the player a set of instructions that have to be done in the same order. In the first level of the game, the player is shown some objects to be collected in order. These objects are displayed on the left side of the screen as shown in Fig. 1. If the player tries to collect an object out of order a hint will be displayed stating the object that should be collected now as shown in Fig. 2a.

Once the player is done with all the instructions for this level, a code snippet in python is displayed as shown in Fig. 2b. The code is equivalent to the steps the player followed to collect some objects from the island. A final congratulation message is then displayed to motivate the player and inform him/her that the current level is completed successfully.

In order to make sure that the player grasped the concept correctly, the second level then asks the player to trace a snippet of code. The code is displayed as shown in Fig. 3a, where the player has to follow it by doing the actions corresponding to the code.

Conditional Levels. A program consists of some events that are controlled by conditionals. In general, conditions control the flow of the program as they have to be achieved in order for some event to be triggered. The conditional statements are expressed in most programming languages using the if-then construct; where the condition evaluates to a boolean state that has to be true for the then part to be done.

(a) Before collecting   (b) After collecting

Fig. 1. Collecting a coconut

(a) Message of collecting out of order object   (b) Level 1 Code snippet

Fig. 2. Messages and code snippets

MiniColon teaches the conditional concept through level 3 and level 4. Level 3 applies this concept by having three chests which the player can open in any order. Upon opening any chest, an object will appear with the equivalent code snippet being displayed. For example, the red chest has a flashlight inside. After opening it, a code snippet saying (`if red_box: collect_flashlight()`) appears, as shown in Fig. 3b. This helps the player to grasp the idea that in order to achieve the then part (in this case collecting a certain object), the condition has to be true (in this case the corresponding box is open).

Level 4 is the code tracing level. This level tests the ability of the players of understanding the sequential algorithm and condition concepts together. This is achieved by having the first line of code to collect a backpack. After that, there are conditions corresponding to each chest. The player has to trace them in order. If he/she tries to open a chest before the required one, or opening the red chest before collecting the backpack, he will be notified with a message to collect or open the required object.

Iterative Levels. In computer programming, an iterative block is a sequence of instructions that is continually repeated. Its main aim is to do a set of instructions repeatedly for a certain number of times, or until the condition of the iterative block is false. The game has two levels for teaching the iterative concept. In level 5 scene the island has many scattered coconuts (more than 4), and on the left side of the screen, there is an image of a coconut with a number attached to it. This number is a counter which is initially four; meaning that

(a) Starting of Level 2   (b) Level 3 Code snippet of Red Chest

Fig. 3. Level 2 and 3 features (Color figure online)

the player has to collect four coconuts to proceed to the next level. Every time the player collects a coconut, the number is decremented by one until it reaches zero. On reaching zero, an equivalent code snippet is displayed. The condition of the while loop says that (`while number_collected < 4:`), which mean that if the `number_collected` is 4, the condition will be false and the iterative block will not be entered.

In Level 6, the students are shown a code snippet and they have to trace it (as in Level 2 and 4). This level combines two concepts, sequential algorithm, and iterative concepts. The players are required to first collect four coconuts then three blackberries. This is achieved by having two iterative blocks in sequence, the first is to collect the coconuts and the second is to collect the blackberries. In addition to the code snippet, there are images on the left of the screen, a coconut, and a blackberry, each has a counter set to zero at the start of the level. The number attached to coconut image is incremented by collecting the coconuts. Once all the four coconuts are collected, the image disappears to indicate that the first iterative block condition is no more satisfied and that the player has to continue to the next instruction i.e. next iterative block.

3.2 Implementation

Motion-based touchless technology is a new trend in the field of human-computer interaction. It can be used to increase student motivation, strengthen their computational thinking and enhance their understanding [1]. "MiniColon" is a motion-based touchless game that was implemented in three stages. The first stage was to implement the game based on the target group. The following stage was implementing the leaning motion using the motion-based touchless technology, which is the Kinect. Finally, the game was integrated with the Kinect. The game is implemented using Unity [7] game engine. The movement of the character is simulated by the leaning gesture; such that leaning to the right is interpreted to move the character to the right direction and the same analogy for the left direction. Leaning is the way of moving the upper part of the body to the right and left, as the upper body makes an angle with the right or left leg depending on the leaning side. It was chosen because it is an easy motion for children to do and does not require a lot of activity to allow them to concentrate on the delivered concepts from each level.

The lean gesture was built using Kinect studio and Kinect visual gesture builder [22]. It was recorded by the camera of the Kinect sensor using Kinect studio software. The act of the motion was recorded several times. The visual gesture builder then uses the recorded motions to train a model using a machine-learning algorithm to create the leaning gesture. The right lean gesture is trained and saved in a database file called Lean. The same is done for the left lean gesture. Thus, the file Lean is the database file containing both right and left lean gesture. To access the database file a C-Sharp class `GestureDetector` is implemented. The class job is to read the database file and compare the tracked gesture with the lean gestures saved in the database.

The integration between the tracked gestures from the Kinect and the game levels is implemented using a script `KinectManager` in C-Sharp language. The functionality of the script is to initialize the Kinect sensor on opening the game. It also passes the tracked gesture from the Kinect to the `GestureDetector` class to be checked if it is leaning right or left.

In order to collect an object, the closed hand state gesture [22] of the right/left hand is checked. The two hands are included to make it easier for the students to interact with the hand which the student has more control of.

Moreover, after finishing the level, the player waves also with his right/left hand to go to the next level. Detecting the wave is implemented by checking the opened hand state [22].

4 Experimental Design

This project experiments the effect of interactive serious games to teach young aged children the main concepts of programming, compared to the traditional methods. This is achieved by implementing MiniColon and testing it with young aged children. This is examined by how much did the children interacted with the game, enjoyed, and learned from the game. The targeted group is children of the age between (8–9). The aim of the experiment is to proof or reject the null hypothesis. The null hypothesis states that there is no difference between the effect of using "MiniColon" and using traditional teaching methods in learning programming. The first hypothesis (H1) states that there is no difference between the learning gain between the two methods. The second hypothesis (H2) claims that there is no difference in the engagement level of the participants between the traditional method and MiniColon.

The model used is a between-group design that has two independent sub-groups: a control group and an experiment group. The experiment group used Kinect interactive game "MiniColon", and control group experienced traditional face-to-face learning method using presentation slides [23]. The slides were designed to be identical to the game flow and structure. The participants for both groups were selected randomly. The only required factor that, they should not have a previous background in programming to ensure homogeneity of the experiment. The experiment for each participant of the experiment group is held individually in a normal room. Hard copied test for the participants, hard copied questionnaires, and presentation slides are the materials used in the experiment. The experiment process consists of four stages, first the pre-quiz, then the experiment method, then the post-quiz, and finally the engagement test.

5   Test and Results

A sample population of 15 children (between the age of 8 and 9) was divided into two groups (an experiment group: n = 8, and a control group: n = 7). Each group was introduced to its assigned learning method. Experiment group participants played the 6 Level game using the Kinect. While the control group participants were taught using face-to-face learning method. This testing approach is inherited from a similar research, that was testing the effectiveness of serious game against traditional methods [23]. The duration for both groups took approximately the same amount of time (between 15 to 20 min). To compare between to two learning methods, learning gain and engagement level of both groups were measured after using the corresponding learning approach. Analyzing the data comparison between the two groups, an independent t-test using SPSS (Statistical Package for the Social Sciences) is applied. The independent sample t-test is used to clarify if there is a significant difference in the learning gain and the engagement level between the control group and the experiment group.

5.1   Learning Gain

Learning gain is how much the participant learned from the activity. It can be tested using oral questions, observations from the participants, and pre and post quizzes. The participant is tested before the activity to know if he has previous knowledge about the activity. After the activity is finished, the participant is tested again to know how much information did he learned from the activity.

Procedure: Before starting the two different learning methods, participants were given a printed pre-quiz. The quiz consists of six questions, divided into three groups, each has two questions. Each group is related to one of the three targeted programming concepts *sequential blocks*, *conditional blocks*, and *iterative blocks* respectively. The quiz has five MCQ questions and a "What is the output?" question. Some of the children required help in reading or understanding the synthesis of the questions. The questions are designed to be compatible with the content of the learning methods. After the participant completes his assigned learning method, he is given an identical copy of the pre-quiz. The learning gain is calculated by subtracting the number of correct answers that the participant got in the pre-quiz from the number of correct answers he got in the post-quiz.

Results: The results of the tests show that the learning gain achieved from the group using the Kinect game (M = 2.75, SD = 1.389) is significantly higher than the group that was introduced to the traditional educational method (M = 0.43,

SD $= 0.787$) (t(8) $= 4.04$, p < 0.05) with a difference of 2.32 and standard error difference of 0.57. This rejects the hypothesis that stated that there is no difference in the learning gain level of the MiniColon game to the traditional learning method (H1).

5.2 Engagement

Engagement is the concept of the presence or the sense of "being there" in the game. Involvement, immersion, arousal, attention, interest, identification, enjoyment, effort, and flow are the factors that defined engagement with the game. There are many approaches that are used to measure engagement, self-reports on questionnaires is the most used to measure the engagement level of the games [15]. Thus, in this experiment self-reported questionnaire is used.

Procedure: This test is held to measure how the two groups differ in the engagement level. It is a questionnaire that consists of 9 items. The answers to the questionnaire are 5-Likert scale. This questionnaire is proposed by [21] to measure the control and enjoyment of the activity, to indicate the overall flow. After completing the assigned learning method, the researcher asks the participant the questions of the questionnaire and then records the answers of the participant in a hand-copied version of the questionnaire. The researcher has to ask the participants the questions of the questionnaire instead of handing it to them to fill it alone. This is due to their young age, which led to some ambiguity in understanding some words. Conclusions about the engagement level of the two learning methods are drawn, by comparing the result of both groups.

Results: The results of the tests show that the engagement revealed from the group using the Kinect game (M $= 4.33$, SD $= 0.428$) is significantly higher than the group that used the traditional educational method (M $= 2.93$, SD $= 0.96$) (t(8) $= 3.5$, p < 0.05) with a difference of 1.4 and standard error difference of 0.397. This rejects the hypothesis that stated that there is no difference in the engagement level of the MiniColon game to the traditional learning method (H2).

5.3 Flow

Flow according to Csikszentmihalyi, is the channel between challenge and skill that the user experience in any activity [18]. Anxiousness is the result of experiencing the high challenge and low skill, while boredom is the result of the opposite case. So the best case is the balance between the two factors. Flow test is used to measure how did the player feel about the flow of the game from the first level passing through all the other levels.

Procedure: After each level of the game, the test of flow is taken by every participant. According to [21], the questionnaire consists of two five Likert scale questions:"How did the participant find this level challenge?" and "Is the skill of the participant appropriate for this level?". After finishing the level, the researcher asks the participant these questions and record the participant's answer on a hand-copied version of the questionnaire, which means 12 answers for each participant.

Results: Fig. 4a illustrates the average of skill and challenge in each level. While the bars in Fig. 4b is calculated according to [21] by the equation.

$$0.25 \times (Skill - Challenge) \tag{1}$$

This graph shows how the flow of each level is far from the optimal flow (zero flow). The figure shows a significant difference at level one, which means that the participants were bored at the start of the game. This is because their skills were higher than the challenge factor of the game. But the more the levels they went through, the more challenging the game. Until the last two levels are reached, the challenge factor gradually decreases. Most of the participants felt that their skills are suitable for the game, with average skill of 3.25 for all levels.

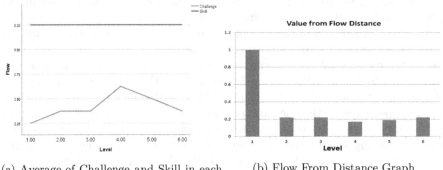

(a) Average of Challenge and Skill in each Level

(b) Flow From Distance Graph

Fig. 4. Flow results

6 Conclusion and Future Work

Using interactive serious games for educating children computational thinking and programming is a growing research field. The main objective of this project was to test the effectiveness of interactive game for computational thinking and programming learning using the Kinect sensor on children's learning gain. "Mini-Colon" is an educational game for children of the age between 8–9 that teaches three main concepts in programming (*sequential blocks, conditional blocks, and iterative blocks*). The game is controlled using the Kinect sensor to add interactivity to the game. The game was designed in a cartoonish and enjoyable way to attract the children. The game was evaluated with two different groups, one group tested the game and the other group was taught in a traditional educational method. The traditional educational method was a teacher who used slides to assist in the education process. The result showed that playing the game has more effect on the learning gain and the engagement level of the children than using a traditional educational method. According to the game flow results, the skill level of the participants was higher than the challenge level of the game. Most of the participants found level 1 not challenging and their skill is suitable for the game. At each level, the challenge level is increasing, but it decreases again when level 5 is reached. Thus, the challenge level of the game needs to be increased especially for level 1. According to the results, adding gesture recognition factor to educating computational thinking using Kinect helps the students to be more engaged in the education process.

More than twenty schools were contacted, however, only one school was interested in trying the project with its children. This is due to cultural reasons for not engaging in modern teaching technologies. Also, some children were not interested in trying the game or joining the activity of the traditional educational method. These led to the lacking number of participants in both groups.

Some of the students suggested that it is better if the main character can move backward. Also, more levels will be implemented to target more advanced concepts in computational thinking and programming such as functions and data structure. We need to do a more extensive long-term study on children, to test the effectiveness of the game in the long run.

References

1. Altanis, I., Retalis, S., Petropoulou, O.: Systematic design and rapid development of motion-based touchless games for enhancing students' thinking skills. Educ. Sci. **8**(1), 18 (2018)
2. Alvarado, C.: CS Ed week 2013: the hour of code. SIGCSE Bull. **46**(1), 2–4 (2014)
3. Armoni, M., Meerbaum-Salant, O., Ben-Ari, M.: From scratch to "real" programming. ACM Trans. Comput. Educ. (TOCE) **14**(4), 25:1–25:15 (2015). https://doi.org/10.1145/2677087
4. Arnold, S., Fujima, J., Jantke, K.P.: Storyboarding serious games for large-scale training applications. In: Foley, O., Restivo, M.T., Uhomoibhi, J.O., Helfert, M. (eds.) CSEDU 2013 - Proceedings of the 5th International Conference on Computer Supported Education, Aachen, Germany, 6–8 May 2013, pp. 651–655. SciTePress (2013)
5. Barr, D., Harrison, J., Conery, L.: Computational thinking: a digital age skill for everyone. Learn. Lead. Technol. **38**(6), 20–23 (2011)
6. Carnegie Mellon University: Alice. https://www.alice.org/. Accessed 3 June 2018
7. Craighead, J., Burke, J., Murphy, R.: Using the unity game engine to develop sarge: a case study. In: Proceedings of the 2008 Simulation Workshop at the International Conference on Intelligent Robots and Systems (IROS 2008) (2008)
8. Dumont, J., Sicard, P., Stum, J., Zanife, O.: Algorithm definition accuracy and specification, vol. 2: CMA altimeter level 2 processing. CNES, Toulouse (2001). SMM-ST-M2-EA-11005-CN
9. Kalelioğlu, F., Gülbahar, Y.: The effects of teaching programming via scratch on problem solving skills: a discussion from learners' perspective. Inform. Educ. **13**(1), 33–50 (2014)
10. Kamnardsiri, T., Hongsit, L.O., Khuwuthyakorn, P., Wongta, N.: The effectiveness of the game-based learning system for the improvement of American sign language using kinect. Electron. J. e-Learn. **15**(4), 283–296 (2017)

11. Kazimoglu, C., Kiernan, M., Bacon, L., Mackinnon, L.: A serious game for developing computational thinking and learning introductory computer programming. Procedia-Soc. Behav. Sci. **47**, 1991–1999 (2012)
12. Kumar, A.N.: Solving code-tracing problems and its effect on code-writing skills pertaining to program semantics. In: Dagiene, V., Schulte, C., Jevsikova, T. (eds.) Proceedings of the 2015 ACM Conference on Innovation and Technology in Computer Science Education, ITiCS 2015, Vilnius, Lithuania, 4–8 July 2015, pp. 314–319. ACM (2015). http://dl.acm.org/citation.cfm?id=2729094
13. Little, P., Wimer, C., Weiss, H.B., et al.: After school programs in the 21st century: their potential and what it takes to achieve it. Issues Oppor. Out-Of-Sch. Time Eval. **10**(1–12) (2008)
14. Maloney, J.H., Peppler, K.A., Kafai, Y.B., Resnick, M., Rusk, N.: Programming by choice: urban youth learning programming with scratch. In: Dougherty, J.D., Rodger, S.H., Fitzgerald, S., Guzdial, M. (eds.) Proceedings of the 39th SIGCSE Technical Symposium on Computer Science Education, SIGCSE 2008, Portland, OR, USA, 12–15 March 2008, pp. 367–371. ACM (2008)
15. Martey, R.M., et al.: Measuring game engagement: multiple methods and construct complexity. Simul. Gaming **45**(4–5), 528–547 (2014)
16. Microsoft: Microsoft Kinect. https://developer.microsoft.com/en-us/windows/kinect. Accessed 15 Mar 2018
17. MIT Media Lab: Scratch. https://scratch.mit.edu/. Accessed 1 June 2018
18. Nakamura, J., Csikszentmihalyi, M.: The concept of flow. In: Csikszentmihalyi, M. (ed.) Flow and the Foundations of Positive Psychology, pp. 239–263. Springer, Dordrecht (2014). https://doi.org/10.1007/978-94-017-9088-8_16
19. Orsini, L.: Kodable teaches kids to code before they learn to read (2013)
20. Parmar, D., et al.: Programming moves: Design and evaluation of applying embodied interaction in virtual environments to enhance computational thinking in middle school students. In: Höllerer, T., Interrante, V., Lécuyer, A., Suma, E.A. (eds.) 2016 IEEE Virtual Reality, VR 2016, Greenville, SC, USA, 19–23 March 2016, pp. 131–140. IEEE Computer Society (2016). http://ieeexplore.ieee.org/xpl/mostRecentIssue.jsp?punumber=7499993
21. Pearce, J.M., Ainley, M., Howard, S.: The ebb and flow of online learning. Comput. Hum. Behav. **21**(5), 745–771 (2005)
22. Rahman, M.: Beginning Microsoft Kinect for Windows SDK 2.0: Motion and Depth Sensing for Natural User Interfaces. Apress, New York (2017)
23. Salah, J., Abdennadher, S., Sabty, C., Abdelrahman, Y.: Super alpha: arabic alphabet learning serious game for children with learning disabilities. In: Marsh, T., Ma, M., Oliveira, M.F., Baalsrud Hauge, J., Göbel, S. (eds.) JCSG 2016. LNCS, vol. 9894, pp. 104–115. Springer, Cham (2016). https://doi.org/10.1007/978-3-319-45841-0_9
24. Stajano, F.: Python in education: raising a generation of native speakers. In: Proceedings of 8th International Python Conference, pp. 2000–2001 (2000)
25. Tsai, C., Kuo, Y., Chu, K., Yen, J.: Development and evaluation of game-based learning system using the microsoft kinect sensor. IJDSN **11**, 498560:1–498560:10 (2015)
26. Wuang, Y.P., Chiang, C.S., Su, C.Y., Wang, C.C.: Effectiveness of virtual reality using Wii gaming technology in children with down syndrome. Res. Dev. Disabil. **32**(1), 312–321 (2011)
27. Wyeth, P., Purchase, H.C.: Tangible programming elements for young children. In: Terveen, L.G., Wixon, D.R. (eds.) Extended abstracts of the 2002 Conference on Human Factors in Computing Systems, CHI 2002, Minneapolis, Minnesota, USA, 20–25 April 2002, pp. 774–775. ACM (2002)

Evaluation of an Augmented Reality Multiplayer Learning Game

Andrea Ortiz, Cristian Vitery, Carolina González[(⊠)], and Hendrys Tobar-Muñoz

Department of Systems, University of Cauca, Popayán, Cauca, Colombia
{andreaortiz, cvitery, cgonzals, fabian}@unicauca.edu.co

Abstract. Augmented Reality Game-Based Learning (ARGBL) has been proposed as the combination of AR and GBL. Studies show that students increase their motivation in learning when they play ARGBL games. Moreover, ARGBL benefits learning processes by allowing social interaction with digital devices within a multiplayer environment. In order to assess the effects of combining ARGBL and a multiplayer approach, an ARGBL multiplayer video game was built guided by a co-creation method. This paper shows the results in terms of learning after using the ARGBL multiplayer video game as part of a classroom activity.

Keywords: Augmented reality · Multiplayer · Game-Based Learning
Co-creation

1 Introduction

Augmented Reality (AR), defined by Azuma [1], is a combination of virtual and real objects that coexist in the same space. In the last decade, studies have shown that AR provides students with greater motivation for learning during classroom activities [2]. Currently there are numerous applications [3–5] that integrate Augmented Reality which are built specifically for the educational environment. Game-Based Learning allows students to learn by new and playful means through video games created for this purpose. Many of the game experiences found in the state of the art [6–8] include AR for learning; nonetheless, they fail to effectively take advantage of the social interaction that Augmented Reality provides [9].

Section 3 describes the video game developed under the Co-CreARGBL method. Section 4 describes the evaluation and analysis process carried out in this study. Finally, Sect. 5 outlines the conclusions and future work.

2 Related Work

The video game showed in this study, named "TerraExplora", was built in context of the SmartSchool project (a project of the University of Cauca, Colombia) following the method Co-CreARGBL [10]. The game aimed to take advantage of AR with social interaction benefitting teaching and learning processes.

© Springer Nature Switzerland AG 2018
S. Göbel et al. (Eds.): JCSG 2018, LNCS 11243, pp. 91–100, 2018.
https://doi.org/10.1007/978-3-030-02762-9_10

The design and development process of "TerraExplora" was described deeply in [10]. Also, that study showed the lessons learned during the process. This paper describes the evaluation and analysis of "TerraExplora" which was conducted in a naturalistic environment setting in a real classroom during a Geography lecture in a rural school in the Colombia's southwest.

3   The Game

"TerraExplora" is an educational video game built using a co-creation method [8] which integrates AR and social interaction. The AR role was the visualization of graphic game elements over a marker-based map of Colombia (Colombian regions, position mark, characters, Colombian resources and climatic events). This video game aims to support learning activities about the Departments (regions) of Colombia and their economic resources, which are the main learning objectives set by primary school teachers. Thanks to the co-creation integrated during each stage of the development process, "TerraExplora" was built and improved considering the input of the teachers trying to fulfill their expectations related to learning and motivation. The game storyline is presented as a competition in which aliens from different planets come to earth looking to know about the Colombian resources. The video game uses marker-based AR which makes the students focusing onto the map as a learning object. The device running "TerraExplora" should be equipped with a webcam with enough resolution to perform marker detection and the Android Operative System.

During the game session, two players face each other to achieve the main objective of the game: fulfill missions. Missions consist of finding natural resources produced in different Departments (regions) of Colombia. Each player has the ability to move through the departments of Colombia, explore them and collect the resources found. These actions can be performed through buttons on a main interface (Fig. 1A). Likewise, these actions have an energy cost and the game is played turn by turn. Players will be affected by several obstacles, such as the opponent player's decisions. For example, players may use cards which can be used to benefit their own game or affect their opponent.

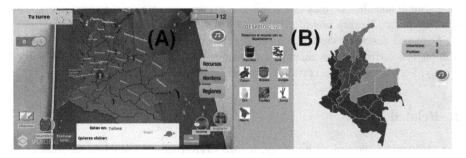

Fig. 1. (A). Main interface of the game. (B). Final challenge interface.

Lastly, a final challenge begins when the missions have been completed. This challenge consists in placing the resources of the missions, with their respective Department. The winner will be the one with the highest total score. Figure 1(B) shows the interface of the final challenge.

For more information, we recommend reviewing the paper "Developing an Augmented Reality Multiplayer Learning Game: Lessons Learned" [10], which deeply describe the design and development process of "TerraExplora".

4 Evaluation

In this section we present the results of the evaluation process conducted on the use of ARGBL and the multiplayer approach through the analysis of "TerraExplora" in a real educational environment. An evaluation based on mixed methods [11] was carried out. The game was deployed in Samsung Galaxy Note 10.1 tablets, with 4.1 Jelly Bean Android Operating System, 3 GB of RAM. In this section we show the problem statement, research design, sampling, data collection and analysis of the results.

4.1 Problem Statement

This stage begins with the definition of the evaluation question. The question that was raised for this project was the following:

Did the students benefit from to the use of ARGBL multiplayer videogames as "TerraExplora"?

4.2 Research Design

The methodology of Mixed Methods [11] provides a number of research designs depending on the characteristics of the research work. That is why the chosen research design in this project was the Concurrent Triangulation Design (DITRIAC) [11], due to the evaluation's aim to corroborate results and carry out a cross-validation between quantitative and qualitative data. On the one hand quantitative approach used an experimental design with the aim of comparing the results of two student groups. On the other hand, the qualitative approach used a case study with the purpose of determining the effect of the video game in terms of learning outcomes.

4.3 Sampling

The sample for this project consisted of 31 sixth grade students from the rural town of "La Cabaña", Department of Cauca, Colombia aged 11 years old on average and a standard deviation of 1.4. A process of simple random probability sampling was carried out, which involved taking the population and divide it into two groups (experimental and control) by selecting their members at random through a table of random numbers without considering any preference of the students.

4.4   Data Collection

To find how the game impacted the learning process, students in the experimental group were asked to interact with the video game during the class. In turn students in the control group took a class activity as they do in their normal school days. The experiment was divided in three stages: (i) test of learning styles, (ii) class activity or gaming activity and (iv) interviews. For the quantitative approach, information was obtained by the participants through questionnaires. The qualitative approach used observations, interviews, audio recordings and photographs. Table 1 shows different activities addressed on the class activities and game activity. Note that the main difference is on activity Book Reading and VideoGame.

Table 1. Summary of stages during the class activity

Activities	Class Activity	Game Activity
Didactic activity	✓	✓
Map	✓	✓
Video	✓	✓
Book reading	✓	–
VideoGame	–	✓
Conclusions and statement	✓	✓

(i) **Test of learning styles**

Based on the study carried out by Chen [12], competition mechanisms are related to the skill of students. The study concluded that the design of competitive learning activities can be improved by considering the preferences of students and their abilities to achieve a more efficient learning process. For this reason, in this project, a test of learning styles was used with the aim of analyzing how the preferences of the students influenced their learning.

We used a test adapted from the "CAPSOL Style Of Learning Assessment" [13], with the objective of determining the learning styles from the students profile ranging low to high preference. In this case we chose the learning styles related to the influential skills in the project, which are: visual, auditory, bodily-kinesthetic, individual, group and written expression.

The test consists of 18 questions whose answers have a numerical value (1–4). Once the test is completed, the respective analysis of the answers is carried out to determine the student's preference for learning styles.

(ii) **Class activity**

The class activity was solely used with the control group. The teacher guided a class carefully observing that the educational content was the same as the content integrated in "TerraExplora". The teacher began with a didactic activity which motivated the students to participate in the class considering their previous knowledge about the topic of interest: Departments of Colombia. The teacher subsequently used a video projector to show the map of Colombia and indicate its regions, as show in Fig. 2. Also, the teacher showed a video explaining the regions of Colombia and its characteristics. At the end of the video the teacher gave the information related to Colombian resources with a document that students transcribed to their notebooks.

Fig. 2. Teacher imparting the class activity to the control group.

A questionnaire designed by the teacher was conducted to assess students' learning, which had questions related to the educational content presented during the class activity.

(iii) Gaming activity

The gaming activity was conducted with the experimental group, the teacher used an instructional activity to guide this session, which was designed to introduce the topics of the educational content and explain the game mechanics. During this activity, the teacher carried out the same traditional didactic activity as well as the presentation of the map of Colombia and the same video explaining the regions of Colombia and their characteristics.

After the video was played, the gaming session began with the support of the teacher, as shown in Fig. 3. The gaming session lasted approximately 25 to 30 min.

During the gaming activity, information was gathered through observations which focused on identifying how multiplayer mechanics and AR cause an increase in student interest and motivation, and consequently better learning. The observation was based on the analysis key factors such as participation, mood, respond timing and amount of accurate answers. Also, it was observed the duration of each turn, the need for help from students and the errors presented in the video game. Once the game activity was

Fig. 3. (A) Gaming activity. (B) Final challenge.

completed, students in the experimental group took a questionnaire to evaluate their learning. This questionnaire is the same one used with the control group.

(iv) **Interviews**

After the class and gaming activity, students were randomly selected from each group to interview them. A third interview was conducted to the teachers in order to know their opinion/perception related to the integration of video games, such as "TerraExplora", in their classes and its influence on the teaching and learning processes.

4.5 Analysis of Results

Learning. The questionnaire was one of the instruments used in the assessment of learning, which was applied to both the control and experimental group. The results were entered into the software for statistical analysis STATA [14], which allowed to analyze the data and gather conclusions. We were not able to find statistical significance probably because of the small sample size. The questionnaire was composed of 7 questions, which were related to the learning objectives set by the teachers. Table 2 shows the results of the questions related to the learning objectives (regions, Departments and resources).

The first question of the questionnaire was related to the Departments of Colombia. The results showed that 75% of the students belonging to the experimental group got good answers against 63.2% of the students belonging to control group. This positive result is considered to be attributed to the gaming mechanics because, in the game, the students had to travel through Colombia and are able to virtually visit the departments.

The sixth question was related to the regions of Colombia. The results showed that 58.3% of the students belonging to experimental group were successful in the response, while no student in the control group was fully successful. It should be noted that no student from the experimental group missed the answer which suggests that they identified at least one region of Colombia. This positive result is considered to be attributed to AR and the gaming mechanics included in "TerraExplora" which allowed the students to visualize the regions of Colombia and foster their learning because the information is presented in a visual and entertaining way capturing their attention and avoiding boredom. The students who recognized the regions of Colombia got an

Table 2. Results of the analysis by group

Question	Group	Scale		
		Good	Regular	Wrong
1	Control	63.2%	36.6%	0%
	Experimental	75%	25%	0%
2	Control	26.3%	36.8%	36.8%
	Experimental	16.7%	16.7%	66.7%
3	Control	31.6%	36.8%	31.6%
	Experimental	50%	25%	25%
4	Control	57.9%	0%	42.1%
	Experimental	75%	0%	25%
5	Control	78.9%	0%	21.1%
	Experimental	91.7%	0%	8.3%
6	Control	0%	68.4%	31.6%
	Experimental	58.3%	41.7%	0%
7	Control	36.8%	21.1%	42.1%
	Experimental	83.3%	0%	16.7%

advantage over their opponent because the game has a set of "clues" which are always related to the regions of the country.

Question seven was related to the resources and its producing Department. The results showed that "TerraExplora" influenced a high number of students (83.3%) form the experimental group. These students were able to relate a resource with the corresponding producing Department. While in the control group most students (42.1%) responded erroneously, this could be related to the lack of motivation during the class. In support of the above, the observations during the game activity indicated that several students struggled to remember the Department where they knew that a specific resource was produced to fulfill a certain mission motivated by competition.

Generally, the result showed that the experimental group was characterized by having a greater number of good answers compared to the control group, as shown in Table 3, suggesting that elements included in "TerraExplora" (AR and social interaction) influenced those results.

Table 3. Overall results related to student learning.

Group	Good	Regular	Wrong
Control	42.1%	28.6%	29.3%
Experimental	64.3%	15.5%	20.2%

The results obtained in the questionnaire were analyzed in order to understand the differences between the control and experimental groups. As shown in Figs. 4(A) and (B).

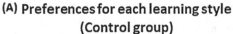

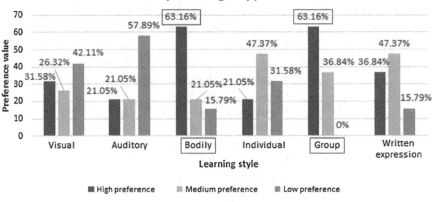

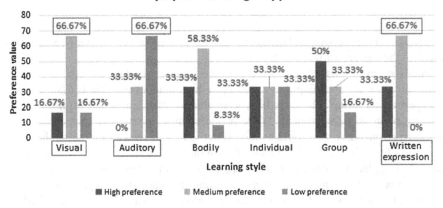

Fig. 4. Preferences for each learning style in control and experimental group

The analysis showed that most students belonging to the control group were inclined towards a bodily-kinesthetic and group learning styles. Regarding the experimental group, the students were inclined towards visual, bodily-kinesthetic, group and written expression learning styles. This suggests that most of the failures in the control group may be due to the fact that a traditional class does not promote their maximum performance because their preferences are inclined to group learning and socialization which are not present in a traditional teacher-to-students lecture. In contrast, the learning styles of the experimental group are more aligned with the game characteristics. The gaming mechanics set in "TerraExplora" are focused on promoting learning by association based on the benefits that provides the AR and social interaction in order to obtain a better student learning. It is considered that students belonging to the control group would obtain better results if they had use "TerraExplora" as the experimental group did, because the physical interaction with the gaming elements helps them remembering and processing information, and the multiplayer mechanics included in the game fits the student's learning styles.

5   Conclusions and Future Work

In this paper, the evaluation of a multiplayer AR Game-Based Learning game has been shown. Regarding the influence of the video game in the learning process, students gave a greater value to the educational content they have to accomplish a game mission. The teaching strategy of Learning by Association played an important role to fulfill the missions in the game. This causes the learning to take place indirectly motivated by the use of components such as AR and social interaction.

As for the influence of learning styles in the results obtained in the questionnaire, it is considered that students belonging to the experimental group obtained a good performance in learning with a 64.3%, compared with the control group with a 42.1%. This may be because most students showed an inclination to a learning style that benefits from the social interaction included in "TerraExplora". On the other hand, it is considered that the students belonging to control group would obtain better results if they will experience with "TerraExplora", because the interaction with the physical elements would help them to remember and process information. Also, the multiplayer mechanics included in the video game benefit this because of the students' high preference for group and bodily-kinesthetic learning styles.

By observing the results, it is concluded that competition integrated in "TerraExplora" allowed students to learn the educational content in a fun way as they looked to get advantage over their opponent, however some students preferred to play in a collaborative way.

Finally, teachers expressed that "TerraExplora" is a support tool to the classes because the students perform the practical part reinforcing the knowledge acquired in class. Teachers emphasized that the use of "TerraExplora" supports learning by association, provides a fun experience that captures the attention of children, increases the motivation and manages an interesting game mechanics for students.

As future work of this research, we propose to include a collaborative experience in the video game, i.e. the possibility of choosing between collaborative or competitive game because some of the students showed preference toward collaboration in their quest to fulfill the missions. Also, the game may be improved to a continuous pace (not turn-based) in order to minimize the gaming time and possible boredom.

Acknowledgments. This work is supported by the Smart School Project: Mobile and Interactive Environment for supporting learning processes. ID. 4565-University of Cauca, Colombia. We want to acknowledge the support the teachers and students who participated in this project.

References

1. Azuma, R.T.: A Survey of Augmented Reality. Hughes Res. Lab., Malibu (1997)
2. Akçayır, M., Akçayır, G.: Advantages and challenges associated with augmented reality for education: a systematic review of the literature. Educ. Res. Rev. **20**, 1–11 (2017)
3. Yilmaz, R.M.: Educational magic toys developed with augmented reality technology for early childhood education. Comput. Hum. Behav. **54**, 240–248 (2016)
4. Kraut, B., Jeknić, J.: Improving education experience with augmented reality (AR). In: 2015 38th International Convention on Information and Communication Technology, Electronics and Microelectronics, MIPRO 2015, pp. 755–760 (2015)
5. Lu, S.J., Liu, Y.C.: Integrating augmented reality technology to enhance children's learning in marine education. Environ. Educ. Res. **21**, 525–541 (2015)
6. Bacca, J., Baldiris, S., Fabregat, R., Kinshuk, Graf, S.: Mobile augmented reality in vocational education and training. In: 2015 International Conference Virtual and Augmented Reality in Education, vol. 75, pp. 49–58 (2015)
7. Pinto, D., Mosquera, J., Gonzalez, C., Tobar-Muñoz, H., Baldiris, S., Fabregat, R.: Augmented reality board game for supporting learning and motivation in an indigenous community. In: Proceedings of the V International Conference on Videogames and Education (2017)
8. Tobar-Munoz, H., Baldiris, S., Fabregat, R.: Co design of augmented reality game-based learning games with teachers using co-CreaARGBL method. In: Proceedings - IEEE 16th International Conference on Advanced Learning Technologies, ICALT 2016, pp. 120–122. IEEE Computer Society, Austin (2016)
9. Sánchez Bolado, J.: El potencial de la realidad aumentada en la enseñanza de español como lengua extranjera. The potential of augmented reality in the teaching of Spanish as a foreign language. EDMETIC, vol. 6, p 62 (2016)
10. Ortiz, A., Vitery, C., González, C., Tobar-Munoz, H.: Developing an augmented reality multiplayer learning game: lessons learned. Lecture Notes in Computer Science (2018, accepted)
11. Sampieri, N.: Capítulo Los métodos mixtos. Chapter mixed methods. McGraw Hill (2014)
12. Chen, Z.H.: Learning preferences and motivation of different ability students for social-competition or self-competition. Educ. Technol. Soc. **17**, 283–293 (2013)
13. Bonacci, J.A., Renaud, L.: An investigation of the test-retest and internal consistency reliability of the computerized assessment program styles of learning (CAPSOL) inventory (1998)
14. STATA: Data Analysis and Statistical Software—Stata. https://www.stata.com/

Prism, a Game to Promote Autism Acceptance Among Elementary School Students

Ridima Ramesh[✉], Xueyang Wang, Daniel Wolpow, Yidi Zhu, Yutian Zheng, Michael Christel, and Scott Stevens

Carnegie Mellon University, Pittsburgh, PA 15213, USA
{ridimar, xueyangw, dwolpow, yidiz, yutianz}@andrew.cmu.edu,
{christel, scottstevens}@cmu.edu

Abstract. Prism was developed to help neurotypical children aged 8 to 10 empathize with their peers who have autism. It is a digital game for the children to play, paired with a discussion framework for instructors that takes the children through the game and how it relates to the children's everyday life. In this paper we describe the development of the game and discussion framework, iteratively working with the stakeholders and interacting with a subject matter expert to create the full experience within 15 weeks.

Keywords: Autism acceptance · Games for behavior change
Games for empathy

1 Introduction

At Beech Bottom Primary School in West Virginia, USA, neurotypical students (students without autism) frequently interact with classmates who have autism. While the children take many classes separately, there are occasions where they take the same class, and many areas where they meet – like during recess or parties. Teachers note that the differences in behavior between the two groups give rise to misunderstandings and difficulties in cooperation. Previous efforts in promoting empathy in neurotypical students involved conversations with the children about autism, sometimes aided with videos. Instances of teasing and mild bullying persisted, however, and the teachers were concerned about the long-term impact of such behavior left unchecked.

Our team of Carnegie Mellon graduate students from the Entertainment Technology Center was tasked with developing a functioning prototype in a 15-week period that could effectively engage neurotypical children with the subject matter and engender empathy for their peers with autism. Our client was interested to see whether an interactive experience would be more effective in getting through to the children. We worked closely with a subject matter expert (SME), Michelle Lubetsky, who is an Educational Consultant at the Allegheny Intermediate Unit (Pennsylvania, USA) to develop the experience. We built the game for web browsers and optimized for Google Chromebooks, later porting it to iOS and Android devices for increased accessibility at schools.

© Springer Nature Switzerland AG 2018
S. Göbel et al. (Eds.): JCSG 2018, LNCS 11243, pp. 101–106, 2018.
https://doi.org/10.1007/978-3-030-02762-9_11

2   Related Work

Autism acceptance and empathy has been promoted through a variety of media. Before we committed to a digital game, we explored the work that had already been done in this area, discussing pros and cons with our SME. Given that we had a 15-week period to create the full prototype, we had only a short span of time to look at other work, focusing on types of interactive experiences we could pursue for our project, or media targeted specifically at our users, like children's books. We met bi-weekly with our SME to keep the experience focused on its goals.

360° Video. Projects employing this media to engender empathy for autism usually simulate the experience of sensory overload to help viewers understand it. Some videos we looked at were the *Autism TMI Virtual Reality Experience* [1] and *The Party* [2]. These applications do not address difficulties with communication and social skills that are typically observed in individuals with autism.

Games. The game *Auti-Sim* [3] allows you to navigate through a playground as a child, focusing on the experience of sensory overload. There are some comments on the game webpage that express positive reception, but other comments emphasize that it is not representative of all autistic experiences. As autism is a wide spectrum, a game set in the real world was a risky endeavor. We also learned to watch for tone, as there are comments and reviews of the game that call it "creepy" or "horrifying". We wanted to ensure that players of our game do not fear or pity their peers with autism.

Installations. An interactive digital poster by BBDO for Autism Speaks [4] addressed the difficulty that children with autism have with making eye-contact. It was used for advertisement purposes and tackled only that one symptom.

Augmented Reality. Heeju Kim created *An Empathy Bridge for Autism* [5] using a smartphone augmented with a specially designed app to simulate autistic vision, earphones to emulate the sound and disposable candy that hinders pronunciation. The creator used low cost materials to address various symptoms of which neurotypical people may not be aware.

Mobile Apps. *The Autism Discovery Tool: Sensory from Within* mobile app [6] dealt with seven senses: vision, hearing, touch, taste, smell, balance and proprioception. The app address both strengths and challenges in these areas. While the platform of a mobile app lends itself well to our users and the wide range of senses provided good coverage, the app functioned as a tool which may not be engaging for children.

Books and Videos. There is a variety of material directed at children through these media. Books like *My Friend With Autism* [7], or the videos *My Autism and Me* [8], *What's up with Nick?* [9] and episodes of *Sesame Street* [10] depict everyday with advice for children on how to navigate them. We also watched episodes of the television show *Mister Rogers' Neighborhood* [11] for insight into constructing a simple story for children and mapping it back to a larger lesson.

3 Design

To flesh out our goals for the player of the game, we used Sabrina Culyba's framework for developing transformational games [12]. The "barriers" we identified i.e. the reasons neurotypical children at the school had trouble empathizing with their autistic peers, were two-fold. First, from the perspective of a neurotypical student, it often seems that there are no apparent stimuli that cause the unusual and sometimes frightening behaviors that their peers with autism exhibit. Second, neurotypical children can have a hard time understanding that their peers with autism must perform conscious social problem-solving on a regular basis to effectively communicate. Extrapolating from these barriers, we developed the goals for the players of our game as follows: First, the game helps the player understand the phenomenon of sensory overload. Second, it helps them understand the difficulty in daily communication that their peers with autism face. And third, the players should understand how they can take actions to be a better friend.

As an informal test, we met with a small group of students at our client school, where we used card sorting with some pictures of different games to understand their preferences. The children expressed a preference for open-world games set in natural settings over more realistic, industrial-like settings. Brainstorming with exploration as a core driver, we arrived at the idea of a having an open-world game set in a forest. We then laid a plot over this structure to make the design address our goals better. The player plays as a nocturnal animal, the fox, who experiences a form of sensory overload in the daytime, and who must communicate with animals unfamiliar to it. This pairs the sensory overload with a series of social interactions, addressing our first two goals. We moved our third goal outside the game, where a teacher leads a discussion about the traits observed in the animals and how it relates to everyday life. We also met with some children a second time, where we asked them for stories about their friends, to help us construct a more relatable narrative. Many stories about friendship revolved around playing together, helping someone who was hurt, or helping someone find a lost object. This helped shape the plot to meet our learning goals (Table 1).

We iteratively tested for development at multiple primary schools, using built-in Google Analytics to evaluate our design choices. We followed all child safety protocol measures as required by the schools with which we worked, as well as CMU's human subject guidelines.

4 Implementation

4.1 Visual and Auditory Distortion

The distortion was in effect during the daytime, which is when the fox would experience a form of "sensory overload." It occurs at regular intervals and the fox must howl to soothe itself. Developing in Unity3D (for WebGL browser deployment, and then iOS and Android apps), we used the bloom filter in combination with grain, depth of field, chromatic aberration and a slight vignette. Initially, we simulated blurry vision, but our SME advised us to instead simulate it as sensitivity to bright light (Fig. 1). For

Table 1. Structure of the plot with associated learning goals

Game plot	Gameplay	Learning goals
The fox meets the owl and the wolf who bring news of the flood and ask the fox to seek help to save the forest	Cutscene, introduction to dialogue selection mechanic	
The bear needs honey before she agrees to help	Soothe visual distortion to read dialogue	Difficulty attending to an auditory message if highly stimulated
A stag and a doe are worried about their lost baby fawn, who is obsessed with fireflies	Select appropriate dialogue options to guide the fawn back	Deliver monologues about a favorite topic rather than allow reciprocal communication
The owl discusses how challenging the daytime can be	Cutscene	Normalizing difficulties, highlighting strengths
An injured boar needs some berries, honey and wheatgrass. The rabbit can help but doesn't seem to be listening	Interacting with the rabbit prompts wheat-grass to appear in her mouth 30 s later	Have difficulty multi-tasking, i.e., talking or listening while doing something else; may need to do one thing at a time
The fox meets a moose who seems unwilling to talk	Repeated interactions encourage non-verbal communication	Desire social interaction, but has difficulty knowing how to initiate and maintain a friendship

the auditory distortion, we used curve smoothing. Since the WebGL platform does not support threads, we were unable to use FMOD for audio playback and mixing, so we created two separate tracks (normal and distorted) and switched between them using the Web Audio API.

Fig. 1. Daytime vision – when soothed and distorted.

4.2   Navigation and Controls

Based on the children's familiarity with games like Minecraft, we initially used a combination of mouse and keyboard for controls. However, this proved to be too difficult for all children to use, so we made the controls keyboard-only, using arrow keys and the spacebar. The players could use the H key to access the Hints menu, and the F key to howl to alleviate distortion. When porting to mobile devices, we changed the F key-press to shaking the device. We added a delay to the effect of the soothing taking place. It created the desired effect of the children repeatedly trying to soothe the fox, without being prompted to do so, seeming effective in simulating the frustration of a sensory overload. The delay in soothing was adjusted based on testing, to make sure that the players were not frustrated enough to stop playing the game.

4.3   Dialogue and Hints System

In lieu of using voice acting, an effort was made to keep the reading level of the dialogue simple using a readability checker [13]. We avoided filling the dialogue box with long lines of text, preferring to break them into smaller sentences.

We found that adding environmental cues for each animal helped the players orient themselves in the world. Consequently, we used a large red tree, fireflies, a pond and large rocks as markers for each animal. A hints menu was added in to provide the players with a visual indicator of progress and gameplay hints. We also added on-screen hints and context-sensitive dialogue hints.

4.4   Discussion Framework and Teacher Resources

In the development of the discussion framework for teachers, we worked closely with our SME who has experience conducting workshops with children for autism acceptance. An accompanying document presents the framework for each animal interaction, consisting of a quick overview of the plot, the learning goal and the questions to be asked. Prior to conducting the workshop, the teachers can watch a series of playthrough videos on our website [14], if they do not wish to play the game.

5   Use in Classrooms

Our client, Beech Bottom Primary, conducted the full workshop with their class of fourth-grade students. The students responded favorably to the post-game discussion, relating the animal scenarios to their real-life experiences. The teacher pointed out that a child known to exhibit some insensitivity on the subject previously took a surprising initiative in the conversation post-game. They theorized it was because he was fond of playing games and looked upon the topic of discussion more favorably when it was presented to him in relation to a game. We also tested the game and workshop at a school that had not seen previous iterations of the game, and without the team physically present in the room. The game was well received and many students took initiative in the post-game discussion. In all tests, the children play the game for 30–35 min, with the follow-up teacher-led workshop running for 25–30 min.

6 Next Steps and Conclusion

Next steps include empirical validation that the game meets its learning goals through formally coding discussions and careful experimental procedures regarding the game plus teacher-led workshop. Our goal with this project was to create a fully-functional working prototype in 15 weeks. We found that our animal world triggered topic appropriate conversations in our pilot tests with two schools. Most efforts in autism acceptance that we examined explain the condition using some version of real-world simulation. However, our unique metaphorical approach also worked well to stimulate conversation. The use of forest animals engaged our players and perhaps made it easier for them to understand the existence of different behaviors. As our developmental focus was the optimization of the game, further research efforts can investigate best-case practices for the post-game discussion.

References

1. Autism TMI Virtual Reality Experience – YouTube. https://youtu.be/DgDR_gYk_a8. Accessed 10 June 2018
2. The Party – YouTube. https://youtu.be/OtwOz1GVkDg. Accessed 10 June 2018
3. Auti-Sim. https://gamejolt.com/games/auti-sim/12761. Accessed 10 June 2018
4. BBDO & Autism Speaks – YouTube. https://youtu.be/UqHrRIwlVm4. Accessed 10 June 2018
5. An Empathy Bridge for Autism. https://vimeo.com/172758926. Accessed 10 June 2018
6. Spectrum Idea Lab Inc. http://www.spectrumidealab.com/. Accessed 10 June 2018
7. Bishop, B., Bishop, C.: My Friend with Autism, 1st edn. Future Horizons Inc., Arlington (2002)
8. My Autism and Me. http://www.bbc.co.uk/newsround/15655232. Accessed 10 June 2018
9. What's up with Nick? – YouTube. https://youtu.be/mtRYKjucDHk. Accessed 10 June 2018
10. Sesame Street: Meet Julia – YouTube. https://youtu.be/dKCdV20zLMs. Accessed 10 June 2018
11. Mister Rogers' Neighborhood Videos. http://pbskids.org/video/mister-rogers/. Accessed 10 June 2018
12. Culyba, S.: The Transformational Framework. Unpublished manuscript (2018). Slide deck of early version available at: https://www.slideshare.net/SeriousGamesAssoc/sabrina-haskell-culyba. Accessed 10 June 2018
13. Readability and keyword density analysis. https://readable.io/. Accessed 10 June 2018
14. Project Prism. https://www.etc.cmu.edu/projects/prism/. Accessed 2018

Game-Based Learning and Teaching

Individuals' Variables in Cognitive Abilities Using a Narrative Serious Game

Elena Parra, Carla de Juan Ripoll, Mariano Alcañiz Raya⬤,
and Irene Alice Chicchi Giglioli(✉)⬤

Instituto de Investigación e Innovación en Bioingeniería (I3B), Universitat
Politècnica de València, Camino de Vera s/n. 46022, València, Spain
{elparvar,malcaniz,alicechicchi}@i3b.upv.es

Abstract. Age, gender, and education represent crucial variables in the assessment and interpretation of traditional neuropsychological measures as regards the executive functions (EF). Currently, traditional measures are showing limitations in capturing real life behaviors and new technologies, such as serious games, are allowing creating more real situations with higher ecological validity. In the present study, we applied a serious game approach to investigate individual variables-related differences in the EF assessment. 268 healthy subjects participated in the study, completing 14 tasks (6 standard tasks; 8 serious games) randomly presented. The results showed that younger participants completed tasks in less time than older and with higher correct answers. Furthermore, males registered shorter reaction times, while females showed higher percentages of correct answers. The university studies group obtained higher total score and correct answers than high school studies group. Finally, since the study involved technology, we divided the group in high and low use technology level, obtaining that participants with a lower level of use technologies reported higher latency times and lower correct answers in high order EF tasks than the group with higher level of use of technology. As the traditional measure, these findings suggest that individuals' differences are critical variables to consider in the development of more ecological measures for the assessment of EFs.

Keywords: Serious game · Executive functions · Age · Education
Gender · Behavioral assessment · Ecological validity

1 Introduction

Executive functions (EFs) are a set of basic and higher-order cognitive processes involved in the monitoring and control of everyday life behaviors for the achievement of established goals [1, 2]. Basic EFs include attention, control inhibition, working memory, and cognitive flexibility, and higher-order EFs involve multi-basic EFs, including planning and problem-solving abilities [3–5]. In addition, EFs do not only play an important role in cognitive behaviors related to the achievement of established goals, but also in emotional and social situations [6]. Currently, the neuropsychological assessment and an accurate interpretation of EFs performance measures are crucial

© Springer Nature Switzerland AG 2018
S. Göbel et al. (Eds.): JCSG 2018, LNCS 11243, pp. 109–119, 2018.
https://doi.org/10.1007/978-3-030-02762-9_12

variables that distinguish normal cognitive functioning from cognitive impairments [1, 7]. For accurate neuropsychological interpretation, the tests are adjusted according to socio-demographic variables such as age, gender, and education that influence cognitive performance [8–10]. Numerous age studies on normal functioning showed that the highest performance of EFs abilities is between 20 and 29 years, weakening progressively in later adulthood [11–13]. Otherwise, educational level has related to higher EFs performance [14–18]. Individuals with higher education performed better than individuals with lower education. Regarding to results on gender, the scientific literature showed more complexity. Some studies, on one hand, showed that women performed better on verbal tasks and men in visual-spatial tasks [19–21]. On other hand, other studies revealed weaker or no differences gender-related on EFs performance [22–24].

Furthermore, the traditional EF tests require simple responses to single stimuli and tend to be decontextualized, and abstract, not reflecting the complex multi-tasks in daily life that demand more composite series of behaviors, limiting in this way their ecological validity [25–27]. Indeed, clinical studies have showed that even if patients are able to perform well as healthy subjects on traditional tests, they experience difficulties in everyday life activities [28–30]. Ecological validity refers to the generalization of the results and individual performance of a research study to real settings of everyday life [25]. Serious games (SG) are games with an established aim that can represent a novel approach to simulate more real-EFs situations and able to capture dynamic performance in real time. Currently, SGs are especially showing efficacy in rehabilitation interventions [31], and less in psychological assessment. The main advantages provided by SGs include appealing, since nowadays technologies are commonly used in daily life, being able to achieve more people [32]; engagement because games are fun and able to increase motivation, decreasing patients' drop-out [33]; and effectiveness since people can experience new behavior in a safe environment [33].

Starting from these premises, the aim of the present study was to assess, through a narrative SG, three distinct domains of EFs involving attentional and inhibition control, planning and cognitive flexibility among healthy individuals with a wide age range of 25–55 years, considering comparative gender and education differences, as well as differences in using technology.

2   Materials and Methods

2.1   Subjects

A total of 268 healthy subjects (Mean age = 39.19; SD = 8.65) participated in this study. Before participating in the study, each participant received written information about the study and was required to give written consent for inclusion in the study. The study obtained ethical approval by the Ethical Committee of the Polytechnic University of Valencia.

2.2   Questionnaire

Participants completed a demographic questionnaire, about their age, gender, education and level of use of technologies.

2.3   Tasks

The tasks were developed using Unity 5.5.1f1 software and completed on a personal computer. The Visual Studio tool was used applying c# programming language. Participants completed a total of 14 tasks (6 standard tasks; 8 serious games) randomly presented. The randomization of the tasks was performed by applying a programming code.

Each of the SGs was designed according to one of the standard tasks (ST). Table 1 shows the ST administered and its correspondent SG.

Table 1. Standard tasks, serious games administered, outcome measures, and cognitive functions assessed

ST	SG	Outcome measures	Cognitive functions assessed
Dot probe task	AT1	Latency times Correct Answers	Attention Inhibition control
	AT2	Latency times Correct Answers	Attention Inhibition control
Go/nogo task	AT3	Latency times Correct Answers	Attention Inhibition control
Stroop test	AT4	Latency times Correct Answers	Attention Inhibition control
Trail making task	CF1	Total times Latency times Correct Answers	Attention Cognitive flexibility
Wisconsin card sorting test	CF2	Latency time Correct answers Perseverative responses	Cognitive flexibility
	CF3	Latency time Correct answers Perseverative responses	Cognitive flexibility
Tower of London	PL1	Total score Initial time Execution time Total time	Planning

2.3.1   Standard Tasks

- Dot probe task [34]
  A neutral version of the arrangement published by Miller and Fillmore [34] was administered. During the task, a black cross appeared in the middle of the screen,

followed by a couple of neutral pictures that were presented together, 3 cm apart. We selected these neutral pictures (20 in total) from the International Affective Picture System (IAPS) [35]. After the images disappear, an "X" emerged on one side of the screen. Participants were instructed to press the "E" key on the keyboard if the target appeared on the left, and the "I" key if the target appeared on the right.

- Go/Nogo Task [36]
  A white rectangle emerged in the middle of the screen. This rectangle could be vertical or horizontal disposed (cue). After the rectangle appeared, it became into blue or green (target). Participants should press the spacebar when the rectangle became into green (go) and they didn't have to press any key if the rectangle became into blue (nogo).
- Stroop Test [37]
  A colored word appeared in the middle of the screen. Participants were asked to indicate the color of the word, between four options, ignoring its meaning.
- Trail making task [36]
  This exercise was divided in two parts. In the first one (A), 25 numbers were randomly distributed along the screen; participants were asked to connect them consecutively (1-2-3, … 25), as quickly as they could and using the mouse. In the second part of the task (B), participants should match numbers and letters alternatively, and in consecutive order (1-a-2-b, … 13).
- Wisconsin Card Sorting Task [38]
  Participants were shown four card piles, with its first card faced up. Each one of these cards had different characteristics: number of elements (one, two, three or four), color (red, yellow, blue or green) and shape (cross, triangle, circle or star). One of these features was the criterion by which a new card should be matched with one of the four piles. Participants should put each new card on the related pile, and the system gave feedback about the correct and wrong answers. The classification criterion changed along the task, in such a way that the participants should deduce the correct criterion in each trial based on the system feedback.
- Tower of London [39]
  Participants were shown a structure made by three sticks of different length connected with base and three colored balls (red, green and blue). Three balls filled in the longer stick, two balls filled in the medium one and only one ball filled in the smaller stick. A combination of balls distributed along the sticks appeared, and participants had to reproduce it using the minimum number of moves that they could.

2.3.2 Serious Games

The narrative SG has been settled in a spaceship and the aim of the game player was to discover a new "earth". The eight games have been created and developed based on the EFs constructs and contextualized in the storytelling:

- AT1: "The takeoff: you are the pilot and you have to take off the spaceship. To take off you should follow the earth planet images that appear in front of you";

- AT3: "Aliens attack: in the space that are a lot of elements and in this moment your spaceship is attacked by aliens and you have to avoid and kill the aliens";
- AT4: "The oxygen valve has broken! You have to repair it but the valve is closed in a strongbox. The strongbox has a code that you have to unlock";
- CF1: "Water and Food: the water and food supply is almost all gone. To obtain water you have to pump up the level and for food you have to cultivate";
- CF2: "The orchard is empty" You have to grow up new plants. You have 4 kinds of plants based on fruit types, number of branches, number of fruits, and color fuits, and you have to decide in which group of plants you joint the new plant";
- CF3: "Without fuel: your fuel supply is finished. To obtain fuel you have to activate the turbine. For activating you have to combine different elements two by two";
- PL1: "Lock up: you are lock up in a room and you have to use and combine different objects that you find in the room to open the door";
- AT2: "Resources: you have achieved the new planet and you have to manage the resources. To manage the resources you should select the correct elements that you need to live".

We developed each task to measure a specific executive function: four of the SGs were designed to measure attention (AT1, AT2, AT3 and AT4), three of them were aimed to assess cognitive flexibility (CF1, CF2 and CF3) and one of the SGs was thought to evaluate planning abilities (PL1). All these tasks started with a brief contextualization, to create a situational context in which the games will fit in.

2.4 Data Analysis

The analyses were performed using SPSS version 22.0 (Statistical Package for the Social Sciences for Windows, Chicago, IL) for PC. After verifying the assumption of normality applying Kolmogorov Smirnov, individual differences between groups were obtained. We calculated the individual differences between groups per age, gender and level of use of technologies using t-test, and we applied ANOVA test for analyzing differences among groups of participants per education.

3 Results

Table 2 shows the descriptive data of participants:

Table 2. Demographic data of participants (n = 268)

Demographic data of participants	Mean (SD) [Range]
Age	39.19 (8.65) [25–55]
Age (18–40/41–64)	147/121
Gender (M/F)	133/135
Education (1 = High School/2 = University/3 = Post-graduate)	107/110/51
Use of technologies level (H/L)	127/141

3.1 Individual Differences Per Gender

Regarding the relation between ST tasks and SG-related, we found significant differences between genders in Stroop Test and the associated SG-AT4. In the Stroop-related SG, males registered shorter reaction times, while females showed higher percentages of correct answers. Furthermore, as concerns the exclusive narrative SG the results showed several significant differences. In the SG-PL1, females expend higher execution time than males while males obtained higher total score. Females registered also higher total time in SG-CF1 (A) (Fig. 1).

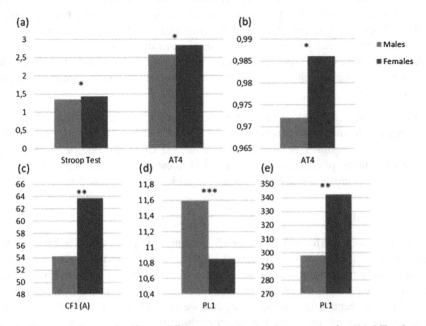

Fig. 1. T-test results on significant differences between groups per gender. (a) LT = Latency time, (b) CA = Correct answers, (c) TT = Total time, (d) TS = Total score, (e) ET = Execution time, (f) PR = Perseverative Responses. *p < .05, **p < .01, ***p < .001

3.2 Individual Differences Per Age

Figure 2 shows the significant differences found among groups per age, ST and SG-related. More in detail, we found analogous significant differences in age between the whole ST tasks and the related SGs: younger participants (18–40) registered lower reaction times and execution times than older subjects (41–64), and higher percentage of correct answers and total score both in the ST tasks and in the SG-related.

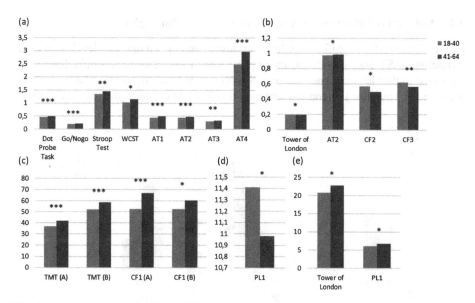

Fig. 2. T-test results on significant differences between groups per age. (a) LT = Latency time, (b) CA = Correct answers, (c) TT = Total time, (d) TS = Total score, (e) ET = Execution time, (f) PR = Perseverative Responses. *p < .05, **p < .01, ***p < .001

3.3 Individual Differences Per Education

Figure 3 shows the significant differences found among groups per education, ST and SG-related. The university studies group obtained higher total score and correct answers than high school studies group both in the WCST ST task and the SG-related, as well as in the Tower of London.

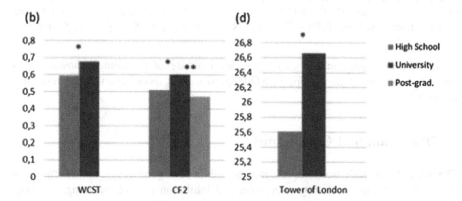

Fig. 3. ANOVA results of significant differences between groups per education. (a) LT = Latency time, (b) CA = Correct answers, (c) TT = Total time, (d) TS = Total score, (e) ET = Execution time, (f) PR = Perseverative Responses. *p < .05, **p < .01, ***p < .001

3.4   Individual Differences Per Level of Use of Technologies

Figure 4 shows the significant differences found among groups per level of use of technologies, ST and SG related. Participants with a low level of use of technologies registered higher latency times between Stroop test and the attentional SGs, as well as between the Tower of London test and the related SG as concerns the execution times.

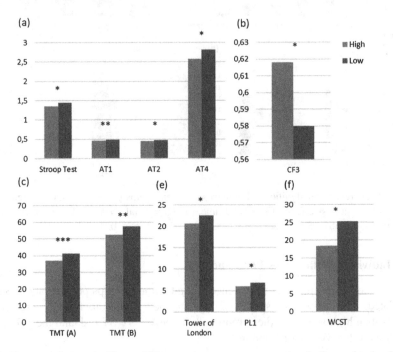

Fig. 4. T-test results on significant differences between groups per level of use of technologies. (a) LT = Latency time, (b) CA = Correct answers, (c) TT = Total time, (d) TS = Total score, (e) ET = Execution time, (f) PR = Perseverative Responses. *p < .05, **p < .01, ***p < .001

Furthermore, participants with a low level of use of technology showed lower percentage of correct answers in the SG-CF3, as well as more perseverative responses in WCST.

4   Discussion and Conclusions

The main of this study was to investigate the influence of gender, age, and education on three EFs' domains, including attentional and inhibition control, planning, and cognitive flexibility comparing traditional and standardized EFs' measures with a narrative SG.

The results on gender revealed differences on latency times of attentional (but not in inhibition control) ST and the SG between men and women, showing shorter reaction times in men. Conversely, women have showed higher latency time and better performance than men. Regarding the exclusive narrative SG, we found on cognitive flexibility higher total time in women than men, as well in planning time, and men showed a better performance than women. These results reflect the complexity in better definition the role of gender in EFs activities, showing consistency with the ambiguity of previous studies [22–24].

Regarding age, our results are consistent with the scientific literature, showing that younger participants registered lower reaction times and execution times than older and higher performance between the whole ST tasks and the related SGs [11–13]. Even results on education reflected coherence with previous works, showing that individuals with higher education performed better than individuals with lower education in ST and the narrative SG [14–18]. More in detail, the main finding about education refers to higher-order EFs performance, as cognitive flexibility and planning abilities, resulting on better performance in participants with higher educational levels. Finally, the level of use of technologies influenced the performance and our findings showed that people with a low level of technologies' use registered higher performance time both the ST and the SG-related. As well, our results showed that lower correct answers and more preservative responses are two possible effects that seem depend on the level of technologies' use, mainly in higher-order EFs.

In conclusion, our study presented two relevant main findings: firstly, we found similar significant differences in gender, age, and education between ST tasks and the related SG, and, secondly, the only narrative SG has been able to detect more significant differences as compared to the ST, especially in higher-order EFs. As a result, if traditionally neuropsychological tests scores are adjusted based on age and education, the new technological approaches, including more ecological measures for the assessment of EFs, should take into consideration also the level of use of technologies as individual variable.

Although, the present study presents some limitations and further studies, including clinical populations, will be need for enhancing the sensitivity, reliability, and validity in using technological approaches for more ecological neuropsychological tests.

Funding. This work was supported by the Spanish Ministry of Economy, Industry and Competitiveness funded project "Advanced Therapeutically Tools for Mental Health" (DPI2016-77396-R).

References

1. Stuss, D.T., Alexander, M.P.: Executive functions and the frontal lobes: a conceptual view. Psychol. Res. **63**(3–4), 289–298 (2000)
2. Diamond, A.: Executive functions. Ann. Rev. Psychol. **64**, 135–168 (2013)
3. Chan, R.C., Shum, D., Toulopoulou, T., Chen, E.Y.: Assessment of executive functions: review of instruments and identification of critical issues. Arch. Clin. Neuropsychol. **23**(2), 201–216 (2008)
4. Lezak, M.D.: The problem of assessing executive functions. Int. J. Psychol. **17**(1–4), 281–297 (1982)

5. Lezak, M.D., Howieson, D.B., Loring, D.W., Fischer, J.S.: Neuropsychological Assessment. Oxford University Press, Oxford (2004)
6. Anderson, P.: Assessment and development of executive function (EF) during childhood. Child Neuropsychol. **8**(2), 71–82 (2002)
7. Jurado, M.B., Rosselli, M.: The elusive nature of executive functions: a review of our current understanding. Neuropsychol. Rev. **17**(3), 213–233 (2007)
8. Gladsjo, J.A., Schuman, C.C., Evans, J.D., Peavy, G.M., Miller, S.W., Heaton, R.K.: Norms for letter and category fluency: demographic corrections for age, education, and ethnicity. Assessment **6**(2), 147–178 (1999)
9. Stricks, L., Pittman, J., Jacobs, D.M., Sano, M., Stern, Y.: Normative data for a brief neuropsychological battery administered to English-and Spanish-speaking community-dwelling elders. J. Int. Neuropsychol. Soc. **4**(4), 311–318 (1998)
10. Beeri, M.S., et al.: Age, gender, and education norms on the CERAD neuropsychological battery in the oldest old. Neurology **67**(6), 1006–1010 (2006)
11. Birch, S.A., Bloom, P.: Understanding children's and adults' limitations in mental state reasoning. Trends Cogn. Sci. **8**(6), 255–260 (2004)
12. De Luca, C.R., et al.: Normative data from the CANTAB. I: development of executive function over the lifespan. J. Clin. Exp. Neuropsychol. **25**(2), 242–254 (2003)
13. Craik, F.I., Salthouse, T.A.: The Handbook of Aging and Cognition. Psychology Press, London (2011)
14. Ostrosky-Solis, F., Ardila, A., Rosselli, M., Lopez-Arango, G., Uriel-Mendoza, V.: Neuropsychological test performance in illiterate subjects. Arch. Clin. Neuropsychol. **13**, 645–660 (1998)
15. Ardila, A., Bertolucci, P.H., Braga, L.W., et al.: Illiteracy: the neuropsychology of cognition without reading. Arch. Clin. Neuropsychol. **25**, 689–712 (2010)
16. Das, S.K., Banerjee, T.K., Mukherjee, C.S., et al.: An urban community-based study of cognitive function among non-demented elderly population in India. Neurol. Asia **11**, 37–48 (2006)
17. Mathuranath, P.S., Cherian, J.P., Mathew, R., George, A., Alexander, A., Sarma, S.P.: Mini mental state examination and the Addenbrooke's cognitive examination: effect of education and norms for a multicultural population. Neurol. India **55**, 106–110 (2007)
18. Liu, K.P., Kuo, M.C., Tang, K.C., et al.: Effects of age, education and gender in the Consortium to Establish a Registry for the Alzheimer's Disease (CERAD)-Neuropsychological assessment battery for Cantonese-speaking Chinese elders. Int. Psychogeriatr. **23**(10), 1575–1581 (2011)
19. Van Hooren, S.A.H., Valentijn, A.M., Bosma, H., Ponds, R.W.H.M., Van Boxtel, M.P.J., Jolles, J.: Cognitive functioning in healthy older adults aged 64–81: a cohort study into the effects of age, sex, and education. Aging Neuropsychol. Cogn. **14**(1), 40–54 (2007)
20. Messinis, L., Tsakona, I., Malefaki, S., Papathanasopoulos, P.: Normative data and discriminant validity of Rey's verbal learning test for the Greek adult population. Arch. Clin. Neuropsychol. **22**(6), 739–752 (2007)
21. Proust-Lima, C., Amieva, H., Letenneur, L., Orgogozo, J.M., Jacqmin-Gadda, H., Dartigues, J.F.: Gender and education impact on brain aging: a general cognitive factor approach. Psychol. Aging **23**(3), 608 (2008)
22. Unger, R.K.: Toward a redefinition of sex and gender. Am. Psycholog. **34**(11), 1085 (1979)
23. Zarghi, A., Zarindast, M.R.: Demographic variables and selective, sustained attention and planning through cognitive tasks among healthy adults. Basic Clin. Neurosci. **2**(3), 58–67 (2011)

24. Bagherpoor, L.S.K., Akbar, A.: The influence of educational type (virtual and non-virtual) and gender on the executive functions (mental flexibility and selective attention) of students. Bull. Environ. Pharmacol. Life Sci. **2014**(3), 360–367 (2014)

25. Chaytor, N., Schmitter-Edgecombe, M., Burr, R.: Improving the ecological validity of executive functioning assessment. Arch. Clin. Neuropsychol. **21**(3), 217–227 (2006)

26. Spooner, D.M., Pachana, N.A.: Ecological validity in neuropsychological assessment: a case for greater consideration in research with neurologically intact populations. Arch. Clin. Neuropsychol. **21**(4), 327–337 (2006)

27. Burgess, P.W., Alderman, N., Volle, E., Benoit, R.G., Gilbert, S.J.: Mesulam's frontal lobe mystery re-examined. Restor. Neurol. Neurosci. **27**(5), 493–506 (2009)

28. Chevignard, M., et al.: An ecological approach to planning dysfunction: script execution. Cortex **36**(5), 649–669 (2000)

29. Barker, L.A., Andrade, J., Romanowski, C.A.J.: Impaired implicit cognition with intact executive function after extensive bilateral prefrontal pathology: a case study. Neurocase **10** (3), 233–248 (2004)

30. Manchester, D., Priestley, N., Jackson, H.: The assessment of executive functions: coming out of the office. Brain Inj. **18**(11), 1067–1081 (2004)

31. Fleming, T.M., et al.: Serious games and gamification for mental health: current status and promising directions. Front. Psychiatry **7**, 215 (2017)

32. Andrade, L.H., et al.: Barriers to mental health treatment: results from the WHO World Mental Health surveys. Psychol. Med. **44**(6), 1303–1317 (2014)

33. Fleming, T.M., et al.: Serious games for the treatment or prevention of depression: a systematic review (2014)

34. Miller, M.A., Fillmore, M.T.: The effect of word complexity on attentional bias towards alcohol-related words in adult drinkers. Addiction **105**, 883–890 (2010)

35. Lang, P.J., Bradley, M.M., Cuthbert, B.N.: International affective picture system (IAPS): affective ratings of pictures and instruction manual. Technical report A-8. University of Florida, Gainesville (2008)

36. Fillmore, M.T., Rush, C.R., Hays, L.: Acute effects of cocaine in two models of inhibitory control: implications of non-linear dose effects. Addiction **101**(132), 3–1332 (2006)

37. Stroop, J.R.: Studies of interference in serial verbal reactions. J. Exp. Psychol. **18**, 643–662 (1935)

38. Grant, D.A., Berg, E.: A behavioral analysis of degree of reinforcement and ease of shifting to new responses in a Weigl-type card-sorting problem. J. Exp. Psychol. **38**(4), 404 (1948)

39. Culberston, W.C., Zillmer, E.A.: Tower of London-Drexel (TOLDX). Examiners's Manual. Research Version. Multi-Health Systems Inc., Toronto (1999)

Does Motivation Enhance Knowledge Acquisition in Digital Game-Based and Multimedia Learning? A Review of Studies from One Lab

Cyril Brom[1]([⊠]), Filip Děchtěrenko[2], Vít Šisler[1,3], Zdeněk Hlávka[1], and Jiří Lukavský[2]

[1] Faculty of Mathematics and Physics, Charles University,
Ke Karlovu 3, Prague, Czech Republic
brom@ksvi.mff.cuni.cz
[2] Institute of Psychology, Czech Academy of Sciences,
Hybernská 8, 110 00 Prague, Czech Republic
[3] Faculty of Arts, Charles University, Nám. Jana Palacha 2,
Prague, Czech Republic

Abstract. In the contexts of digital game-based and multimedia learning, little is known about the strengths of associations between positive affective-motivational factors elicited during a study session and the quality of knowledge acquisition. Here, we take a step forward in filling this gap by re-analyzing our 11 experiments carried out between 2009–2017, featuring digital games, a simulation, animations, or a computerized presentation (total $N = 1{,}288$; primarily Czech and Slovak high school and university learners). The correlational meta-analysis showed that the overall relationship between positive affective-motivational variables and learning outcomes was significant, but relatively weak. The weaker relationship was found for enjoyment and generalized positive affect compared to flow. The finding corroborates the idea that affective-motivational states may be differentially related to learning outcomes. Future research should investigate why some affective-motivational states seem to play relatively limited roles in learning from multimedia instructional materials.

Keywords: Digital game-based learning · Multimedia learning
Motivation · Flow · Learning outcomes

1 Introduction

Digital game-based learning (DGBL) refers to learning partly or fully through computerized games. DGBL can be viewed as a subfield of multimedia learning, which is learning from materials combining words and pictures [25]. Digitalized multimedia learning materials are, for example, animations or computerized slides.

Recent major meta-analyses of studies comparing the effectiveness of the DGBL approach to "traditional" educational approaches demonstrated a small superiority of games [e.g., 12, 40]. In theory, the reasons for the games' superiority are numerous,

© Springer Nature Switzerland AG 2018
S. Göbel et al. (Eds.): JCSG 2018, LNCS 11243, pp. 120–132, 2018.
https://doi.org/10.1007/978-3-030-02762-9_13

[e.g., 2, 15, 29, 34; see also 25, pp. 13–15]. In practice, they are generally unknown. This superiority can in fact be only seeming; it could have arisen because of a methodological artifact. For instance, both meta-analyses showed that the positive effects of games tend to attenuate in studies with random assignment. Elevated positive affective-motivational states of learners (motivational states throughout for brevity) are also one possible reason for the games' alleged superiority. However, despite the hype about DGBL motivational benefits, the meta-analyses made it clear that only a fraction of the DGBL studies measured both motivational and learning outcome variables (see below for examples). Narrative DGBL reviews [e.g., 11, 22] also did not provide information on the strength of the relationship between learning outcomes and motivational variables. Still very little is known about this issue.

In the general multimedia learning field, motivational factors have only recently started to be studied [e.g., 18, 24, 37], and incorporated into multimedia learning theories [e.g., 27]. Syntheses of literature point to the fact that augmenting learning materials by using appealing bits of extraneous information, which elicit interest but are not needed for comprehending the key learning message (i.e., seductive or extraneous details), generally hampers learning [26, Chap. 4; 30]. Beyond that, little is known about the motivational–learning relationship in the context of learning from computerized multimedia (similar to the DGBL field).

From a methodological perspective, in comparative studies, the correlations between learning outcome variables and motivational variables depend on two things: on the experimental manipulation (which may have effects both on cognitive and motivational domains) and on underlying motivational–learning associations (which are detectable also in a correlational study). Information is insufficient about the possible strengths of either of those two influences.

From the perspective of educational psychology, this situation is not surprising. First, the key variables of interest are the learning outcomes (rather than motivational self-reports), because they are objective. Motivational variables are thus not always measured. Second, concerning comparative studies, it is now generally accepted that DGBL approaches (and additions of interesting embellishments to multimedia learning materials in general) can influence learning processes in two opposing ways, [e.g., 1, 10, 37]. They can enhance learning through positively activating and energizing learners: learners will invest more into learning. This idea is framed, for example, by the cognitive-affective theory of learning by media [27]. However, these approaches can also hamper learning by distracting attention away from learning (i.e., via the seductive details embellishing the instructional message, which, in the case of DGBL, is often the game's entertainment feature). This idea is outlined, for instance, in the cognitive load theory [36]. Depending on how well the game/multimedia is designed and how well the learning and playing/interesting parts are integrated, the positives may (but also may not) outweigh the negatives.

Third, the level of distraction may play a moderating role (on motivational–learning link) also in single-group correlational studies, provided learners can relatively easily ignore the supposedly interesting part of the learning material. Consider a learning game, for example. When the gaming part is not well integrated with the learning part, the learners motivated by the gameplay will end up playing rather than learning. Whereas, the less motivated learners may ignore the gaming part and just learn (because they were told to do so), eventually outperforming the game-motivated learners in terms of learning outcomes.

Motivational–learning correlations can thus be confounded by different levels of distraction caused by different intervention designs. As a result, null-to-negative [e.g., 14, 21, see also 1], null [e.g., 38], null-to-positive [e.g., 16, 18], as well as positive [e.g., 32, see also 13, 17] associations have been reported in DGBL and multimedia learning literature.

In this paper, we re-analyze our 11 multimedia learning experiments dating from 2009–2017. The participants were primarily Czech and Slovak high school and university learners (total $N = 1288$). We focused on correlational outcomes in order to obtain information about the nature of motivational–learning association in the context of learning through digital games and related multimedia. These studies in particular used digital learning games ($n = 689$), complex interactive simulations ($n = 140$), brief animations ($n = 278$), and computerized slides ($n = 181$) as treatments. Despite the fact that all our studies were comparative, we focused primarily on the underlying motivational–learning associations rather than the effects of experimental manipulations. This is because the majority of our studies yielded null results (i.e., with two exceptions, there were no robust effects of experimental manipulations). The interventions were reasonably optimized by so-called multimedia learning principles [26] and, in the case of games, we paid special attention not to separate the gaming and learning parts. The studies were conducted by the same lab using the same/similar research methods. Therefore, at least a certain level of consistency across studies with respect to possible cognitive distraction (and methodological artifacts) can be guaranteed, and the general correlational trend can indicate how motivational variables are related to learning outcomes in DGBL-like contexts.

2   Method

2.1   Study Characteristics, Participants

The studies (Table 1) used experimental design with two or three groups. They either compared a DGBL approach to a different type of learning on the same topic (i.e., so-called media comparison studies [25]) or they compared interventions that differed in a single feature or a few features (i.e., so-called value-added studies [25]). Participants were typically above-average, high school or college learners from the capital city of the Czech Republic (see Table 1 for mean age).

2.2   Interventions

The interventions ranged from using static computerized slides to a complex digital learning game (see Table 1).

In a set of three value-added studies [3, 4, 9], we compared different versions of a 2-h interactive simulation on the topic of beer brewing (Fig. 1). Participants studied how to brew beer using on-screen instructions, practiced key steps in the simulation, and eventually brewed beer in the simulation. We researched the added value of

Table 1. Pearson's correlations between motivational and learning outcome variables.

Experiment/intervention	Type, manipulation	N[a]	No. of groups	Mean Age (SD)	Enjoyment Immediate Reten. | Trans.	Enjoyment Delayed Reten. | Trans.	Generalized positive affect Immediate Reten. | Trans.	Generalized positive affect Delayed Reten. | Trans.	Flow Immediate Reten. | Trans.	Flow Delayed Reten. | Trans.
Simulation – beer brewing [3]	Value-added, pers. principle	75 (70)	2	22.1 (2.3)[b]	.45***|.37***	.40***|.22†	.27*|.33**	.32*|.15	.41**|.45***	.40***|.37***
Simulation – beer brewing [9]	Value-added, gamification	98 (97)	3	23.1 (2.53)	.10|.13	.11|.05	.23*|.18†	.25*|.18†	.31**|.27**	.40***|.30**
Simulation – beer brewing [4]	Value-added, motivating topic	65 (64)	2	23.6 (3.75)	-.09|-.06	-.00|-.04	-.06|.01	.05|.05	.31*|.33**	.31*|.30*
Animations[c] **[6]**	Value-added, pers. principle									
- **Lightning** (college)		57	2	22.2 (2.7)	.03|-.20	-	-	-	-	-
- **Lightning** (high school)		73	2	17.3 (0.7)	.19|.12	-	-	-	-	-
- **Wastewater** (college)		74	2	22.1 (2.5)	.16|.08	-	-.14|.04	-	.25*|.36*	.23*
- **Wastewater** (high school)		74	2	17.1 (0.9)	.14|.11	-	.05|.18	-	.06|.27*	.25*
Game – Europe [10][d]	Media comp., DGBL	325 (287)	3	16.8 (2.1)	.16**	.30***	.26***	.42***	.21***	.30***
- subgr.: digital game		n = 103 (93)	subgroup	-	.01	.18	.04	.37**	.12	.30**
- subgr.: non-digital game		n = 96 (84)	subgroup	-	.13	.43***	.32**	.48**	.13	.23*
- subgr.: discussion		n = 126 (110)	subgroup	-	.18†	.21*	.30**	.32**	.26**	.25*
Game – Animal Training [8]	Media comp., DGBL	100 (100)	2	16.0 (0.9)	.24*,.05[e]	.18†,.12[e]			.28*|.32**	.29*|.29*
Game – Animal Training, Genetics [7]	Media comp., DGBL	166 (166)	2	16.8 (0.6)						
- Animal Training		n = 93 (93)	2	-	.08|.06	.14|.13	-	-	-	-
- Genetics		n = 73 (73)	2	-	.28*|.03	.23†|.13	-	-	-	-
Slides – Influenza [35]	Value-added, anthropom.	181 (167)	5 (partial 2 x 3)	22.2 (3.4)	.17|.13	.07|.04	.05|.09	.09|.06	.28*|.32**	.29*|.29*
Summary Correlation, 95% CI					.134*** [.074, .194]	.160*** [.072, .246]	.141** [.040, .239]	.213** [.042, .372]	.269*** [.206, .329]	.314*** [.244, .381]
Q					12.72	12.33†	12.29†	18.44***	5.09	0.79
I^2, τ^2					13.5%, .0016	43.2%, .0069	51.2%, .0092	78.3%, .0298	0.0%, 0	0.0%, 0

Notes: †$p < .10$ *$p < .05$ **$p < .01$ ***$p < .001$ (not corrected for multiple comparisons). [a]Number of participants attending the delayed testing session shown in brackets. [b]Also, one 40-year-old outlier (not counted in the average) was included. [c]No delayed testing session. [d]The *Europe 2045* experiment did not distinguish between retention and transfer tests but between four different types of tests. Here, correlations with the overall score are presented. [e]Spearman correlation coefficients. The animal training experiment featured two types of test questions: a) on general animal training knowledge, b) on positive reinforcement knowledge, practiced in the game; the correlations are given in this order. Both types were a mixture of retention and transfer test questions. [f]Whole-sample correlations are summarized using the DerSimonian–Laird (DSL) random-effect meta-analytical approach; 95% confidence intervals in square brackets.

instructional texts in a conversational rather than a formal style (i.e., the so-called personalization principle: [26, Chap. 12]), the effects of an intrinsically motivating topic, and the added value of several gamification elements (e.g., points).

In another study [6], which consisted of four different experiments, we once again studied the personalization principle. We used about 7-min-long, self-paced animations. In two experiments, one with high school and the other with university students, participants studied how lightning forms. In the remaining two experiments, they studied how a biological wastewater treatment plant functions.

In a set of three media comparison studies [7, 8, 10], we compared a DGBL approach to a non-game instructional method, keeping the content and the length of exposure the same. In one case, we used the *Europe 2045* computer game (Fig. 1). This is a complex, team role-playing game on the topic of European Union policies. The non-game control condition was organized around discussions that replicated in-game discussions but removed all game mechanics. In the second case, we used a 20-min simulation mini-game on how to train animals (Fig. 1). After an expository lecture on the animal training topic, participants either played the game or received a complementary lecture with videos on animal training. In the final study, after an expository lecture, students either played a mini-game individually at computers, or the teacher played it, while showing it to the whole class on a projector and prompting students on how to proceed with the game. One half of learners were exposed to the animal training mini-game, and the other half to a 20-min simulation mini-game on Mendelian genetics [28].

In the final study [35], we used 10-minute-long, self-paced instructional slides as a treatment. We researched the added value of augmenting schematic graphics by adding black-and-white or colorful anthropomorphic faces to non-human elements. This type of instructional redesign is called emotional design [37].

2.3 Variables

Learning Outcomes. Our studies generally tested mental model acquisition. In the multimedia learning field (including DGBL), quality of acquired mental models is typically measured by so-called retention and transfer knowledge tests [26]. **Retention** tests assess "superficial" learning; i.e., whether the learner was able to memorize the material without necessarily understanding the core process/model in question (e.g., "Based on the animation you just saw, describe in detail how biological wastewater treatment works."). **Transfer** tests assess "deep" learning; i.e., if learners truly understand the point and are thus able to "transfer" and use what they learnt into new contexts (e.g., "What would happen if a fungus first appeared in the wastewater treatment plant and then bacteria? Write down all consequences that come to mind based on the animation you saw today."). We typically measured learning outcomes immediately after the treatment and three or four weeks later (i.e., delayed tests).

Motivational Variables. There are indications that different positive motivational variables are differently related to learning outcomes [4]. Therefore, we report here correlations for individual variables rather than for a synthetic, composite variable:

Fig. 1. Screenshots from the beer brewing simulation, animal training game, and Europe 2045.

enjoyment (n = 1,288), flow (n = 892), and generalized positive affect (n = 892). We measured **enjoyment** typically on a 4-, 6- or 8-point Likert scale with 1–3 items (e.g., "I enjoyed today's lesson.", "This activity was appealing for me."). These items correspond to items from intrinsic motivation inventories [e.g., 20]. We did not use the whole inventories for brevity. **Generalized positive affect**, called positive affect here for brevity, was measured by a PANAS (Positive and Negative Affect Schedule [39]). Participants had to rate their current feelings on a 5-point Likert scale. The list of feelings included 10 positive feelings (e.g., interested, excited, strong) and 10 negative feelings (e.g., distressed, upset, scared – these are not analyzed here). **Flow** was measured using ten, 7-point Likert items from the Flow Short Scale [31] (e.g., "I feel just the right amount of a challenge.", "My thoughts run freely and smoothly.", "I don't notice time passing."). Internal consistencies were generally good for all variables (Cronbach α generally > .8).

2.4 Procedures

Two studies [7, 8] took place in school settings. The rest was organized in a lab setting. In general, the studies followed the following procedure. After the introduction and filling in prior questionnaires, participants were randomly assigned to one of the conditions. Thereafter, they completed the intervention. In three cases [3, 4, 9], motivational variables were measured during the treatment and after it. The values were then averaged. In other cases, the variables were measured only once; typically, right after the treatment ended. Afterwards, participants filled in retention and transfer tests. With one exception [6], they attended a delayed testing session three/four weeks later and completed the tests once again. They were not informed in advance that the purpose of the delayed session was to assess their knowledge. Many of them probably guessed the purpose of the session; however, the majority of them reported back they did not study for the tests beforehand, even though they had a hunch they would be tested. Data collection was anonymized. The test performance had no consequences for students (e.g., did not impact their grades).

2.5 Data Treatment

Correlations between motivational variables and learning outcome variables are reported across the whole sample for each study, because subgroups are generally small ($\sim$30 per cell). Whole-sample correlations reflect both general motivational–learning associations and the effects of experimental interventions. However, only two studies [4, 10] found robust between-group differences: both in motivational and learning outcome variables. Special attention will be paid to these two studies. For one of them [10], the sample is actually so large (around 100 per cell) that correlations within subgroups can be considered for meaningful contrasting of whole-sample correlations to subgroup correlations. Other studies generally reported null results as concerns motivational variables as well as for learning outcomes (only 4 out of a total 52 between-group comparisons were significant at $p < .05$ level).

We summarized the correlation results across reported studies using the DerSimonian-Laird (DSL) random-effect meta-analytical approach. We used a *metacor* [23] and *meta* [33] packages for calculations. Because not all studies used strict retention and transfer tests (see Table 1), but all used immediate knowledge assessments and all but one used delayed knowledge assessments, we decided to obtain one correlation value per (1) each motivational variable and immediate learning outcome variable, and (2) each motivational variable and delayed learning outcome variable. Therefore, in studies featuring separate retention and transfer correlations, we transformed the values in Fisher's z scale and we used their average (i.e., one average for immediate and another for delayed knowledge assessments). In addition to individual correlations, we report summary correlations, their 95% confidence intervals, corresponding p values, and dispersion measures (Q, I^2, τ^2).

3   Results

All correlations are reported in Table 1. As is apparent, there is a general trend for weaker and less stable associations (with learning outcomes) for enjoyment and positive affect compared to flow. At the whole sample level, correlations range from $-.20$ to $.45$ (median = $.13$) for enjoyment, from $-.14$ to $.48$ (median = $.165$) for positive affect, and from $.06$ to $.45$ (median = $.30$) for flow. This pattern does not change when correlations with immediate learning outcomes and delayed learning outcomes are considered separately, nor when the whole-sample correlations are summarized using the meta-analytic approach (see Fig. 2 and the last rows of Table 1). Even the weaker associations concerning enjoyment and positive affect are significant though (see Table 1). In correlations between positive affect and delayed learning outcomes we saw an evidence for substantial variability – it is likely the true effect sizes differ across the included studies.

Do these correlations reflect the effects of experimental manipulations or general motivational–learning associations? First, as already said, with the exception of two studies [4, 10], no robust between-group differences with respect to experimental comparisons emerged (i.e., generally, the studies reported null results; see Sect. 2.5). Second, when correlations at the subgroup level of the *Europe 2045* study [10] (Table 1) are contrasted to whole-sample correlations, the general pattern of results

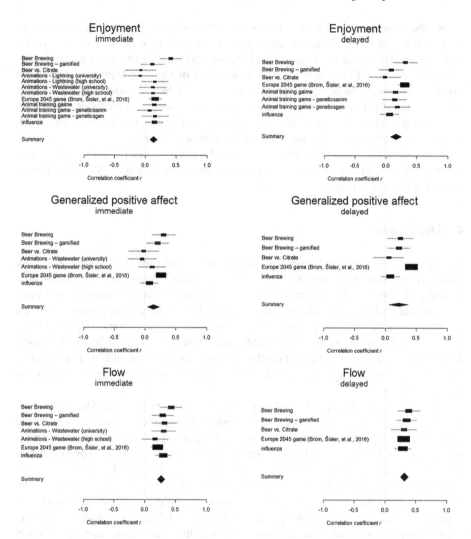

Fig. 2. Correlations and summary effects between learning outcomes and motivation variables.

remains the same; although that particular study was the only one in which flow correlations were weaker than positive affect correlations.[1] Thus, the strength of the underlying motivational–learning associations (i.e., without the effects of experimental manipulations) is indeed within the range reported in the last column of Table 1.

---

[1] Although confidence intervals for correlations are quite large for sample sizes of around 30 participants, we point out that for the study [4] ($n = 35 + 30$), the subgroup-level correlations also show this pattern: roughly medium positive correlations for flow and zero/small negative correlations for enjoyment and positive affect.

At the same time, in the two studies that reported between-group differences, we showed that experimental manipulations (i.e., a low vs. a high intrinsically motivating topic: [4]; a discussion vs. a game: [10]) influenced both motivational variables and learning outcomes. Flow partly mediated the effect of topic on learning outcomes in [4]. Positive affect, but not flow, partly mediated the effect of game play on learning outcomes in [10]. In neither case was enjoyment confirmed as a mediator. Therefore, there is also some evidence that motivational states can be experimentally elevated and, at the same time, they can be associated with enhanced learning.

It is also worth noting that one of the beer brewing studies [3] is the only one in which enjoyment correlations were consistently moderate to strong. We will return to this point in the discussion.

4 Discussion

This review has found that, in eleven experiments conducted by the same lab, with relatively homogeneous samples and with treatments "optimized" by multimedia learning principles, whole-sample associations between learning outcomes and three motivational variables (enjoyment, positive affect, flow) tended to be positive. Average correlations, across all experiments, were all positive and significant. Enjoyment and positive affect correlations were less stable and weaker compared to flow correlations. This pattern of results corroborates results from our study [4] that indicated directly that flow may be more strongly associated with learning outcomes compared to enjoyment and positive affect.

On the theoretical level, the following point is worth mentioning. Questions from the flow questionnaire are most closely linked (compared to positive affect and enjoyment questions) to focused attention on the learning content and increased cognitive activation, which have been posited to be the key causes of improved learning [e.g., 27]. Learners who are focused on learning (as indexed by flow) may still experience neutral rather than positive feelings (as indexed by enjoyment and positive affect). On the other hand, learners having positive feelings may not necessarily be cognitively focused on learning; especially in DGBL-like contexts, wherein enjoyment/positive affect may originate from playing rather than learning. In other words, flow-based questionnaires may better capture slight changes in cognitive activation and attention processes (which are very difficult to measure directly but are essential for successful learning).

We wish to emphasize that this pattern of results is provisional. Despite the fact that the studies were relatively similar, there were some confounding factors. This is an inevitable limitation. For example, in two studies above [3, 10], a learning–enjoyment relationship was still notable. What could be the reason for this? We believe that the culprit is the different (uncontrolled) heterogeneity of participants in terms of developed interest in the instructional domain, i.e., participants' relatively stable predisposition to re-engage with particular types of content [19]. Specifically, we think more heterogeneous samples could have been recruited for these two studies, explaining generally stronger correlations. To corroborate this idea, in one unpublished study ($N = 128$; young adults; learning by means of a *non*-digital game; [5]), we intentionally recruited participants who were diverse in their developed domain interest: the enjoyment–learning outcome correlations were moderate-to-strong $(r = .36 - .43)$, even somewhat stronger than flow $(r = .25 - .35)$ or positive affect correlations $(r = .19 - .35)$. This adds another dimension of complexity to thinking about the relationship between situational motivational factors and quality of knowledge acquisition. When a generally neutral developed domain interest can be expected for a particular sample and a learning situation, the motivational–learning correlations would then be influenced primarily by situational factors. When differing developed domain interests can be expected (e.g., an electromechanical topic), the correlations may also be influenced by this type of (stable) interest. The same can be said with respect to use of media through which the learning message is presented. For instance, computerized slides (i.e., the medium as such) would unlikely trigger hatred or affection in present-day college learners; unlike a new, complex educational game (some may love it, others will hate it).

That said, the methodological implication is that care should be taken when considering what motivational measures are used in future DGBL and multimedia learning studies. Using multiple measures at the same time is advisable, as is controlling for developed domain interest and attitude toward instructional media.

Given the arguments above in this section and in the introduction, can one expect that our results generalize to different contexts (e.g., different labs, different intervention types, different levels of distraction, different age groups, different measures)? This is not guaranteed. Still, it is worth noting that, in this report, flow–learning correlations were in the range previously reported in the context of interest–academic achievement associations [42] and the relation between interest and learning from texts [41]. It can thus be speculated that these correlations reflect general motivation–learning associations rather than something specific to game-based/multimedia learning. Future research should focus more on this issue.

At the same time, we also showed in two studies [4, 10] that motivational states induced by re-design of the intervention can be connected to better learning outcomes. Additional evidence supporting the idea that this is possible exists in DGBL [e.g., 13, 17] and multimedia learning [e.g., 37, 43] contexts. This means that motivational states elevated by specific DGBL/multimedia learning approaches can facilitate learning after all. However, whether they do so depends on the quality of the re-design in question.

Acknowledgement. We thank to numerous collaborators who participated on the studies; most notably, T. Stárková, T. Hannemann, and D. Klement. We also thank Laboratory of Behavioral and Linguistic Studies in Prague, where part of the studies was conducted. Studies were primarily supported by the Czech Science Foundation (GA ČR) (Projects nr. P407/12/P152, 15-14715S). During writing this review, C.B. and V.Š. were supported by the project PRIMUS/HUM/03. V.Š. was further supported by the European Regional Development Fund-Project "Creativity and Adaptability as Conditions of the Success of Europe in an Interrelated World" (No. CZ.02.1.01/0.0/0.0/16_019/0000734) and Charles University Program Progress Q15. F.D. and J.L. were supported by Czech Academy of Sciences (RVO 68081740 and research program Strategy AV21). Z.H. was partially supported by Charles University Program – Progress Q49.

References

1. Adams, D.M., Mayer, R.E., MacNamara, A., Koenig, A., Wainess, R.: Narrative games for learning: testing the discovery and narrative hypotheses. J. Educ. Psychol. **104**, 235–249 (2012)
2. Barab, S., Thomas, M., Dodge, T., Carteaux, R., Tuzun, H.: Making learning fun: quest atlantis, a game without guns. ETRD **53**, 86–107 (2005)
3. Brom, C., Bromová, E., Děchtěrenko, F., Buchtová, M., Pergel, M.: Personalized messages in a brewery educational simulation: is the personalization principle less robust than previously thought? Comput. Educ. **72**, 339–366 (2014)
4. Brom, C., Děchtěrenko, F., Frollová, N., Stárková, T., Bromová, E., D'Mello, S.K.: Enjoyment or involvement? Affective-motivational mediation during learning from a complex computerized simulation. Comput. Educ. **114**, 236–254 (2017)
5. Brom, C., Dobrovolný, V., Děchtěrenko, F., Stárková, T., Bromová, E.: It's Better to Enjoy Learning than Playing: Motivational Effects of an Educational Larp (submitted)
6. Brom, C., Hannemann, T., Stárková, T., Bromová, E., Děchtěrenko, F.: The role of cultural background in the personalization principle: Five experiments with Czech learners. Comput. Educ. **112**, 37–68 (2017)
7. Brom, C., Levčík, D., Buchtová, M., Klement, D.: Playing educational micro-games at high schools: Individually or collectively? Comput. Hum. Behav. **48**, 682–694 (2015)
8. Brom, C., Preuss, M., Klement, D.: Are educational computer micro-games engaging and effective for knowledge acquisition at high-schools? A quasi-experimental study. Comput. Educ. **57**, 1971–1988 (2011)
9. Brom, C., Stárková, T., Bromová, E., Děchtěrenko, F.: Gamifying a Simulation: Null Effects of a Game Goal, Choice, Points and Praise (preprint; psyarxiv.com/uwrjb)
10. Brom, C., Šisler, V., Slussareff, M., Selmbacherová, T., Hlávka, Z.: You like it, you learn it: affectivity and learning in competitive social role play gaming. Int. J. Comput.-Support. Collab. Learn. **11**, 313–348 (2016)
11. Boyle, E.A., Hainey, T., Connolly, T.M., et al.: An update to the systematic literature review of empirical evidence of the impacts and outcomes of computer games and serious games. Comput. Educ. **94**, 178–192 (2016)
12. Clark, D.B., Tanner-Smith, E.E., Killingsworth, S.S.: Digital games, design, and learning a systematic review and meta-analysis. Rev. Educ. Res. **86**, 79–122 (2016)
13. Cordova, D.I., Lepper, M.R.: Intrinsic motivation and the process of learning: beneficial effects of contextualization, personalization, and choice. J. Educ. Psychol. **88**, 715–730 (1996)
14. Echeverría, A., Barrios, E., Nussbaum, M., Améstica, M., Leclerc, S.: The atomic intrinsic integration approach: a structured methodology for the design of games for the conceptual understanding of physics. Comput. Educ. **59**, 806–816 (2012)
15. Gee, J.P.: What Video Games Have to Teach Us About Learning and Literacy. Palgrave/St. Martin's, New York (2003)
16. Giannakos, M.N.: Enjoy and learn with educational games: examining factors affecting learning performance. Comput. Educ. **68**, 429–439 (2013)
17. Habgood, M.J., Ainsworth, S.E.: Motivating children to learn effectively: exploring the value of intrinsic integration in educational games. J. Learn. Sci. **20**, 169–206 (2011)
18. Heidig, S., Müller, J., Reichelt, M.: Emotional design in multimedia learning: differentiation on relevant design features and their effects on emotions and learning. Comput. Hum. Behav. **44**, 81–95 (2015)

19. Hidi, S., Renninger, K.A.: The four-phase model of interest development. Educ. Psychol. **41**, 111–127 (2006)
20. Isen, A.M., Reeve, J.: The influence of positive affect on intrinsic and extrinsic motivation: facilitating enjoyment of play, responsible work behavior, and self-control. Motiv. Emot. **29**, 295–323 (2005)
21. Iten, N., Petko, D.: Learning with serious games: is fun playing the game a predictor of learning success? Br. J. Edu. Technol. **47**, 151–163 (2014)
22. Jabbar, A.I.A., Felicia, P.: Gameplay engagement and learning in game-based learning: a systematic review. Rev. Educ. Res. **85**(4), 740–779 (2015)
23. Laliberté, E.: metacor: Meta-analysis of correlation coefficients. R package version 1.0-2 (2011)
24. Magner, U.I., Schwonke, R., Aleven, V., Popescu, O., Renkl, A.: Triggering situational interest by decorative illustrations both fosters and hinders learning in computer-based learning environments. Learn. Instr. **29**, 141–152 (2014)
25. Mayer, R.E.: Computer Games for Learning: An Evidence-Based Approach. The MIT Press, Cambridge (2014)
26. Mayer, R.E.: Multimedia Learning. Cambridge University Press, Cambridge (2009)
27. Moreno, R.: Instructional technology: promise and pitfalls. In: Technology-Based Education: Bringing Researchers and Practitioners Together, pp. 1–19. Information Age Publishing (2005)
28. Novak, M., Wilensky, U.: NetLogo Bird Breeder model. Center for Connected Learning and Computer-Based Modeling, Northwestern University, Evanston (2007)
29. Prensky, M.: Digital Game-Based Learning. McGraw-Hill, New York (2001)
30. Rey, G.D.: A review of research and a meta-analysis of the seductive detail effect. Educ. Res. Rev. **7**, 216–237 (2012)
31. Rheinberg, F., Vollmeyer, R., Engeser, S.: Die Erfassung des Flow-Erlebens [in German]. In: Steinsmeier-Pelster, J., Rheinberg, F. (eds.) Diagnostik von Motivation und Selbstkonzept, pp. 261–279. Hogrefe (2003)
32. Sabourin, J.L., Lester, J.C.: Affect and engagement in game-based learning environments. IEEE Trans. Affect. Comput. **5**, 45–56 (2014)
33. Schwarzer, G.: meta: an R package for meta-analysis. R News **7**(3), 40–45 (2007)
34. Squire, K.: Replaying history: learning world history through playing civilization III. Ph.D. thesis, Indiana University (2004)
35. Stárková, T., Lukavský, J., Javora, O., Brom, C.: Anthropomorphisms in Multimedia Learning: Are They Universally Effective? (submitted)
36. Sweller, J., Ayres, P., Kalyuga, S.: Cognitive Load Theory. Springer, New York (2011). https://doi.org/10.1007/978-1-4419-8126-4
37. Um, E.R., Plass, J.L., Hayward, E.O., Homer, B.D.: Emotional design in multimedia learning. J. Educ. Psychol. **104**, 485–498 (2012)
38. van der Meij, H.: Developing and testing a video tutorial for software training. Tech. Commun. **61**, 110–122 (2014)
39. Watson, D., Clark, L.A., Tellegen, A.: Development and validation of brief measures of positive and negative affect: the PANAS scales. J. Pers. Soc. Psychol. **54**, 1063–1070 (1988)
40. Wouters, P., van Nimwegen, C., van Oostendorp, H., van der Spek, E.D.: A meta-analysis of the cognitive and motivational effects of serious games. J. Educ. Psychol. **105**, 249–265 (2013)

41. Schiefele, U.: Interest and learning from text. Sci. Stud. Read. **3**, 257–279 (1999)
42. Schiefele, U., Krapp, A., Winteler, A.: Interest as a predictor of academic achievement: a meta-analysis of research. In: The Role of Interest in Learning and Development, pp. 183–211. Lawrence Erlbaum Associates (1992)
43. Schneider, S., Nebel, S., Beege, M., Rey, G.D.: Anthropomorphism in decorative pictures: benefit or harm for learning? J. Educ. Psychol. **110**, 218–232 (2018)

Predicting Learning Performance in Serious Games

Michael D. Kickmeier-Rust[(⊠)]

Institute for Educational Assessment, University of Teacher Education,
St. Gallen, Switzerland
michael.kickmeier@phsg.ch

Abstract. The prediction of learning performance is an important task in the context of smart tutoring systems. A growing community from the field of Learning Analytics and Educational Data Mining investigates the methods and technologies to make predictions about the competencies and skills, learners may reach within a specific course or program. Such performance predictions may also enrich the capabilities and the effectiveness of serious games. In game-based assessment, predictions add a novel dimension for the personalization and adaption in games for which these functions may provide a valuable data basis. The Learning Performance Vector (LPV) allows utilizing information about the learning domain (i.e., the competencies and the structure of competencies) and log file information from games to make performance predictions. In a simulative study based on existing datasets, we explored the characteristics of the approach and compared it to a linear regression model. The results indicate that the LPV is a promising method, specifically in data rich game-based scenarios with limited external information.

Keywords: In-game assessment · Performance prediction · Learning analytics
Competence-based Knowledge Space Theory

1 Introduction

The assessment of learning performance plays a crucial role in many serious games. Specifically adaptive games require a certain understanding of competencies of the learners and their learning progresses. Accordingly important is a sound, valid, and theoretically grounded assessment. The evidences, thereby, may be divided into performance related aspects, emotional-motivational as well as personality related aspects [1]. The performance related aspects include measuring, gathering, analyzing, and interpreting scores, task completion rates, completion times, success rates, success depths (the quality or degree to which a ask has been accomplished), etc. [2]. The approaches to in-game assessment, stealth assessment, and non-invasive adaptation of games have been refined significantly over the past decade [3, 4]. There exist structural models (related to KST and micro-adaptivity [5]), cognitive diagnosis models [6, 7], Bayesian approaches [8], latent variable models [9] and methods from the field of learning analytics (LA) research [10]. A concept that is not as popular in the context of serious games as assessment approaches are, is the prediction of learning performance

© Springer Nature Switzerland AG 2018
S. Göbel et al. (Eds.): JCSG 2018, LNCS 11243, pp. 133–144, 2018.
https://doi.org/10.1007/978-3-030-02762-9_14

in games. Performance prediction has a long(er) tradition in the context of Learning Analytics, for example.

In the context of serious games, prediction of learning performance may be important in two areas. The one is game-based assessment, the assessment of certain performance constructs on the hand of games or simulations. A prominent example is the National Observational Teaching Exam (NOTE) by the Educational Testing Service (ETS) [11]. NOTE is a test instrument for teacher's abilities based on simulated classroom scenarios, accredited in the USA. Meanwhile already a number of commercial psychometric games exist. Prediction of achievements may be a valuable dimension of such games and simulations. The second area is assessment for games, for example to inform personalization and adaption of games. An example is the approach of micro-adaptivity [5], which is a probabilistic, non-numerical framework to build believe models about learner performance on the basis of fine grained activities in the game. This paper describes an extension of the micro-adaptivity concept, aiming at the prediction of a so-called learning horizon of a learner. This concept refers to the likelihood with which a particular learner will achieve the learning goals in the domain of the learning game. This approach is specifically interesting for serious games because with each action of a learner in the game, the prediction model can be updated and the prediction gets more accurate. By this means, the game may predict possible achievements already at a comparably early stage and the right didactic consequences can be drawn (e.g., an adaptation of the game at an early stage).

2 Predictive Learning Analytics

The prediction of academic success has a longer tradition, for example in the context of university entry exams, which in the end aim to predict the performance and the chances to graduate. This research basically focuses on two types of predictors: cognitive ability or traditional measures, and non-cognitive, affective or non-academic factors. Cognitive factors usually refer to measures such as high school grades and standardized test scores whereas non-cognitive measures are related to psychological factors, like social support and academic related skills [12]. Of course, there are mixed approaches as well [13]. Often, very simple measures – such as engagement – predict study success best [14]. In general, one has to distinguish the attributes and variables on which predictions are based and, second, the methods how these variables are processed. The most frequent methods to process variables are classifications, regressions, and categorizations. In a review [15] list and describe the following methods: Decision Tree, Artificial Neural Networks, Naive Bayes, K-Nearest Neighbor, and Support Vector Machine. These authors conclude that Neural Network and Decision Tree approaches have the highest prediction accuracy. [16] provide an overview of approaches over the past fifteen years. These authors also demonstrate the effectiveness and the limitations of four approaches (Logistic Regression, Naïve Bayes, Support Vector Machine) in the context of an early alert system. An interesting comparison of eight methods (ranging from K-Nearest Neighbor to Decision Tree algorithms) along a variety of learning factors was published by [17] who found only fair prediction accuracy (60 to 80%). Also, the various algorithms did not differ substantially. [18]

compared different methods from data mining and from the field of recommender systems such as Bayesian Probabilistic Matrix Factorization and Bayesian Probabilistic Tensor Factorization and could demonstrate that the methods are, in principle, equally accurate [19] demonstrated, that prediction accuracy can be improved when binary regression algorithms are extended to partial credit models and when the algorithms includes penalties for hints and attempts.

Using multiple and continuously changing sources of data are the basis for predictions, which perfectly suits the nature of serious games. [20] discuss how the predictive capacity of different sources of data changes as the course progresses and also how a student's pattern of behavior changes during the course, which in turn affects predictions. [16] conclude that prediction and risk detection approaches do work, however, they have their strengths in large lecture-style electronic courses. It remains unclear though, to what extend these methods are helpful in smaller, perhaps more limited games.

In conclusion, an overview of the literature indicates that a number of sophisticated prediction models do exist and that the accuracy of the methods is widely acceptable. The different prediction models and methods appear to have a lower impact on the accuracy in comparison to the underlying data basis (the variables and attributes of students). A critical factor, obviously, is the settings within which the methods can be applied. Only few studies outside "ideal" settings such as (i) a general forecast of academic success (likelihood of completing a course or school) or (ii) as MOOCs or distance learning scenarios report a practical success. This argument is mirrored by studies that yielded that conventional methods could not predict student success (e.g., [20–22]). A number of researchers argue that further work is needed to investigate the applicability of methods in small scale, heterogeneous scenarios with incomplete data basis (e.g., [16]). The literature indicates that a differentiating factor is whether predictions are made over a long period (e.g., by predicting college success at the time of the enrollment) or on a short scale (e.g., a course or a game, cf. [20]). In general, such settings reveal the limitations of prediction methods in general. With this paper, I want to introduce a different approach of predicting student performance, originating from the community of probabilistic and combinatorial test theory.

3 Competence Spaces

We developed a combinatorial approach to educational personalization in games, which is called micro-adaptivity. In projects such as ELEKTRA and 80Days (www.eightydays.eu) we introduced and evaluated the usefulness of this approach. The goal was to complement the widely bottom-up driven, data mining and statistics focused methods of assessment and adaptation with a top-down approach, driven by psycho-pedagogical theories. At the same time, we attempted to work towards solutions for the areas, within which typical methods have certain weaknesses (as discussed above). One direction, micro-adaptivity pursued was Competence-based Knowledge Space Theory (CbKST), which is an extension of Knowledge Space Theory (KST) established by [23, 24]. KST is a set-theoretic framework for addressing the relations among problems (e.g., test items). It provides a basis for structuring a domain of knowledge and for representing the knowledge based on prerequisite relations. Similar to Item Response Theory (IRT), KST attempts to order test items and problems. As opposed to IRT, which establishes linear orders, KST allows for multiple dimensions. It establishes a Knowledge Structure by identifying relationships between the items. While KST focuses only on the items – or rather whether learners are able to master the item (performance), CbKST introduces a separation of observable performance and latent, unobservable knowledge and competences, which determine the performance [25]. Very briefly, the fundamental idea of CbkST is to assume a set of atomic competencies and a so-called Prerequisite Relation between them. Such relation is, in fact, a pedagogical model that explains the course of learning and development in a specific domain and the structural relations in the domain. As an example, one such relationship is to assume that adding integers is a prerequisite to learn multiplying integers. An individual learner can have none, all, or a specific set of competencies of a domain (e.g., being able to add, subtract, and multiply integers) – this is called the learner's Competence State. By a combinatorial permutation, the Prerequisite Relation induces a so-called Competence Space, the collection of all possible Competence States (cf. Fig. 1). Due to the pedagogical model, not all possible combinations of competencies are meaningful states; for example being able to multiply integers but not to add them is not reasonable state. This happens on a latent, conceptual level; the knowledge, the competencies and skills, the aptitude of a learner cannot be observed directly. CbKST now links the performance to the competence level on a stochastic level by so-called Representation Functions. Concrete test items and problems serve as behavioral indicators. Mastering an item increases the probabilities of all those Competence States that include the associated competencies. By this means, the probability distribution over the Competence Space is updated on the basis of a continuous interpretation of all sorts of behavioral indictors. Each gaming activity, each achievement, each learning activity contributes to CbKST's believe model. [5] demonstrate that this approach can be broken down to a very fine granularity and that it can be utilized in the context of serious games.

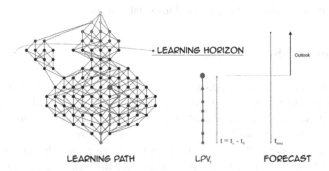

Fig. 1. The left part shows a Competence Space including the admissible learning paths. The red path may be that of a particular student. The left part of the figure illustrates the prediction principle of the LPV. (Color figure online)

4   The Learning Performance Vector

In the game context, it might be important to estimate the competence states a learner may reach within a reasonable time span of gaming. This helps, for example, preventing the learner to fail in reaching the goals of a game. As outlined initially, a good portion of the existing methods are statistics-based data mining techniques. These perform well on a general, statistical basis however have clear weaknesses when operating on a level of individual learners. Also, many statistical approaches build upon a set of (at least) debatable statistical assumptions and decision criteria. In this paper, we introduce a first evaluation study, comparing a simple statistical prediction method with a CbKST-based one, we term Learning Performance Vector (LPV). The purpose is to elucidate primarily the prediction characteristics of the method.

The origin of the prediction algorithm is a Competence Space. This space gives us a model of the learning domain, starting from having no competencies in a domain, leading to the complete mastery. This allows us to identify the progress of a particular learner given the timeline of a course. Mathematically speaking, we have the set of all admissible learning paths. This indicates the average learning efforts, given that transitions have specific difficulties or weights. We have a set of competencies $Q = \{a, b, c, \ldots\}$ with a relationship $c \leq c'$ among the competencies, which establishes the Competence Space. The sum of the resulting Competence States is $\sum(|Q|r)$. Given that the transitions from one competence state to another has a difficulty parameter, which in turn is the average of the difficulty parameters of the competencies being a part of the state, we have a set of tuples of the initial state, the end state, and the difficulty $\tau = [s_1, s_2, w]$. This results in a set of such tuples for the entire Competence Space $T = \sum(r|Q)$. In addition, we have a set of indicators providing evidences for competencies: $I = \{e_i, \{c\} * w\}$, with a given weight w. Based on the evidences we can estimate the likelihood of each competency. The probability of a Competence State is the average of its competencies $p(s) = \sum(\pi)/n$. To identify the learning path of a person, we identify the states with the highest probability at each assessment point. For each step, we compute the difficulty (as a value between 0 and 1). The sum of the values gives us an indicator of the efforts a student spent on her learning history (the individual learning path). In a next step, given the concrete Competence State of the learner, we have to identify the possible paths towards the final learning goal, which is a (rather small) subset of all possible paths. Equal to the computation of the difficulty to reach the current state, we can compute the potential difficulties of all possible paths towards the goal. This now is an indicator for the efforts that are necessary for an individual learner to reach the learning goal.

As illustrate in Fig. 1, considering the progress of a student within a given span of time, we can make a prediction about how far a student can come within the remaining time (of a course, for example). So, as a final step, we can identify exactly those states (and therefore the competencies) a particular learner will be able to reach within the time limits. We call the set of the reachable Competence States the learning horizon.

5 Identifying the Prediction Characteristics

The purpose of this study was to investigate the characteristics of the prediction method as opposed to an existing, well-elaborated approach. To judge the accuracy, it is necessary to compare the predictions with – what often is called – "ground truth". Therefore, we simulated the learning performance of excellent, medium, and poor learners. On this basis, we made systematic comparisons. Since no particular examples exists for the prediction with games, we used a conventional test data set.

5.1 Data Set

The first step for this study is to select an appropriate data set. To build upon a realistic data we selected a data set from Carnegie Mellon's DataShop. It is a data set of "Assistments Math 2004–2005", data set id 92 (accessible at pslcdatashop.web.cmu. edu/DatasetInfo?datasetId=92). This data set covers mathematics (which offers an easy 'playground' because it is a well-defined domain) and includes the data of 912 students. The data set is based on in total 80 competencies (knowledge components). For the simulation study, we selected a subset of 11 competencies and established a compe-tence model (see Fig. 2). The weights are derived from the inverse solution frequencies of the real data set. Furthermore, we selected 12 item types and 111 items from the data set. These cover one or more of the selected competencies, partially also other com-petencies (Fig. 2). Based on the real data set, we simulated prototypical learners, taking the characteristics of 912 students and the item solution frequencies into account. The ability parameter was defined on a scale from 1 to 10, while 1 means no knowledge in the domain and 10 means having all competencies. The parameters were simulated based on a normal distribution, assuring the medium level abilities are most common and extreme position rather seldom. Finally, because this study is about prediction, we simulated 9 time points with the assumption that in the time intervals learning occurs, depending on the student abilities. In summary, we simulated the answer patterns of 15 students across 9 time points in 111 fictitious test items, covering 12 competencies. The simulated data set consists of 1665 data points. The following chart shows the pro-totypical simulated results of an excellent learner (squares), a medium learner (circles), and a poor learner (diamonds) (Fig. 3a). The values show the relative increase in correctly solved items over the 9 time intervals. The bold black diagonal indicates the optimal increase, so that with each of the 9 points in time 1/9 of the items is solved correctly – or in other terms, 1/9 of the competencies have been acquired.

The results show that the increase is determined by the student abilities, due to error rates (lucky guesses and careless errors) we see that the optimal learner is a bit below the ideal diagonal while thee poor learner still shows a slight increase.

5.2 A Simple Linear Prediction Model

To evaluate the characteristics of the LPV, we established a baseline prediction model. The model is a simple linear regression model based on a retrospective view of a particular student's performance. The model considers the performance of a particular student and predicts the future performance on the basis of the slope the general

Competencies		
ID	Competence	Weight
1	Addition	0.10
2	Subtraction	0.15
3	Multiplication	0.27
4	Division	0.40
5	Fraction	0.45
6	Division /w decimals	0.55
7	Fraction multiplication	0.66
8	Fraction division	0.70
9	Fraction percent	0.80
10	Fraction /w decimals	0.89
11	Comb. Equation	0.93

Test Items	
Item Type	Competencies
1	1
2	1,2
3	1,3
4	2
5	1,2,3
6	1,2,3,4
7	1,2,3,4,5
8	1,2,3,4,6
9	1,2,3,4,5,7
10	1,2,3,4,5,6,7,8,9
11	1,2,3,4,5,6,7,8,10
12	1,2,3,5

Students	
Student ID	Ability Level (1 – 10)
1	2
2	9
3	3
4	3
5	4
6	5
7	5
8	6
9	7
10	7
11	8
12	8
13	9
14	5
15	4

Competence Model

Fig. 2. From left to right: the selected competencies, the selected test items, the simulated students, and the derived competence model (prerequisite relation).

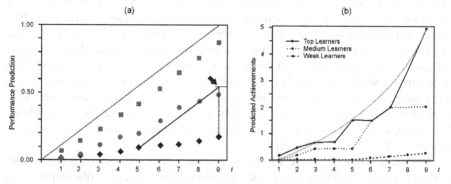

Fig. 3. Panel (a) shows the simulated results of three prototypical students as opposed to the ideal learning performance. Panel (b) shows the prediction results of the CbKST approach for a good (bold line), medium (dotted line) and poor (dashed line) student.

regression lines. This is demonstrated in Fig. 3. The low performing (diamonds) student reached a solution frequency of 0,054 at the end of interval 4. The model prediction is indicated in the grey line. This, however, is a significant overestimation of a student's abilities. There is a strong discrepancy between the results of a student and such estimations (dotted line in the figure). Figure 4 reports the predictive power of this approach over time. The left panel shows the predicted final achievements over the time intervals for the good (bold line) and the poor (dashed line) students. The right panel shows the accuracy (difference of simulated end values and predictions) of the approach. It is evident that the method overestimates the achievements by far, even for a nearly optimally performing student. This optimal and average linear increase is a problematic approach, obviously.

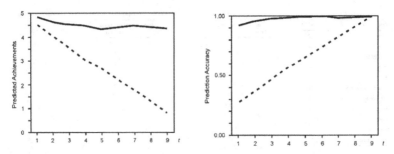

Fig. 4. The left panel shows the predicted achievements over time; the right panel shows the accuracy of the prediction method over time. The bold line refers to the LPV, the dashed line to the linear model.

5.3 The CbKST-Based LPV

The regression model, of course, is over simple. Methods that are more sophisticated are available, as introduce in this paper. These methods use more information about student performance and establish more complex, non-linear models. The contribution of CbKST is to use the multidimensional domain and learner models (the Competence Spaces) to add information about the nature of a learning domain to the model. This information includes the number and complexity of competencies as well as the relationships between them. Moreover, since the Competence Space is composed of the admissible Competence States, the lines between the states indicate the set of different learning paths that are possible – starting from having none of a domain's competencies to having all (cf. Fig. 1, left part).

The prediction logic of the LPV is to assume a finite number of learning paths leading from the trivial Competence State of having no competencies (the empty set) to the trivial state of having all competencies (the full set). We assume a well-graded space, claiming that in each step in the learning paths only one competency is acquired. The set of learning paths a learner is on can be identified on the basis of the current and past answer patterns (i.e., which item types were mastered and which not). The various paths can be characterized by their complexity, which is determined by the weights of the individual steps, which in turn result from the item solution frequencies in the original data set. The advantage is that we have a specific instance of the prediction model for each individual learner and her specific learning paths. In other words, mastering many easy items at an early stage is a weak indicator because major challenges are still ahead for the student. In turn, mastering highly complex items (with high weights and perhaps a larger number of prerequisites) is a very strong indicator because all prerequisite items are assumed to be possessed by the learner. The following figure shows the prediction results for the same simulated data set and the same students. In this example, the sum of weights assigned to the competence structure is 4.98 (the grey curve in Fig. 3b indicates the average prediction of this approach, contrasting the linear approach we described above). The curves show the performance of the three prototypical students across the 9 time intervals.

Figure 5(a and b) illustrates the final values predicted at each point in time. For the low performing student (dashed line) we obtain a clear overestimation of achievements but this overestimation is decreasing very quickly; after time interval 5, the prediction is very low – which is an accurate prediction. In case of a high performer (bold line) we have similar predictions as for the low performer and we see the same decrease in the predicted achievements. This decrease is much smaller and after time interval 5 the prediction becomes quite accurate also for the high performer. Figure 5b shows the accuracy, defined as the difference of predicted and actual achievements. When ana-lyzing the different answer patterns (which items were processed in which order) for the 12 item types in our data, we found that the order of item types strongly influences the prediction characteristics (the predictive accuracy) of the LPV approach. If items that are more difficult are presented already at an early stage, the accuracy of the LPV can be increased, while such item order effects do not affect the accuracy of a linear model. Figure 5c illustrates the accuracy depending on the item order. With difficult items in the beginning, the accuracy of the LPV is very high already after 3 time intervals and superior to the linear model (Fig. 5c). In turn, the linear model has higher accuracy only when the order of item presentation strictly follows the assumption of an evenly distributed linear increase of item difficulty (Fig. 5d).

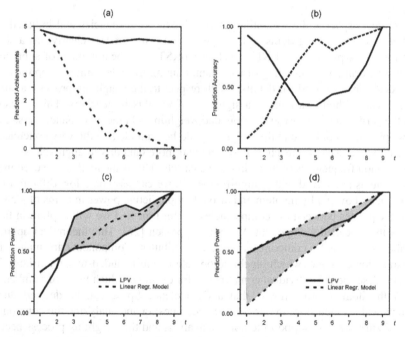

Fig. 5. Panel (a) shows the predicted performance over time, panel (b) the method's accuracy. The bold line displays an optimal student, the dashed line a poor student. Panels (c) and (d) show a comparison of predictive power (LPV vs. linear).

6 Discussion

The aim of this simulation study was to identify the characteristics of the LPV and if and to what extent the LPV is a suitable method to predict learning performance in serious games. The simulation-based study, developed on the basis of a real data set, allowed us to explore the characteristics and dependencies of the method in its application to various data characteristics. In this paper, we described the main findings.

As benchmark, we used a simple, linear regression model. Although there are much more sophisticated methods available, for the prediction of performance within a single course and without additional information about the learner, only few suitable methods exist [20]. Considering the development of the LPV as a robust prediction method, at this stage of our research, we avoided to involve too many student attributes. And certainly, one of the main goals of the LPV is to provide a performance prediction method that operates in scenarios with little to no background data available, with a shallow and incomplete data basis, and that allows a continuous monitoring of performance. Insofar, we obtained promising results. The information added to the prediction model – the domain structure and the weights of competencies – allows a more accurate performance prediction and the predictions converge quicker to a reasonable accuracy.

A critical aspect is the weighting process for the competencies and indirectly the test items (by associating items and competencies). This process clearly has a strong influence on the predictions. KST as well as CbKST describe a number of approaches for the structuring and weighting of a domain, ranging from data mining approaches to expert decisions (see [25] for details). With respect to the weighting process, a simple but practical method is a manual assignment of weights by teachers. This, however, bears the peril of an arbitrary and unfounded weighting. On the other hand, the strength of this approach could be that the weights would be grounded on the very concrete and practical experiences of a teacher. A second and more data driven approach is to refer to the solution frequencies of items in large data sets. This is the method we used in this study. If items are solved with a high frequency, we can assume a low difficult of the competencies covered by the item and also a low predictive power in terms of CbKST-type prerequisites between the competencies. A third method we will explore in future work is the so-called Component Attribute Approach [26]. This theoretical approach describes test items by components and their attributes. Components are major characteristics, for example, which algebraic operations are included in a math item. The attributes describe the individual components, for example, which types of numbers are part of the item. It was shown, that a Competence Space can be derived due to mathematical set inclusion. In our context decomposing and analyzing the components and their attributes can support the domain analysis and the weighting process because for typical course settings, usually elaborated curricula are available. A forth method is to analyze existing test items on the basis of their cognitive depth. This refers back to the famous taxonomy of Benjamin Bloom, revised by [27]. In the so-called Concept – Action Verb approach. Bloom proposed six such levels. An example would be "understand that a house has windows and apply this understanding in a new situation".

The taxonomy also separates the knowledge dimensions factual, conceptual, procedural, and metacognitive knowledge, which in the end established a two-dimensional hierarchy. In our context, this taxonomy provides a scaffolding to analyze the items, to identify the covered competencies, and to rank the competencies according the taxonomy – which in the end specifies the weights.

Certainly, the LPV presented in this paper stands in close relationship to other game analytics and game learning analytics (GLA) solutions [28]. Gaming Learning Analytics refers to analyzing gaming behaviors of students to obtain the relevant information about the learning process of the student. The goal is to understand how a student learns something new and how to help students achieve a higher outcome of their interaction with it – either in form of new designs or in-game adaptions. Several complex frameworks have been proposed and realized [28]. The aspect of the prediction of learning performance, however, was not necessarily in the focus of the systems. Instead they rather provide the information necessary for the predictions to stakeholders (students, teachers), for example in form of dashboards. Future steps will demonstrate the use of the LPV (and other predictive analytics approaches) in the context of a math game, developed by the Technical University of Graz. Moreover, we will formally extend the micro-adaptivity concept for serious games by performance predictions. In conclusion, the recent initiatives of introducing assessment, prediction, and adaptation methods from fields such as psychometrics and Learning Analytics should be intensified to make games stronger and more reliable means of educational assessment.

References

1. Kickmeier-Rust, M.D., Albert, D. (eds.): An Alien's Guide to Multi-Adaptive Educational Games. Informing Science Press, Santa Rosa (2012)
2. Wiemeyer, J., Kickmeier-Rust, M.D., Steiner, C.M.: Performance assessment in serious games. In: Dörner, R., Göbel, S., Effelsberg, W., Wiemeyer, J. (eds.) Serious Games: Foundations, Concepts and Practice, pp. 273–302. Springer, Berlin (2016). https://doi.org/10.1007/978-3-319-40612-1_10
3. Bellotti, F., Kapralos, B., Lee, L., Moreno-Ger, P., Berta, R.: Assessment in and of serious games: an overview. Adv. Hum.-Comput. Interact. (2013)
4. Shute, V.J., Ventura, M.: Stealth Assessment. Measuring and Supporting Learning in Video Games. The MIT Press, Cambridge (2013)
5. Kickmeier-Rust, M.D., Albert, D.: Micro adaptivity: protecting immersion in didactically adaptive digital educational games. J. Comput. Assist. Learn. 26(2), 95–105 (2010)
6. Heller, J., Stefanutti, L., Anselmi, P., Robusto, E.: Erratum to: on the link between cognitive diagnostic models and knowledge space theory. Psychometrika 81, 250–251 (2016)
7. Heller, J., Stefanutti, L., Anselmi, P., Robusto, E.: On the link between cognitive diagnostic models and knowledge space theory. Psychometrika 80, 995–1019 (2015)
8. Käser, T., et al.: Design and evaluation of the computer-based training program Calcularis for enhancing numerical cognition. Front. Psychol. 4, 289 (2013)
9. Mislevy, R.J.: Evidence-centered design for simulation-based assessment. Mil. Med. 178 (10), 107–114 (2013)

10. Kickmeier-Rust, M.D. (ed.): Learning analytics for an in serious games. In: Proceedings of the Joint workshop of the GALA Network of Excellence and the LEA's BOX project at EC-TEL 2014, 17 September 2014, Graz, Austria (2014). http://css-kmi.tugraz.at/mkrwww/leas-box/ectel2014.htm

11. Sandberg, H.: The Good and the Bad of Game-Based Assessment. ETS, Focus on R&D, Issue 1, April 2016. https://www.ets.org/research/policy_research_reports/focus_on_rd/issue1

12. Ma, Y., Liu, B., Wong, C., Yu, P., Lee, S.: Targeting the right students using data mining. In: Proceedings of the 6th International Conference on Knowledge Discovery and Data Mining (KDD), Boston, Massachusetts, USA, 20–23 August, pp. 457–464 (2000)

13. Shahiria, A.M., Husaina, W., Rashid, N.A.: A review on predicting student's performance using data mining techniques. Procedia Comput. Sci. **72**, 414–422 (2015)

14. Christian, T.M., Ayub, M.: Exploration of classification using nbtree for predicting students' performance. In: Proceedings of the International IEEE Conference on Data and Software Engineering (ICODSE), pp. 1–6 (2014)

15. Romero, C., López, M.I., Luna, J.-M., Ventura, S.: Predicting students' final performance from participation in on-line discussion forums. Comput. Educ. **68**, 458–472 (2013)

16. Jayaprakash, S.M., Moody, E.W., Lauría, E.J.M., Regan, J.R., Baron, J.D.: Early alert of academically at-risk students: an open source analytics initiative. J. Learn. Anal. **1**(1), 6–47 (2014)

17. Gray, G., McGuinness, C., Owende, P., Hofmann, M.: Learning factor models of students at risk of failing in the early stage of tertiary education. J. Learn. Anal. **3**(2), 330–372 (2016)

18. Sahebi, S., Huang, Y., Brusilovsky, P.: Predicting student performance in solving parameterized exercises. In: Trausan-Matu, S., Boyer, K.E., Crosby, M., Panourgia, K. (eds.) ITS 2014. LNCS, vol. 8474, pp. 496–503. Springer, Cham (2014). https://doi.org/10.1007/978-3-319-07221-0_62

19. Ostrow, K., Donnelly, C., Heffernan, N.: Optimizing partial credit algorithms to predict student performance. In: Proceedings of Educational Data Mining (EDM) 2015 (2015)

20. Wolff, A., Zdrahal, Z., Herrmannova, D., Knoth, P.: Predicting student performance from combined data sources. In: Peña-Ayala, A. (ed.) Educational Data Mining. SCI, vol. 524, pp. 175–202. Springer, Cham (2014). https://doi.org/10.1007/978-3-319-02738-8_7

21. Strang, K.D.: Can online student performance be forecasted by learning analytics? Int. J. Technol. Enhanc. Learn. **8**(1), 26–47 (2016)

22. Papamitsiou, Z., Economides, A.: Learning analytics and educational data mining in practice: a systematic literature review of empirical evidence. Educ. Technol. Soc. **17**(4), 49–64 (2014)

23. Doignon, J.-P., Falmagne, J.-C.: Spaces for the assessment of knowledge. Int. J. Man-Mach. Stud. **23**, 175–196 (1985)

24. Doignon, J.-P., Falmagne, J.-C.: Knowledge Spaces. Springer, Berlin (1999). https://doi.org/10.1007/978-3-642-58625-5

25. Albert, D., Lukas, J. (eds.): Knowledge Spaces: Theories, Empirical Research, and Applications. Lawrence Erlbaum Associates, Mahwah (1999)

26. Heller, J., Steiner, C., Hockemeyer, C., Albert, D.: Competence-based knowledge structures for personalized learning. Int. J. E-Learn. **5**, 75–88 (2006)

27. Anderson, L.: Taxonomy for Learning, Teaching, and Assessing: A Revision of Bloom's Taxonomy of Educational Objectives. Pearson Education, Boston (2013)

28. Freire, M., Serrano-Laguna, Á., Iglesias, B.M., Martínez-Ortiz, I., Moreno-Ger, P., Fernández-Manjón, B.: Game learning analytics: learning analytics for serious games. In: Spector, M., Lockee, B., Childress, M. (eds.) Learning, Design, and Technology. Springer, Cham (2016). https://doi.org/10.1007/978-3-319-17727-4_21-1

Connecting Theory and Design Through Research: Cognitive Skills Training Games

Jan L. Plass[1](✉) ⓘ, Bruce D. Homer[2] ⓘ, Shashank Pawar[1],
and Frankie Tam[1]

[1] New York University, New York, NY 10012, USA
jan.plass@nyu.edu
[2] The Graduate Center, CUNY, New York, NY 10016, USA

Abstract. How can the effectiveness of games for learning be enhanced? In this paper, we present an approach that connects theory and research to enhance the design of games that train cognitive skills. Specifically, we combine our model for designing games for learning with Value-Added Design Research, which can provide design guidance for decisions that the model alone cannot provide. We applied this method in the context of designing games to train executive functions, an application area that is highly promising but nevertheless has produced many games that are not effective. We discuss three examples of design research studies we conducted, including the emotional design of the game, the use of an adaptive algorithm, and the design of level progressions privileging either speed or accuracy in learners' responses. We conclude that this approach is able to contribute to both the enhancement of CHI related design challenges and to theory.

Keywords: Game design methodology · Value added research
Executive functions

1 Introduction

There is an increasing recognition that playing games can have benefits that go beyond entertainment [45]. Practical examples for such games as well as related research of the games' effectiveness to benefit players have been produced in areas such as games for health [37, 50], exergames [5, 40], games for cognitive skills training [38], and games for learning [11, 30], among others.

For the design of such games for impact, different design methods need to be applied to ensure their effectiveness than are used for entertainment games [43]. These methods should be based on a model of designing games for learning such as proposed in [45], which includes the different design factors that need to be considered. These factors include cognitive factors, affective factors, motivational factors, and socio-cultural factors. We argue that existing game design models need to be expanded to include the consideration of theoretical and research insights from the specific area the game aims to address, such as research on behavioral change, research on training of cognitive skills, or research on how we learn.

© Springer Nature Switzerland AG 2018
S. Göbel et al. (Eds.): JCSG 2018, LNCS 11243, pp. 145–158, 2018.
https://doi.org/10.1007/978-3-030-02762-9_15

In this paper, we present an approach to design research for games that we have used successfully at our research and development lab for the past decade. We use the term *design research* to describe empirical research that informs specific design decisions for a game. This approach combines different research methods in order to provide empirical evidence based on which game design decisions can be made, especially those related to the player's interaction with the game. We will discuss how the outcome of such research can benefit the CHI community in two ways. One is in user experience and interaction design of the game with which it was conducted, in our case, the design of games to train cognitive skills. The other contribution is to our theoretical understanding of processes related to cognitive skills training.

2   Designing Games for Learning

In many ways, the design of games for learning follows models of game design in general, as described, for example, by [19], perhaps with modifications for games for learning as proposed by [42]. However, unlike entertainment games, which are defined as being "outside ordinary life" and "not serious" [24], these games have an actual goal, and are therefore quite well connected to ordinary life and are serious in that they seek to enhance the human condition. Consequently, there is a need to design games for learning in a way that these goals can in fact be met.

Among the many ways to increase the likelihood that games for learning meet their intended goals are three we will mention here. The first is the use of an appropriate design process and a design team that has expertise in the learning sciences in addition to game design [42, 43]. The second is to base the design of games for learning, and especially of the interactions within the game, on relevant theoretical models of play, cognition, learning, emotion, and motivation [45]. The learning game model proposed in [45] shows how the different forms of engagement in games are facilitated by different game features. The model includes affective, social, cognitive and motivational engagement factors that are based on a broad range of relevant theories, and identifies relevant game features that can be used to promote different types of engagements (Fig. 1).

The third and final method to design interactions that enhance the effectiveness of games to meet their learning goals is to use design research for those decisions that cannot be addressed by the other two methods. It is this method we will discuss further in the present paper. For many of the design factors shown in the model in Fig. 1, a range of different forms of implementation in a game are possible that would have an effect on the effectiveness of the factors to obtain the desired outcome. Although the model cannot provide insights specific enough to inform which form of implementation to choose, it can be used to derive design factors to investigate in an empirical study.

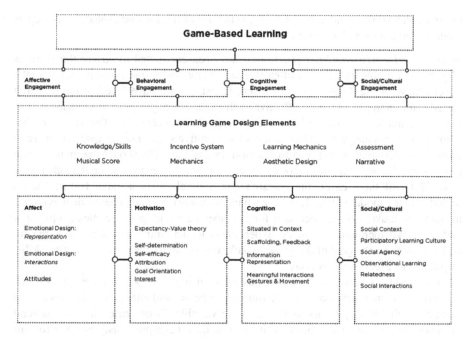

Fig. 1. Model for games for learning

3   Research Methods for Design Research for Games

In our work of designing games for a broad range of subject areas, contexts, and learners, we have used a variety of design research methods, each focusing on different research questions that arise during the design process. The learning sciences and CHI communities have developed many methods that can be used for this purpose, including game usability research [25], design-based research [21], and participatory research [55]. In our research project to design games to train cognitive skills describe we have particularly used three types of methods, Ideation, Playtesting, and Value Added Research.

Ideation Research. Ideation research is conducted in order to identify problems to solve and to imagine and communicate methods of how to solve them [53]. During the ideation phase, it may not even be clear whether a game is in fact a meaningful way to address the problem at hand. Ideation involves participation from various stakeholders, observations, literature review, and other qualitative methods. The outcome of successful ideation research is a clear understanding of the problem and of possible approaches to potential solutions.

Playtesting. If a decision was made to design a game to address a specific learning-related issue, playtesting is used to verify whether the approach identified and developed during the ideation process is in fact one that resonates with the target audience, but also whether the game was implemented in a way that users were able to comprehend its features and use them successfully. Playtesting methods include player observations, surveys and user log analysis, the use of think-aloud protocols, as well as video observations and video coding [48].

Value Added Research. After playtesting has been conducted to ensure the game is playable and usable, researchers often still face many design questions that relate to the effectiveness of the design factors chosen. Questions we have faced in our research include, for example: (1) How effective is the adaptive algorithm we implemented in our game, and for whom? (2) How does the use of game characters that induce higher emotion arousal change the effectiveness of a cognitive skills training game compare to game characters that do not lead to emotion arousal? and (3) Should the game's level progression favor speed of responses over accuracy of responses, or the other way around? In all three cases, the research question relates to a game feature that is included in the model in Fig. 1, but for which there wasn't sufficient empirical evidence available to make a design decision for this specific game, genre, context, topic, and audience. We therefore conducted experiments to determine the value each feature added to achieve the goal of the game, which was to enhance learners' cognitive skills, in particular, executive functions.

Value added research studies are experiments using a pre/post-test design with two or more treatment conditions. The measure given before and after game play has to be a valid and reliable way to assess the outcome variable. In our case, there are several measures for executive functions available that have been previously normed for our target audience [17, 52, 61]. In other cases, such a measure may have to be developed and normed. The treatment conditions need to be designed to allow for a comparison of the game design feature under investigation. This requires some special attention in the context of games as other features may create confounds. For example, when we investigated the effect of the emotional design of game characters, we had to make sure the adaptive algorithm of the game was disabled to ensure that emotional design was the only variable for which the game play differed. Below we will describe for each of the variable why it was important, how it was studied, and what we found.

4   Application Area: Training Executive Functions

Executive functions (EF) are a set of cognitive skills required to plan, monitor and control cognitive processes. EF, which develop throughout childhood into adolescence and early adulthood [7, 14], are related to a number of important outcomes, including externalizing behavioral problems [60], social functioning [31], and academic success [6, 59]. There is also considerable evidence of the importance of EF for educational outcomes. For example [6] found that EF skills in preschool uniquely predicted children's math and literacy skills in kindergarten.

Of the theoretical models that describe EF, the unity/diversity model by Miyake et al. [32] is especially useful for our work as it proposes a distributed structure of EF. According to this model, EF is comprised of three component skills that are closely related yet distinguishable: updating, shifting, and inhibition. *Updating* is defined as updating and monitoring of working memory representations, such as replacing old irrelevant information in working memory with new task-relevant information. *Shifting* is defined as shifting between tasks or mental sets, such as switching from one perspective to another. *Inhibition* is defined as the ability to suppress a dominant or prepotent response and allows us to control our attention, behaviors, thoughts, and emotions [32].

Because of the importance of EF, there has been considerable research on the topic, and great interest in developing successful interventions for improving EF. Reviews have found mixed results for the effectiveness of digital games as interventions for improving EF [30, 49], but there is nevertheless evidence of their potential. One approach has been "brain training" games–essentially gamified versions of EF tasks. Some research found significant improvements in EF in older adults who played the brain-training game, *Brain Age*, for 15 min a day, 5 days per week over a 4-week period as compared to a control group [25]. However, other studies have not found significant effects. One researcher recruited a large online sample and found that participants who were trained with EF tasks got better only at those specific tasks–the effects did not transfer to other tasks [36].

We argue that one of the reasons for these inconsistent findings of the effectiveness of games to train EF may lie in their design and the extent to which design research was conducted to support specific design decisions. In the following sections, we will describe how we used value added research to address the questions described above.

5   Value-Added Design Studies for EF Training Games

Value added research studies are experiments that provide empirical evidence whether a specific design feature of a learning game contributes to an enhanced learning outcome. In other words, this research helps designers decide whether or not to include this feature in the final release. Figure 1 shows how many possible features could be designed based on the different theories underlying the design of games for learning, and related to the different game design features that could be used to implement them. We selected three of these features for this report, namely adaptivity, emotional design, and level progressions, all of which are described in more detail below.

5.1   Adaptivity

Our first question concerned the adaptivity with the game. Adaptive technologies are designed to cater to individual differences of users. Studies have shown that factors like prior knowledge [2, 56], emotional states such as frustration, boredom, motivation, and confidence [9, 12, 41, 51] and differences in demographic and sociocultural factors [10, 13] are strong predictors of learning outcomes. To overcome the gap created by these differences, adaptive systems can optimize game parameters at a cognitive, affective, socio-cultural or motivational level [47]. However, the existing literature lacks clarity in defining the specific purpose of adaptive systems [22, 33, 58]. In the present case, we focus on adaptivity at a cognitive and affective level for our EF training game. The purpose of adaptivity, in our case, is to adjust the difficulty of the training task to facilitate optimal cognitive engagement and to avoid disengagement and frustration due to extraneous cognitive load. This is managed by manipulating task difficulty in real-time based on player performance. The adaptive engine in our EF training game reacts to player performance and manipulates the training task to maintain task difficulty at a level that provides optimal cognitive engagement.

Previous research has shown that adaptive difficulty adjustment plays a pivotal role in cognitive training tasks [1]. If a task is of low difficulty for a player, their cognitive capacity is underwhelmed, leading to boredom and disengagement. Similarly, if a task is too difficult for a player, their cognitive capacity is overwhelmed, leading to frustration and disengagement. Both of these conditions are suboptimal for cognitive skill training as they fail to fully tap into the cognitive resources of the user. Despite strong theoretical support for this design feature [15, 22, 27], existing empirical evidence consists of inconclusive findings [58]. This value-added study investigates this design feature and explores the impact of adaptive difficulty adjustment on the enhancement of EF skills through game-based training.

Participants and Design. Participants were recruited from middle and high schools from a large urban city in Northeastern United States (N = 119) and from the mturk platform (N = 100 adults located in the United States, 4,999+ completed HITs, approval ratings > 97%). Data collection was completed using DREAM, an online experimentation platform. The study used an experimental design with two treatment conditions further explained below.

Materials and Procedure. We used the *Alien game* (Fig. 2) hosted on the online experiment platform DREAM. The game is designed to develop the EF subskill of *switching* as identified by the Unity/Diversity model of EF [32]. Players are faced with the task of feeding incoming aliens with the either food or drinks. However, these rules keep changing, forcing players to apply changing and increasingly difficult sets of rules. To measure EF skills, we used the Dimensional change card sorting (DCCS) task, which is a widely-accepted measure for *switching* skills [61] and the Flanker task, which measures *inhibition* skills [16, 34]. In addition to the game and the EF measures, the participants also completed a demographic survey and a short survey about their gameplay experience. Participants were randomly assigned to either the treatment group, which received the adaptive version of the game, or the control group, which received the non-adaptive version. They then finished a demographic survey followed by the DCCS and the Flanker task as a pretest of their EF skills. The participants then completed a 20-min gameplay session of the *Alien game*. After gameplay, participants completed a posttest measure of EF skills with the DCCS and Flanker task.

Results. Results supported the positive impact of adaptivity on EF skills training. Both adolescent and adult participant groups showed significant improvements in their switching skills as measured by the DCCS task. The differences of pretest and posttest scores were significant with an effect size of $d = .53$ for adolescents and $d = .20$ for adults. For adult participants, we found a significant difference in EF gains between group, where the adaptive group outperformed the control group. For adolescents, despite the improvement in EF skills for both groups, no significant difference was associated with the treatment condition.

Conclusions. The results informed our design by emphasizing the role of age in determining the impact of adaptive difficulty adjustment on EF training. They also

Fig. 2. Screen shots from the Alien game, showing explanation of rule changes

highlight the need to consider factors like the thresholds for triggering adaptive difficulty adjustment, the granularity of change in difficulty, and the duration of gameplay in the design and development of adaptive systems. There appears to be a need to adjust the adaptive algorithm for adolescents, conduct additional playtesting, and run another value-added study to verify whether these changes led to improvements of the adaptive version. On the theoretical side, the study contributed to insights into the developmental nature of EF.

5.2   Emotional Design

A second area of interest was the emotional design of the EF training game. Theoretical approaches suggest that emotions, cognition, and learning are inherently interdependent constructs [26, 39, 46], which is backed by empirical studies investigating the impact of positive and negative emotions on cognition [28] and on learning [44, 57]. To leverage the positive effects of emotions on cognition and learning, learning environments can be designed to induced emotions conducive to learning [57].

For EF training, research suggests that emotionally charged cognitive training yields better outcomes compared to emotionally neutral training [62]. An emotionally charged training task, 'hot EF,' requires higher levels of cognitive control and emotional regulation than 'cool EF,' i.e., tasks with a lower emotional charge. Emotional design of EF training games can help generate 'Hot EF' tasks and interaction in games to improve cognitive training outcomes. However, despite this theoretical justification, there is lack of empirical evidence supporting this phenomenon. This second value-added study therefore investigates the effect of emotional design on player emotions and on their EF gains.

Participants and Design. 239 participants were recruited from middle and high schools in a large urban area in Northeastern United states. Out of these 239 participants, 129 were assigned to the control group (Cool EF version) and 110 were assigned to the treatment group (Hot EF version). The study used an experimental design with two treatment conditions, see below. Similar to the first study, all participants completed the experiment on-site in a laboratory setting.

Materials. For this study, we used a game called *All you can E.T*, a newer version of the *Alien game* described in the previous section. With the exception of visual elements and the development platform, both games are identical in gameplay. For this experiment, we created a 'Hot EF' version and a 'Cool EF' version of the game. The 'Hot EF' version consisted of characters with warm colors and round shapes, the characters displayed strong emotional reactions to player actions, reacting with either joyful or sad facial expressions based on correct or incorrect actions of players. The 'Cool EF' version consisted of grayscale characters with square shapes. The characters in this version had neutral emotional reactions to player actions, see Fig. 3. Except the differences mentioned above, both versions of the game were identical. All other measures were identical to the previously mentioned study. We used the DCCS [61] and the Flanker [52] tasks as measures of *switching* and *inhibition* respectively, a demographics survey for participant details, and another short survey to examine the participants' gameplay experience.

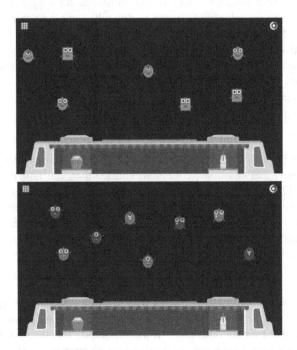

Fig. 3. Cool EF (top) and Hot EF (bottom) variants of the EF training game

Procedure. The procedure for this study was comparable to the adaptivity study mentioned previously. Participants were randomly assigned to the treatment or the control group in the beginning of the experiment. First, all participants completed a demographics survey. Then, all participants completed pretests by performing the

DCCS and Flanker task. The pretest was followed by 20 min of gameplay of *All you can E.T.* For this part, the treatment group was assigned to play the 'Hot EF' version and the control group was assigned to play the 'Cool EF' version. After gameplay, all participants completed the posttest by performing the DCCS and Flanker task followed by a short gameplay survey.

Results. Results support the claim that game-based training can lead to enhanced EF [23, 38]. Participants from both groups showed significant improvements in their *switching* skills, indicated by significant improvements in DCCS scores, $d = .28$. We also found that the 'Hot EF' game is more effective than 'Cool EF' game, $d = .17$.

Conclusions. This study contributes to the theoretical as well as design literatures on cognitive training games. It provides empirical evidence on the effect of emotional design of game characters on emotional arousal of players, which can inform character-design choices and enhance the fidelity of cognitive training games. The study also contributes to the literature supporting benefits of 'Hot EF' training by providing empirical evidence for this effect. Results support our decision to create an emotionally appealing game to enhance EF training outcomes.

5.3   Level Progressions: Speed Vs Accuracy

A third question concerns the level progression within our game. Inhibition control is an EF subskill that describes the ability to control or suppress dominant or prepotent responses [32], which allows us to inhibit an incorrect or inappropriate response when facing multiple sources of information under time pressure [4, 18, 54]. Inhibition ability is related to processing speed [20]. Inhibition control is often measured by speed and accuracy of individual's response [8, 29], but no guidance exists on whether to privilege speed or accuracy in the level progression. The goal of this value-added study was therefore to compare the effectiveness of level progressions that focus on speed versus progressions that focus on accuracy in a game specifically designed to train EF skill of inhibition.

Participants and Design. Participants ($N = 120$) were recruited from middle and high schools in a large urban area in Northeastern United states. The study employed an experimental design with two treatment conditions, see below.

Materials and Procedure. For this study, we used the *Gwakkamole* game hosted on our online experiment platform DREAM. The objective of the game is similar to whack-a-mole game where players are instructed to hit two types of target as they appear while at the same time trying to avoid hitting two types of non-targets on screen. The targets have the color and shape of an avocado. Normal and hardhat-wearing avocados are the targets to hit, while avocados with spiky helmets or with bombs are to avoid (Fig. 4). The game consists of a series of level with a different combination of target and non-target with increased difficulty. Participants are required to achieve a certain accuracy ratio in order to progress to the next level. This study asks whether the difficulty of the next level should be increased with priority on speed (reaction times) or with priority on accuracy of responses.

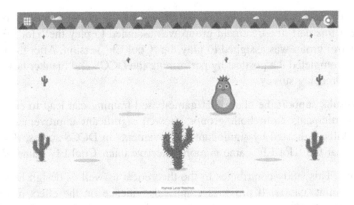

Fig. 4. EF training game *Gwakkamole* to train inhibition, Avocado with Spiky Helmet

The entire study was completed in approximately 50 min. Participants were randomly assigned to either speed or accuracy condition. In speed condition, game increases difficulty by increasing speed of the target. In accuracy condition, accuracy requirements increase by using higher percent accuracy criteria. Participants first completed a demographic survey and pretest measures of EF: Letters and Numbers (LN) task as a measure for working memory/updating [52], the Flanker task as a measure of inhibition [17] and the DCCS task as a measure of switching [61]. They then played the game for 20 min. Finally, they completed posttest LN, Flanker and DCCS tasks.

Results. The results revealed that playing the game significantly improved participant's EF skill overall. There was also a significant effect of age on EF gains, where younger participants demonstrating a substantially greater improvement from EF pre- to posttest than the older adolescent or adult participants. We also found an interaction effect of the EF pretest score and treatment group, which suggests that participants with lower prior EF scores benefited more from the speed condition while participants with higher prior EF scores benefited from the accuracy condition. Finally, computing the switching costs for the LN task, we found that participants with lower prior EF benefited more from accuracy condition, while participants with higher prior EF benefited more from the speed condition.

Conclusion. The results from this value-added study have theoretical as well as practical implications. On the theoretical side, they contribute to the EF literature by providing empirical evidence for the developmental nature of EF, as well as to the question which aspect of EF, speed v. accuracy, develops at which age. As practical implications, findings suggest that a focus on gradual increases in reaction time has a cognitive benefit for learners with lower EF, whereas those with higher EF benefit from increase in demands on accuracy.

6   General Discussion and Conclusion

The main message in this paper is that we want to highlight the usefulness of value-added research in the arsenal of designers of gaming experience where the goal goes beyond entertainment. We argued that a combination of a theory-based approach and a range of empirical methods has the potential to furnish insights that theory alone cannot provide. These insights can be used, as we have shown in our case examples, to increase the effectiveness of the game to achieve its intended goal. In our case, this goal was to increase the players' gains in executive functions, an important cognitive skill. We investigated three specific design factors that were included in the model of game-based learning (Fig. 1), but for which insufficient empirical research existed in order to make specific design decisions. In each case, the value-added research we conducted after ideation and playtesting research provided us with highly valuable insights that guided our design to improve the effectiveness of the game, often targeting learners with specific characteristics. One of the key benefits of this kind of research is that it does not only help with such practical design decisions, it also provided theoretical insights that contributed to the academic literature. Studies of this nature can therefore benefit the learning game design community on a theoretical as well as a practical level.

Acknowledgments. This work was partially supported by IES Grant R305A150417, "Focused Computer Games that Promote Executive Functions Skills, and by PSC-CUNY Award #60816-00 48: Virtual Reality and Emotional Design for the Development of Executive Functions in Adolescents.

References

1. Ahissar, M., Hochstein, S.: The reverse hierarchy theory of visual perceptual learning. Trends Cogn. Sci. **8**(10), 457–464 (2004)
2. Alexander, P.A., Judy, J.E.: The interaction of domain-specific and strategic knowledge in academic performance. Rev. Educ. Res. **58**(4), 375–404 (1988)
3. Alexander, M., Stuss, D.: Disorders of frontal lobe functioning. Semin. Neurol. **20**, 427–437 (2000)
4. Baddeley, A.D.: Exploring the central executive. Q. J. Exp. Psychol. **49A**, 5–28 (1996)
5. Biddiss, E., Irwin, J.: Active video games to promote physical activity in children and youth: a systematic review. Arch. Pediatr. Adolesc. Med. **164**(7), 664–672 (2010)
6. Blair, C., Razza, R.P.: Relating effortful control, executive function, and false belief understanding to emerging math and literacy ability in kindergarten. Child Dev. **78**(2), 647–663 (2007)
7. Blakemore, S.J., Choudhury, S.: Development of the adolescent brain: implications for executive function and social cognition. J. Child Psychol. Psychiatry **47**(3–4), 296–312 (2006)
8. Bogacz, R., Wagenmakers, E.J., Forstmann, B.U., Nieuwenhuis, S.: The neural basis of the speed–accuracy tradeoff. Trends Neurosci. **33**(1), 10–16 (2010)
9. Conati, C.: Probabilistic assessment of user's emotions in educational games. Appl. Artif. Intell. **16**(7–8), 555–575 (2002)

10. Conchas, G.: The Color of Success: Race and High Achieving Urban Youth. Teachers College Press, New York (2006)
11. Connolly, T.M., Boyle, E.A., MacArthur, E., Hainey, T., Boyle, J.M.: A systematic literature review of empirical evidence on computer games and serious games. Comput. Educ. **59**(2), 661–686 (2012)
12. Craig, S., Graesser, A., Sullins, J., Gholson, B.: Affect and learning: an exploratory look into the role of affect in learning with AutoTutor. J. Educ. Media **29**(3), 241–250 (2004)
13. Desimone, L.: Linking parent involvement with student achievement: do race and income matter. J. Educ. Res. **93**(1), 11–30 (1999)
14. Diamond, A.: Executive functions. Annu. Rev. Psychol. **64**, 135–168 (2013). https://doi.org/10.1146/annurev-psych-113011-143750
15. Diamond, A., Lee, K.: Interventions shown to aid executive function development in children 4 to 12 years old. Science **333**(6045), 959–964 (2011)
16. Eriksen, B.A., Eriksen, C.W.: Effects of noise letters upon the identification of a target letter in a nonsearch task. Atten. Percept. Psychophys. **16**(1), 143–149 (1974)
17. Eriksen, C.W.: The flankers task and response competition: a useful tool for investigating a variety of cognitive problems. Vis. Cogn. **2**(2–3), 101–118 (1995)
18. Friedman, N.P., Miyake, A., Young, S.E., Defries, J.C., Corley, R.P., Hewitt, J.K.: Individual differences in executive functions are almost entirely genetic in origin. J. Exp. Psychol. **137**(2), 201–225 (2009)
19. Fullerton, T.: Game Design Workshop: A Playcentric Approach to Creating Innovative Games. CRC Press, Boca Raton (2014)
20. Hedden, T., Yoon, C.: Individual differences in executive processing predict susceptibility to interference in verbal working memory. Neuropsychology **20**(5), 511–528 (2006)
21. Hoadley, C.M.: Methodological alignment in design-based research. Educ. Psychol. **39**(4), 203–212 (2004)
22. Holmes, J., Gathercole, S.E., Dunning, D.L.: Adaptive training leads to sustained enhancement of poor working memory in children. Dev. Sci. **12**(4), F9–F15 (2009)
23. Homer, B.D.: Using video games to enhance executive functions across the lifespan. In: Invited Symposium at Annual Meeting of the Jean Piaget Society, San Francisco (2017)
24. Huizinga, J.: Homo Ludens Versuch Einer Bestimmung des Spielelementest der Kultur. Pantheon Akademische Verlagsanstalt, Amsterdam (1939)
25. Isbister, K., Schaffer, N.: Game Usability: Advancing the Player Experience. CRC press, Boca Raton (2015)
26. Izard, C.E.: Basic emotions, natural kinds, emotion schemas, and a new paradigm. Perspect. Psychol. Sci. **2**, 260–280 (2007)
27. Klingberg, T., et al.: Computerized training of working memory in children with ADHD – a randomized, controlled, trial. J. Am. Acad. Child Adolesc. Psychiatry **44**(2), 177–186 (2005)
28. Lench, H.C., Flores, S.A., Bench, S.W.: Discrete emotions predict changes in cognition, judgment, experience, behavior, and physiology: a meta-analysis of experimental emotion elicitations. Psychol. Bull. **137**(5), 834–855 (2011)
29. MacKay, D.G.: The problems of flexibility, fluency, and speed–accuracy trade-off in skilled behavior. Psychol. Rev. **89**(5), 483 (1982)
30. Mayer, R.E.: Computer Games for Learning: An Evidence-Based Approach. MIT, Cambridge (2014)
31. Miller, M., Hinshaw, S.P.: Does childhood executive function predict adolescent functional outcomes in girls with ADHD? J. Abnorm. Child Psychol. **38**(3), 315–326 (2010)
32. Miyake, A., Friedman, N.P., Emerson, M.J., Witzki, A.H., Howerter, A., Wager, T.D.: The unity and diversity of executive functions and their contributions to complex "frontal lobe" tasks: a latent variable analysis. Cogn. Psychol. **41**(1), 49–100 (2000)

33. Morrison, A.B., Chein, J.M.: Does working memory training work? The promise and challenges of enhancing cognition by training working memory. Psychon. Bull. Rev. **18**(1), 46–60 (2011)
34. Mullane, J.C., Corkum, P.V., Klein, R.M., McLaughlin, E.: Interference control in children with and without ADHD: a systematic review of Flanker and Simon task performance. Child Neuropsychol. **15**(4), 321–342 (2009)
35. Nouchi, R., et al.: Brain training game improves executive functions and processing speed in the elderly: a randomized controlled trial. PLoS ONE **7**(1), e29676 (2012)
36. Owen, A.M., et al.: Putting brain training to the test. Nature **465**(7299), 775–778 (2010)
37. Papastergiou, M.: Exploring the potential of computer and video games for health and physical education: a literature review. Comput. Educ. **53**(3), 603–622 (2009)
38. Parong, J., Mayer, R.E., Fiorella, L., MacNamara, A., Homer, B.D., Plass, J.L.: Learning executive function skills by playing focused video games. Contemp. Educ. Psychol. **51**, 141–151 (2017)
39. Pekrun, R.: The impact of emotions on learning and achievement: towards a theory of cognitive/motivational mediators. Appl. Psychol. **41**(4), 359–376 (1992)
40. Peng, W., Lin, J.H., Crouse, J.: Is playing exergames really exercising? A meta-analysis of energy expenditure in active video games. Cyberpsychol. Behav. Soc. Netw. **14**(11), 681–688 (2011)
41. Picard, R.W.: Affective Computing. MIT Press, Cambridge (1997)
42. Plass, J.L., Homer, B.D.: Popular game mechanics as inspirations for learning mechanics and assessment mechanics. Paper Presented at the Game Developers Conference, 5–9 March 2012, San Francisco (2012)
43. Plass, J.L., Perlin, K., Nordlinger, J.: The games for learning institute: research on design patterns for effective educational games. Paper Presented at the Game Developers Conference, 9–13 March 2010, San Francisco (2010)
44. Plass, J.L., Heidig, S., Hayward, E.O., Homer, B.D., Um, E.: Emotional design in multimedia learning: effects of shape and color on affect and learning. Learn. Instr. **29**, 128–140 (2014)
45. Plass, J.L., Homer, B.D., Kinzer, C.K.: Foundations of game-based learning. Educ. Psychol. **50**(4), 258–283 (2015)
46. Plass, J.L., Kaplan, U.: Emotional design in digital media for learning. In: Emotions, Technology, Design, and Learning, pp. 131–161 (2015)
47. Plass, J.L.: A taxonomy of adaptivity in learning. In: Panel on Personalized and Adaptive Learning Systems, CRESSTCON 2016, Los Angeles, CA, 20 September 2016 (2016)
48. Plass, J.L.: Basing the design of cognitive skills training games on developmental psychology. In: Invited Symposium Using Video Games to Enhance Executive Functions Across the Lifespan, Annual Meeting of the Jean Piaget Society, San Francisco, CA (2017)
49. Powers, K.L., Brooks, P.J., Aldrich, N.J., Palladino, M.A., Alfieri, L.: Effects of video-game play on information processing: a meta-analytic investigation. Psychon. Bull. Rev. **20**(6), 1055–1079 (2013)
50. Primack, B.A., et al.: Role of video games in improving health-related outcomes: a systematic review. Am. J. Prev. Med. **42**(6), 630–638 (2012)
51. Qu, L., Wang, N., Johnson, W.L.: Detecting the learner's motivational states in an interactive learning environment. In: Looi, C.K., et al. (eds.) Artificial Intelligence in Education, pp. 547–554. IOS Press, Amsterdam (2005)
52. Rogers, R.D., Monsell, S.: Costs of a predictable switch between simple cognitive tasks. J. Exp. Psychol. Gen. **124**(2), 207–231 (1995)
53. Shah, J.J., Smith, S.M., Vargas-Hernandez, N.: Metrics for measuring ideation effectiveness. Des. Stud. **24**(2), 111–134 (2003)

54. Smith, E.E., Jonides, J.: Storage and executive processes in the frontal lobes. Science **283**, 1657–1661 (1999)
55. Squire, K.: Open-ended video games: a model for developing learning for the interactive age. In: Salen, K. (ed.) The John D. and Catherine T. MacArthur Foundation Series on Digital Media and Learning, pp. 167–198. MIT Press, Cambridge (2008)
56. Tobias, S.: Interest, prior knowledge, and learning. Rev. Educ. Res. **64**(1), 37–54 (1994)
57. Um, E., Plass, J.L., Hayward, E.O., Homer, B.D.: Emotional design in multimedia learning. J. Educ. Psychol. **104**(2), 485 (2012)
58. Von Bastian, C.C., Eschen, A.: Does working memory training have to be adaptive? Psychol. Res. **80**(2), 181–194 (2016)
59. Yeniad, N., Malda, M., Mesman, J., van IJzendoorn, M.H., Pieper, S.: Shifting ability predicts math and reading performance in children: a meta-analytical study. Learn. Individ. Differ. **23**, 1–9 (2013)
60. Young, S.E., et al.: Behavioral disinhibition: liability for externalizing spectrum disorders and its genetic and environmental relation to response inhibition across adolescence. J. Abnorm. Psychol. **118**(1), 117 (2009)
61. Zelazo, P.D.: The Dimensional Change Card Sort (DCCS): a method of assessing executive function in children. Nat. Protoc. **1**(1), 297 (2006)
62. Zelazo, P.D., Carlson, S.M.: Hot and cool executive function in childhood and adolescence: development and plasticity. Child. Dev. Perspect. **6**(4), 354–360 (2012)

Modeling Consumers' Observational Learning in Digital Gaming: A Conceptual Model

Amir Zaib Abbasi[1]([⊠]), Ding Hooi Ting[2], Helmut Hlavacs[3],
and Muhammad Shahzeb Fayyaz[2]

[1] Faculty of Management Sciences, Shaheed Zulfiqar Ali Bhutto Institute of
Science and Technology (SZABIST), Islamabad, Pakistan
amir_zaib_abbasi@yahoo.co.uk
[2] Department of Management and Humanities, Universiti Teknologi Petronas,
Bander Seri Iskander, 31750 Tronoh, Perak, Malaysia
[3] Research Group Entertainment Computing, University of Vienna,
Vienna, Austria

Abstract. The present study intends to develop a conceptual model predicting videogame consumers' observational learning that is initiated through the playful-consumption experience of a digital game. To meet this objective, authors employed the hedonic theory of consumption experience and observational learning theory to propose a conceptual model demonstrating that it is the gamer's playful-consumption experience of a digital game which actually influences videogame consumers to observe and learn from the digital game. This study is first among others as it takes the theoretical support from hedonic theory of consumption experience, particularly the playful-consumption experience in predicting the videogame consumers' observational learning in the videogame environment. The study is based on the conceptual model and hence, another empirical study is under way to prove its validation in the videogame setting.

Keywords: Hedonic theory · Playful-consumption experience
Observational learning · Digital game

1 Introduction

Pong was the initial videogame that was developed by Atari in 1972. The huge success of Pong stimulated a spate of competitors and Atari to develop the first-generation of home consoles comprising Magnavox Odyssey, Taito's Gunfight, and the Home Pong [1]. Since then, each consecutive generation of gaming-consoles has pushed the medium forward, with achieving various key milestones for instance, 3D graphics and etc. that have boomed the videogame industry [1]. Authors further added that the term videogame now covers many subgroups that have grown rapidly such as arcade games, PC games, mobile games etc.

In literature, there is no agreed definition of the term videogame that everyone needs to follow in his or her study. However, a number of videogame definitions can be found in a review study by Stenros [2] in which he discussed all possible definitions of

© Springer Nature Switzerland AG 2018
S. Göbel et al. (Eds.): JCSG 2018, LNCS 11243, pp. 159–168, 2018.
https://doi.org/10.1007/978-3-030-02762-9_16

a videogame. In this study, we follow the definition of a videogame given by Aarseth [3] as *games are facilitators that structure player behavior, and whose main purpose is enjoyment* [2]. A videogame means any digital game/electronic game that is played by a consumer/player on a personal computer, smartphone, tablet, handheld device or dedicated video gaming console. Aarseth [3] further added that a theory in videogame playing should focus on player behavior instead a videogame.

According to entertainment software association report, videogame has several genres such as action, shooter, arcade, strategy, role-playing, racing, arcade, adventure, flight, fighting, family entertainment, children's entertainment, causal, sports games and other videogames/compilations [4].

Recently, Jason Allaire, associate professor of psychology and co-director of the gains through gaming lab added that now all ages of people play video games irrespective of age and gender, meaning that can be your boss, grandparent, or even your institutional professor [4]. Therefore, it has become an essential part of our routine life. Katie Salen, executive director of institute of play, stated that videogames offer a wonderful platform to videogame consumers for play and learning [4]. This viewpoint is consistent with the definition of a videogame given by Aarseth [3] in two ways: first, both authors have believed that a videogame provides a platform, whereby consumers play or enjoy playing a videogame. Second, both authors have talked about learning or shaping player behavior that derive from videogame playing. In this study, authors followed this viewpoint and conducted extant reviews of literature to address prior studies that have investigated how videogame playing has impacted on player or consumer behavior.

During an extant review of literature, the study found two main communities of researchers: one community of scholars investigated the negative outcomes of videogame playing on player behavior. Their studies reported the following negative effects of videogame playing on player's behavior such as impulsivity, attention problems, sleep deficiency, risk-taking, academic performance, musculoskeletal health problems and increased food consumption [5–12]. While some studies examined the effects of violent game playing on consumer's aggressive behavior and their results were proven to have association with playing violent games and player's aggressive behavior [5, 6, 13–15]. Few other scholars measured the role of online game addiction and its detrimental efffects on consumer behavior and their findings showed that depression, academic achievement, and conduct problems were significant with online game-addiction [16].

Another community of researchers focused on the potential benefits of videogame playing on consumer's skills and behavior. Their findings stated that videogame playing increases prosocial behavior, skills in social-cooperation, motivation and strengthen the skills to continue at stages of failure, and also enhances visuospatial skills and social involvement, which in turn reduces the moods of depression [17–22].

However, the present study is different from earlier studies as we do not focus on the positive or negative aspects of videogame playing on gamers or consumer behavior. Instead, we mainly look into the learning process, especially the observational learning process that how videogame consumers actually observe and learn from the videogame environment. For this reason, we aim to use the hedonic theory of consumption experience as it can capture playful hedonic experiences comprising the imaginal, emotional, and sensory that originate from the computer-mediated settings such as videogames. More importantly, this theory is utilized to propose a conceptual model predicting videogame consumers' observational learning. The next section debates on the use of both theories such as hedonic theory of consumption experience and observational learning to develop a conceptual model.

2 Hedonic Theory of Consumption Experience

The article by Hirschman and Holbrook [23] is one of the earliest works to criticize the current literature for ignoring key facets of the consumption experience in the context of marketing and consumption. In their work, the authors coined the experiential aspects of consumption as being titled *"hedonic consumption"* to make the terminology distinct from the more recognized form of utilitarian consumption. Scholars have further argued that consumer behavior is not only restricted to buying decisions, but it also involves various and often important hedonic components *(fantasies, fun, and feelings)* which are derived from experiences when using products/services or even thinking about using products/services. Few studies have defined the term hedonic consumption as *"those features of consumer behavior that explain the multisensory, fantasy and emotive facets of one's experience with the product"* [23, 24]. Hence, hedonic consumption is described by fantasies, multisensory features, and emotional motives that are derived from the consumption of hedonic products. Several studies have explained that hedonic products are those goods that have the potential to arouse a consumer's feelings, fantasies, and multisensory aspects [25] and playing a videogame comes under the umbrella of hedonic products [26].

2.1 The Videogame is a Hedonic Product

According to Marchand and Hennig-Thurau [21], videogames are defined as hedonic products, as their playful consumption involves emotional responses, constructs imaginary, and entails the multisensory aspects. Voss et al. [27] also classified videogames as high-hedonic/low-utilitarian products. Some studies have conceptualized videogames as being interactive and computer-mediated structures, which facilitating the experience of videogame play [28, 29]. The experience of videogame play is also explained by Salem and Zimmerman [30] as *"playing a videogame is truly considered as experiencing a videogame."* However in the literature of marketing and videogame, a few scholars [28, 31–33] have conceptualized the videogame playing experience as playful-consumption experience.

2.2 Playful Consumption Experience

In the field of hedonic consumption, consumer scholars have revealed the importance of theorizing the playful-consumption and defined the construct of playful consumption as "intrinsically motivating, active and self-based consumer behavior" that is executed for its own sake and pleasure [23, 28, 31, 34]. Moreover, these scholars have also stated that such playful-consumption behavior also involves the three main playful hedonic experiences feelings, sensory and fantasy arising from the consumption of hedonic products. In their seminal article, Holbrook, et al. [31] argued that playful-consumption falls into the broad category of intrinsically motivated consumer behavior comprising hobbies, esthetic appreciation, creativity, sports, and games. Most recently, Buchanan-Oliver and Seo [28] have reported that the perspective of playful-consumption has become mainly important for the unique kinds of play, which is facilitated by computer-mediated settings such as videogames.

In the field of marketing and videogame literature, few studies have conceptualized the act of playing a videogame as playful-consumption experience [28, 31, 34]. Therefore, this study follows the definition of playful-consumption given by these scholars [28, 31, 34] and define as playful-consumption experience is an intrinsically, motivating, active, and self-based videogame playing behavior that is executed for a player's own sake and pleasure, which in turn involves a player to get playful hedonic experiences (feelings, sensory and fantasy) [33].

In literature, Wu and Holsapple [35] were the first authors who applied the hedonic theory of consumption experience, especially the role of imaginal and emotional experiences in predicting the system-use behavior but they ignored to study sensory experience in their research. Later, we have found another study in which they have shown the importance of gamers' playful-consumption experiences of a digital game comprising imaginal, emotional, and sensory experience influencing on multiple engagement states (cognitive, affective, and behavioral) of consumer videogame engagement [36]. More recently, the authors have proposed another conceptual model demonstrating that it is the player's overall playful-consumption experience of a digital game which influences on the overall consumer videogame engagement [32]. After reviewing both studies, we have found that one study has focused on the sub-dimensions of constructs and whereas, the other study has only emphasized on the use of higher-order level of constructs.

In another study by Mukherjee et al. [34] added that playful-consumption experience of digital gaming influences players' mastery, skill development, and learning. Several other studies have also stated that gaming experience has the potential to impact on players' decision-making processes, thought and learning and to enhance gamer's knowledge, problem solving and learning skills [37–39]. Through previous studies, it has been proven that videogame playing experience is a source of player's learning. Therefore, this study develops a hypothesis stating that videogame consumers interact with digital gaming environment and attain their playful-consumption experience of gaming, which in turn provide them an opportunity to observe and learn though videogame elements.

H_1: *Playful-consumption experience of gaming positively influences consumers' observational learning.*

3   The Theory of Observational Learning

The observational learning theory is originated from the stimulus-response (S-R) behaviorist psychology which is termed as social learning theory by Albert Bandura and his colleagues in the period of 1960s [40–42]. As per this theory, people learn actions or behaviors via noticing the model and then repeating the learnt actions in either the exact manner or in the new shape of a behavior. Authors consider the social learning theory as a comprehensive model to realize a human behavior [43]. We in this study, mainly emphasis on the use of observational learning theory and its basics to understand the modeling process in digital gaming context.

According to observational learning theory, behavioral responses are instigated through modeling-based stimulus [40, 44]. Within this theory, there are three main modeling-based stimulus comprising direct, verbal, and symbolic-based modeling. In symbolic-based modeling, individuals learn a behavior through observing a behavior that is portrayed in the media which comprise television, movie, dramas, videogame and etc. In this paper, we have a focal concern with the symbolic-based modeling using a videogame as a medium.

3.1 Video Games as Symbolic-Based Modeling

The main justification for selecting a videogame as symbolic-based modeling is, videogame product is created for pleasure, fun, and entertainment purposes [45]. Despite having the pleasure oriented attributes of digital gaming, a videogame playing has the ability to hold consumers for longer duration and hence, capturing their whole attention [46]. It has been witnessed that when consumers gain playful-consumption experience of a videogame, they get involved in the videogame environment that they consider themselves as a main role player in the videogame [46]. This in turn, influences consumers to play videogames for longer span of time [46]. Such a longer engagement in videogames help consumers learn via noticing the models portrayed in videogame settings [40].

This is due to the fact that nowadays every videogame has story-based environment whereby different role-plays or characters are involved which have become the basis for gamers to learn through the observation of models [45] and hence, impacting the behavioral learning in forms of behaviors, skills or knowledge acquisition [47].

4   Hypothesis Development

Korkealehto and Siklander [48] have also discussed that videogames and technologies are capable of triggering players' attention and increasing their motivation level, which in turn influence the players to learn from videogames. For instance, Zarzycka-Piskorz [49] applied the use of language games to assess whether the students were able to learn the language and authors found the satisfactory results. The playful-consumption experience of a videogame is one of the triggers that can engage and motivate videogame consumers to learn from videogame contents that are accessible via a range of narratives, virtual characters, environments, and multimedia elements [49, 50]. Abdul Jabbar and Felicia [50] further added that such videogame related elements are integrated to gain players' attention and interest. As a result, players' engagement in videogame playing is initiated and due to which they get more opportunities to observe and learn from videogame elements.

Few other authors have stated that the playful-consumption experience of a videogame is one of the important elements of human development and vital for human cultural advancement [51]. Coyne et al. [52] have studied the co-playing digital games with family outcomes, and the authors resulted that gamers have developed their prosocial behaviour. Baabdullah [53] has evidenced that videogames now provide a platform through which many players get interacted, learn from other players, and enhance social relationships among players. Several authors have debated that the playful experience of educational videogames has generated positive learning outcomes, especially in the literacy learning [54], in science [55], and mathematics [56].

The common thing we have noticed in the above studies is, the playful-consumption experience of a videogame is producing some kinds of learning but how such learning is initiated in videogame playing has never been discussed by any studies. Hence, the current study is interested in developing a conceptual model to explicate the learning process in videogame literature. For this purpose, the conceptual model as shown in Fig. 1, has developed with the help of playful-consumption experience and observational learning theories. Utilizing both theories, we have proposed a conceptual model stating that when videogame consumers interact with a digital game environment and they gain playful-consumption experience of a videogame play. Their playful-consumption experience further provides them with an opportunity to observe and learn through videogame elements. On this basis, we have developed the hypothesis stating that videogame consumers' observational learning is instigated through playful-consumption experience of a videogame.

Fig. 1. Modeling videogame consumer's observational learning

5 Conclusions

In this study, authors observed that many studies have been conducted on either positive or negative changes on the gamer's behavior in form of personality traits. However, it has never been discussed that how such a change actually happen in the gamers' behavior. We have motivated from this point and aimed to develop a conceptual model that can illustrate the process of change or learning in the gamers' behavior. A conceptual model has been developed on the basis of hedonic theory of consumption experience and observational learning theory. Within the hedonic theory of consumption experience, we took the aspect of playful-consumption experience of a videogame in predicting consumers' observational learning in the videogame environment. While using the observational learning theory, we focused on the symbolic-based learning that occurs through observing the models shown in the videogame play. On the basis of both theories, we have developed a conceptual model that with gaining the playful-consumption experience of a digital game, consumers get an opportunity to observe the models such as role-plays, characters or story-based environment as shown in the videogame environment and learn either the same behavior or new pattern of the behavior.

6 Contribution and Future Work

This study contributes to almost every single study that has previously stated that videogame playing has positive and negative changes. For instance; authors found that videogame playing has adverse effects on teenagers' behavior such as aggressive behavior [14, 57, 58]. These studies have only shown that teenagers become more aggressive with playing videogames but these studies have not shown any mechanism through which such a change occur in the gamers' behavior. However, our conceptual model has the potential to contribute in their studies through giving an overview of the learning process that may have incurred during the videogame play. Teenagers may have gained the playful-consumption experience of a videogame that has violent content related things. During the videogame play, teenagers may have observed the models such as characters, role-plays or story-based environment performing the violent related behaviors, which in turn may have caused gamers to act either in the same manner or a new pattern of the behavior such as aggressive thoughts or behavior. Our study conceptual is applicable to every single videogame that is bringing a change in the gamers' behavior. Entertainment industry can adopt this conceptual model to bring a change in the gamers' behavior, especially in accordance to the developers' mindset. The present study is a conceptual study and therefore, a future empirical study is required to validate the conceptual model.

References

1. Kuo, A., Hiler, J.L., Lutz, R.J.: From Super Mario to Skyrim: a framework for the evolution of video game consumption. J. Consum. Behav. **16**, 101–120 (2017)
2. Stenros, J.: The game definition game a review. Games Cult. (2016). https://doi.org/10.1177/1555412016655679
3. Aarseth, E.: I fought the law: transgressive play and the implied player. In: Situated Play, Proceedings of DiGRA, pp. 24–28 (2007)
4. ESA: Essential Facts About the Computer and Video Game Industry. Entertainment Software Association (2014)
5. Anderson, C.A., Dill, K.E.: Video games and aggressive thoughts, feelings, and behavior in the laboratory and in life. J. Pers. Soc. Psychol. **78**, 772 (2000)
6. Gentile, D.A., Lynch, P.J., Linder, J.R., Walsh, D.A.: The effects of violent video game habits on adolescent hostility, aggressive behaviors, and school performance. J. Adolesc. **27**, 5–22 (2004)

7. Jaruratanasirikul, S., Wongwaitaweewong, K., Sangsupawanich, P.: Electronic game play and school performance of adolescents in Southern Thailand. Cyberpsychol. Behav. **12**, 509–512 (2009)
8. Chaput, J.-P., Visby, T., Nyby, S., Klingenberg, L., Gregersen, N.T., Tremblay, A., et al.: Video game playing increases food intake in adolescents: a randomized crossover study. Am. J. Clin. Nutr. **93**, 1196–1203 (2011)
9. Gentile, D.A., Swing, E.L., Lim, C.G., Khoo, A.: Video game playing, attention problems, and impulsiveness: evidence of bidirectional causality. Psychol. Popul. Media Cult. **1**, 62 (2012)
10. Lui, D.P., Szeto, G.P., Jones, A.Y.: The pattern of electronic game use and related bodily discomfort in Hong Kong primary school children. Comput. Educ. **57**, 1665–1674 (2011)
11. Nakatsu, R., Rauterberg, M., Ciancarini, P.: Handbook of Digital Games and Entertainment Technologies. Springer, Heidelberg (2017). https://doi.org/10.1007/978-981-4560-50-4
12. Tazawa, Y., Okada, K.: Physical signs associated with excessive television-game playing and sleep deprivation. Pediatr. Int. **43**, 647–650 (2001)
13. Anderson, C.A., et al.: Violent video game effects on aggression, empathy, and prosocial behavior in eastern and western countries: a meta-analytic review. American Psychological Association (2010)
14. Busching, R., Krahé, B.: Charging neutral cues with aggressive meaning through violent video game play. Societies **3**, 445–456 (2013)
15. Kumarasuriar, V., Pangiras, G., Sinnapan, S., Koran, S.: A study of the relationship between violent video game playing and aggression among adolescents in the Klang Valley, Malaysia, vol. 20, pp. 74–79 (2011)
16. Brunborg, G.S., Mentzoni, R.A., Frøyland, L.R.: Is video gaming, or video game addiction, associated with depression, academic achievement, heavy episodic drinking, or conduct problems? J. Behav. Addict. **3**, 27–32 (2014)
17. Brooks, F.M., Chester, K.L., Smeeton, N.C., Spencer, N.H.: Video gaming in adolescence: factors associated with leisure time use. J. Youth Stud. **19**, 36–54 (2016)
18. Ferguson, C.J., Rueda, S.M.: The hitman study. Eur. Psychol. **15**, 99–108 (2010)
19. Gentile, D.A., Anderson, C.A., Yukawa, S., Ihori, N., Saleem, M., Ming, L.K., et al.: The effects of prosocial video games on prosocial behaviors: international evidence from correlational, longitudinal, and experimental studies. Pers. Soc. Psychol. Bull. **35**, 752–763 (2009)
20. Granic, I., Lobel, A., Engels, R.C.: The benefits of playing video games. Am. Psychol. **69**, 66 (2014)
21. Marchand, A., Hennig-Thurau, T.: Value creation in the video game industry: industry economics, consumer benefits, and research opportunities. J. Interact. Mark. **27**, 141–157 (2013)
22. Sweetser, P., Wyeth, P.: GameFlow: a model for evaluating player enjoyment in games. Comput. Entertain. (CIE) **3**, 3 (2005)
23. Hirschman, E.C., Holbrook, M.B.: Hedonic consumption: emerging concepts, methods and propositions. J. Mark. **46**, 92–101 (1982)
24. Alba, J.W., Williams, E.F.: Pleasure principles: a review of research on hedonic consumption. J. Consum. Psychol. **23**, 2–18 (2013)
25. Zhong, J.Y., Mitchell, V.-W.: A mechanism model of the effect of hedonic product consumption on well-being. J. Consum. Psychol. **20**, 152–162 (2010)
26. Venkatesh, V., Brown, S.A.: A longitudinal investigation of personal computers in homes: adoption determinants and emerging challenges. MIS Q. **25**, 71–102 (2001)
27. Voss, K.E., Spangenberg, E.R., Grohmann, B.: Measuring the hedonic and utilitarian dimensions of consumer attitude. J. Mark. Res. **40**, 310–320 (2003)

28. Buchanan-Oliver, M., Seo, Y.: Play as co-created narrative in computer game consumption: the hero's journey in Warcraft III. J. Consum. Behav. **11**, 423–431 (2012)
29. Eskelinen, M.: Towards computer game studies. Digit. Creat. **12**, 175–183 (2001)
30. Salem, K., Zimmerman, E.: Rules of Play. MIT Press, Cambridge (2004)
31. Holbrook, M.B., Chestnut, R.W., Oliva, T.A., Greenleaf, E.A.: Play as a consumption experience: the roles of emotions, performance, and personality in the enjoyment of games. J. Consum. Res. **11**, 728–739 (1984)
32. Abbasi, A.Z., Abu Baker, S.A.J.: Playful-consumption experience of videogame-play influences consumer video-game engagement: a conceptual model. Glob. Bus. Manag. Res.: Int. J. **9**, 9 (2017)
33. Abbasi, A.Z., Ting, D.H., Hlavacs, H.: Playful-consumption experience in digital game playing: a scale development. In: Munekata, N., Kunita, I., Hoshino, J. (eds.) ICEC 2017. LNCS, vol. 10507, pp. 290–296. Springer, Cham (2017). https://doi.org/10.1007/978-3-319-66715-7_32
34. Mukherjee, S., Mukherjee, S., Lau-Gesk, L., Lau-Gesk, L.: Retrospective evaluations of playful experiences. J. Consum. Mark. **33**, 387–395 (2016)
35. Wu, J., Holsapple, C.: Imaginal and emotional experiences in pleasure-oriented IT usage: a hedonic consumption perspective. Inf. Manag. **51**, 80–92 (2014)
36. Abbasi, A.Z., Ting, D.H., Hlavacs, H.: Proposing a new conceptual model predicting consumer videogame engagement triggered through playful-consumption experiences. In: Wallner, G., Kriglstein, S., Hlavacs, H., Malaka, R., Lugmayr, A., Yang, H.-S. (eds.) ICEC 2016. LNCS, vol. 9926, pp. 126–134. Springer, Cham (2016). https://doi.org/10.1007/978-3-319-46100-7_11
37. Qian, M., Clark, K.R.: Game-based learning and 21st century skills: a review of recent research. Comput. Hum. Behav. **63**, 50–58 (2016)
38. von Gillern, S.: The gamer response and decision framework a tool for understanding video gameplay experiences. Simul. Gaming **47**, 666–683 (2016)
39. Griffiths, M.D., McLean, L.: Content effects: online and offline games. In: The International Encyclopedia of Media Effects (2017)
40. Bandura, A.: Social Foundations of Thought and Action, vol. 1986. Prentice Hall, Englewood Cliffs (1986)
41. Bandura, A.: Observational learning. Encycl. Learn. Mem. **2**, 482–484 (2003)
42. Bandura, A., McClelland, D.C.: Social learning theory (1977)
43. Lee, D., LaRose, R.: A socio-cognitive model of video game usage. J. Broadcast. Electron. Media **51**, 632–650 (2007)
44. Yi, M.Y., Davis, F.D.: Developing and validating an observational learning model of computer software training and skill acquisition. Inf. Syst. Res. **14**, 146–169 (2003)
45. Abbasi, A.Z., Ting, D.H., Jamek, A.B.S.A.: An integrated conceptual model for predicting behavioral learning triggered by video-game engagement: a mediating role of observational learning. Game Phys. Mech. Int. Conf. (GAMEPEC) **2015**, 11–15 (2015)
46. Baranowski, T., Buday, R., Thompson, D.I., Baranowski, J.: Playing for real: video games and stories for health-related behavior change. Am. J. Prev. Med. **34**, 74–82. e10 (2008)
47. Garris, R., Ahlers, R., Driskell, J.E.: Games, motivation, and learning: a research and practice model. Simul. Gaming **33**, 441–467 (2002)
48. Korkealehto, K., Siklander, P.: Enhancing engagement, enjoyment and learning experiences through gamification on an English course for health care students. Seminar. net **14**, 13–30 (2018)
49. Zarzycka-Piskorz, E.: Kahoot it or not? can games be motivating in learning grammar? Teach. Engl. Technol. **16**, 17–36 (2016)

50. Abdul Jabbar, A.I., Felicia, P.: Gameplay engagement and learning in game-based learning: a systematic review. Rev. Educ. Res. **85**, 740–779 (2015)
51. Pecchioni, L.L., Osmanovic, S.: Play it again, grandma: effect of intergenerational video gaming on family closeness. In: Zhou, J., Salvendy, G. (eds.) ITAP 2018. LNCS, vol. 10926, pp. 518–531. Springer, Cham (2018). https://doi.org/10.1007/978-3-319-92034-4_39
52. Coyne, S.M., Padilla-Walker, L.M., Stockdale, L., Day, R.D.: Game on… girls: associations between co-playing video games and adolescent behavioral and family outcomes. J. Adolesc. Health **49**, 160–165 (2011)
53. Baabdullah, A.M.: Factors influencing adoption of mobile social network games (M-SNGs): The Role of awareness. Inf. Syst. Front., 1–17 (2018)
54. Schmitt, K.L., Hurwitz, L.B., Duel, L.S., Linebarger, D.L.N.: Learning through play: the impact of web-based games on early literacy development. Comput. Hum. Behav. **81**, 378–389 (2018)
55. Herodotou, C.: Mobile games and science learning: a comparative study of 4 and 5 years old playing the game Angry Birds. Br. J. Educ. Technol. **49**, 6–16 (2018)
56. McLaren, B.M., Adams, D.M., Mayer, R.E., Forlizzi, J.: A computer-based game that promotes mathematics learning more than a conventional approach. In: Gamification in Education: Breakthroughs in Research and Practice, pp. 415–437. IGI Global (2018)
57. Anderson, C.A., Bushman, B.J.: Effects of violent video games on aggressive behavior, aggressive cognition, aggressive affect, physiological arousal, and prosocial behavior: a meta-analytic review of the scientific literature. Psychol. Sci. **12**, 353–359 (2001)
58. Elson, M., Ferguson, C.J.: Twenty-five years of research on violence in digital games and aggression. Eur. Psychol. **19**, 47 (2014)

Design of a BCI Controlled Serious Game
for Concentration Training

Augusto Garcia-Agundez[✉], Eduard Dobermann, and Stefan Göbel

Multimedia Communications Lab, Technische Universitaet, Darmstadt, Germany
{Augusto.garcia,stefan.goebel}@kom.tu-darmstadt.de

Abstract. The goal of this work is to design a BCI that can then be used to control a serious game for concentration training. A 32-Electrode cap system was used, in addition to a bandpass and notch filter, t-SNE dimension reduction, standard deviation outlier detection as well as a SVM classifier. A maximum classification accuracy of 80% was achieved when using a four class classification system. Our BCI-Controlled Serious Game is viable and we thus plan to evaluate our application in a pilot test.

Keywords: BCI · Serious Games · Concentration · Games for health
EEG

1 Introduction and Related Work

A brain-computer interface (BCI) is a system able to interpret the brain activity and issue corresponding control commands for a certain application, in our case, a serious game. Serious Games is a term used for video games that pursue a characterizing goal besides entertainment within a certain application area, for example, promoting health (Göbel et al. 2010) or cognitive remediation (Garcia-Agundez et al. 2017). Considering that the brain can be affected by mental exercise, for example with meditation, (Malinowski 2013), a BCI serious game may be used for training purposes, for example, increasing concentration. The goal of the present work is to develop a BCI to control a serious game designed for concentration training.

There are already several Game-based BCIs available. For example, the game "Brain Arena" (Bonnet et al. 2013) is a collaborative/competitive BCI football game. The goal of this game is to control a ball towards a target by imagining hand movements. The extraction of features is realized with Common Spatial Pattern (CSP). (Coyle et al. 2011) generated an automatic method for parameter search. In addition, they added a data recording technology to the BCI, based on a spaceship game. In it, the goal is to dodge asteroids by moving a spaceship. While playing the assignment of data to the classes is performed and both are recorded. Another BCI system (Belkacem et al. 2015) extracted EOG signals from a two-sensor EEG and uses them for the control of a 2D Plattformer game. The purpose of the game is to dodge meteors with an avatar.

Regarding signal processing methods, several procedures can be used to improve EEG signal quality. Outlier detection seems necessary to filter muscular movements,

S. Göbel et al. (Eds.): JCSG 2018, LNCS 11243, pp. 169–174, 2018.
https://doi.org/10.1007/978-3-030-02762-9_17

which may be removed by using the standard deviation factor method or a moving average filter (Leys et al. 2013). Afterwards, dimension reduction may improve accuracy. For this purpose, parametric t-SNE (t-Distributed Stochastic Neighbor Embedding), as suggested by (Li et al. 2016), may be applied, since it provides better results than Principal Component Analysis or no dimension reduction at all. For feature extraction, relative energy (Amin et al. 2015), static Energy (Li et al. 2016) and Fast Fourier Transform (FFT) features (Akin 2002) may provide good results. For the final classification, Support vector machines (SVM) seem to be an optimal approach (Alomari et al. 2013).

2 Methods

In order to capture the EEG, we used the USBAmp biosignal amplifier system designed by g.Tec with a 32-electrode wearable cap using the 10–20 system (Ramadan and Vasilakos 2017), acquiring data with the Matlab Simulink software. The data is filtered with a 50 Hz notch filter and a bandpass filter with cutoff frequencies of 0.5 and 60 Hz. Once processed, we tested several postprocessing techniques: Outlier detection, dimension reduction, feature extraction, and finally classification.

We implemented the standard deviation method suggested by (Leys et al. 2013) as well as a moving average filter. For feature extraction, we implemented t-SNE from (Li et al. 2016) in combination with the wavelet transform method (Amin et al. 2015). Finally, we focused on all three sets of features: Relative Energy, Static Energy as well as FFT. We decided to implement SVM for classification, and compare it to two other methods, Multilayer Perceptron (MLP) and Random Forests (RF).

Once the methods were decided upon, we programmed an application in Java for data collection and visualization, following the work of (Bernard et al. 2016). This tool implements the Weka machine learning algorithms, t-SNE and the Wavelet/Fast Fourier Transform implementation presented on (Scheiblich et al. 2011). This application allows us to study different parameters of the data processing, as well as training and classification. The training and test data are assembled and tested in a cross-consolidation.

To determine the viability of our approach, we wanted to study the accuracy of designing a game that uses up to eight classes. That is seven possible commands, and a neutral state. We implemented orders for controlling each of the four limbs (left arm, right arm, left leg, right leg), a combination of two of them (both arms, both legs) as well as an "extra action". A total of five users, two male, participated in our evaluation, we thus performed 5-fold cross validation on the captured data.

Recording was performed following a pattern of a two-second relaxation phase and a five-second recording period. Motion stimuli are to be prevented during the relaxation phase. At the start of the recording phase, a symbol is presented to represent one of the eight chosen classes, positioned accordingly. For example, the class "left hand" would be represented by a left hand displayed towards the left of the screen to allow for an intuitive recognition. After a test run, each class was presented five times following a random pattern. Between recordings, users could rest shortly.

We began our result analysis by testing the ideal duration of both reaction time (from 0 to 1000 ms) and interval length of the EEG signal window (from 250 to 4000 ms). We found interval length works best from two seconds onwards, and has a significant impact on final accuracy. Reaction times show no fundamental impact on accuracy. Therefore, we chose an interval time of two seconds and reaction time of 0.2 s. Regarding outlier detection, we tested a moving average filter with 0 to 25 data elements, but it did not have any impact on accuracy on either the static or relative energy features. On the other hand, the standard deviation factor method does improve accuracy by up to 4%. We decided to classify an element as an outlier with a standard deviation factor of 2.

The static energy features provide the best results in average. The Fourier transform energy features perform better than the relative energy features, but considering both methods perform worse than static energy and take significantly more time to extract, it seems using stating energy features exclusively is the best option.

We thus proceeded to evaluate the classifiers. These were tested with parameters in an interval through several iterations. In each iteration, an interval for a parameter with an appropriate step size was evaluated according to the data of all volunteers. The parameter with the best result was firmly held-for the next iteration, and another parameter was tested. If all influential parameters are passed through the test, a small interval was selected and tested. For the SVM, both the PUK kernel and RBF kernel were tested in addition to the preset poly kernel. However, the SVM showed better results with the poly kernel. Thus, SVM with default Weka parameters seems to be the best candidate for this application. Maximum achieved accuracies were 73.3% for both RF and MLP and 80% for SVM.

To conclude our evaluation, we tested the accuracy when considering different classes with the design decisions made so far. Results are presented on Fig. 1. As expected, accuracy is reduced as the number of classes increase. For this particular case, accuracy is around 55–57% on average when considering two classes (plus the neutral state), 43–45% when considering three, 31% for four classes and 29% for five classes. There are significant differences depending on which class we choose, for example when considering "both hands", "both feet" and "tongue" we can achieve an average accuracy of 80%.

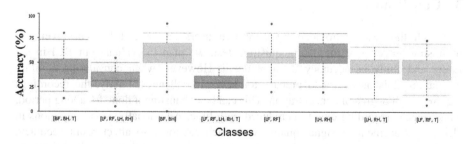

Fig. 1. Evaluation of different class compositions. (T: Tongue, BF: Both Feet, BH: Both Hands, L and R are left and right respectively)

Considering game development, a simple game with intuitive controls is the best approach in order to minimize distractions and cognitive load. In addition, players should be given time for reflection between actions that do not affect the game, as they may be misinterpreted by the BCI. Following these ideas, we conceived a climbing game where the user controls a frog avatar and is required to choose different limb combinations in order to continue climbing. As an "extra" action, the frog can eat flies with its tongue when they are on the way. The limbs have a maximum distance allowed between each other in order to limit the possible options to climb further, this ensures players have to think of different commands in order to progress further and also ensures the classifier is processing the orders accurately (Fig. 2).

Fig. 2. Image capture of the game. The UI is as minimal as possible to avoid distractions.

To indicate to the player when the recording is in progress, the frog torso for that period is colored gray. During movement or preparation time, the frog retains its green color. Finally, new orders during an ongoing movement of the limbs are not processed. In order to evaluate game progress, a score is calculated as a sum of correct movements and flies eaten. This number of points is designed to be used for a future evaluation, since a higher score means the player was able to progress further.

3 Conclusions

Although the results provided by only five users are indeed limited, given the promising outcome of the data acquisition test, we plan to evaluate our BCI in the future and study its accuracy in more detail. However, when considering a future evaluation, it is necessary to prepare for several challenges. Firstly, the recordings require a high degree of concentration. This can be exhausting if done for a long period, which means recording quality is reduced with time. Additionally, small variations in electrode placement or signal quality with each session also affect result accuracy. Thirdly, the conductive gel used on the electrodes dries over time, which also affects signal quality. For these reasons it is necessary to capture all training data in one session. The recording time for the training data was approximately 10.5 min, during which we could approximately capture 70 records per class, which should suffice to obtain acceptable quality.

Another important limitation of the present BCI system is that a parameter to determine the quality of the BCI system is required. In this sense, related work stresses the importance of user training and BCI usage as a trainable skill (McFarland and Wolpaw 2018). We chose the game score purposely as means to be able to calculate player progress and progress speed, and use these variables as a measure of BCI accuracy. In order for the game to have any impact on concentration, follow-up evaluations on the same subjects over a longer period of time will be required. Comparing the individual evaluations using time series parameters would then provide an indicator of the improvement in concentration.

References

Akin, M.: Comparison of wavelet transform and FFT methods in the analysis of EEG signals. J. Med. Syst. **26**(3), 241–247 (2002)

Alomari, M.H., Samaha, A., AlKamha, K.: Automated classification of L/R hand movement EEG signals using advanced feature extraction and machine learning. arXiv preprint arXiv: 1312.2877 (2013)

Amin, H.U., et al.: Feature extraction and classification for EEG signals using wavelet transform and machine learning techniques. Australas. Phys. Eng. Sci. Med. **38**(1), 139–149 (2015)

Belkacem, A.N., et al.: Real-time control of a video game using eye movements and two temporal EEG sensors. Comput. Intell. Neurosci. **2015**, 1 (2015)

Bernard, J., Dobermann, E., Bögl, M., Röhlig, M., Vögele, A., Kohlhammer, J.: Visual-interactive segmentation of multivariate time series. Paper Presented at the EuroVis Workshop on Visual Analytics (EuroVA). Eurographics (2016)

Bonnet, L., Lotte, F., Lécuyer, A.: Two brains, one game: design and evaluation of a multiuser BCI video game based on motor imagery. IEEE Trans. Comput. Intell. AI Games **5**(2), 185–198 (2013)

Coyle, D., Garcia, J., Satti, A.R., McGinnity, T.M.: EEG-based continuous control of a game using a 3 channel motor imagery BCI: BCI game. Paper Presented at the 2011 IEEE Symposium on Computational Intelligence, Cognitive Algorithms, Mind, and Brain (CCMB) (2011)

Garcia-Agundez, A., Folkerts, A.-K., Konrad, R., Caseman, P., Göbel, S., Kalbe, E.: PDDanceCity: an exergame for patients with idiopathic Parkinson's disease and cognitive impairment. Mensch und Computer 2017-Tagungsband (2017)

Göbel, S., Hardy, S., Wendel, V., Mehm, F., Steinmetz, R.: Serious games for health: personalized exergames. Paper Presented at the Proceedings of the 18th ACM International Conference on Multimedia (2010)

Leys, C., Ley, C., Klein, O., Bernard, P., Licata, L.: Detecting outliers: do not use standard deviation around the mean, use absolute deviation around the median. J. Exp. Soc. Psychol. **49**(4), 764–766 (2013)

Li, M.-A., Luo, X.-Y., Yang, J.-F.: Extracting the nonlinear features of motor imagery EEG using parametric t-SNE. Neurocomputing **218**, 371–381 (2016)

Malinowski, P.: Neural mechanisms of attentional control in mindfulness meditation. Front. Neurosci. **7**, 8 (2013)

McFarland, D.J., Wolpaw, J.R.: Brain–computer interface use is a skill that user and system acquire together. PLoS Biol. **16**(7), e2006719 (2018)

Ramadan, R.A., Vasilakos, A.V.: Brain computer interface: control signals review. Neurocomputing **223**, 26–44 (2017)

Scheiblich, C., Banucu, R., Reinauer, V., Albert, J., Rucker, W.M.: Parallel hierarchical block wavelet compression for an optimal compression of 3-D BEM problems. IEEE Trans. Magn. **47**(5), 1386–1389 (2011)

A Concept of a Training Environment for Police Using VR Game Technology

Polona Caserman$^{(\boxtimes)}$ (ID), Miriam Cornel, Michelle Dieter, and Stefan Göbel

Multimedia Communications Lab - KOM, Technische Universität Darmstadt,
Darmstadt, Germany
{polona.caserman,stefan.gobel}@kom.tu-darmstadt.de,
{miriam.cornel,michelle.dieter}@stud.tu-darmstadt.de

Abstract. Serious games and simulations can be used to support or supplement training, especially when training scenarios are too complex. With the novel Virtual Reality technology, training can be partially replaced and complemented by a virtual environment. This paper focuses primarily on the design of the police training. The requirements for the serious game were raised in cooperation with policemen. A virtual training environment for traffic control was developed. The initial user evaluation revealed importance of full-body tracking and intelligent virtual agents. Due to the variability of the training scenario, the effectiveness can be increased and the skills learned within the serious games are transferable to the real work tasks.

Keywords: Serious games · Training environment
Police traffic control · Immersive virtual reality

1 Introduction

Traditional emergency training is complex, costly, and often includes only a small variety of scenarios [1]. With the novel Virtual Reality (VR) technologies, new possibilities arise to train certain action sequences and procedures in the virtual environment, that are not always possible in the current existing training. Head-Mounted Displays (HMDs), such as HTC Vive or Oculus Rift enable external tracking, creating a full 360° immersion and allowing the user to physically move in a large area. Recent studies provide significant evidence that room-scale VR games lead to a higher immersion [9].

Due to recent improvements in VR, not only game industry but also the government and corporate organizations can benefit from the training environment that serious games provide [10]. Serious games are digital games that are designed to entertain and have an additional characterizing goal (e.g., a learning/training effect) [4]. Safe VR-based training environments allow making mistakes without serious consequences in order to gather experiences, that help to avoid bad decisions in the future [3,6]. In comparison with the traditional training, virtual environments have various advantages, e.g., they are less expensive,

© Springer Nature Switzerland AG 2018
S. Göbel et al. (Eds.): JCSG 2018, LNCS 11243, pp. 175–181, 2018.
https://doi.org/10.1007/978-3-030-02762-9_18

can be easily set up and training sessions can be performed even when the team members are geographically far apart [3]. Playful training and simulations are a major field of serious games, mainly used for collaborative training, e.g., military training [10], police training [1,6], and crime scene investigation [3,5]. Moreover, previous studies reported that intelligent virtual agents in training environments are helpful, e.g., for leadership training and decision making in stressful situations [8] or to reduce the chances of accidents and failures [2]. A positive impact on training results in serious games could be proven in some studies [6]. However, the context must always be considered and it is difficult to make general statements about the effects of serious games.

In this paper, we present a concept of an immersive, virtual training environment for traffic control. A demo can be seen here[1]. The requirements analysis for the training and the initial user evaluation were done in cooperation with the policemen. We want to show how the VR technology could be used for the police training in the future. Due to the variability of the scenario, the quality of training can be increased. In particular, trainees can be supported in their individual training and can receive immediate feedback on completed activities.

2   Concept

Training in a virtual environment can be effective to learn particular behaviors and strategies. We raised requirements for the training in cooperation with ten policemen (eight men, average age of 27). A police training is usually practiced in a team. In the traditional training settings, scenes of everyday police work life are recreated and the behavior of the policemen in these situations is then evaluated. Such a training requires at least two participants and must be additionally assessed by an expert. Frequent training of different situations is thus often not possible.

We identified various scenarios, e.g. routine activities such as traffic control, shoplifting, and search of a person. Further examples include situations where the policemen themselves are in danger, such as knife attach and domestic violence. Some complex situations were named, e.g., accidents with many persons involved, demonstrations, rampaging football fans, and bank robberies.

2.1   Virtual Training for the Police Traffic Control

We focus on general police traffic control because this is a common situation in the daily routine of a policeman and it requires from the policeman to follow a certain procedure. Nevertheless, the work processes have to be trained regularly, as new situations may occur.

The following scenarios should not be considered as complete. Each federal state and country can provide a different approach. In the scenario, the vehicle already stopped and the policeman stands next to the car. The player must

---

[1] https://youtu.be/H8AP_S8x6A0, last visited on May 31st, 2018.

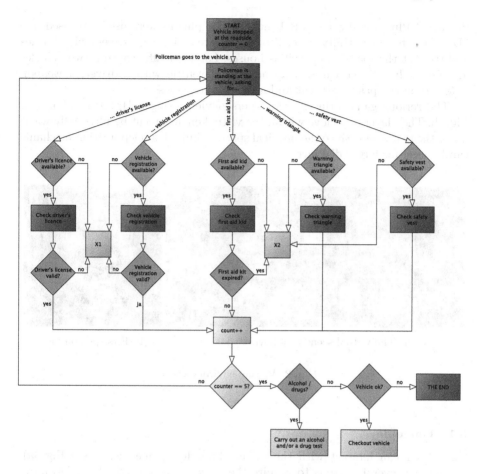

Fig. 1. Flowchart of the general traffic control

inspect the driver's license, the vehicle registration, the first-aid kit, the warning triangle and the safety vest. To increase the quality of the training and to train varied situations, the items which have to be inspected vary. Figure 1 shows the flowchart of the general traffic control. In addition, the general condition of the driver (e.g., an influence of alcohol or drugs) and the vehicle (e.g., the lights and tire condition) must be examined. The states marked with "X" serve as placeholders for special cases, e.g., situations that involve a warning or even an arrest. Parallel, the policemen have to ensure their own safety, e.g., look for a weapon and other dangerous items.

3 Implementation

The virtual environment, as it can be seen in Fig. 2a, was built using the Unity3D game engine. To facilitate integrating the device and controller interaction, the

SteamVR Plugin and SteamVR Unity Toolkit plugins were used. We used free 3D models from the Unity Asset Store to create a city, e.g., streets with bushes and trees at the roadside as well as houses. For the traffic control, two vehicles are included: a police car and an additional vehicle with a driver, a weapon (PM-40) on the passenger seat and a cat on the back seat.

The serious game utilizes a first-person view using a HMD, as shown in Fig. 2b. The player can move within the virtual environment by physically walking in the real world. Since the physical space is limited, a teleportation mechanic can be used for larger distances.

(a) The virtual scene top-down layout   (b) First-person view

Fig. 2. Virtual environment

3.1   Gameplay

The player can interact with the driver through a game menu (see Fig. 3a). It contains several buttons to require the driver's license, vehicle registration, warning triangle, safety vest and first aid kit. To specify the items as "OK" or "Not OK", the player can drag the items to the green checkmark or the red cross. To increase the variability, the items are randomly created, e.g., the driver will either have the permission to drive a car or only a scooter, the car color in the vehicle registration will change, and the first aid kit will either expired or not. When the quit button is pressed, the feedback for the player appears (see Fig. 3b). The feedback system consists of a "thumbs up" or "thumbs down" icon for each interaction item.

In the car, dangerous or unsecured items are hidden. To increase the training effect, these items are generated randomly. A dangerous item can be weapon lying on the passenger seat (see Fig. 3c). An unsecured item can be a cat in the footwell of the rear seats.

4   Evaluation

An evaluation was conducted to review the game concept and to collect ideas for future developments. Three policemen (aged between 27 and 34)

(a) Game menu   (b) Feedback   (c) The hidden weapon

Fig. 3. Game design

participated in the evaluation. First, the game concept was explained briefly. This was followed by an introduction of the interaction possibilities (teleportation, assignment of the items). HTC Vive HMD with two associated controllers were used to gain the first-person view of the virtual environment. During the evaluation, the policemen were encouraged to express their thoughts (think-aloud method). Two observers were asked to take notes of what participants say and do.

The impression of the VR was consistently positive. None of the subjects experienced cybersickness. The controls were perceived as simple and intuitive. The participants also liked the fact that the cat and the weapon are not immediately visible. Only the resolution rate of the headset was perceived as too low and too blurry, which caused some details to be hard to read, e.g., text on the driver's license and vehicle registration.

The analysis has revealed the importance of full-body tracking in VR. The visualization of only Vive controllers was irritating and the participants were missing the representation of the own body. This finding corresponds with the recent work, showing that visualizing of a controller or floating hands will break the immersion [7].

The current implementation supports only a single-player. However, in the real life the policemen (in Germany) usually always work in pairs (or teams). The participants suggested a multiplayer mode so that the second player can secure the vehicle on the passenger side as in a real control situation. In such a virtual team training, the players can inhabit the same virtual world and learn to perform tasks as a team. To still enable single-player mode, an intelligent virtual agent could provide feedback and help. Non-player characters could furthermore simulate additional characters, e.g. a passenger. Moreover, traffic can be simulated so that the player must be careful not to be hit by a car.

To improve the level of immersion, sound effects, such as engine noise should be created. Speech control would furthermore improve training efficiency, e.g., to show the driver's license and the vehicle documents.

However, our study has some limitations. The current implementation includes only a small scenario for the general traffic control. The current implementation can be easily expanded by creating additional interfaces for the interaction items, e.g. a stolen license plate. Furthermore, the total number of three participants is too low for any statistical conclusions. A significantly greater evaluation should be carried out in a future work.

5   Conclusion

We developed a serious game in order to show how VR technology could be a part of the police training in the future. We raised the requirements for the training scenario in cooperation with the policemen. We evaluated the game with policemen to review the game concept and to identify the limitations. Our results are promising and show that immersive VR can be used for the effective training. The evaluation results showed that our game is fun, motivating and could be used in police training in the future.

Further research will focus on body tracking since this would improve the presence in VR. To increase the effectiveness of the training and to support complex collaborative tasks, a multiplayer mode is needed. Furthermore, in the future work, we also want to support speech recognition. For a more advanced training scenario, intelligent virtual agents should be incorporated.

References

1. Bertram, J., Moskaliuk, J., Cress, U.: Virtual training: making reality work? Comput. Hum. Behav. **43**, 284–292 (2015)
2. Brasil, I.S., et al.: An inteligent agent-based virtual game for oil drilling operators training. In: 2011 XIII Symposium on Virtual Reality, pp. 9–17 (2011)
3. Conway, A., James, J.I., Gladyshev, P.: Development and initial user evaluation of a virtual crime scene simulator including digital evidence. In: James, J.I., Breitinger, F. (eds.) ICDF2C 2015. LNICST, vol. 157, pp. 16–26. Springer, Cham (2015). https://doi.org/10.1007/978-3-319-25512-5_2
4. Dörner, R., Göbel, S., Effelsberg, W., Wiemeyer, J.: Serious Games: Foundations, Concepts and Practice. Springer, Heidelberg (2016). https://doi.org/10.1007/978-3-319-40612-1
5. Ebert, L.C., Nguyen, T.T., Breitbeck, R., Braun, M., Thali, M.J., Ross, S.: The forensic holodeck: an immersive display for dorensic crime scene reconstructions. Forensic Sci. Med. Pathol. **10**(4), 623–626 (2014)
6. Lukosch, H., van Ruijven, T., Verbraeck, A.: The participatory design of a simulation training game. In: Proceedings of the 2012 Winter Simulation Conference (WSC), pp. 1–11 (2012)
7. Mendes, D., et al.: Mid-air modeling with Boolean operations in VR. In: 2017 IEEE Symposium on 3D User Interfaces (3DUI), pp. 154–157 (2017)
8. Rickel, J.: Intelligent virtual agents for education and training: opportunities and challenges. In: de Antonio, A., Aylett, R., Ballin, D. (eds.) IVA 2001. LNCS (LNAI), vol. 2190, pp. 15–22. Springer, Heidelberg (2001). https://doi.org/10.1007/3-540-44812-8_2

9. Shewaga, R., Uribe-Quevedo, A., Kapralos, B., Alam, F.: A comparison of seated and room-scale virtual reality in a serious game for epidural preparation. IEEE Trans. Emerg. Top. Comput., 1–14 (2017). https://ieeexplore.ieee.org/document/8017559
10. Zyda, M.: From visual simulation to virtual reality to games. Computer **38**(9), 25–32 (2005)

The Virtual House of Medusa: Guiding Museum Visitors Through a Co-located Mixed Reality Installation

Jürgen Hagler⬤, Michael Lankes(✉)⬤, and Andrea Aschauer⬤

Department of Digital Media, University of Applied Sciences Upper Austria,
4232 Hagenberg, Austria
{juergen.hagler,michael.lankes,andrea.aschauer}@fh-ooe.at
https://www.fh-ooe.at/

Abstract. In our submission we introduce a novel approach to guide Virtual Reality (VR) players and spectators via a Mixed Reality (MR) guidance tool trough a museum installation called the Virtual House of Medusa. The installation features an overview display, a VR headset for the player and a MR guidance tool (tablet with a VR-tracker) for the museum guide. This setup enables museum guides to support the VR player and to present the VR installation to a large audience. Our work deals with the issue that existing VR installations for museums are mainly designed as a single user VR experience and without any forms of spectators and player guidance. We argue that the interaction between the VR museum guide, the VR player, and the spectators has the potential to create a unique experience and to facilitate the feeling of being together in the VR world.

Keywords: Mixed reality museum installation
Head-mounted display · Co-located interaction

1 Introduction

Virtual Reality (VR) technologies have gained importance in recent years and are employed in various fields of application: Apart from health, entertainment, education and many other areas, these technologies have also found their way in the museum's context. In contrast to traditional approaches (such as info screens, installations with limited interaction functionalities, etc.), VR-based experiences in museums yield several benefits, such as providing the audience scientific data on cultural heritage. Although there are numerous positive aspects of VR-based solutions for museums, several design challenges have to be tackled. One of these issues can be seen in the fact that a majority of VR-based experiences

Supported by the University of Applied Sciences Upper Austria, the Kunsthistorisches Museum Wien and the Federal Monuments Authority Austria.

S. Göbel et al. (Eds.): JCSG 2018, LNCS 11243, pp. 182–188, 2018.
https://doi.org/10.1007/978-3-030-02762-9_19

in museums, in particular installations using head-mounted displays (HMDs), are mainly tailored for single user experiences.

VR installations for museums have the potential to provide a more engaging experience for visitors including an educational value. Furthermore, they can be used for a wide variety of applications form cultural heritage to natural science. The first VR museum installations can be found in the early 90s. In most cases HMDs were employed, but also Cave systems [1] were used. The Cave is a multi-person, room-sized, VR environment and can be considered as a co-located VR installation that allows museum educators to guide visitors through virtual environments.

Museum guides can be visually represented through avatars in VR [2]. If they share the same physical space with other players, this co-located hybrid between real and virtual is defined as Mixed Reality (MR) [3]. A much cheaper and space-saving solution for museums are HMDs. Whereas Cave systems can be used by a large number of museum visitors, HMDs offer single user experiences. As robust and affordable VR technologies, like the Oculus Rift [4] and the HTC Vive [5], are now available, they are being increasingly utilized in museums. Recent examples for instance are Tate Modern [6] or the VRLab at Ars Electronica Center (AEC) Linz [7].

Current museum installations with HMDs are usually offering an overview display for the audience, showing the perspective of the VR player or providing an overview of the VR installation (see Fig. 1). But so far, VR players cannot share the experiences with others, as seen at recent examples of VR museum installations on cultural heritage [8,9]. This problem is known as "Perspective Gap" [10]. Research on shared, co-located MR settings with HMDs [10,11] and on remote MR collaboration [12] is still at its very beginning.

Based on these limitations, we propose a novel MR approach for guiding museum visitors through a VR experience: first, it includes the spectators of a VR installation by giving the guide a MR guidance tool (tablet that is connected to the VR space) to explain relevant events and mechanisms in VR, and, secondly, the VR player is supported by the museum guide through our solution. In the following sections the MR guidance tool will be explained in detailed, and several use cases will be presented to highlight the usefulness and flexibility of our solution.

2   Our Approach

In general, research on co-located VR installations is still in its infancy in general, especially in the museum application context. VR museum installations using current HMDs are single user VR experiences and offer no interaction possibilities neither for museum guides nor for visitors. This is quite surprising, as on the one hand museum installations are usually tailored for multiple participants, and on the other hand interactive VR installations have to be introduced by the museum staff. Especially for museum guides, additional interaction and guidance possibilities that support their explanations appear to be useful.

Following this notion, we propose a novel MR approach for guiding museum visitors through an VR experience: first it includes the spectators of a VR installation by giving the guide a MR guidance tool (tablet that is connected to the VR space) to explain relevant events and mechanisms in VR, and, secondly, the VR player is supported by the museum guide through our solution.

Based on this concept, a playful co-located VR museum installation called Virtual House of Medusa (VHM) was developed [13]. The installation enables interactions between the VR player, the museum guide, and the spectators and supports different player roles: VR player (VR device), museum guide (MR guidance tool), spectators (overview display).

2.1   The Installation: The Virtual House of Medusa

The VHM is a playful co-located VR museum installation about a Roman villa and its wall paintings [14]. These fresco fragments were found at the Danubian Limes in Upper Austria. The game prototype was developed in collaboration with the Federal Monuments Authority Austria [15] and designed as a seated VR installation for multiple exhibition scenarios (see Fig. 2). The VHM offers four playful virtual workstation: VR players can assemble collected wall fragments like puzzle pieces into nearly complete paintings and can explore a reconstruction of the villa and its wall paintings in multiple ways.

With the MR guidance tool the museum guide can look into the VR environment, can provide support for the VR player, and is able to introduce the experience to the spectators in detail. This is achieved with a Vive tracker, mounted on a tablet device. Furthermore, the installation consists of a VR headset (HTC Vive) with one VR controller. For reasons of simplicity only the trigger button of the VR controller is used.

Figure 1 shows the physical devices of the two actors (guide and VR player) and the rendered screen view of each device. The MR guidance tool user (guide) is visualized as an avatar and can touch objects by touching the tablet screen. With a wiping gesture from the top edge of the tablet, a menu appears. The menu contains multiple functions: reset of the installation, switch between different visualizations of the museum guide, switch between the four workstations, switch between different cameras (Camera Player, Camera Audience, etc.), controls of the avatar (wave, nod or shake head, wink), showing hints or additional functions (tutorial, language, etc.).

The VHM was exhibited in different museum settings, at the art museum Kunsthistorisches Museum Wien (KHM) [16] and at the media art museum AEC, in the VRLab [7] and in the Deep Space [17], to identify design potentials and implications. These settings differ how the audience and the guides are integrated in the VR experience and will be discussed in the next sections.

2.2   Virtual House of Medusa at the AEC VRLab

The VRLab is a special exhibition at AEC, showcasing the latest VR, Augmented Reality (AR) and MR technologies. At 6 VR stations each supported

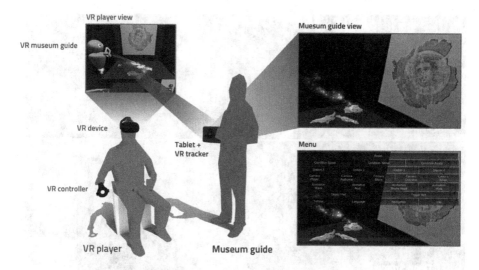

Fig. 1. Technical setup: VR player (red), seated VR experience with a HMD (Vive); museum guide (blue) can look into the virtual world and can touch virtual objects via a tablet, equipped with a VR tracker; trough a menu the museum guide can navigate the VR player and spectators trough the VHM. The museum guide is visualized in VR as an abstract avatar (green). (Color figure online)

with overview screens a broad range of different VR applications from art to industry use cases are presented. Hands-on experience and active involvement are a basic pillar at AEC. To achieve that, museum staff supports visitors in the entire exhibition. If a visitor wants to explore the VHM a museum guide introduces the installation. An additional overview screen shows the perspective of the VR player. The museum guide uses that screen to guide the VR players; further visitors can follow the journey. Neither the museum guide nor the spectators are actively involved. They can observe the VR player's perspective and can talk to him/her. In this setup the VR player is sitting in front of the others with his/her back turned, which does not ensure a perfect communication between the VR player and the museum guide (see Fig. 2).

2.3   Installation at the KHM

The VHM was fist presented at the KHM in Vienna as a co-located VR installation as part of the special exhibition of the original artifacts of the House of Medusa. Figure 2 shows the setup with one tablet device and an overview display at the back of the VR player. The installation was introduced by museum guides with the help of the MR guidance tool. Unlike the setup at the VRLab the museum guide is facing the VR player. The visual representation of the guide (VR museum guide) supports the communication between VR player, guide and spectators. Spectators can follow the virtual journey on the screen. After the

Fig. 2. The VHM was exhibited at three different museum settings: AEC VRLab: Museum guide introduces the installation to the VR player exclusively by talking to the him/her. Spectators observe the interaction process via an overview display. KHM: Museum guide introduces the installation using the MR guidance tool. Spectators can follow via an overview display. AEC Deep Space: A Museum guide navigates the VR player through VHM. A big audience can watch the journey through time via a large overview projection (16 × 9 m).

introduction phase the VR tablet was handed over to a museum visitor. Together with the VR player a co-located playful VR experience can be achieved.

2.4   Installation at the Deep Space, AEC

The setup at the Deep Space at AEC illustrates the potential for a large audience. The museum guide introduces the installation using the MR guidance tool and a head microphone (see Fig. 2). Up to 150 spectators can follow the time travel back to the Roman Age on a large screen (16 × 9 m). With additional tablet devices spectators can also actively participate in the virtual trip. Preliminary presentations have shown that the MR guidance tool is a big support for the museum guide and fosters the communication between VR player and spectators. In a further prototype a stereoscopic 3D projection for the audience and an enhancement of the user interface for the guide is in the planing.

3   Conclusion and Future Design Directions

In this paper we proposed a novel approach of guiding museum visitors through a VR experience: It features a unique MR guidance tool and is conceptualized as a playful installation with multiple virtual workstations. The proposed solution grants museum staff to guide both the VR player and the spectators. As described in the previous sections, the installation was presented at several occasions. However, until now the potentials and design implications have not been investigated: Regarding the next steps, currently a study is carried out that focuses on the co-playing experience. Here, it is aimed to find out how participants with multiple roles supported by the MR guidance tool experience the installation. We are especially interested in the communicative acts among visitors. Via observations and questionnaires, it is anticipated that the presence of the MR guidance tool will have a positive impact on the social experience.

References

1. Cruz-Neira, C., Sandin, D.J., DeFanti, T.A., Kenyon, R.V., Hart, J.C.: The CAVE: audio visual experience automatic virtual environment. Commun. ACM. **35**(6), 64–72 (1992)
2. Multi Mega Book (1995). https://www.digitalartarchive.at/database/general/work/multi-mega-book.html. Accessed 10 June 2018
3. Milgram, P., Kishino, F.: A taxonomy of mixed reality visual displays. IEICE Trans. Inf. Syst. E77-D, 1321–1329 (1994)
4. Oculus Rift. https://www.oculus.com/rift/. Accessed 10 June 2018
5. HTC Vive. https://www.vive.com/. Accessed 10 June 2018
6. Modigliani VR The Ochre Atelier. http://www.tate.org.uk/whats-on/tate-modern/exhibition/modigliani/modigliani-vr-ochre-atelier. Accessed 10 June 2018
7. VRLab, Ars Electronica. https://www.aec.at/center/en/ausstellungen/vrlab/. Accessed 10 June 2018
8. Ferrari, F., Medici, M.: The virtual experience for cultural heritage: methods and tools comparison for Geguti Palace in Kutaisi, Georgia. In: Proceedings of the International and Interdisciplinary Conference IMMAGINI?, vol. 1, 10 pp. (2017)
9. Sierra, A., de Prado, G., Ruiz Soler, I., Codina, F.: Virtual reality and archaeological reconstruction: be there, back then. MW2017: museums and the Web (2017).   https://mw17.mwconf.org/paper/virtual-reality-and-archaeological-reconstruction-be-there-be-back-then-ullastret3d-and-vr-experience-in-htc-vive-and-immersive-room/. Accessed 10 June 2018
10. Ishii, A., et al.: ReverseCAVE: providing reverse perspectives for sharing VR experience. In: ACM SIGGRAPH 2017 Posters (SIGGRAPH 2017), Article 28, 2 p. ACM, New York (2017)
11. Masson, T., Perlin, D.K.: HOLO-DOODLE: an adaptation and expansion of collaborative holojam virtual reality. In: ACM SIGGRAPH 2017 VR Village (SIGGRAPH 2017), Article 9, 2 p. ACM, New York (2017)
12. Piumsomboon, T., Day, A., Ens, B., Lee, Y., Lee, G., Billinghurst, M.: Exploring enhancements for remote mixed reality collaboration. In SIGGRAPH Asia 2017 Mobile Graphics & Interactive Applications, SA 2017, pp. 16:1–16:5. ACM, New York (2017) https://doi.org/10.1145/3132787.3139200
13. Hagler, J., Lankes M., Aschauer A.: The virtual house of medusa: playful co-located virtual archaeology. Tagungsband FFH 2018, Salzburg, Österreich, 2018, 8 p. (2018)
14. Santner, M. (ed.): Fokus Denkmal 8: Das Haus der Medusa. Römische Wandmalereien in Enns. Berger & Söhne, Ferdinand (2017)

15. Federal Monuments Authority Austria. https://bda.gv.at/de/. Accessed 10 June 2018
16. Kunsthistorisches Museum Wien. https://www.khm.at/. Accessed 10 June 2018
17. Deep Space, Ars Electronica Center Linz. https://www.aec.at/center/ausstellungen/deep-space/. Accessed 10 June 2018

Game Development – Serious Games Design, Models, Tools and Emerging Technologies

Recognition of Full-Body Movements in VR-Based Exergames Using Hidden Markov Models

Polona Caserman$^{(\boxtimes)}$(iD), Thomas Tregel, Marco Fendrich, Moritz Kolvenbach, Markus Stabel, and Stefan Göbel

Multimedia Communications Lab - KOM, Technische Universität Darmstadt, Darmstadt, Germany
{polona.caserman,thomas.tregel,stefan.goebel}@kom.tu-darmstadt.de
{marco.fendrich,moritz.kolvenbach,markus.stabel}@stud.tu-darmstadt.de

Abstract. Due to recent improvements in Virtual Reality (VR) regarding the potential of full-body tracking, the number of VR-based exergames has been increasing. However, such applications often depend on additional tracking technology, e.g., markerless or marker-based. On the one hand, tracking approaches, such as the Kinect device are limited by either high latency or insufficient accuracy. On the other hand, motion capture suits are expensive and create discomfort. In this paper we present an accurate motion recognition approach, using only the HTC Vive HMD with their associated Controllers and Trackers. The recognition is based on an Hidden Markov Model, that has been trained in advance for a specific movement. The results suggest that our system is capable of detecting a complex full-body gesture, such as yoga *Warrior I* pose, with an accuracy of 88%. In addition, audible feedback is provided, so that the user can immediately hear if the particular exercise has been executed correctly. Such a system can be used to assist players in learning a particular movement and can be applied in various serious games applications, e.g., for training purposes or rehabilitation.

Keywords: Full-body tracking · Motion recognition
Machine learning · Hidden Markov model · Virtual reality · Exergames
Serious games

1 Introduction

Recognition of body movements is attracting increasing research interest. However, most publications using Hidden Markov Models (HMMs) are recognizing only a part of the body, e.g., hand gestures [4,12–14,18,24] or arm movements [17,20]. Only a little research regarding full-body recognition in VR-based exergames using machine learning approaches has been made.

© Springer Nature Switzerland AG 2018
S. Göbel et al. (Eds.): JCSG 2018, LNCS 11243, pp. 191–203, 2018.
https://doi.org/10.1007/978-3-030-02762-9_20

On the one hand, many publications trying to recognize full-body motions are using markerless tracking technologies, such as the Microsoft Kinect device[1] which provides the joint orientation for the player's skeleton. However, the Kinect suffers from occlusion, low precision, and inaccuracy [8]. On the other hand, more precise motion capture technologies, such as Optitrack[2] or Vicon[3], are based on multiple markers attached to the player's suit which are tracked by multiple cameras. Even though such a system is more accurate, it can create discomfort since the user has to wear a tight suit [21]. Moreover, multiple Inertial Measurement Units (IMUs) can be attached to the user's body in order to recognize body motions [7]. However, since multiple sensors must be worn by the user, such a system may also be considered intrusive.

In contrast to Kinect, our approach is designed to recognize full-body motions reliably. Furthermore, the recognition algorithm should be independent of the execution speed (i.e. how fast or slow the user performs a pose) as well as user's size (i.e. the height of the user). According to Raheja et al. [20], HMM are scale-invariant. In other words, the recognition algorithm using HMM works regardless of the student's height performing a movement. Unlike suit-based motion capture systems, we use only a small number of devices. Some advantages of the reduced sensor amount include ease of use, detection reliability and less potential for error. With two HTC Vive Controllers, the hands' movements are tracked. With the three additional HTC Vive Trackers, we determine the position of the lower back as well as both legs.

There are basically three main criteria that our approach should meet:

– The approach must be computationally efficient and must recognize the motion in real-time
– The motion recognition algorithm must be reliable:
  • It should be independent of the player's movement speed
  • It should provide similar results regardless of the player's height
– Only a small number of devices must be used

The paper is organized as follows: Sect. 2 presents relevant related work. In Sect. 3, the concept of the proposed approach using HMM in VR is presented. In Sect. 4, implementation details are provided in order to specify the parameters of the HMM. Section 5 presents the results of the full-body recognition. These results are discussed in Sect. 6. Finally, Sect. 7 concludes this paper.

2   Related Work

In the field of motion detection in VR there exist already a number of applications. However, to the best of our knowledge, none of this work uses the Vive Tracker in conjunction with supervised machine learning, such as HMM.

---

[1] https://www.xbox.com/en-GB/xbox-one/accessories/kinect, last visited on May 25th, 2018.

[2] http://optitrack.com, last visited on May 29th, 2018.

[3] https://vicon.com, last visited on May 29th, 2018.

2.1   Motion Recognition in VR

Chan et al. [3] used a motion capture suit to follow the movements of the virtual teacher in order to learn how to dance. The suit with several attached markers can capture the full-body movements. The resulting data is then compared with "correct" reference data to give the student feedback about the correctness of her or his movement. Similar, Jiang et al. [11] presented a novel action recognition algorithm based on neural network. The researchers could reconstruct various full-body motions, such as walking, jogging, jumping, crouching and turning by only using Vive HMD and two associated Controllers.

Motion recognition in VR can also be done using a single Kinect sensor. The developers can easily exploit Microsoft Visual Gesture Builder NUI tool[4] in order to perform real-time gesture detection. Past work showed, that Kinect can be utilized to recognize motions in VR, e.g., for remote posture guidance during sports [10], for efficient strength training [22] or for efficiently dancing training [23]. In the approach proposed by Lee et al. [16], posing and acting is used as input to personalize furniture. The users can specify dimensions with simple speech commands while indicating a distance with their arms. However, speech recognition was performed using a trained operator, thus no machine learning approach was applied. Since the field of view of the Kinect is small, Rhodin et al. [21] attached a pair of fisheye cameras to the VR headset to increase the visibility of body parts in order to estimate the full-body pose. Furthermore, hand gestures can be recognized using a Leap Motion[5] device [6] or a Myo[6] armband [9,15] to enable natural interaction in VR.

Furthermore, IMUs can be advantageous for motion detection. Fitzgerald et al. [7] integrated nine Xsens inertial-based sensors[7] to develop a biofeedback system for the instruction and analysis of sport rehabilitation exercises. However, the sensor data were stored in order to do offline analysis by comparing the data of the player and the expert. Another study used integrated sensors of a HMD to detect steps in real-time by applying a Gaussian low-pass filter [2]. With the recognition algorithm, the avatar's feet could be synchronized with the user's feet while walking on a treadmill.

2.2   Hidden Markov Models

Previous work showed that machine learning approaches and more specifically HMMs are widely and successfully applied in the field of speech and hand gesture recognition. First work has been already presented in the 80's and 90's, e.g., for automatic speech [19] or handwriting [24] recognition. Later on, Chen et al. [4] developed a real-time system to recognize hand gesture from a 2D video

---

[4] https://docs.microsoft.com/en-us/previous-versions/windows/kinect/dn785304(v %3dieb.10), last visited on May 25th, 2018.

[5] https://www.leapmotion.com, last visited on May 28, 2018.

[6] https://www.myo.com, last visited on May 28th, 2018.

[7] https://www.xsens.com/functions/human-motion-measurement/, last visited on May 28th, 2018.

input. To reduce the complexity of hand detection in the images, markers were used in order to separate the hand from the background [14]. Similar, in the study conducted by Just and Marcel [12], the user had to wear two colored gloves to facilitate hand tracking while recognizing two-handed gestures. Kao and Fahn [13] proposed an approach, where a single hand or both hands, as well as the face, have to be detected in each video frame in order to recognize hand gestures accurately. Hand gesture recognition can also be done based on recorded tracking data provided by a three-axis accelerometer embedded in a handheld device [18].

Other researchers collected body movement data with a Kinect in order to train the HMM [17,20]. Even though the Kinect device is capable of tracking a full-body, both publications used this device to only recognize the upper body or more precisely to track gross arm movements.

3   Concept

The proposed recognition approach based on HMMs can be used to assist the player to learn a particular movement. A player can supervise own improvements. Another possible application example would be a training scenario where therapists can monitor the patient's recovery.

To determine the HMM, a teacher is needed to repeat the movement so that reference data can be gathered (ground truth). Since the recognition works regardless of the height of the teacher performing the posture [20], our model is generalized and independent of the size variance. Obtained data are then utilized to decide if the student performed the motion correctly. The VR environment provides visual and audible feedback to the student, informing her or him whether the executed movement was right or wrong.

3.1   Hidden Markov Model

The HMM was chosen since this approach showed good results for movement recognition in previous works (see Sect. 2). Motion recognition using HMMs essentially works in five steps (see Fig. 1), as adapted from Yang and Xu [24].

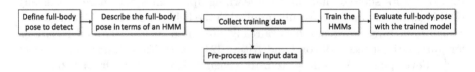

Fig. 1. Block diagram of the motion recognition-based system

In the *first step*, a pose or gesture, which should be recognized, must be defined. We want to show that our approach is able to recognize full-body motions in VR. Therefore, a pose must be selected, where the position of the hands and feet are important.

In the *second step*, the full-body pose must be described in terms of an HMM. The HMM is described as $\lambda = (S, V, A, B, \pi)$ as proposed by Rabiner [19]:

- $S = (s_1, ..., s_N)$, the set of N possible hidden states, i.e. possible values of q_i
- $V = (v_1, ..., v_M)$, the set of M possible observations, i.e. values of o_i
- $A \in \mathbb{R}^{N \times N}$, the transition matrix between the states, where the elements a_{ij} of the matrix indicate the probability for the transition from the state s_i to s_j, i.e. $a_{ij} = P(q_{t+1} = s_j | q_t = s_i)$
- $B \in \mathbb{R}^{N \times M}$, the distribution matrix, which indicates with which probability a state s_i leads to the observation v_j, i.e. $b_{ij} = b_i(j) = P(o_t = v_j | q_t = s_i)$
- $\pi \in \mathbb{R}^N$, the initial probability, i.e. a vector whose elements indicate with which probability s_i is the starting state: $\pi_i = P(q_1 = s_i)$

In this step only the structure of A and B are determined. The values of elements in A and B will be first estimated in the training process (Step 4). An overview is given in Fig. 2.

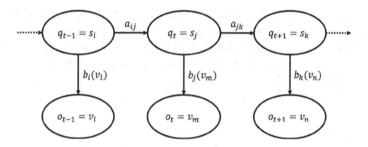

Fig. 2. Schematic representation of an HMM

In the *third step*, before the training data is collected, the raw input data has to be pre-processed. In order to train the HMM, several executions of the correct movement must be recorded and saved in a file. Since the HTC Vive provides global positions of the VR devices, this data has to be first transformed into a local coordinate system. Otherwise, the result would be distorted. Hence, the local orientation and position vector of all VR devices have to be continuously stored while the actual motion is being performed. Because the motion detection should work regardless of body height and execution speed, the data must be furthermore normalized.

In the *fourth step*, the HMMs should be trained using the collected data from the previous step. A console application, called *HMM-Trainer* allows the user to select training sequences and adjust the HMM parameters to train the model. The model parameters should be adjusted so that the likelihood $P(O|\lambda)$ can be maximized for the given training dataset. Therefore, the Baum-Welch algorithm is used to iteratively improve the values of λ to achieve the local maximum. In addition, the forward-backward algorithm to calculate the probability of a given HMM emitting a given observation sequence must be implemented.

Finally, in the *fifth step*, the full-body pose must be evaluated with the trained HMM. The trained model is then used to classify a full-body pose.

3.2 Feedback

In addition to the recognition of a full-body movement in VR, a constructive feedback is provided so that the student can improve the movement. Depending on whether the pose is recognized as correct or incorrect, the student gets audible feedback (e.g., "Your movement was correct" or "Your movement was wrong"). For a more detailed feedback about each individual Vive Controller/Tracker, a text is displayed on the PC and saved in a file. The student is informed whether the executed movement was right or wrong and if necessary, which position of the Controller/Tracker was recognized as correct or incorrect.

4 Implementation

The motion detection is implemented using the *Body Tracking Framework*[8] which was previously developed by KOM - Multimedia Communications Lab at the TU Darmstadt. To achieve maximal performance, the framework is based on the low-level game API and hardware abstraction library *Kore*[9] (C++). Audio files are created using IBM's speech synthesis software Watson[10] to provide audible feedback to the student. A demo can be viewed online[11].

```
1 N= 1242
2 HMD 41.8893 0.0018896 1.81965 0.00109858
3 lhC 41.8893 0.0708489 0.723469 0.122266
4 rhC 41.8893 -0.0718539 0.71499 -0.147675
5 bac 41.8893 0.207485 1.18198 0.160868
6 lfT 41.8893 0.227679 0.0898545 0.223854
7 rfT 41.8893 0.113464 0.112596 0.0269231
```

Fig. 3. An example of collected motion capture data. The first line indicates the number of data points. The followed rows indicate data points with a prefix, time and position vector (x, y, and z-axis).

First, the training data has to be collected by a teacher. When the virtual environment is loaded, the sensor data for the training of an HMM is recorded by pressing the "trigger" button on the Controller. The data is stored in a text file, as shown in Fig. 3. Each line indicates positional data of a VR device at a

---

[8] https://github.com/CatCuddler/BodyTracking, last visited on May 22th, 2018.

[9] https://github.com/Kode/Kore/, last visited on May 22th, 2018.

[10] https://text-to-speech-demo.ng.bluemix.net, last visited on May 22th, 2018.

[11] https://youtu.be/q-yKLtrTodA, last visited on May 30th, 2018.

certain time. The prefix at the beginning of the line is an identifier to associate the data with the VR devices: "lhC" and "rhC" correspond either the left or right Controller held in the hands, "bac" corresponds to the Tracker on the lower back (or hip), and "lfT" as well as "rfT" corresponds either to the left or right Tracker attached to the foot. In each row, time in seconds (equal for all six entries) and values for x, y, and z-axis are saved. The x and z-axis are defined as horizontal and the y-axis vertical. In addition, the number of data points is saved in the first line.

For training and evaluation, the Vive Trackers have to be attached to the teacher's and student's body. As it can be seen in Fig. 4, two of the three additional Trackers are attached on the outside of the legs right above the ankle. It should be ensured that the Trackers are mounted as tight as possible in order to avoid falsification of the data by shaking. The third Tracker is fastened with a belt at the lower back. The Controllers are held in the hands and the HMD is worn on the head.

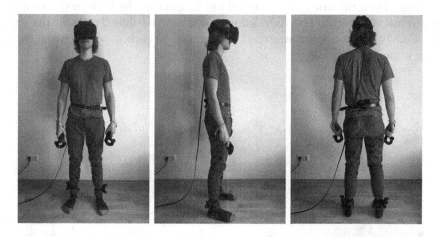

Fig. 4. Attached HTC Vive Tracker to the body.

To define the HMM, we have to characterize the number of hidden states, the number of clusters, and the depth of the left-to-right matrix. We use *k-means clustering* to partition the observations of the data matrix into k cluster. For the initial estimation of the parameters, a teacher performed 17 correct and 30 incorrect versions of the yoga *Warrior I* pose. We deliberately chose this pose because it is well defined (only one correct possible execution). In other words, with another teacher, the correct movement should look very similar. The data was divided into a training and test set. We observed the result data of 6 to 16 hidden states, 8 to 100 cluster with random initial parameters and bounded left-to-right depth from 1 to 3. The HMMs were trained in order to calculate the log probability. By analyzing these log probabilities and standard deviations, some quantities could be calculated to adjust the HMM parameters. The first results of the test set indicate, that the smaller number of clusters (between 8 and 12) achieved better results. As expected, our model is overfitting due to a larger number of clusters approaching the number of actual data points (measurement values, i.e. position vector). The number of states, however, does not seem to have much influence. With six or eight hidden states the results are slightly better. Observing the left-to-right depth, the completely random initial parameters (depth of 0) yielded worse results. By increasing the depth parameter (i.e. depth of 2 or 3), better results were achieved.

5   Results

The HMM should be used to demonstrate that our concept is able to recognize complex full-body movements. To complete the pose correctly (see Fig. 5), the student starts the movement while standing and takes a step backward with his left foot. Both heels should lie on one line and the rear foot should be turned outwards. Then the arms are stretched out in front of the body and the upper body remains upright. The right knee should now be directly above the right heel. Finally, the arms are stretched out parallel to each other with the palms facing inwards.

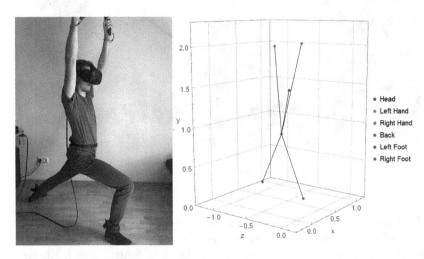

Fig. 5. The final position of the yoga *Warrior I* pose (left) and visualization of the test data (right).

5.1   Training

In the initial tests (see Sect. 4), no explicit ideal HMM parameters could be determined. Therefore, a total number of further 100 correct movements of the yoga *Warrior I* pose were collected (training set). Two final HMMs were trained and finally tested to find the best model. The first HMM has six hidden states (HMM6) and the second HMM 10 hidden states (HMM10). For HMM6 we use 8 clusters and left-to-right depth of 2 while for the HMM10 100 clusters and left-to-right depth of 3 are used.

5.2   Testing

To test the final HMMs, a test set of 40 correct movements and 40 incorrect movements was used. We furthermore divided the test set of the incorrect movements into 20 partially correct or similar movements (e.g., only the legs were correctly positioned, however, the arms were stretched to the side rather than up or the arms were correctly positioned and the legs not) and 20 totally incorrect movements (e.g., either legs nor arms were correctly positioned). Here the motions are recognized in real-time and the student gets audible feedback right after the motion is completed. The results can be obtained from the Table 1. For the evaluation, we furthermore introduced the second condition. We wanted to evaluate if false positives are recognized when the Tracker/Controller do not move during the exercise. Thus, HMM6* and HMM10* will recognize a movement as wrong as soon as one Tracker/Controller remains in the same cluster during the entire movement.

Table 1. The results with the four final HMMs. In each case, the probability of correctly recognized movements (either right or wrong) is given.

	Positive	Similar	Negative	Total
HMM6	97,5% (39/40)	50% (10/20)	100% (20/20)	86.25%
HMM6*	90% (36/40)	75% (15/20)	100% (20/20)	88.75%
HMM10	0% (0/40)	100% (20/20)	100% (20/20)	50%
HMM10*	0% (0/40)	100% (20/20)	100% (20/20)	50%

The results clearly show that neither HMM10 nor HMM10* is suitable for detecting *Warrior I* movement, as none of the correct motions are detected. The reason for this is that the current implementation of the forward algorithm is not robust to underflow. Thus, even with the correct (*positive*) movements and despite the fact that input data is normalized, the HMM10 is not able to recognize the movements. As described by Blunsom [1] we could avoid underflow by using a scaling coefficient c_t, that only depends on t and can keep the probability values in the dynamic range of the machine.

A significantly better result is provided by HMM6 or even HMM6*. These two models can recognize all completely wrong (*negative*) movements. Analyzing the partially correct movements (*similar*), the recognition rate of HMM6 drops to 50%. With HMM6*, the accuracy of similar poses is increased to 75%. Compared to the HMM6 (with the accuracy of 97,5%), the detection of the correct movement decreases to 90% when using HMM6*. We believe this happens because the right foot and back do not move much while performing *Warrior I* pose. Therefore, HMM6 should be used for movements, where the positions of all extremities differ much between the initial and final position. For other movements, HMM6* should be used.

6 Discussion

The results presented in the previous Section show that the proposed concept can be used to recognize a complex pose. Therefore, we believe that our method can also be used to detect additional full-body movements: it can be used for exergames where the player is motivated to move or to learn a certain movement pattern. The results suggest that our concept is able to detect complex movements, such as yoga *Warrior I* pose. This movement takes advantage of all existing sensors (Vive HMD, two Controllers, and three Tracker). We demonstrated that a full-body movement can be detected with a probability of over 88%. We believe that our system is able to recognize various full-body movements in VR.

Compared to related work using HMM, we could obtain similar results. In the evaluation conducted by Chen et al. [4] an accuracy of 85% was achieved, while Raheja et al. [20] achieved a recognition success rate of over 90%. Other researchers detected more than 95% of the movements [13,14,17,18] or even more than 99% [24] as correct. The step detection algorithm using a Gaussian low-pass filter provided an accuracy of up to 98.7% while walking at different speeds [2]. Recognition of various hand gestures using Support Vector Machine reached an accuracy of 80%[12]. However, in most publications, only motions of one body part (e.g., only hand gestures or steps) were recognized and not a full-body pose as in our approach. Furthermore, some works also only compare gestures and do not take the detection of wrong movements into account.

To make the current HMM reliable in terms of player's execution speed and height, we normalize the tracking data. To improve our approach, a *Dynamic Time Warping* could be furthermore used, as the one proposed by Raheja et al. [20]. Alternatively, a promising approach of *Conversive Hidden non-Markovian Models* has recently been developed that can explicitly consider information about the speed of a movement [5]. With this approach, it would be possible to recognize movements which differ in execution speed even more accurately. For further improvements, calibration may also be necessary.

Additionally, since we want to reduce the sensor amount (currently using five VR tracking devices in addition to the HMD), only the position and orientation of the extremities (e.g., hands and feet) are known. To additionally track other joints (e.g., elbow and knee) we do not need to increase the number of sensors. By solving the Inverse Kinematics (IK), the position and orientation of every joint can be estimated. Using the IK solution we could distinguish between different

---

[12] https://tzuchanchuang.itch.io/gesture-recognition-input-method-for-ar, last visited on June 6th, 2018.

full-body movements, where the positions/orientations of a large number of joints are crucial.

7   Conclusion

In this paper, we present a concept to recognize full-body movements in VR using only a small number of VR devices: a HTC Vive HMD, two Vive Controllers and three Vive Trackers which have to be attached to the body. Thus, the head, both hands, and both feet, as well as the upper body, are tracked. The positions of all these body parts are important for the motion recognition. Furthermore, the students get immediate feedback about the motion performance and can thus easily improve their execution. Further work could include extended feedback, describing the detailed improvements for the movement.

Our approach allows to train the model for various full-body gestures/poses easily and without much extra effort. The trained model is independent of the player's movement speed and it provides similar results regardless of the player's height. The evaluation showed that we can recognize a full-body movement, such as yoga *Warrior I*, with an accuracy of 88.75%. However, we evaluated our HMM with only one pose. In the future work, various additional movements should be trained, e.g. dancing or gestures for locomotion (walking in place, swimming).

Further research will focus on optimizing HMM parameters to improve the average recognition rate. We also want to improve the VR experience. For a better visual performance, a virtual mirror could be used so that the student can see her or his movements as well as the movements of the teacher. The movements can be represented through an avatar using IK approaches to provide real-time feedback.

References

1. Blunsom, P.: Hidden Markov models. Lecture Notes, vol. 15, pp. 18–19, August 2004
2. Caserman, P., Krabbe, P., Wojtusch, J., von Stryk, O.: Real-time step detection using the integrated sensors of a head-mounted display. In: 2016 IEEE International Conference on Systems, Man, and Cybernetics (SMC), pp. 3510–3515, October 2016
3. Chan, J.C.P., Leung, H., Tang, J.K.T., Komura, T.: A virtual reality dance training system using motion capture technology. IEEE Trans. Learn. Technol. 4(2), 187–195 (2011)
4. Chen, F.S., Fu, C.M., Huang, C.L.: Hand Gesture recognition using a real-time tracking method and hidden Markov models. Image Vis. Comput. 21(8), 745–758 (2003)
5. Dittmar, T., Krull, C., Horton, G.: A new approach for touch gesture recognition: conversive hidden non-Markovian models. J. Comput. Sci. 10, 66–76 (2015)
6. Ferracani, A., Pezzatini, D., Bianchini, J., Biscini, G., Del Bimbo, A.: Locomotion by natural gestures for immersive virtual environments. In: Proceedings of the 1st International Workshop on Multimedia Alternate Realities, AltMM 2016, pp. 21–24. ACM (2016)

7. Fitzgerald, D., et al.: Development of a wearable motion capture suit and virtual reality biofeedback system for the instruction and analysis of sports rehabilitation exercises. In: 2007 29th Annual International Conference of the IEEE Engineering in Medicine and Biology Society, pp. 4870–4874, August 2007

8. Han, J., Shao, L., Xu, D., Shotton, J.: Enhanced computer vision with microsoft kinect sensor: a review. IEEE Trans. Cybern. **43**(5), 1318–1334 (2013)

9. Han, P.H., et al.: Moving around in virtual space with spider silk. In: ACM SIGGRAPH 2015 Emerging Technologies, SIGGRAPH 2015, pp. 19:1–19:1. ACM, New York (2015)

10. Hoang, T.N., Reinoso, M., Vetere, F., Tanin, E.: Onebody: remote posture guidance system using first person view in virtual environment. In: Proceedings of the 9th Nordic Conference on Human-Computer Interaction, NordiCHI 2016, pp. 25:1–25:10. ACM, New York (2016)

11. Jiang, F., Yang, X., Feng, L.: Real-time full-body motion reconstruction and recognition for off-the-shelf VR devices. In: Proceedings of the 15th ACM SIGGRAPH Conference on Virtual-Reality Continuum and Its Applications in Industry, VRCAI 2016, vol. 1, pp. 309–318. ACM, New York (2016)

12. Just, A., Marcel, S.: A comparative study of two state-of-the-art sequence processing techniques for hand gesture recognition. Comput. Vis. Image Underst. **113**(4), 532–543 (2009)

13. Kao, C.Y., Fahn, C.S.: A human-machine interaction technique: hand gesture recognition based on hidden markov models with trajectory of hand motion. Procedia Eng. **15**, 3739–3743 (2011). CEIS 2011

14. Keskin, C., Erkan, A., Akarun, L.: Real time hand tracking and 3D gesture recognition for interactive interfaces using HMM. In: ICANN/ICONIPP 2003, pp. 26–29 (2003)

15. Koniaris, B., et al.: IRIDiuM: immersive rendered interactive deep media. In: ACM SIGGRAPH 2016 VR Village, SIGGRAPH 2016, pp. 11:1–11:2. ACM, New York (2016)

16. Lee, B., Cho, M., Min, J., Saakes, D.: Posing and acting as input for personalizing furniture. In: Proceedings of the 9th Nordic Conference on Human-Computer Interaction, NordiCHI 2016, pp. 44:1–44:10. ACM, New York (2016)

17. Nguyen-Duc-Thanh, N., Lee, S., Kim, D.: Two-stage hidden Markov model in gesture recognition for human robot interaction. Int. J. Adv. Robot. Syst. **9**(2), 39 (2012)

18. Pylvänäinen, T.: Accelerometer based gesture recognition using continuous HMMs. In: Marques, J.S., Pérez de la Blanca, N., Pina, P. (eds.) IbPRIA 2005. LNCS, vol. 3522, pp. 639–646. Springer, Heidelberg (2005). https://doi.org/10.1007/11492429_77

19. Rabiner, L.R.: A tutorial on hidden Markov models and selected applications in speech recognition. Proc. IEEE **77**(2), 257–286 (1989)

20. Raheja, J., Minhas, M., Prashanth, D., Shah, T., Chaudhary, A.: Robust Gesture Recognition Using Kinect: A Comparison Between DTW and HMM. Optik - International Journal for Light and Electron Optics **126**(11), 1098–1104 (2015)

21. Rhodin, H., et al.: EgoCap: egocentric marker-less motion capture with two fisheye cameras. ACM Trans. Graph. **35**(6), 162:1–162:11 (2016)

22. Tanaka, Y., Hirakawa, M.: Efficient strength training in a virtual world. In: 2016 IEEE International Conference on Consumer Electronics-Taiwan (ICCE-TW), pp. 1–2, May 2016

23. Yan, S., Ding, G., Guan, Z., Sun, N., Li, H., Zhang, L.: OutsideMe: augmenting dancer's external self-image by using a mixed reality system. In: Proceedings of the 33rd Annual ACM Conference Extended Abstracts on Human Factors in Computing Systems, CHI EA 2015, pp. 965–970. ACM, New York (2015)
24. Yang, J., Xu, Y.: Hidden Markov model for gesture recognition. Technical report, Robotics Institute, Carnegie-Mellon University, Pittsburgh, May 1994

A Review of Serious Games
for Programming

Michael A. Miljanovic and Jeremy S. Bradbury$^{(\boxtimes)}$

University of Ontario Institute of Technology,
2000 Simcoe St N, Oshawa, ON L1H 7K4, Canada
{michael.miljanovic,jeremy.bradbury}@uoit.ca

Abstract. A large number of games are available to students and instructors that aid in developing a basic understanding of how to read and write programs. In this paper we review the existing serious programming game literature and examine the educational content and game evaluations of 49 games. First, we assess all games with respect to the programming fundamentals specified in the ACM 2013 Computer Science Curricula guidelines. Next, we review how each game is evaluated with respect to likability, accessibility, learning effect and engagement. In addition to the evaluated research questions, we also review the research methods used in the evaluations. Based on the results of our survey we conclude by identifying a number of open problems in the serious programming games literature.

Keywords: Computer science · Education · Game evaluation
Programming · Serious games · Survey · Systematic review

1 Introduction

Within the field of game-based Computer Science learning, a large number of games have been developed that focus on computer programming [55]. Unfortunately, serious programming games are often developed independently; existing work does not focus on methods that improve gameplay, and there is a need to analyze the use of games to support introductory programming [27]. This means games may be created without learning from existing games, especially if games are not available via open-source licensing or other methods. Additionally, many serious games that claim to have positive outcomes for players lack any scientific validation [44]. Without any supporting evidence, it is difficult to compare serious games and judge which are the most effective learning tools.

In this paper we survey 49 serious programming games with respect to both game content and evaluation. Specifically, we survey these games to answer the following research questions:

© Springer Nature Switzerland AG 2018
S. Göbel et al. (Eds.): JCSG 2018, LNCS 11243, pp. 204–216, 2018.
https://doi.org/10.1007/978-3-030-02762-9_21

- *What programming knowledge is covered by existing serious games?*
- *How are serious programming games evaluated?*

The games included in our survey are exclusively games that involve reading and/or writing programs in order to help players develop computer programming skills. The goal of our review is to provide a comprehensive overview of the state-of-the-art research in these serious programming games while also identifying open research problems. The open problems we identified fall into two categories: new opportunities for serious games development and new opportunities for enhancing evaluation best practices. Our review methodology is described in Sect. 2 followed by our review results in Sect. 3. Related work is discussed in Sect. 4. Finally, we discuss our results and present open problems in Sect. 5.

2 Methodology

2.1 Identification and Selection Criteria

We used different selection criteria for our categories of research and commercial games. The search term we used for both was "introductory programming games". Research games were first gathered using the top 200 results from a Google Scholar web search in English, then pruned based on our exclusion criteria. We then selected games that were discussed in the related works sections of those papers that fit our criteria. For inclusion in the study, research games must have an associated peer-reviewed paper or be the subject of a thesis project. Games developed by researchers with no oversight were excluded. Unfortunately, not all research games were available to be played and we therefore had to evaluate some based only on their descriptions and not a first-hand evaluation. Commercial games were collected using a Google web search and through online game stores [1]. This includes games like Code Hunt [53], which is a game developed by Microsoft Research, but has been discussed in several peer-reviewed papers.

2.2 Classification Criteria

Audience. The targeted audiences for serious programming games is broken down into four separate categories:

- Children (age 5–13)
- High school students (age 14–17)
- Undergraduate novices (age 18+, no programming experience)
- Undergraduate adepts (age 18+, programming experience)

---

[1] Commercial sources such as the iOS game store, Google Play Store, HourOf-Code.com, and Tynker.com offer over 100 different programming games, typically aimed at children. However, many of these games follow a similar approach or share visual programming environments. We chose to only include a small sample from these websites due to the high degree of game overlap and similarity.

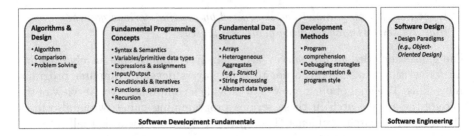

Fig. 1. ACM computer science curricula 2013 knowledge areas [7]

Educational Content. The 2013 ACM Curriculum Guidelines for Undergraduate Degree Programs in Computer Science [7] include areas of knowledge for students learning programming (see Fig. 1). The concepts we selected were from the Tier 1 list of knowledge areas for computer science, meaning that the topics are intended to be introduced to students in their first or second years of study at the undergraduate level.

We focused on the Software Development Fundamentals (SDFs) and Software Engineering (SE) knowledge areas. SDFs are critical for students to become both competent at programming and knowledgeable about designing and analyzing algorithms. The other software-oriented knowledge areas discussed in the ACM Curriculum require students to have strong foundations in SDFs. In addition, a number of games have been developed to help students understand the object-oriented paradigm; we chose to include this specific section of Software Engineering to acknowledge the multitude of games that included or focused on object-oriented development. Due to space limitations, we chose to exclude knowledge areas and concepts that were not included in more than two games.

We differentiate between the inclusion of educational content with a primary focus versus a secondary focus. Educational content that is classified as being a primary focus of a given serious game indicates that the game designers emphasize that their game is designed to teach that content. In cases where the primary focus is not explicitly stated, we make a determination based on play testing or on a description of the game play. Alternatively, if educational content is present in a serious game but not emphasized, we classify this as having a secondary focus. Content with a secondary focus may be introduced in the game or may need to be learned prior to playing.

Evaluation. When available, we also review and classify the evaluation of a serious game[2]. First, we identify which games evaluate learning outcomes, player engagement, positive feedback, and accessibility. Second, we classify the evaluation methods used, ranging from informal player feedback and game results to full empirical studies about learning outcomes.

---

[2] Serious games with evaluations are primarily a subset of those that have accompanying research papers, technical reports or theses.

3   Results

We identified 49 serious programming games that met our selection criteria –
36 research games and 13 commercial games. Approximately half (23) of these
games can be downloaded or played online.

3.1   Audience

The largest audience of the surveyed games was undergraduate novices with
no programming experience (21 games) followed by undergraduates with some
programming experience (17 games), children (seven games) and high school
students (four games).

3.2   Educational Content

The educational content in each game was assessed based on the knowledge areas
identified in the ACM Computer Science Curricula 2013 (see Table 1):

– **Algorithms and Design:** this SDF unit covers the importance of algorithms
  in problem-solving, including mathematical functions and divide-and-conquer
  strategies. The comparison of algorithms in the surveyed serious games was
  not widely covered. An exception was the Human Resource Machine game
  in which players are incentivized to minimize the number of instructions and
  steps taken to complete tasks. When algorithm comparison was included, it
  was often done informally and without any mention of algorithmic complexity. Interestingly, only 21 of the 49 games had an emphasis on problem solving. For example, Robocode [36] is not problem solving-based but is instead
  competition-based with players completing programming challenges against
  opponents.
– **Fundamental Programming Concepts:** these are the most commonly
  targeted topics for serious programming games, which is consistent with the
  goal of introducing students to programming and helping them learn how to
  read and write code. 'Syntax and Semantics' was the most commonly covered
  concept with 30 games using some sort of written programming language; the
  remaining games used a drag-and-drop block interface for creating programs,
  or use a high-level language with little room for error (e.g. Gidget [33]).
  The next most widely covered concept was 'conditionals and iteratives' with
  28 games, followed by 'variables and primitive data types' with 23 games.
  Not all games required fundamental concepts like variables. For example,
  PlayLogo 3D [43] does not include variables as players need only submit
  individual commands with functions to play the game. While 'Recursion' was
  the primary focus of several games [9,14,32], it was one of the least covered
  concepts along with 'Input and Output.' This result was surprising given that
  the target audience for many of the games was university students with some
  programming experience.

Table 1. Classification of serious programming games based on educational content

| Game | ACM Computer Science Curricula 2013 – System Development Fundamentals & Software Engineering |||||||||||||||||| |
	Algorithm Comparison	Problem Solving	Non-specific Programming Concepts	Syntax & Semantics	Variables & Primitive Data Types	Expressions & Assignments	Input & Output	Conditionals & Iteratives	Functions & Parameters	Recursion	Arrays	Heterogeneous Aggregates	String Processing	Abstract Data Types	Program Comprehension	Debugging Strategies	Documentation & Program Style	OO Design Paradigms
Children																		
Minecraft: Hero's Journey [2]																		
Code Combat [3]																		
ToonTalk [26]																		
PlayLogo 3D [43]																		
Software KIDS [48]																		
Cquest [50]																		
World of Variables [64]																		
High School																		
Unnamed RPG [13]																		
May's Journey [23]																		
Co.Co.I.A. [45]																		
RoboBuilder [59]																		
University (no programming experience)																		
Super Markup Man [3]																		
Human Resource Machine [5]																		
Unnamed Maze [8]																		
Unnamed Puzzle [16]																		
Wu's Castle [20]																		
BOTS [22]																		
Pythia [25]																		
Program Your Robot [27]																		
IRPG [30]																		
Leek Wars [31]																		
Gidget [33]																		
Train B&P [34]																		
LightBot 2.0 [38]																		
Robot ON! [39]																		
Prog&Play [41]																		
Cube Game [46]																		
The Catacombs [47]																		
Project Orion [49]																		
No Bug's Snack Bar [56]																		
Bomberman Game [60]																		
Capital Tycoon [62]																		
University (programming experience)																		
Codingame [1]																		
Code Fights [4]																		
Saving Sera [9]																		
Ruby Warrior [10]																		
EleMental [14]																		
Screeps [15]																		
Resource Craft [24]																		
Critical Mass [32]																		
Unnamed Prototype [35]																		
RoboCode [36]																		
CMX [37]																		
RoboBUG [40]																		
Super Mario Collaborative [52]																		
Code Hunt [53]																		
Pex4Fun [54]																		
Soccercode [58]																		
Program Pacman [63]																		

Column group headers: *Algorithms & Design* (Algorithm Comparison, Problem Solving); *Fundamental Programming Concepts* (Non-specific Programming Concepts, Syntax & Semantics, Variables & Primitive Data Types, Expressions & Assignments, Input & Output, Conditionals & Iteratives, Functions & Parameters, Recursion); *Fundamental Data Structures* (Arrays, Heterogeneous Aggregates, String Processing, Abstract Data Types); *Development Methods* (Program Comprehension, Debugging Strategies, Documentation & Program Style); *Soft. Des.* (OO Design Paradigms).

LEGEND: ■■■■■ PRIMARY FOCUS   □□□□□ SECONDARY FOCUS

- **Fundamental Data Structures:** the most common data structure concepts were 'arrays and lists' (13 games) and 'heterogeneous structures' (12 games). Few research papers explicitly stated a focus on data structures, and our identification was primarily the result of game testing and reading game play descriptions. 'Abstract data types' were not included in most games. Exceptions include Critical Mass [32], which required players to navigate a tree structure. Finally, 'string processing' was only a secondary focus of three games, and other ACM concepts including 'linked lists' and 'referencing' were not targeted by any of the games.
- **Development Methods:** 'debugging' was the most commonly targeted development concept, with 12 games featuring some focus on debugging code. However, this does not include all of the ACM's program correctness topics (e.g. test-case generation, unit testing). Even the games that choose to focus on debugging [33, 40] are not comprehensive with respect to debugging topics. 'Program comprehension' was the focus of a few games, but the vast majority of games required players to write their own code. CodeFights is an example of a game where players must interpret code written by someone else and develop program comprehension skills through trying to understand foreign code. Although games with real programming languages allow for commenting, very few games focused on documentation and program style, and only did so as a secondary focus. Other development methods, including refactoring and the use of software libraries, were not covered by the games.
- **Software Design:** the majority of software design areas presented by the ACM are intended for learners above the beginner level. However, the curriculum indicates that software design should be covered at an early stage. IBM's Robocode [12,21,36,42] has a strong focus on software design – specifically object-oriented (OO) design, as players learn about abstraction through the use and modification of the game's robot objects.

3.3   Learning Focus

Identifying the primary focus of serious programming games was especially difficult when not explicitly stated by the game designers. When not stated, we based our identification of a primary focus from playing the available games and inferring based on the content of the research papers. In the end we found that 18 games focused primarily on general introductory programming, without a specific topic. Most of these 18 games included other fundamental programming concepts, but there were some research papers that introduced a game for learning introductory programming without detailing specific content. Problem solving was the second most common focus, with 7 different games. One example of this is Lightbot 2.0 [38], where players do not learn a programming language but do develop an understanding of sequencing and implementation of algorithms. The general trend of programming games that focus on problem solving is that they target simple problems and program-based solutions, with limited or no emphasis on formality.

Table 2. Classification of serious programming games based on evaluations methods

	Game	Research Questions				Method of Evaluation					
		Did the users have positive feelings about the game?	Was the game accessible?	Were users engaged while playing the game?	Was there a learning effect from playing the game?	Informal Feedback	Survey/Questionnaire	Formal Interview	Skill Tests	Game Play Statistics	Expert Feedback
Children	ToonTalk [26]		✓							●	
	PlayLogo 3D [43]		✓								●
	Software KIDS [48]	✓					●				
	Cquest [50]	✓				●					
High School	Unnamed RPG [13]				✓		●		●		
	May's Journey [23]	✓					●			●	
	Co.Co.I.A. [45]			✓		●					
	RoboBuilder [59]			✓		●					
University (no programming experience)	Unnamed Maze [8]			✓			●			●	
	Unnamed Puzzle [16]			✓			●				
	Wu's Castle [20]				✓		●		●		
	BOTS [22]				✓				●		
	Pythia [25]		✓				●				
	Program Your Robot [27]	✓					●				
	IRPG [30]	✓				●					
	Gidget [33]			✓	✓				●	●	
	Train B&P [34]			✓	◆		●			●	
	LightBot 2.0 [38]	✓			✓		●				
	Robot ONI [39]	✓			✓		●	●	●		
	Prog&Play [41]	✓	✓		◆		●		●	●	
	The Catacombs [47]	✓	✓	✓	◆		●	●	●	●	
	Project Orion [49]	✓	✓		◆		●				
	No Bug's Snack Bar [56]	✓				●					
	Capital Tycoon [62]			✓	◆		●				
University (programming experience)	Saving Sera [9]	✓	✓	✓	◆		●	●	●	●	
	EleMental [14]	✓			✓		●		●	●	
	Resource Craft [24]				✓		●			●	
	Critical Mass [32]	✓					●			●	
	Unnamed Prototype [35]			✓				●			
	RoboCode [36]	✓		✓	✓		●				
	CMX [37]	✓					●				
	RoboBUG [40]	✓	✓		◆		●		●		
	Code Hunt [53]	✓				●					
	Pex4Fun [54]	✓				●					
	Soccercode [58]	✓				●					
	Program Pacman [63]	✓					●				

EMPIRICAL EVIDENCE FOR A GIVEN RESEARCH QUESTION WAS POSITIVE (✓) or INCONCLUSIVE (◆)
DATA WAS COLLECTED & ANALYZED USING A GIVEN RESEARCH METHOD (●)

3.4   Evaluation

A variety of evaluation methods were used in the surveyed games (see Table 2) – 23 surveys, 11 sets of game play statistics, 10 skill tests, four sets of interviews and one evaluation using expert feedback. 21 games used only one evaluation method while 14 used multiple methods. The most common evaluation subject matter was positive feedback. There were 21 cases of participants reporting that they liked a game, often through a survey. 16 games were evaluated for learning effects on the players, but unfortunately seven of these did not have a statistically significant learning effect. Although many of the papers cited engagement as a motivation for using serious games, only 11 were actually evaluated for player engagement. Finally, only eight of the games were tested for accessibility.

4   Related Work

Although there are reviews that investigate the impact of serious games [17,19], there is very little research focusing on serious programming games. One exception is a review by Vahldick et al. [55], that focuses specifically on games for improving introductory programming skills. The review categorizes 40 games by type (Logo-based, adventure, general), platform (Windows, iOS, Java, Web, Android, Linux), competency (writing, reading, debugging), topic (including some of the ACM 2013 CS curricula topics from SDFs), and language (Textual/visual block graphics, Java/Javascript, C/C++/C#, and others).

Our work has two similarities with the Vahldick et al. review – first, 15 games are included in both studies and second, both studies survey the learning topics or content of the games. With regard to this overlap, we have included 34 games in our study that were not included by Vahldick et al. Furthermore, 25 games included in their study were not included in ours. Reasons for exclusion include: 13 games were outside of our selection criteria (e.g., non-english, not focused on learning programming), four games were extremely similar to other games in the survey, and eight games were no longer available online and did not have published papers. Our initial intention was to include as many of the previously studied games as possible in order to reproduce and validate the learning portion of the Vahldick et al. results. However, this was not possible as many of the overlapping games have been updated in the three years since their study and we no longer have access to the versions of games surveyed. The main difference between our work and the Vahldick et al. review is that we have surveyed a wider selection of games with the intention of assessing the learning aspects of the games (learning content and learning evaluation) as opposed to the game characteristics (e.g., platform, language, genre).

5   Discussion and Conclusion

Our results show that the 49 serious programming games surveyed focus primarily on a subset of the ACM computing knowledge areas. Unfortunately, many of the games are not released publicly and we were unable to independently verify the learning content of these games through play testing. The lack of access is problematic for both researchers developing computer science educational games and instructors seeking to find effective learning tools. The surveyed serious games focus largely on the problem solving and fundamental programming concepts knowledge areas. There are a lack of games that focus on data structures, development methods and software design. Furthermore, while the primary learning focus of many games was introductory programming, few of the games appear to cover all of the ACM's SDFs. This indicates **a need to determine if new serious programming games can bridge the curricula gaps**. It is possible that some SDFs are not well suited for game-based learning.

With respect to game design, we observed that the majority of the games were not multiplayer. There is **a need for further research on the learning benefits of competitive and collaborative serious games for programming**. We also observed that while a number of games were designed with accessibility and inclusivity in mind (e.g. Saving Sera [9], May's Journey [23]), many did not include any detail on these important aspects of design. This maybe an indicator that **best practices for accessible and inclusive design of serious programming games need to be adopted.**

With respect to the evaluation of serious program games, we were unable to observe common methodological practices other than a tendency to assess if players liked a game. This indicates a **need for the establishment of best practices in evaluating serious programming games**. We believe that the use of alternative evaluation methods in addition to in-class studies would be beneficial. In particular, it may be helpful to consider controlled experiments and expert feedback (e.g. used only in PlayLOGO 3D [43]) in combination with playability heuristics [18]. Finally, in addition to establishing best practices for evaluation, there is a **need for third-party evaluations**. Third-party evaluations do not suffer from self-confirmatory bias, provide valuable data that can independently validate a serious game's learning effects, and can lead to wider adoption of serious games in Computer Science education.

Acknowledgment. This research was partially funded by the Natural Sciences and Engineering Research Council of Canada (NSERC).

References

1. Codingame: Coding games and programming challenges to code better. https://www.codingame.com/ (2012). Accessed 12 Apr 2017
2. CodeCombat: Learn how to code by playing a game. https://codecombat.com/ (2013). Accessed 12 Apr 2017
3. Super Markup Man. http://store.steampowered.com/app/502210/ (2013). Accessed 12 Apr 2017
4. Codefights: Test your code. https://codefights.com/ (2015). Accessed 12 Apr 2017
5. Human Resource Machine. https://tomorrowcorporation.com/humanresourcemachine (2015). Accessed 12 Apr 2017

6. Minecraft: Hour of code tutorials. https://code.org/minecraft (2017). Accessed 12 Apr 2017
7. ACM/IEEE-CS Joint Task Force on Computing Curricula: Computer science curricula 2013. Technical report, ACM Press and IEEE Computer Society Press, December (2013)
8. Adamo-Villani, N., Haley-Hermiz, T., Cutler, R.: Using a serious game approach to teach 'operator precedence' to introductory programming students. In: Proceedings of the International Conference on Information Visualisation (IV 2013), pp. 523–526 (2013)
9. Barnes, T., Powell, E., Chaffin, A., Lipford, H.: Game2Learn : improving the motivation of CS1 students. In: Proceedings of the 3rd International Conference on Game Development in Computer Science Education (GDCSE 2008), pp. 1–5 (2008)
10. Bates, Ryan: Ruby warrior: popular free ruby programming tutorial game. https://www.bloc.io/ruby-warrior/ (2010). Accessed 13 April 2017
11. Begel, A.: LogoBlocks: a graphical programming language for interacting with the world. Master's thesis, Electrical Engineering and Computer Science, MIT (1996)
12. Bonakdarian, E., White, L.: Robocode throughout the curriculum. J. Comput. Sci. Coll. **19**(3), 311–313 (2004)
13. Buckley, C.: Design and implementation of a genre hybrid video game that integrates the curriculum of an introductory programming course. Master's thesis, Clemson University (2012)
14. Chaffin, A., Doran, K., Hicks, D., Barnes, T.: Experimental evaluation of teaching recursion in a video game. In: Proceedings of the 2009 ACM SIGGRAPH Symposium on Video Games, vol. 1, pp. 79–86 (2009)
15. Chivchalov, A., Chivchalov, A., Gunyakov, S.: Screeps. https://screeps.com/ (2016). Accessed 12 Apr 2017
16. Coelho, A., Kato, E., Xavier, J., Gonçalves, R.: Serious game for introductory programming. In: Ma, M., Fradinho Oliveira, M., Madeiras Pereira, J. (eds.) SGDA 2011. LNCS, vol. 6944, pp. 61–71. Springer, Heidelberg (2011). https://doi.org/10.1007/978-3-642-23834-5_6
17. Connolly, T.M., Boyle, E.A., MacArthur, E., Hainey, T., Boyle, J.M.: A systematic literature review of empirical evidence on computer games and serious games. Comput. Educ. **59**(2), 661–686 (2012)
18. Desurvire, H., Wiberg, C.: Game usability heuristics (PLAY) for evaluating and designing better games: the next iteration. In: Ozok, A.A., Zaphiris, P. (eds.) OCSC 2009. LNCS, vol. 5621, pp. 557–566. Springer, Heidelberg (2009). https://doi.org/10.1007/978-3-642-02774-1_60
19. Dondlinger, M.J.: Educational video game design: a review of the literature. J. Appl. Educ. Technol. **4**(1), 21–31 (2007)
20. Eagle, M., Barnes, T.: Experimental evaluation of an educational game for improved learning in introductory computing. In: Proceedings of the 40th ACM Technical Symposium on Computer science education (SIGCSE 2009), pp. 321–325 (2009)
21. Hartness, K.: Robocode: using games to teach artificial intelligence. J. Comput. Sci. Coll. **19**(4), 287–291 (2004)
22. Hicks, A.: Towards social gaming methods for improving game-based computer science education. In: Proceedings of the Fifth International Conference on the Foundations of Digital Games - FDG 2010, pp. 259–261 (2010)
23. Jemmali, C., Zijian, Y.: May's journey: a serious game to teach middle and high school girls programming. Master's thesis, Worcester Polytechnic Institute (2016)

24. Jiau, H.C., Chen, J.C., Ssu, K.F.: Enhancing self-motivation in learning programming using game-based simulation and metrics. IEEE Trans. Educ. **52**(4), 555–562 (2009)

25. Johnsen, A.L., Ushakov, G.: Python programming game. Master's thesis, Norwegian University of Science and Technology (2011)

26. Kahn, K.: A computer game to teach programming introduction to ToonTalk. In: Proceedings of the National Educational Computing Conference, pp. 127–135 (1999)

27. Kazimoglu, C., Kiernan, M., Bacon, L., Mackinnon, L.: A serious game for developing computational thinking and learning introductory computer programming, vol. 47, pp. 1991–1999. Elsevier (2012)

28. Kelleher, C., Cosgrove, D., Culyba, D., Forlines, C., Pratt, J., Pausch, R.: Alice2: programming without syntax errors. In: Proceedings of the 15th International Symposium on User Interface Software and Technology (UIST 2002) - Demonstrations, pp. 35–36 (2002)

29. Kelly, J.O., Maynooth, N.U.I., Gibson, J.P.: RoboCode & problem-based learning: a non-prescriptive approach to teaching programming. ACM SIGCSE Bull. **38**(3), 217–221 (2006)

30. Khenissi, M., Essalmi, F., Jemni, M.: Presentation of a learning game for programming languages education. In: Proceedings of IEEE 13th International Conference on Advanced Learning Technologies (ICALT 2013), pp. 324–326 (2013)

31. Laupretre, P.: Leek wars. https://leekwars.com/ (2016). Accessed 12 Apr 2017

32. Lawrence, R.: Teaching data structures using competitive games. IEEE Trans. Educ. **47**(4), 459–466 (2004)

33. Lee, M.J., Ko, A.J.: Investigating the role of purposeful goals on novices' engagement in a programming game. In: Proceedings of IEEE Symposium on Visual Languages and Human-Centric Computing, VL/HCC, pp. 163–166 (2012)

34. Liu, C.C., Cheng, Y.B., Huang, C.W.: The effect of simulation games on the learning of computational problem solving. Comp. and Edu. **57**(3), 1907–1918 (2011)

35. Ljungkvist, P., Mozelius, P.: Educational games for self learning in introductory programming courses - a straightforward design approach with progression mechanisms. In: Proceedings of the 6th European Conference on Games Based Learning, pp. 285–293 (2012)

36. Long, J.: Just for fun: using programming games in software programming training and education - a field study of IBM robocode community. J. Inf. Technol. Educ. **6**, 279–290 (2007)

37. Malliarakis, C., Satratzemi, M., Xinogalos, S.: CMX: implementing an MMORPG for learning programming. In: Proceedings of the 8th European Conference on Games Based Learning (ECGBL2014), pp. 346–355 (2014)

38. Mathrani, A., Christian, S., Ponder-Sutton, A.: PlayIT: game based learning approach for teaching programming concepts. Educ. Technol. Soc. **19**(5), 5–17 (2016)

39. Miljanovic, M.A., Bradbury, J.S.: Robot ON!: a serious game for improving programming comprehension. In: Proceedings of the 5th International Workshop on Games and Software Engineering, pp. 33–36 (2016)

40. Miljanovic, M.A., Bradbury, J.S.: RoboBUG: a serious game for learning debugging techniques. In: Proceedings of the 2017 ACM Conference on International Computing Education Research (ICER 2017), pp. 93–100 (2017)

41. Muratet, M., Delozanne, E., Torguet, P., Viallet, F.: Serious game and students' learning motivation: effect of context using Prog&Play. In: Proceedings of the 11th International Conference on Intelligent Tutoring Systems (ITS 2012), pp. 123–128, Jun 2012

42. O'Kelly, J., Gibson, J.P.: RoboCode & problem-based learning : a non-prescriptive approach to teaching programming. In: Proceedings of the Annual Conference on Innovation and Technology in Computer Science Education (ITiCSE 2006), pp. 26–28 (2006)
43. Paliokas, I., Arapidis, C., Mpimpitsos, M.: Game based early programming education: the more you play, the more you learn. In: Pan, Z., Cheok, A.D., Müller, W., Liarokapis, F. (eds.) Transactions on Edutainment IX. LNCS, vol. 7544, pp. 115–131. Springer, Heidelberg (2013). https://doi.org/10.1007/978-3-642-37042-7_7
44. Pandeliev, V.T., Baecker, R.M.: A framework for the online evaluation of serious games. In: Proceedings of the International Academic Conference on the Future of Game Design and Technology, pp. 239–242. ACM (2010)
45. Pellas, N.: Exploring interrelationships among high school students engagement factors in introductory programming courses via a 3D multi-user serious game created in open Sim. J. Univers. Comput. Sci. 20(12), 1608–1628 (2014)
46. Piteira, M., Haddad, S.R.: Innovate in your program computer class: an approach based on a serious game. In: Proceedings of the Workshop on Open Source and Design of Communication, pp. 49–54 (2011)
47. Ralph, T., Barnes, T.: The Catacombs: a study on the usability of games to teach introductory programming (2006)
48. Ramirez-Rosales, S., Vazquez-Reyes, S., Villa-Cisneros, J.L., De Leon-Sigg, M.: A serious game to promote object oriented programming and software engineering basic concepts learning. In: Proceedings of the 4th Interenational Conference in Software Engineering Research and Innovation (CONISOFT 2016), pp. 97–103 (2016)
49. Romo, E.K.: Game design for a serious game to help learn programming. Master's thesis, Faculdade de Engenharia da Universidade do Porto (2011)
50. Singh, J., et al.: Designing computer games to introduce programming to children. In: Proceedings of the 4th International Conference on Information Technology and Multimedia, pp. 643–647 (2008)
51. Tessler, J., Beth, B., Lin, C.: Using cargo-bot to provide contextualized learning of recursion. In: Proceedings of the 9th Annual International ACM Conference on International Computing Education Research (ICER 2013), pp. 161–168 (2013)
52. Theodorou, C., Kordaki, M.: Super Mario: a collaborative game for the learning of variables in programming. Int. J. Acad. Res. 2(4), 111–118 (2010)
53. Tillmann, N., Bishop, J.: Code hunt: searching for secret code for fun. In: Proceedings of the 7th International Workshop on Search-Based Software Testing (SBST 2014), pp. 23–26 (2014)
54. Tillmann, N., Halleux, J.D., Bishop, J.: Teaching and learning programming and software engineering via interactive gaming. In: Proceedings of the International Conference on Software Engineering (ICSE 2013), pp. 1117–1126 (2013)
55. Vahldick, A., Mendes, A.J., Marcelino, M.J.: A review of games designed to improve introductory computer programming competencies. In: Proceedings of the Frontiers in Education Conference (FIE 2014), pp. 1–7. IEEE (2014)
56. Vahldick, A., Mendes, A.J., Marcelino, M.J.: Analysing the enjoyment of a serious game for programming learning with two unrelated higher education audiences. In: Proceedings of the European Conference on Games-based Learning, pp. 523–531 (2015)
57. Vassilev, T.I., Mutev, B.I.: An approach to teaching introductory programming using games. In: Proceedings of the International Conference on e-Learning, pp. 246–253 (2014)

58. Wang, M., Hu, X.: SoccerCode: A game system for introductory programming courses in computer science. In: Proceedings of the World Congress on Engineering and Computer Science (WCECS 2011), pp. 282–287, Oct 2011
59. Weintrop, D., Wilensky, U.: RoboBuilder: video game program-to-play constructionist. Proc. Constr. **2012**, 1–5 (2012)
60. Wong, W., Chou, Y.: An interactive Bomberman game-based teaching/learning tool for introductory C programming. In: Proceedings of the International Conference on Technologies for E-Learning and Digital Entertainment, pp. 433–444 (2007)
61. Yan, L.: Teaching object-oriented programming with games. In: Proceedings of the 6th International Conference on Information Technology: New Generations, pp. 969–974. IEEE (2009)
62. Yeh, K.c.M., Chen, W.f.: WIP: Using a computer gaming strategy to facilitate undergraduates' learning in a computer programming course: an experimental study. In: Proceedings of the 41st ASEE/IEEE Frontiers in Education Conference, pp. 11–12 (2011)
63. Yue, W.S., Wan, W.L.: The effectiveness of digital game for introductory programming concepts. In: Proceedings of the 10th International Conference for Internet Technology and Secured Transactions (ICITST 2015), pp. 421–425 (2015)
64. Zapušek, M., Rugelj, J.: Learning programming with serious games. EAI Endorsed Trans. Game-Based Learn. **13**(1), 1–8 (2013)

Examining Approaches for Mobility Detection Through Smartphone Sensors

Thomas Tregel[1(✉)], Andreas Gilbert[2], Robert Konrad[1],
Petra Schäfer[2], and Stefan Göbel[1]

[1] TU Darmstadt, Darmstadt, Germany
{thomas.tregel,robert.konrad,
stefan.goebel}@kom.tu-darmstadt.de
[2] Frankfurt University of Applied Sciences, Frankfurt, Germany
{andreas.gilbert,petra.schaefer}@fbl.fra-uas.de

Abstract. The ubiquity of smartphones with integrated positioning systems, and multiple sensors for movement detection made it possible to develop context-sensitive applications for both productivity and entertainment. Location-based games like Ingress or Pokémon Go have demonstrated the public interest in this genre of mobile-only games – games that are exclusively available for mobile devices due to their sensor integration. For these games mobility is a key component, which defines and influences the game's flow directly.

In this paper we compare different approaches and available frameworks for mobility detection and examine the frameworks' performances in a scenario-based evaluation.

Based on our finding we present our own approach to differentiate between different modes of public transport and other common modes of movement like walking, running or riding a bicycle. Our approach already reaches an accuracy of 87% with a small sample size.

Keywords: Mobility · Mobility detection · Machine learning

1 Introduction

The purpose of recognized types of movement is diverse. Depending on the application, different levels of detail are required in the recognition. If the user is to be animated solely for more exercise in the fresh air and thereby improve his health, the recognition of different types of mobility such as walking or running, cycling and skating is needed. Distinctions regarding different types of vehicles are not necessary. If, however, it is possible to differentiate between different emission levels, additional vehicles must be distinguished from each other. So there are in addition to the usual cars with combustion engine electric cars or cars with hybrid drive. There are also motorbikes and public transport such as trams and buses. In order for the respective level of pollutant emissions to be approximately assigned, a precise distinction of the vehicles is required. Although there are two implementations for mobility detection for Android in the form of an API and a framework, the distinction with these

© Springer Nature Switzerland AG 2018
S. Göbel et al. (Eds.): JCSG 2018, LNCS 11243, pp. 217–228, 2018.
https://doi.org/10.1007/978-3-030-02762-9_22

implementations is not sufficiently detailed possible. These allow at most a distinction between non-existent mobility, walk, run, drive and ride a bicycle.

Our goal in this paper is to show possibilities and limitations of mobility detection with Android smartphones in both literature and open available frameworks. To this end, existing approaches are first examined and compared, and relevant components from comparable approaches are analysed. Subsequently, existing implementations for Android are examined, implemented and compared with each other. In addition to the accuracy of the recognition, particular attention should be paid to resource consumption.

From the results obtained, a concept is created and implemented that can more quickly differentiate more modes of transport. This implementation is checked for accuracy in detail. The goal is to be able to distinguish vehicles from each other and to operate with greater accuracy than in existing implementations.

In the context of Location-based games or mobile-only games this system enables the use personalization and adaptation methods with respect to the user's mobility behaviour.

2   Mobility Detection Using Smartphones

The following approaches have been developed in the current decade. At the beginning of the decade, Nokia was the most popular operating system for smartphones with Symbian operating system versions, but Android and iOS also became more relevant in the marketplace than at the end of the last decade [1]. The following approaches are in chronological order.

2.1   "Movement Recognition Using the Accelerometer in Smartphones"

The approach of Sian Lun Lau and K. David studied below was designed in 2010 [2]. As hardware the Nokia N95 8 GB with the operating system Symbian S60 3rd edition FP1 was used. Built into this is an accelerometer that measures the acceleration on three different axes in the x, y and z directions.

The data was first collected using a Python script for the appropriate operating system. Another script combined the collected data to determine the mode of travel. The chosen modes of movement were running, standing, sitting and running down and running up a staircase. As a condition to maintain the Accelerometer data, it was determined that the smartphone is in your pocket. Two different situations were examined. The first situation (S1) stated that the smartphone is in a fixed and predetermined position in the right pocket, while in the second situation (S2) the smartphone did not need to have a fixed position in any trouser pocket. Sampling rates of 60 Hz to 70 Hz have been achieved with the Nokia N95 8 GB by obtaining the accelerometer data. However, in this approach 32 Hz was considered sufficient for mobility detection, so higher sampling rates were not investigated. Sampling rates of 5 Hz, 10 Hz, 20 Hz and 40 Hz were compared with an accuracy of more than 90% already achieved for 5 Hz to 20 Hz. The extracted features were the average $\bar{x}$ and the standard deviation σ of both the accelerometer raw data and the Fast Fourier Transform (FFT) components of the data. There were three combinations of features for this. The first combination (C1) included the average and standard deviation of the individual and aggregate axes of the accelerometer. The second combination (C2) included the average and standard deviation of the FFT components of each axis and the combination of axes. The third combination (C3) contained all features for each axis and for the combination of all axes.

For extracting the features, the sliding window approach was used. Compared window sizes were 5, 10, 20, 40, and 80 samples per window, so along with the sampling rates, these window sizes are equivalent to 0.5, 1, 2, and 4 s between getting new data. The windows also had an overlap of 50%. The classification was based on the rule-based learner JRip and the Supervised classifiers Decision Tree, Bayesian Network, Naive Bayes, K Nearest Neighbor (k-NN) and Support Vector Machine (SVM). Sequential Minimal Optimization (SMO) was used for the comparison. It was evaluated with 10-fold Cross Validation. Weka was used for the classification. The accuracy of the results was determined by the percentage of correctly classified mobility types on the total number of types of mobility occurring.

With the combinations of the classifiers C1 and C3 the best results were achieved with 99.27% for S1 and 96.59% for S2. In addition, higher accuracy was achieved if all axes were combined rather than considered individually. In addition, the classifier KNN was the most accurate. The best combination of samples and window sizes was a sampling rate of 20 Hz with 80 samples per window with the classifiers KNN, Bayesian Networks, Naive Bayes and JRip, as well as 10 Hz with 40 samples and 40 Hz with 80 samples. The highest accuracy reached was 99.27%. In addition, the results were tested against a new data set with S1. Here an accuracy of 91.95% was achieved, with levels achieved a lower accuracy than the other modes of mobility. Other modes of transport had an accuracy of almost 100%. Here the combination of C1 with KNN and Bayesian Networks with 10 Hz and 20 Hz as sampling rate and a window length of four seconds gave the highest accuracy.

2.2 "Activity Detection on Smartphones"

The following examines a Wirtl and Nickel approach from 2011, with which various activities can be distinguished directly on the smartphone [3].

Two smartphones with Android operating system were used. These include the HTC G1 from 2008 with Android 1.6 and the Motorola Defy from 2010 with Android 2.1. The HTC G1 averaged a sampling rate of 43 Hz, and the Motorola Defy one of 137 Hz. The accelerometer was used for detection. The devices should be horizontally attached to the belt in this approach, while the sensor data used were generated on a flat and straight path.

There were six classifying features, which were also considered separately from the sensor axis. To address the problem that an exact sample rate cannot be specified with Android, the data was interpolated before the features were extracted. The interpolation was achieved on the one hand through the assumption of the nearer value and on the other hand through a linear interpolation. The six characteristics were the time between extreme values TBP, the mean AVG, the standard deviation STD, the average absolute difference, the average resulting acceleration AAD and the class division BIN. The time between the extreme values is calculated as the absolute difference between the minima i and maxima A, which in turn are recorded by a change from slopes to positive or negative values.

The average difference is calculated using $aad = \frac{1}{n}\sum_{i=1}^{n} |a_i - \bar{a}|$ and the resulting average acceleration using $ara = \frac{1}{n}\sum_{i=1}^{n} \sqrt{x_i^2 + y_i^2 + z_i^2}$.

Classification is the division of the span between the maximum and minimum into ten equally sized classes and the subsequent counting of the values that can be assigned to an axis by a class. First, a one-way test was performed on the computer with one-third of the data. This related to the classification algorithm, the features, the interpolated sample rate, the duration of the data acquisition and the type of interpolation. In this case, raw data was also compared to preprocessed data in order to be surer of the effect of preprocessing. The 18 algorithms available at the time of this approach in Weka were run with all feature combinations and sample rates of 50 Hz, 100 Hz and 150 Hz with a data acquisition duration of 2 s, 5 s, 10 s and 15 s and the two interpolation data. In addition to classifying up-to-date data from the Accelerometer, the training of the Classifier has been implemented on the smartphone to optionally use newly acquired data to improve the classifier.

The activities were classified with Weka, maintaining the default parameters. There were 151 records, of which 51 were intended for fast walking, 49 for normal walking and 51 for slow walking. The data was collected from 51 subjects who were walking on level ground with the HTC G1 for about 17 s without any turns. The REPTree algorithm achieved the best result when using the test data with a data collection time of 10 s. Thus, this combination was used for implementation on smartphones.

The classification took 0.29 s with the Motorola Defy and 0.79 s with the HTC G1. The former detected 80% of the correct mode of mobility in a test by 20 subjects and 75% with the latter.

2.3 "Accelerometer-Based Transportation Mode Detection on Smartphones"

In the approach of Hemminki et al. [4] investigates techniques for discriminating modes of transport travel using smart phone sensors on Android devices.

The GPS receiver is not used in this approach, as it is efficient with the existing signal, but consumes a lot of battery and is dependent on uninterrupted view to the satellites. This can be a problem not only in buildings, but also on a route through subway stations, or even in vehicles where the user sits too far away from a window. Another problem with using the GPS receiver is only mediocre accuracy, should many different vehicle rides be distinguished. Instead, the accelerometer is mainly used for this approach because it does not have the aforementioned problems. Because it is consumed with this less battery, there is no dependence on external information sources such as satellites and it was a particularly fast and detailed query possible. For more accurate results, gravity is estimated. As a result, the horizontal speed can be determined more accurately, which is to be used to distinguish start-up and braking sequences. For the estimation an own algorithm was presented, which in contrast to the simple formation of the average is more robust against sudden changes of the orientation of the smartphone. These sequences are different from means of mobility to means of transportation. In addition, new features called 'peak features' are introduced, which are intended to model patterns of acceleration and deceleration and to increase the performance of recognition. The process of mobility detection is divided into four different classifiers in this approach. First of all, the 'Kinematic Motion' Classifier attempts to detect the general mode of mobility. Depending on the outcome of this classifier, it will be passed to one of the three more specific classifiers for 'Walking', 'Stationary' or 'Motorized'. With "Stationary" is to be distinguished whether the user is in a vehicle or in a fixed location. If the former is the case, it is forwarded to the classifier "Motorized", with which a distinction from the means of transportation bus, train, tram, metro and car is provided. Between modes of travel in vehicles, a segment is assumed on foot, in which the user runs to the next means of transportation. To increase the accuracy, no frames are used for the classification of the raw data, but segments, which are formed depending on the types of mobility. The raw data is first revised with a low-pass filter to reduce noise. Then the data is aggregated with a sliding window approach with 50% overlap and a length of 1.2 s. The length was chosen to be able to react quickly to a change of mobility types and to distinguish them. Afterwards the calculated gravity is calculated with the accelerometer data and the result uses the integral as the current speed. The algorithm is an improvement to the simpler approach of Mizell et al. thought.

Preprocessing is followed by extracting features. This approach extracts frame-based features, peak-based features, and segment-based features, each applied to the appropriate situations. Frame-based features are designed to differentiate types of mobility on the basis of higher frequencies of the data, as they occur when walking on foot. Here, 27 features were calculated in the vertical and horizontal directions by, for example, average $\bar{x}$, variance, double integral, entropy, and sum of FFT coefficients. Peak-based features should characterize lower frequencies for mobility detection by extracting regions with strong changes through a stream-based algorithm. Segment-based features are used to characterize patterns of acceleration and deceleration. It identifies the frequency of accelerations and brakes, the frequency and duration of intermediate pauses in mobility, and the variance of individual peak-based features. Subsequently, the data is used for classification. AdaBoost is used to improve the learning algorithms. Decision trees with a depth of two were used for the Kinematic Motion classifier. Also in the Motorized classifier AdaBoost is used along with decision trees with a depth of two.

2.4 "Activity Recognition Using Smartphone Sensors"

The approach described below was developed in 2013 by Anjum and Ilyas [5].

It was implemented on an Android smartphone, which in this case was a Samsung Galaxy Y with Android 2.3.3. No exact orientation of the smartphone was given.

The activities 'walking', 'running', 'climbing stairs', 'going down stairs', 'driving', 'cycling' and 'being inactive' should be differentiated. For detection, a classifier with the best found configurations is developed. This classifier was implemented in an Android application that performs real-time activity detection using this classifier. Initially, a dataset with 510 activity shots was created, for which an Android application was written that enabled data collection. In this application, additional user information such as size, age, gender and the most used smartphone position were queried. The recorded sensor data was divided by a comma into a file specially written for this activity. The written data consisted of the three axes for the accelerometer and for the gyroscope, and the GPS data based on longitude, latitude and speed. In the Android version used in this approach, the sampling rates in 'Normal' with 5 Hz, 'UI' with 15 Hz, 'Game' with 50 Hz and 'Fastest' with platform-dependent 50 Hz to 100 Hz were selected. In this case, the 'UI' mode was used because a Nyquist rate of 15–16 Hz would allow a maximum signal frequency of 8 Hz to distinguish it from human activity. To compensate for the dependence on the orientation of the smartphone, the data was rotated to selected axes d1, d2 and d3.

The data was collected by 10 different people aged 12 to 25 years. The data from four of these people were used to train the classifier while the remaining data was used for testing.

Existing data was divided into ten different datasets using 10-fold Cross Validation. Different classifiers were trained, with the most performant, judged by iterating over all ten sets of data with the test set, used for the implementation. The examined classifiers used the algorithms C4.5, Naive Bayes, KNN and SVM. The classifier with method C4.5 had the best performance with a true positive rate of 95.2%, a false positive rate of 1.1%, a precision of 94.4% and a recall rate of 94.2%.

2.5 Comparison

In the following assessment of the approaches, a comparison of the existing approaches as well as relevant aspects of other approaches will be made. Based on this comparison, the approaches for their usability are evaluated for our own approach (Table 1).

The above table compares existing approaches in their significant points. Significant for the assessment were the hardware used, the recognizable mobility types, the sampling rates, the window sizes in seconds, and the overlapping of the windows in which Weka was used, as well as the algorithms examined for the classification. The highlighted entries indicate favoritism by the authors of the approaches, which were assessed by evaluations.

In the table it can be seen that there is no mode of mobility, which is recognizable from all examined approaches. In addition, specifications for data entry are made in all approaches, which are differentially restrictive depending on the approach. The approach described in [2] was to carry the smartphone in your pocket. In addition, two different situations were examined, which specified the orientation and the side of the smartphone in one case and, in the other case, allowed any orientation and side. As a result of these restrictive requirements, an accuracy of almost 100% was achieved, in particular with an exact specification of the position of the smartphones in the trouser pocket. Even with a rotation of the device or a change of the side of the trouser pocket, the accuracy dropped by about three percent from 99.27% to 96.59%. In the approach in [3] the devices were attached vertically to the belt and a flat and straight path was chosen, while in [4] the subjects were given whether the smartphone should be in the bag, trouser pocket or jacket pocket. In the approach described in [5], the data was collected with an indication of how the user transports the smartphone in most cases.

Table 1. Comparison of existing approaches in related work.

Approach	Hardware	Movement types	Sampling rates	Window size	Overlap	Features	Classifier
(1)	Nokia N95 with Symbian S60	Walking, Standing, Sitting, Stairs up, Stairs down	5 Hz **10 Hz 20 Hz** 40 Hz	0.5 s 1 s 2 s **4 s**	50%	$\bar{x}$, σ of raw data, FFT	Decision Tree, BN, NB, KNN, SVM + 10-Fold Cross Validation, JRip, SMO
(2)	HTC Android 1.6 and 2.1	Fast, normal, slow walking	50 Hz 100 Hz 150 Hz	2 s 5 s **10 s** 15 s	–	T_e, $\bar{x}$, σ, average absolute difference, average resulting acceleration	**REPTree** & all other Weka classifiers
(3)	Nexus S, Galaxy S2 & S3	Standing, Running, Car, Bus, Tram, Train, Metro	60 Hz, 100 Hz	1.2 s	50%	Lowpass 90% & own Frame-/Peak-/Segment-based features	AdaBoost
(4)	Samsung Galaxy Y with Android 2.3.3	Walking, Running, Stairs up, Stairs down, Bike, Vehicle, None	15 Hz	5 s	–	$\bar{x}$, σ, Acceleration-magnitude, FFT	**C4.5 Decision Tree**, NB, KNN, SVM + 10-Fold Cross Validation

Here, for example, a trouser pocket, shirt pocket, handbag and hand were distinguished. This approach also uses user data to include size, weight, and gender. In this approach, the accuracy was not nearly 100%, but decreased to 94% −95%.

The sampling rates are also very different. The choice was justified in the approach in [2] and the approach in [5]. In the former, the rates of 10 Hz and 20 Hz are based on the evaluation results, while in the latter; the 15 Hz is due to the Nyquist frequency, which allows a maximum recoverable signal frequency of 8 Hz. These 8 Hz were considered sufficient to detect human mobility. Also the window sizes vary depending on the approach. In the approach described in [3], a duration of ten seconds was considered best after evaluation, while in [2] four seconds were chosen as a result of evaluation. In half of the approaches, an overlap of the windows was mentioned, which in both cases had a size of 50%. Also half of the approaches used for coaching and using the classifier Weka. For this purpose, different features were extracted from approach to approach. The use of raw data and the use of Fourier transforms was also compared in [2]. The result of this comparison was that it was more accurately classified with raw data. Most commonly, the mean and standard deviation were used as features, with additional features defined in [3]. In [4], the noise in the data was reduced with a low-pass filter with 90% energy. As versatile as the selected features are the classifiers. For this comparison, the following table with classifiers is also included in further comparable approaches.

3 Existing Frameworks

In comparison to the previously presented approaches the following two frameworks can be directly integrated and evaluated on mobile devices. In contrast to the previous approaches the decision-making process is not described. We aim to compare them regarding their prediction accuracy and the time required to identify and switch towards the real type of movement.

3.1 Awareness API

Google introduced the Awareness API at the Google I/O 2016 conference [6]. With this API the context recognition has to be implemented in a resource-saving way. There are seven different types of contexts to distinguish. These seven types are local time, location and location, headset state, weather, mobility, and nearby interesting places called beacons. The distinct modes of mobility are *vehicle*, *bi*cycle, standing, *running*, *walking*, *without movement* and *unknown*. A detailed distinction between vehicles does not take place.

The Awareness API consists of two different APIs. The Snapshot API can be used to make a request about the user's current context. The Fence API, on the other hand, defines so-called fences for describing a context to be observed. If the user enters such a fence, the app will be notified without having to open it. For continuous detection of mobility types, notification of a change makes the Fence API more suitable than the Snapshot API. However, if you only need to know the mode of travel at that particular time at certain times, the Snapshot API can also be used to actively run a query.

3.2 Neura SDK

The NeuraLabs Neura SDK [7] provides comprehensive context recognition for both iOS and Android. The time of origin can be assumed according to the code on Github5 at the end of 2016. In addition other contextual information, the user's mode of travel may determine whether the user has just started or stopped walking, running, or driving a vehicle. Thus, it is the modes of travel, on foot 'and' drive vehicle 'distinguishable. In addition, after one hour and two hours, a notification can be received that the user has not moved during this period. These types of mobility can be used when including the Neura SDK named *userStartedRunning*, *userFinishedRunning*, *userStartedWalking*, *userFinishedWalking*, *userStartedTransitByWalking*, *userFinishedTransitByWalking*, *userIsIdleFor1Hour*, *userIsIdleFor2Hours*, *userStartedDriving* and *userFinished Driving*.

3.3 Comparison

In a 40-minute-long test scenario we used the presented frameworks in parallel and logged the identified mobility types. Figure 1 shows that mobility detection by no means works perfectly.

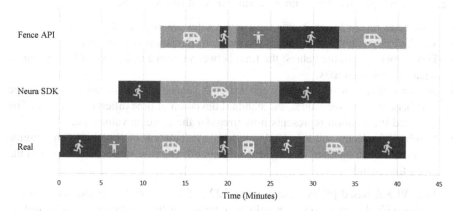

Fig. 1. Comparison of a test scenario over 45 min using two available Android frameworks.

Waiting times cannot be detected by the Neura SDK, so they are ignored. This is particularly evident in the longer journey in a vehicle, which is detected instead of the switch to the tram. The Fence API more reliably detects the changeover between modes of transport. The part of the tram ride in which the tram has been waiting was considered missing. In addition, the detection of a change of mobility takes place only after a time delay. Based on the test results, the Neura SDK has a minimum delay of five minutes and a maximum delay of seven minutes. For the Fence API, the minimum delay is one minute, while the maximum delay is four minutes.

In summary, it can be seen that the Awareness API for mobility detection offers more advantages due to more detailed distinctions, less extensive implementation, less impact on application design, lower resource consumption, and less delay in recognition than the Neura SDK. In addition, if only an active query of the current mode of transport is required, the Snapshot API would be preferred to the Fence API, in particular due to less implementation effort. But even the Awareness API does not provide a sufficient distinction for the mobility detection, since in particular no vehicles can be differentiated among themselves.

4 Consolidated Approach

For our own approach the goal is to be able to distinguish between the different modes of transportation like bike, car, bus or tram.

The identification of the modes of movement in this concept should refer exclusively to the data of these sensors. The use of GPS data was reported by (3) is considered inappropriate because the collection of data places restrictive conditions on the environment. Thus, the user may not be in a subway or train station or other building, and should sit as close to the window as possible in a car for a clear view of the satellites delivering the GPS data.

In order to differentiate between these modes of transportation we choose similar features as these presented in the related work, with all of them being calculated in a parameterized time window with a default value of five seconds:

- Arithmetic mean: for each axis the mean values are calculated
- Standard deviation: for each axis the standard deviation is calculated
- Time between extreme values: the time between minima and maxima is determined separated for each axis.
- Standard deviation of time between extreme values: instead of using the average time between extreme values, the standard deviation of time differences is used. The extracted information represents how irregular the extreme values are.
- Number of extreme values: Analogue to the calculation of time between extreme values and their standard deviation the number of extreme values is extracted in the given time window.

In a WEKA-based [8] evaluation using 722 collected samples spread across seven categories with the main focus on vehicular modes of transportation we achieved an accuracy of 87% using 10-fold cross validation on both a random forest and an IBk algorithm as shown in Table 2. While these algorithms have comparable accuracy the mean absolute error for the k-nearest neighbors-based algorithm with IBk is substantially smaller.

Table 2. Algorithm performance using 10-fold cross validation

Algorithm	Accuracy	Mean absolute error	Root mean squared error
JRip (rule-based)	79.499%	0.0713	0.217
J48 (decision-tree)	85.133%	0.0498	0.1994
IBk (k-NN)	87.167%	0.0392	0.1904
Random forest	86.698%	0.0735	0.1721

Going into detail it can be seen from the classifiers' confusion matrix in Table 3 that a differentiation, in particular between car and bus, is not exact. With 10-fold cross evaluation, about 8% of the car's records were classified as a bus, while about 22% of the bus's records were classified as cars. In the case of rail, the misclassification as a car or bus is less than about 6% less. A misclassification of the vehicles as a lack of mobility has also occurred, but more misclassifications were expected here as busses, trains or cars often stop at traffic lights or intersections. The reason for this may be that in this time the engine is on and the vibration of the vehicle can be detected by the sensors, so that a difference to the lack of mobility can be detected here. The only class without misclassification is the one to classify standing still.

Table 3. Confusion matrix for the best random forest classifier

	Bike	Car	Bus	Tram	On foot	Still	Unknown
Bike	121	2	1	0	0	0	0
Car	1	259	21	0	0	0	0
Bus	0	41	144	0	0	1	1
Tram	0	3	2	23	1	0	2
On foot	0	4	0	3	19	0	0
Still	0	0	0	0	0	66	0
Unknown	0	2	0	0	0	2	5

5   Conclusion

In this paper we examined and compared six approaches for mobility detection. All four scientific approaches present different features and parameters that promise good detection results. However, because the frameworks are not openly available for testing they cannot be evaluated in a comparative study. For the two openly available frameworks our evaluation has shown problems regarding live detection of mobility change due to minute-long delays in detection. Additionally, neither of the presented systems is able to distinguish between different vehicle-based modes of transportation like car, bus, tram or train.

We presented an approach designed to distinguish between these vehicle-based modes of transportation in addition to those covered by the existing approaches.

Our approach can be improved in accuracy by collecting more sensor data over a longer period of time. Another aspect that can be implemented with today's common resources is the comparison of the isolated classifier presented in this work with a combination with Markov chains or automata. This would allow the start and stop sequences, which are significant for buses and trams, to be included in the classification.

The integration into a mobility-based mobile game is the next step to follow in order to provide an appealing game experience and furthermore to collect additional data to improve prediction accuracy.

Acknowledgment. The research presented in this paper was partially funded by the LOEWE initiative (Hessen, Germany) within the research project "Infrastruktur – Design – Gesellschaft" as project mo.de.

LOEWE

Exzellente Forschung für
Hessens Zukunft

References

1. Schonfeld, E.: Mobile OS 2009 market share (2017). https://techcrunch.com/2010/02/23/smartphone-iphone-sales-2009-gartner/. Accessed 15 June 2018
2. Lau, S.L., David, K.: Movement recognition using the accelerometer in smartphones. In: Future Network and Mobile Summit (2010)
3. Wirtl, T., Nickel, C.: Aktivitätserkennung auf Smartphones. In: International Conference of the Biometrics Special Interest Group (2011)
4. Hemminki, S., Nurmi, P., Tarkoma, S.: Accelerometer-based transportation mode detection on smartphones. In: Proceedings of the 11th ACM Conference on Embedded Networked Sensor Systems (2013)
5. Anjum, A., Ilyas, M.U.: Activity recognition using smartphone sensors. In: IEEE 10th Consumer Communications and Networking Conference (2013)
6. Google: Google Awareness API (2016). https://developers.google.com/awareness/. Accessed 15 June 2018
7. Neura: Neura SDK (2017). https://dev.theneura.com/. Accessed 15 June 2018
8. Holmes, G., Donkin, A., Witten, I.H.: Weka: a machine learning workbench. In: Proceedings of the 1994 Second Australian and New Zealand Conference on Intelligent Information Systems (1994)

Towards a More Reflective Social Media Use Through Serious Games and Co-design

Barbara Göbl[1], Dayana Hristova[2], Suzana Jovicic[3], Thomas Slunecko[4], Marie-France Chevron[3], and Helmut Hlavacs[1(✉)]

[1] Faculty of Computer Science, University of Vienna, Vienna, Austria
helmut.hlavacs@univie.ac.at
[2] Department of Philosophy, University of Vienna, Vienna, Austria
[3] Department of Social and Cultural Anthropology,
University of Vienna, Vienna, Austria
[4] Department of Psychology, University of Vienna, Vienna, Austria

Abstract. This paper presents an interdisciplinary co-design approach for a serious game that elaborates on social media's diverse potentials and underlying design principles. The contribution of the following methods to our game design are discussed: workshops, interviews, group discussions, participant observations and surveys. We argue that an informed approach to the use of social media can promote a more reflective involvement with it.

Keywords: Mobile serious games · Effects of social media · Co-design

1 Introduction

Digital technologies are increasingly interlinked with our lives. Especially among adolescents, the so called "digital natives" [24], smartphones and accompanying apps have become an essential factor in everyday situations. According to surveys, social media apps such as WhatsApp and YouTube score above 80% and SnapChat and Instagram around 60% in reported use among Austrian adolescents [1,23].

Considering this regular and highly frequent use, it seems even more noteworthy that social media can influence behavior and emotional experiences [16, 31]. Social media platforms, such as Facebook, Snapchat or Instagram, have been associated with eliciting feelings of jealousy and with both de- and increasing self-esteem [29,30]. Furthermore, feeling obliged to participate in social networking is reported to be an issue for teenagers [18].

Additionally, studies suggest that users are often not aware of the terms and conditions of their media use. A Viennese study provided selected clauses from

Supported by a DOC-team grant of the Austrian Academy of Sciences (2017–2020).

Facebook's terms and conditions and found that only 1% of the participants were aware that they agreed to all of them. 37% reported that they knew about their data being collected and used [25]. An experiment with a fictitious social networking site found that three quarters of participants skipped reading its terms of service altogether [20]. A mere 15% of the participants in this study reported concerns with intentionally disadvantageous policies, containing clauses such as free disposal over data to be shared with e.g. government agencies or agencies that assess eligibility for bank loans or university access.

2   Game Concept

To address above mentioned issues, our interdisciplinary team, consisting of an anthropologist, a computer scientist and a cognitive scientist, is developing a mobile serious game. It aims to promote transparency for adolescents concerning social media design principles and privacy issues and to inspire a more reflective usage. Respective education is shown to be a prime method to support coping with negative experiences and increase resilience and well-being [11,26,32].

Teenagers, aged 14–19 years, will be involved as informants and co-designers during game development. Co-designing is based on the continuous involvement and active contributions of users in the design process [27]. Such participatory methods are particularly helpful when designing serious games, as developers and target users often strongly differ in age, gaming preferences or other important characteristics [4,5]. Regarding access and familiarity, mobile platforms such as smartphones are a suitable choice as they are the most available devices, with 90% of Upper Austrian adolescents owning their personal smartphone [23].

3   Interaction Design

Speech interfaces have been recognized as a natural and engaging approach to human-computer interaction [7,33] and have been used to help learners reflect on their knowledge and progress [13]. Hence, in addition to graphical interfaces we use natural language interfaces for our game. We consider this feature particularly promising, as communication via text and natural language is a prominent interaction pattern among adolescents. 70–85% of our target users report using WhatsApp or other text-based communication on their phones [1,23].

During our co-design sessions, we will also discuss and integrate slow interactions to balance a fun game experience with space for reflection. For instance, in LunchTime [21], a game promoting healthy food choices, game rounds can take up to 12 h with only one new challenge per day to allow for research and thoughtful choices. The Reef Game [19] aims to raise awareness on issues concerning the Great Barrier Reef's ecosystem. Its approach is to blend fast, fun gameplay with slow, exploratory settings where restrictions and distracting activities are removed to make way for reflection. Such approaches will serve as a starting point for further development during the co-design process.

4   Methods

To adapt our game design, we gather a broad range of data. The following mix of conventional and co-design methods is applied to involve our future users: workshops, interviews, discussion groups and observations.

4.1   Workshops

Each workshop consists of several sessions and handles a variety of topics ranging from privacy to design models applied to generate addictive behavior [6,28]. We try to pinpoint and alleviate knowledge gaps using interactive methods such as *quizzes* and *discussions*, as well as to focus on topics that are relevant to adolescents and their social media activities. Discussing both domain knowledge and introducing game design principles is considered an important step to address a common issue of participatory design in a serious game context, namely that a lack of knowledge in either discipline may limit possible contributions [14]. Methods such as *brainstorming* and *storyboarding*, as discussed in [9], will further add to our game design. Initial workshops will be concluded by creating and pitching *paper prototypes*, which enable easier collaboration, require little technical knowledge and allow for quicker iterations and initial development [8].

4.2   Interviews

Semi-structured interviews, based on [31], aim to provide an insight into the broader context of social-media use. This method gathers information about the use of different social media platforms (e.g. duration, intensity, priority), details about the use of the most relevant platforms (e.g. social/content type context, features used), as well as critical incidents. The second type of interviews designed for this project are *think-alouds* based on the micro-explicative work of [22] and [15]. Informants are invited to share their experience in real-time as they are viewing their last incoming message (text, picture or audio) and to comment on the aspects that they are paying attention to.

4.3   Expert Boards - Group Discussions

The group discussion method [3] is selected for two purposes. Firstly, it supports the process of co-designing by providing opportunities for constant feedback loops. Hence, a close dialogue regarding the features of the serious game is established with a stable group of experts (diverse group of individuals aged 14–19). Secondly, the discussion groups provide an insight into qualitative data regarding their experiences and habits of games and social media use. The setting offers an opportunity to capture the process of group specific dynamics and active meaning making regarding the social experience of social media. This is particularly relevant given the emergence and negotiation of new social norms pertaining to the usage of new media technologies [10].

4.4   Participant Observation

Participant observation is a qualitative, ethnographic method. By participating in the everyday activities, the goal is to experience the field in the "natural" environment, as opposed to the laboratory or staged interview and group setting [17]. In this case, the researcher spends extended periods of time within a school and youth clubs, observing and participating in online and offline activities [10], paying attention to everyday practices and initiating informal conversations. The overall goal is to supplement the isolated data from the workshops, interviews, group discussions and surveys by contextualizing the practices and perspectives of the informants in a wider social, cultural, political and economic context.

4.5   Surveys

Based on the findings of our workshops and interviews, surveys will be used to gather a broader range of data determining social media usage, associated experiences and pre-existing knowledge. Surveys will also investigate knowledge gaps and preferences of Austrian adolescents concerning game genres, goals and other elements.

5   Method Integration

The combinations of these methods will provide an extensive set of data that can be integrated into game design. As Kayali et al. [12] have demonstrated, a combination of qualitative and quantitative methods provides a solid base for serious game development and can support the selection of game setting, characters or game worlds. Furthermore, continuous workshops and discussion groups provide a suitable way to involve target users in later stages, for example by using a digital prototype to discuss mechanics and additional game elements [14]. Adolescents' experiences that are explored in our early design phase, using interviews, workshops and observation, will then be integrated in our game and evaluated during further workshops, play testing and discussion groups. One of the main challenges during co-design will be to ensure the application of suiting serious game mechanics to achieve our purpose of learning and reflection [2].

6   Conclusion

Literature suggests a complex range of consequences of social media use, findings that our first workshop sessions have confirmed as adolescents report empowering, yet sometimes stressful experiences. Social media has become an essential tool to them, which they use to find new friends, entertain themselves or find inspiration. The intention of our game will not be to point out negative consequences but to provide our users with strategies to handle potential issues and equip them with respective knowledge. Our data gathering comprises various situations, settings and techniques. The game will be built using the most available platform (mobile) and preferred user interaction patterns (e.g. natural language interfaces), and co-designed by adolescents regarding game content, mechanics and elements.

References

1. Jugend-Internet-Monitor (2018). https://www.saferinternet.at/jugendinternet monitor. Accessed 23 Apr 2018
2. Baalsrud Hauge, J.M., Lim, T., Louchart, S., Stanescu, I.A., Ma, M., Marsh, T.: Game mechanics supporting pervasive learning and experience in games, serious games, and interactive & social media. In: Chorianopoulos, K., Divitini, M., Baalsrud Hauge, J., Jaccheri, L., Malaka, R. (eds.) Entertainment Computing - ICEC 2015. LNCS, pp. 560–565. Springer International Publishing, Cham (2015). https://doi.org/10.1007/978-3-319-24589-8_57
3. Bohnsack, R.: Gruppendiskussion. In: Flick, U., von Kardoff, E., Steinke, I. (eds.) Qualitative Forschung. Ein Handbuch, pp. 369–383. Rowohlt Taschenbuch Verlag, Reinbek b. Hamburg (2000)
4. Danielsson, K., Wiberg, C.: Participatory design of learning media: designing educational computer games with and for teenagers. Interact. Technol. Smart Educ. 3(4), 275–291 (2006). https://doi.org/10.1108/17415650680000068
5. Dörner, R., Göbel, S., Effelsberg, W., Wiemeyer, J.: Serious Games: Foundations, Concepts and Practice. Springer, Heidelberg (2016). https://doi.org/10.1007/978-3-319-40612-1
6. Eyal, N.: Hooked, 3rd edn. Redline, München (2017)
7. Følstad, A., Brandtzæg, P.B.: Chatbots and the new world of HCI. Interactions 24(4), 38–42 (2017). https://doi.org/10.1145/3085558
8. Gibson, J.: Introduction to Game Design, Prototyping, and Development: From Concept to Playable Game with Unity and C#. Addison-Wesley, Boston (2014)
9. Hall, L., Woods, S., Dautenhahn, K., Sobreperez, P.: Using storyboards to guide virtual world design. In: Proceedings of the 2004 Conference on Interaction Design and Children: Building a Community, IDC 2004, pp. 125–126. ACM, New York (2004). https://doi.org/10.1145/1017833.1017853
10. Hine, C.: Ethnography for the Internet: Embedded, Embodied and Everyday. Bloomsbury Publishing, London (2015)
11. Horn, A.B., Pössel, P., Hautzinger, M.: Promoting adaptive emotion regulation and coping in adolescence: a school-based programme. J. Health Psychol. 16(2), 258–273 (2011). https://doi.org/10.1177/1359105310372814
12. Kayali, F.: Design considerations for aserious game for children after hematopoietic stem cell transplantation. Entertain. Comput. 15, 57–73 (2016). https://doi.org/10.1016/j.entcom.2016.04.002
13. Kerly, A., Hall, P., Bull, S.: Bringing chat bots into education: towards natural language negotiation of open learner models. Knowl.-Based Syst. 20(2), 177–185 (2007). https://doi.org/10.1016/j.knosys.2006.11.014
14. Khaled, R., Vasalou, A.: Bridging serious games and participatory design. Int. J. Child-Comput. Interact. 2(2), 93–100 (2014). https://doi.org/10.1016/j.ijcci.2014.03.001. Special Issue: Learning from Failures in Game Design for Children
15. Kimmel, M., Hristova, D., Kussmaul, K.: Sources of embodied creativity: interactivity and ideation in contact improvisation. Behav. Sci. 8(6), 52 (2018)

16. Kramer, A.D.I., Guillory, J.E., Hancock, J.T.: Experimental evidence of massive-scale emotional contagion through social networks. Proc. Natl. Acad. Sci. **111**(24), 8788–8790 (2014). https://doi.org/10.1073/pnas.1320040111

17. Lüders, C.: Beobachten im Feld und Ethnographie. In: Flick, U., von Kardoff, E., Steinke, I. (eds.) Qualitative Forschung. Ein Handbuch, pp. 384–401. Rowohlt Taschenbuch Verlag, Reinbek b. Hamburg (2000)

18. Madden, M., et al.: Teens, social media, and privacy (2013). http://www.pewinternet.org/2013/05/21/teens-social-media-and-privacy/. Accessed 7 May 2018

19. Marsh, T.: Slow serious games, interactions and play: designing for positive and serious experience and reflection. Entertain. Comput. **14**, 45–53 (2016). https://doi.org/10.1016/j.entcom.2015.10.001

20. Obar, J.A., Oeldorf-Hirsch, A.: The biggest lie on the internet: Ignoring the privacy policies and terms of service policies of social networking services. In: The 44th Research Conference on Communication, Information and Internet Policy. TPRC 44 (2016). https://doi.org/10.2139/ssrn.2757465

21. Orji, R., Vassileva, J., Mandryk, R.L.: LunchTime: a slow-casual game forlong-term dietary behavior change. Pers. Ubiquitous Comput. **17**(6), 1211–1221 (2013). https://doi.org/10.1007/s00779-012-0590-6

22. Petitmengin, C.: Describing one's subjective experience in the second person: an interview method for the science of consciousness. Phenomenol. Cogn. Sci. **5**(3), 229–269 (2006). https://doi.org/10.1108/10748120110424816

23. Pfarrhofer, D.: Medienverhalten der Jugendlichen aus dem Blickwinkel der Jugendlichen. https://www.edugroup.at/fileadmin/DAM/Innovation/Forschung/Dateien/Charts_Jugendliche_2017.pdf. Accessed 1 May 2018

24. Prensky, M.: Digital natives, digital immigrants part 1. On Horiz. **9**(5), 1–6 (2001)

25. Rothmann, R., Buchner, B.: Der typische Facebook-Nutzer zwischen Recht und Realität. Datenschutz und Datensicherheit - DuD **42**(6), 342–346 (2018). https://doi.org/10.1007/s11623-018-0953-x

26. Ruini, C.: School intervention for promoting psychological well-being in adolescence. J. Behav. Ther. Exp. Psychiatry **40**(4), 522–532 (2009). https://doi.org/10.1016/j.jbtep.2009.07.002

27. Sanders, E.B.N., Stappers, P.J.: Co-creation and the new landscapes of design. CoDesign **4**(1), 5–18 (2008). https://doi.org/10.1080/15710880701875068

28. Schüll, N.D.: Addiction by Design: Machine Gambling in Las Vegas. Princeton University Press, Princeton (2012)

29. Utz, S., Muscanell, N., Khalid, C.: Snapchat elicits more jealousy than Facebook: a comparison of Snapchat and Facebook use. Cyberpsychology Behav. Soc. Netw. **18**(3), 141–146 (2015). https://doi.org/10.1089/cyber.2014.0479

30. Wang, R., Yang, F., Haigh, M.M.: Let me take a selfie: exploring the psychological effects of posting and viewing selfies and groupies on social media. Telemat. Inform. **34**(4), 274–283 (2017). https://doi.org/10.1016/j.tele.2016.07.004

31. Weinstein, E.: The social media see-saw: positive and negative influences on adolescents' affective well-being. New Media & Society (2018). https://doi.org/10.1177/1461444818755634

32. Wittchen, H.U., Hoyer, J.: Klinische Psychologie & Psychotherapie, 2nd edn. Springer, Heidelberg (2011). https://doi.org/10.1007/978-3-642-13018-2

33. Zadrozny, W., Budzikowska, M., Chai, J., Kambhatla, N., Levesque, S., Nicolov, N.: Natural language dialogue for personalized interaction. Commun. ACM **43**(8), 116–120 (2000)

Development of a Wii Balance Board Array System for Exergames

Augusto Garcia-Agundez[1]([⊠]), Florian Baumgartl[2], Fritz Kendeffy[2],
Robert Konrad[1], Hendrik Wunsch[2], and Stefan Göbel[1]

[1] KOM, TU Darmstadt, Rundeturmstr. 10, 64283 Darmstadt, Germany
augusto.garcia@kom.tu-darmstadt.de
[2] m2m Germany, Am Kappengraben 18, 61273 Wehrheim, Germany

Abstract. The goal of this work is to present and describe the development of a
6-Wii Balance Board array system for its use in exergaming scenarios. To avoid
the main problem, which is connection stability and latency, we developed a
board using a microcontroller from SILABS and a Bluetooth Stick was used to
synchronize data acquisition and minimize data latency. Our data demonstrates
that, under the described experimental conditions, the developed system is
functional and is capable of delivering the data of 6 Wii Balance Boards in real
time.

Keywords: Wii Balance Board · Exergames · Parkinsons Disease
Serious games · Rehabilitation

1 Introduction

Parkinson's Disease (PD) is a neurodegenerative malady caused by the progressive
degeneration of dopaminergic neurons in the substantia nigra pars compacta. Its
diagnosis is determined by motor symptoms, such as slow movements, rigidity, and
hand tremor, but cognitive dysfunction is also common (Aarsland et al. 2011). Currently, there is no strategy to prevent cognitive decline in PD patients (Weintraub et al.
2016). However, recent research suggests employing cognitive training (Petrelli et al.
2014) or a combination of physical and cognitive training (Rahe et al. 2015). Research
also suggests that, when combining both training methods, transfer effects can be
expected (Hindle et al. 2013), for example in symptoms such as freezing of gait
(Walton et al. 2014).

For this combined training scenario, exergames as an extension of traditional
cognitive and motor training for PD is under consideration (Kalbe and Folkerts 2016),
but so far, clinical trials are scarce (Barry et al. 2014). Some findings point towards
improvement in balance (Harris et al. 2015), gait (Mhatre et al. 2013) as well as
cognition (Ogawa et al. 2016). Thus, to the knowledge of the authors, there is no
available exergames program adapted to the needs of PD patients with MCI or
dementia.

S. Göbel et al. (Eds.): JCSG 2018, LNCS 11243, pp. 235–240, 2018.
https://doi.org/10.1007/978-3-030-02762-9_24

For this purpose, the PDExergames[1] project, funded by the German Ministry of Research and Education, was created. In the framework of this project, we previously developed a game that presents this task duality which seems to be optimal for PD patients. (Garcia-Agundez et al. 2017). However, the game is currently controlled by a simple dance mat. This simple digital control allows for little relevant feedback to be used for medical purposes. To obtain more relevant information from patients, we considered using a commercial sensor, such as the Wii Balance Board (WBB).

Since the usable area of a balance board is only about twice that of a personal scale, we came to the idea of building a matrix of such boards. In order to produce a square with even sizes, a total of six boards is required. This corresponds to 6 × 4 scales or load cells and, from a theoretical point of view, allows quite a good recording of movement/dynamics during game scenarios. Each weighing sensor from the balance boards is a highly sensitive sensor whose data is processed by the Wii boards and output via 6 wireless interfaces.

2   Methods

The goal of this work was to implement a 6-WBB array system to control a game as presented on Fig. 1 and to develop methods to overcome the inherent difficulties of implementing such a system. We decided to name this array Extended Balance Board (EBB). In terms of collecting data, the main difficulty lies in bundling the connections of the six WBBs. In order to prevent the game from later on degrading its functionality and adversely affecting the user experience, it is necessary to read out and transfer the information provided by the WBBs in near real-time.

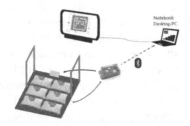

Fig. 1. Schematic of the EBB

A WBB consists of a total of four weighing sensors, which are installed underneath each foot of the board. When started, the WBB opens two radio channels. This means that every integrated board has two duplex channels in operation in the Bluetooth Classic Band. For the EBB, this means twelve wireless connections are requested. On the opposite side, twelve devices/assemblies must be available to enable the radio design and the connection. Here we encountered some difficulties. Firstly, it is

---

[1] www.pdexergames.de.

cumbersome to open twelve stable Bluetooth Classic radio channels and then receive data. Again and again individual radio channels break off and then the logical data stream of the matrix is suspended. This is particularly difficult in a tightly networked scenario, such as an office. The latency in the radio link is an additional issue that needs to be addressed. If a single or two WBBs are used, the setup is mostly hassle-free. However, with more than two WBBs in use, the latency, which is mainly due to the radio link, increases significantly and becomes irregular, making the game unplayable.

Once connected, the reports generated by the WBB consist of 8 bytes, which identify the data format shown in Table 1. The calibration values follow the same pattern using a total of 24 bytes (0 kg values, 17 kg values and 34 kg values, that is, 3 times 8 bytes). A determination of the load or the weight of a single weighing sensor (at a certain point in time) requires the interpolation of two values.

Table 1. WBB data structure

Byte	Content
0	Top right <15:8>
1	Top right <7:0>
2	Bottom right <15:8>
3	Bottom right <7:0>
4	Top left <15:8>
5	Top left <7:0>
6	Bottom left <15:8>
7	Bottom left <7:0>

In order to connect the WBBs to a computer, we used the Blue-1000 Bluetooth stick developed by m2m[2]. It has a range of up to 1000 meters and uses BR/EDR. In the Bluetooth stack of the Blue-1000, a maximum of 8 parallel connections are possible. A Wii Balance Board requires two independent Bluetooth connections. The first connection (input) is responsible for the transmission of control commands and the second connection (output) provides all information in the form of event messages. This means we were confronted with a problem, since it is only possible to connect a total of four WBBs with such a Bluetooth stick.

A solution was designed to circumvent these interference factors. The basic idea is to circumvent and replace the twelve-fold radio channel as much as possible. A board analysis was performed to locate the interfaces that precede or underlie the radio channel. The interfaces (UART interfaces) were located as serial channels and tests were successfully performed with a PC and serial terminal program running on it. Thanks to this, instead of twelve Bluetooth wireless connections, we have six UART interfaces for further use. It was therefore necessary to resort to a specially developed module. The radio links have been deactivated without affecting the user data or the active user data stream.

---

[2] www.m2mgermany.de.

The core of this newly designed module is a microcontroller from the manufacturer Silicon Labs[3], which provides six UART channels/interfaces. Silicon Labs was chosen given we had extensive previous experience with the manufacturer. The illustration below shows the structure of the Board. The board includes the interface-channels, which were each supplemented by a level-converter circuit, as well as test points to debug interfaces for verification and diagnostics. Furthermore, the board includes voltage regulation as well as the actual power supply (Fig. 2).

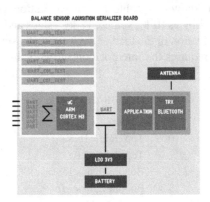

Fig. 2. Schematic of the acquisition board

The sum signal of the serial data streams/UART signals captured from the six WBBs is output by the microcontroller in a seventh position and converted from UART to Bluetooth by an onboard radio module. Using the WiiUse Library (Laforest 2009), we connected the WBBs to the Blue-1000 adapter to decode raw WBB data. The data streams were transparently passed to a UDP/TCP socket. Depending on the operating mode and configuration of the WBB, the sensor information can be retrieved approximately every 50 ms. A record in the current version consists of 85 bytes. For six WBBs we incur in 510 bytes per 50 ms, that is 0.01 megabytes per second. This data has to be compressed before being sent to the computer. The data can then be analyzed in the background, while the user plays the game.

To conclude our design, we built a frame to provide users with a completely flat surface. The frame holds the WBBs in place and covers them with a plastic sheet to cover the small holes between them. This sheet was tested to ensure it did not affect the accuracy of the measurements (Fig. 3).

---

[3] www.silabs.com.

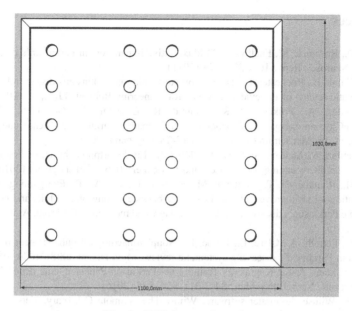

Fig. 3. EBB frame schematic

3 Results and Outlook

The final system is able to connect all six boards to the computer and indeed receive data from all boards simultaneously. A sample of this data is presented below in Table 2. When receiving data, each board has a unique identifier (Board ID) to identify which position it occupies in the array, from 1 to 6. This allows us to separate the information as it is received via UDP and construct an array of all sensor data in real time. In a future publication, we plan to evaluate this sensor with PD patients and attempt to link movement parameters, such as balance and time between inputs, with UPDRS scores and physical improvement. Finally, this sensor may also be of interest to expand such rehabilitation modules to remote scenarios (Garcia-Agundez et al. 2016).

Table 2. Example of the data sent by the EBB

Data type	Int	Int	Float	Float	Float	Float	Int	Int	Int	Int	Float
Description	MAC	Board ID	Top left sensor IW	Top right sensor IW	Bot left sensor IW	Bot right sensor IW	Top left sensor RV	Top right sensor RV	Bot left sensor RV	Bot right sensor RV	Weight (KG)
Example	58bda3a9cd6f	3	30.022	26.871	16.94	16.052	10265	5522	4800	9157	89.887

References

Aarsland, D., Brønnick, K., Fladby, T.: Mild cognitive impairment in Parkinson's disease. Curr. Neurol. Neurosci. Rep. **11**(4), 371–378 (2011)

Barry, G., Galna, B., Rochester, L.: The role of exergaming in Parkinson's disease rehabilitation: a systematic review of the evidence. J. NeuroEngineering Rehabil. **11**(1), 33 (2014)

Garcia-Agundez, A., Folkerts, A.-K., Konrad, R., Caseman, P., Göbel, S., Kalbe, E.: PDDanceCity: an exergame for patients with idiopathic Parkinson's disease and cognitive impairment. In: Mensch und Computer 2017-Tagungsband (2017)

Garcia-Agundez, A., Sharma, S., Dutz, T., Göbel, S.: Ein Smartphone-basiertes Framework für Patientenfernüberwachung. In: Mensch und Computer 2016–Workshopband (2016)

Harris, D.M., Rantalainen, T., Muthalib, M., Johnson, L., Teo, W.-P.: Exergaming as a viable therapeutic tool to improve static and dynamic balance among older adults and people with idiopathic Parkinson's disease: a systematic review and meta-analysis. Front. Aging Neurosci. **7**, 167 (2015)

Hindle, J.V., Petrelli, A., Clare, L., Kalbe, E.: Nonpharmacological enhancement of cognitive function in Parkinson's disease: a systematic review. Mov. Disord. **28**(8), 1034–1049 (2013)

Kalbe, E., Folkerts, A.-K.: Kognitives Training bei Parkinson-Patienten–eine neue Therapieoption? Fortschr. Neurol. Psychiatr. **84**(S 01), S24–S35 (2016)

Laforest, M.: Wiiuse. Computer software. Wiiuse-The Wiimote C Library. Vers. 0.12. GNU. Web, 6 (2009)

Mhatre, P.V., et al.: Wii Fit balance board playing improves balance and gait in Parkinson disease. PM&R **5**(9), 769–777 (2013)

Ogawa, E.F., You, T., Leveille, S.G.: Potential benefits of exergaming for cognition and dual-task function in older adults: a systematic review. J. Aging Phys. Act. **24**(2), 332–336 (2016)

Petrelli, A., et al.: Effects of cognitive training in Parkinson's disease: a randomized controlled trial. Park. Relat. Disord. **20**(11), 1196–1202 (2014)

Rahe, J., Petrelli, A., Kaesberg, S., Fink, G.R., Kessler, J., Kalbe, E.: Effects of cognitive training with additional physical activity compared to pure cognitive training in healthy older adults. Clin. Interv. Aging **10**, 297 (2015)

Walton, C.C., Shine, J.M., Mowszowski, L., Naismith, S.L., Lewis, S.J.: Freezing of gait in Parkinson's disease: current treatments and the potential role for cognitive training. Restor. Neurol. Neurosci. **32**(3), 411–422 (2014)

Weintraub, D., Hauser, R.A., Elm, J.J., Pagan, F., Davis, M.D., Choudhry, A.: Rasagiline for mild cognitive impairment in Parkinson's disease: a placebo-controlled trial. Mov. Disord. **31**(5), 709–714 (2016)

Building a Hybrid Approach for a Game Scenario Using a Tangible Interface in Human Robot Interaction

Vinicius Silva[1] (ID), Filomena Soares[1,2(✉)] (ID), João Sena Esteves[1,2] (ID),
and Ana Paula Pereira[3] (ID)

[1] Algoritmi Research Centre, University of Minho, Guimarães, Portugal
a65312@alunos.uminho.pt, {fsoares,sena}@dei.uminho.pt
[2] Department of Industrial Electronics, University of Minho, Guimarães,
Portugal
[3] Research Center on Education, Institute of Education, University of Minho,
Braga, Portugal
appereira@ie.uminho.pt

Abstract. Understanding others intention can be a very difficult task for some individuals, in particular, individuals with Autism Spectrum Disorder (ASD). ASD is characterized by difficulties in social communication and restricted patterns of behaviour. In order to mitigate the emotion recognition impairments that individuals with ASD usually present, researchers are employing different technological strategies. Among those technological solutions, the use of assistive robots and Objects based on Playware Technology (OPT) in context of serious games are getting more attention. Following this trend, the present work targets a novel hybrid approach using a humanoid robot and one OPT. The proposed approach consists of a humanoid robot capable of displaying social behaviours, particularly facial expressions, and an OPT called PlayCube. The system was designed for emotion recognition activities with children with ASD. To evaluate the proposed approach, two pilot studies were performed: one with typically developing children and another with children with ASD. Overall, the different evaluations demonstrated the possible positive outcomes that this child-OPT-robot interaction can produce.

Keywords: Playware · Human robot interaction · Autism Spectrum Disorders

1 Introduction

In any communication, humans generally express their intents effortlessly. Conversely, automatic understanding of social signals is a very difficult task for some individuals, especially for children with Autism Spectrum Disorder (ASD) [1]. Nowadays, distinct technological strategies have been used to try to mitigate the emotion recognition impairments that usually individuals with ASD present, mainly through the use of Objects based on Playware Technology (OPT) and assistive robots [2, 3].

Playware is defined as intelligent technology for children's play and playful experiences for the user [2]. Henrik Lund suggested the term "playware" as a

S. Göbel et al. (Eds.): JCSG 2018, LNCS 11243, pp. 241–247, 2018.
https://doi.org/10.1007/978-3-030-02762-9_25

combination of intelligent hardware and software that aims at producing play and playful experiences among users [2]. There have been few related works in the field of OPT. The work developed by Henrik Lund [2] consisted in designing interactive tiles as a modular robotic playware with the goal of being flexible in both set-up and activity building for the end-user, allowing easy creation of games. A set of experiments was performed with a group of 7 children with ASD. The authors concluded that the results provided by the research offers an interesting novel research direction to investigate playware as playful tools for cognitive challenged children, giving the children a playful experience and automatically investigate the playful interaction to provide insight (and possible a diagnosis).

Concerning assistive technologies, assistive robots can be an exceptional tool for interacting with children with ASD. Research with assistive robots have showed that, in general, individuals with ASD express elevated interest while interacting with robots [4]. The research in this area have moved to using facial expressive robots with humanoid design, since it can promise a great potential for generalisation, especially in tasks of imitation and emotion recognition which can be harder if the robot does not present a human form [5–7].

Following this trend, the present work proposes a new approach of using both technologies (OPT and assistive robots) with the goal of promoting social interaction with children with ASD. None of the related works in the literature, to the authors' knowledge, present a similar approach. Therefore, the present work consists in the development of an OPT to be used as an add-on to the human-robot interaction with children with ASD in emotion recognition activities. In order to evaluate the proposed approach, two pilot studies were conducted one with typically developing children and other with children with ASD. The purpose of these pilot studies was to evaluate both the game scenario and the OPT rather than to quantify and evaluate the performance of the child. The present paper is organized as follow: Sect. 2 presents the proposed approach; Sect. 3 shows and discusses the results obtained; the conclusions and future work are addressed in Sect. 4.

2   Developed Framework

The framework, depicted in Fig. 1, is composed of a humanoid robot capable of displaying facial expressions, a computer, and a new OPT called PlayCube. The Zeno R50 RoboKind humanoid child-like robot ZECA is a robotic platform that has 34 degrees of freedom. The robot is capable of expressing facial cues thanks to the servo motors mounted on its face and a special material, Frubber, which looks and feels like human skin, being a major feature that distinguishes Zeno R50 from other robots. Concerning the PlayCube, the present design approach consisted in developing an OPT that can offer a tangible experience and adapt to different games scenarios, as well as to provide immediate feedback. The concept of tangible interaction refers to enabled technological objects that can be physically manipulated [8]. A two-way Bluetooth communication protocol was developed to allow communication between the robot and the PlayCube.

The developed device, PlayCube (7 cm × 7 cm × 7 cm), has an OLED RGB display, Inertial Measurement Unit (IMU), a small development board (ESP32) that already has built-in Bluetooth and Wi-Fi communication, an RGB LED ring, a Linear Resonant Actuator (LRA), and a Li-Po battery. Additionally, the top face of the cube is a touch sensitive surface. Thus, interacting with the PlayCube just means, touching the physical object and manipulating it via natural gestures (e.g. rotation, shake, tilt, among others).

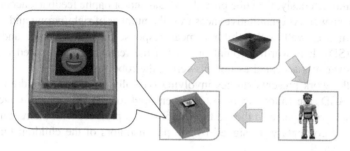

Fig. 1. Experimental setup. Starting from the left bottom: PlayCube (the final prototype), computer, and the humanoid robot.

In order to design the play experience in all its fullness, feedback is a key feature in guiding the children through the play activity. Furthermore, the immediate feedback feature can be a very important factor specially when designing OPT devices for children with impairments [9]. Additionally, the type of feedback must be configurable for different children as some types of feedback can be unenjoyable for some individuals, e.g., in the case of children with ASD, in general, a sound feedback can be unpleasant for them [1].

Following this idea, both the humanoid robot and the PlayCube offer immediate feedback to the children actions. For ensuring immediate feedback for the PlayCube, a ring with a total of sixteen multicolour and equal spaced LEDs is used. A haptic driver is used to enable haptic control of an LRA actuator. These actuators can provide haptic and/or visual feedback to the user. Additionally, the display can also provide visual feedback. Concerning the robot feedback, the reinforcement that is given is based on a previous study [7] and consists in a combination of verbal, movement, and sound reinforcements (e.g. the robot says "Congratulations!" while waving its arms in the air).

3   Results and Discussion

In order to evaluate the present approach, two studies were conducted in a school environment. The goal of the pilot study with typically developing children was to detect the system constraints in an intervention session. Concerning the pilot study with children with ASD, the main goal was to verify if the system can implement a procedure that makes the children able to interact in a comfortable and natural way. The experiments were performed individually in a triadic setup, i.e., child-robot-researcher with a duration of five minutes. The activity played was the recognize game scenario where ZECA randomly performs a facial expression and its associated gestures, representing one of the five basic emotions (happiness, sadness, anger, surprise, and afraid), plus neutral. After, ZECA asks the children to identify the performed emotion. Then, the children have to manipulate the cube by tilting it back or forward in order to scroll through the facial expressions displayed on the cube. When the child selects an answer, by touching the top touch sensitive surface of the cube, ZECA verifies if the answer is correct and prompts a reinforcement accordingly to the correctness of the answer. Simultaneously, the cube provides visual and/or haptic feedback accordingly to the child's answer. As quantitative measures, the number of right/wrong and no answer was quantified as well as the children mean response time, in seconds, and standard deviation (SD). It is worth to point out that if the response time exceeded 60 s, the child's answer was accepted as not answering the robot prompt.

Since the work presents studies involving typically developing children and children with ASD, the following issues were ensured to meet the ethical concerns: the school which participated in the studies established a protocol with the research group and informed consents were signed by the parents/tutors of the children that participated in the studies.

3.1 Pilot Study with Typically Developing Children

A set of preliminary experiments were carried out involving eight children aged between six and seven years old. The results obtained with the eight typically developing children are presented in Table 1.

Table 1. Children answers to the robot prompts where C1 to C8 is the number of the child.

	C1	C2	C3	C4	C5	C6	C7	C8
Right	7	3	3	6	2	4	5	7
Wrong	2	1	2	3	1	1	1	2
NoAnswer	0	3	3	0	4	2	2	0

Children 1, 4, 6, 7, and 8 showed an overall better performance. Children 2, 3 and 5 manifested more difficulties. Nevertheless, it is interesting to notice that the children answered the robot prompts giving a strong indication that in general the participants understood the game, and consequently interact with the robot by successfully manipulating the OPT (PlayCube). Furthermore, the mean response time for the unsuccessful answers was higher when comparing this value for the successful answers – 42.79(8.73) and 37.66(2.70) seconds, respectively. This higher value might be related to the children thinking and considering all options that they have available. Additionally, the children response time to the robot prompts decreased along the session – from 46.38(8.36) to 39.09(8.42) – indicating that the children responded faster to the robot prompts and were able to manipulate the OPT.

3.2   Pilot Study with Children with ASD

A pilot study with three high-functioning children with ASD (two females and one male) aged between 6 and 9 years old was carried out during four sessions in a school environment with the goal of evaluating the suitability and comprehension of the game scenario and the OPT. Analyzing each participant performance (Table 2), it is possible to conclude that child A performance improved much more along the four sessions when compared with the other participants. Furthermore, the mean response time of child A decreased along the session which can indicate that she understood the activity and how to manipulate the OPT in order to answer the robot prompts.

Table 2. Children answers and mean response time to the robot prompts during the four sessions (SD): RT – response time (s), RA – right answer, WA – wrong answer, NA – no answer.

Child	Session	RT	RA	WA	NA
A	S1	45.15(7.87)	3	4	0
	S2	44.85(14.26)	5	1	0
	S3	36.11(5.64)	8	1	0
	S4	28.45(3.08)	9	2	0
B	S1	43.53(13.99)	4	3	1
	S2	54.36(13.90)	3	1	2
	S3	50.54(10.21)	4	2	1
	S4	51.69(13.02)	4	1	1
C	S1	42.01(7.66)	1	5	0
	S2	36.26(8.55)	3	3	0
	S3	34.48(3.84)	4	5	0
	S4	34.26(4.67)	7	2	0

Concerning child B, she does not present an evolutive pattern in the first two sessions. However, in the last two the number of wrong answers decreased, maintaining the number of right answers. It is also worth to point out that the response time, for this participant, is longer. The results from the last two sessions suggests that this participant may need more sessions, which is consistent with the difficulties that these children present when discovering new activities or interests [1]. Even though child C had more difficulties answering the prompts, his performance improved in the last session and the child mean response time also decreased. When comparing the children mean response time along the four sessions and the number of total prompts (Table 2), it is possible to observe that in general the number of prompts increased along the four sessions as the children mean response time decreased along the sessions, considering that the session time is always five minutes. Additionally, it is worth to mention that none of the children that participated in this study abandoned the game. All children repeatedly touched gently the robot and in general manipulated correctly the OPT when prompted by the robot. Furthermore, as they answered the robot prompt they were particularly attentive to the cube feedback, lights and the images displayed in the screen for correct and incorrect answers.

4 Conclusions and Future Work

Recently, researchers are using technological tools such as OPT and assistive robots to try to mitigate the emotion recognition impairments that individuals with ASD present. Thus, the present work proposes a novel and hybrid approach for robot-assisted play. It combines the use of a OPT and a humanoid robot capable of displaying facial expressions with a serious game focused on improving the emotion recognition skills of children with ASD.

By analysing the results of the typically developing children it is possible to conclude that they interacted/responded well to the robot and understood the mechanics of the OPT and the game. One of the system constraints detected was the placement of the robot support that caused the children to always have to look up towards the robot face. In the pilot study with children with ASD this was corrected by placing the robot in a similar height to the children face. In general, the children with ASD reacted positively to the activity which can indicate that the developed approach allowed the children to interact in a comfortable and natural way with the system.

Future work includes further development and improvement of this approach. Additionally, a study will be conducted with a larger sample of children with ASD, aiming to understand if and how the presented hybrid approach can be used as a valuable tool to develop skills of emotional labelling by children with ASD.

Acknowledgements. The authors thank to COMPETE: POCI-01-0145-FEDER-007043 and FCT – Fundação para a Ciência e Tecnologia within the Project Scope: UID/CEC/00319/2013. Vinicius Silva also thanks FCT for the PhD scholarship SFRH/BD/ SFRH/BD/133314/2017. The authors thank the teachers and students of the Elementary School of Gualtar (EB1/JI Gualtar) in Braga for the participation.

References

1. American Psychiatric Association: Diagnostic and Statistical Manual of Mental Disorders, 5th edn. (DSM-5). Diagnostic and Statistical Manual of Mental Disorders, 4th edn., TR, p. 280 (2013)
2. Lund, H.H., Dam Pedersen, M., Beck, R.: Modular robotic tiles: experiments for children with autism. Artif. Life Robot. **13**(2), 394–400 (2009)
3. Pennisi, P., et al.: Autism and social robotics: a systematic review. Autism Res. **9**(2), 165–183 (2016)
4. Kim, E., Paul, R., Shic, F., Scassellati, B.: Bridging the research gap: making HRI useful to individuals with autism. J. Hum. Robot Interact. **1**, 26–54 (2012)
5. Begum, M., et al.: Measuring the efficacy of robots in autism therapy. In: Proceedings of the Tenth Annual ACM/IEEE International Conference on Human-Robot Interaction – HRI 2015, pp. 335–342 (2015)
6. Mazzei, D., Lazzeri, N., Hanson, D., De Rossi, D.: HEFES: an hybrid engine for facial expressions synthesis to control human-like androids and avatars. In: Proceedings of IEEE RAS EMBS International Conference on Biomedical Robotics and Biomechatronics, pp. 195–200 (2012)

7. Costa, S., Soares, F., Santos, C., Pereira, A.P., Hiolle, A., Silva, V.: Social-emotional development in high functioning children with autism spectrum disorders using a humanoid robot. Interact. Stud. (2018, accepted for publication)
8. Hornecker, E., Buur, J.: Getting a grip on tangible interaction: a framework on physical space and social interaction. In: Proceedings of the SIGCHI Conference on Human Factors in Computing Systems, pp. 437–446 (2006)
9. Schuetze, M., Rohr, C.S., Dewey, D., McCrimmon, A., Bray, S.: Reinforcement learning in autism spectrum disorder. Front. Psychol. **8**, 1–15 (2017)

Game Design Principles in a Game Programming Framework

Robert Konrad$^{(\boxtimes)}$, Thomas Tregel, and Stefan Göbel

Multimedia Communications Lab - KOM, Technische Universität Darmstadt,
Darmstadt, Germany
{robert.konrad,thomas.tregel,stefan.goebel}@kom.tu-darmstadt.de

Abstract. Programming game engines threatens to become an elitist activity with the industry split between the professional studios which are pushing for more direct but also more difficult to program hardware access and hobbyists using ready-made game-engines with little focus on understanding their inner workings. This paper presents an attempt to make game engine programming more accessible via a game programming framework which focuses explicitly on the programmers learning path in a similar manner to how video games are typically designed.

Keywords: Kha · Kore · Game programming · Game engines

1 Introduction

Game programming covers a very broad spectrum of expertise starting with gameplay programmers who implement simple gameplay triggers in visual scripting languages and culminating in game engine programming, requiring expert knowledge in debugging and optimizing C/C++ and GPU programming languages and specific disciplines of mathematics and physics. Today's broad adoption of ready-made game engines makes it hard for newcomers to walk the way from a gameplay programmer to a professional engine developer - the most common engines and accompanying tools do explicitly not provide a learning path towards game engine development.

Kha is a portable low-level programming framework which is designed amongst other things to accompany game-engine development courses and Kha or its components were used to teach hundreds of students. Being used in the realm of game development it seemed obvious to use game design patterns to make the programming framework more motivating to use. Instead of adding gamification components we try to foster the intrinsic motivation of game programmers to support the personal long term investment required to reach expert levels of expertise.

2 Related Work

Making games has become a widely popular hobby and consequently a broad range of game engines is easily available, from tool-sets specialized on build-

© Springer Nature Switzerland AG 2018
S. Göbel et al. (Eds.): JCSG 2018, LNCS 11243, pp. 248–252, 2018.
https://doi.org/10.1007/978-3-030-02762-9_26

ing complex, interactive 3D worlds like Unreal Engine 4 and Unity to game engines which specifically focus on beginners, providing visual tools to make programming accessible to non-programmers like GameMaker and Stencyl. Kha in contrast is not a game engine per se but only provides the most basic building blocks for constructing a game engine, freeing developers from the need to take care of any platform specific details. Game engine programming courses most commonly use a combination of OpenGL for graphics programming and a system integration library like SDL or SFML for all other system access. OpenGL in particular though is not designed for learning and its design is primarily defined by its long history going back more than 25 years to its predecessor IrisGL. To the best of our knowledge no comparable libraries exist which specifically focus on teaching game engine programming from a hobbyist level up to a professional level.

3 Expertise Based API Levels

Maybe the most well known aspect of game design for single-player games is the structural and carefully planned increase in difficulty over the course of a play-through. In many games this is accentuated by the player's avatar becoming more powerful while the game progresses (leveling up).

It is uncommon for game programming tools to even have a planned learning path and in fact from a game-design perspective things seem to be mixed up in the most popular tools as they focus on making the most powerful tools (big, complex 3D world management and rendering) available to beginners and hiding away the more basic building blocks. The path to understanding the inner workings of those 3D engines is therefore hard to impossible - in particular Unity does not provide the source code to the engine and in Unreal Engine 4 the lower level source code is mostly undocumented.

Kha on the other hand provides multiple APIs designated by the required experience level to provide an explicit learning path while making every aspect of the underlying implementations easily accessible and changeable.

3.1 Graphics

Graphics programming in modern computers has become very complex. New APIs like Vulkan are known for requiring a huge amount of work for the most basic tasks [1] and are conceptualized for the needs of professional game engine development teams. The graphics APIs in Kha are therefore designed to support programmers in approaching the complexity of APIs like Vulkan and Direct3D 12 step by step in a logical way.

Graphics 1. For beginners Kha provides a graphics API which only includes a single function called "setPixel". Setting the color of a singular pixel arguably the most basic graphics task a computer can perform [2] and is useful for teaching any rendering algorithm from the ground up without distracting students with the details of modern GPUs. Nonetheless most game programming frameworks are missing any similar API, likely because setting color values pixel by pixel is not directly supported in modern operating systems and therefore requires workarounds in the underlying implementation.

Graphics 2. Kha's second graphics API is a basic but very fast API for 2D graphics, providing functions to draw images and simple geometry. It is an easy introduction to matrix-based graphics transformations and homogeneous coordinates [3]. Complex 2D games can be built with little effort, typically outperforming larger engines in this discipline.

Graphics 3 to 5. are 3D APIs which roughly follow the development of low level 3D APIs like OpenGL and Direct3D. Those APIs became more difficult over time, allowing more and more programmability [4] and more direct hardware access. Today's graphics programming experts naturally learned about 3D graphics by following this timeline and due to its increasing difficulty it also matches the learning-needs of new graphics programmers. Programming with Kha provides the additional benefit of including the source code to show how the lower level graphics APIs are implemented based on the higher level APIs. Kha's Graphics 5 API in particular is similar to Vulkan and Direct3D 12, marking the goal of current graphics development courses.

3.2 Audio

Audio programming is fundamentally much simpler than graphics programming because specialized hardware support is absent on most modern systems. On the most basic level audio software just directly provides the discretized audio samples which are sent to the audio hardware in fixed time steps to drive the audio speakers [5]. However low level audio programming is not widely understood as demonstrated by the broad usage of complex audio libraries for very simple audio tasks - many games' audio needs do not exceed occasional "playAudioFile" calls to stream music and sound effects to the audio subsystem.

Audio 1. The entry level audio API in Kha consequentially provides the aforementioned, basic functionality required by most games to merely play pieces of audio data at defined points in time. The play calls return channel objects which allow further modifications of currently playing audio data. All audio mixing and synchronization of the audio thread is handled automatically.

Audio 2. The second audio API directly exposes a sample streaming interface which is ideal for learning low-level audio programming. It also includes the source code for an implementation of the Audio 1 API, making the transition easier.

4   Explorable Programming Environments

Game worlds exhibit certain qualities which makes it easy for gamers to get used to a game easily and to learn its inner logics without frustration. Kha tries to replicate the most important of these qualities to improve engagement with the programming APIs.

4.1   Easy Access

The most popular games are playable everywhere - on PCs, game consoles, mobile devices and in a web browser. Kha currently provides two IDEs. Kode Studio is a fork of Visual Studio Code which works on regular PCs. Kode Garden works directly in modern web browsers. Both IDEs can work on the same projects which can be moved freely from on to another. A third IDE for mobile devices is currently in a conceptual phase.

Games which foster the creation and sharing of user-created content like Mario Maker, Little Big Planet and Minecraft also make easy access to that content a priority. Similarly Kode Garden projects can be shared via a simple string of 40 characters. This string is created for every change by hashing the very last project change and the previous project hash and is long enough to unambiguously identify every project state with a negligible probability of hash collisions without any need to synchronize multiple Kode Garden servers.

4.2   Initial Familiarity

Most games are clearly defined by one of the widely known game genre like realtime-strategy games, ego-shooter games and jump 'n' runs and most of them go to great lengths to at least initially feel familiar to players who are used to the particular genre [6]. Control schemes in particular are largely standardized among game-genres.

Kha tries to strike a similar balance by using the Haxe programming language which is conceptually very similar to Java - the most popular language for teaching computer science. Java itself is not used because of its problematic multi-platform support which for example resulted in Minecraft being reimplemented in C++ from the ground up. Professional game programmers however tend to use C++ and therefore Kha provides an easy upgrade path via its sister project Kore which provides very similar features and APIs to Kha but is implemented and programmed in C++.

4.3   Direct Feedback

In most games learning predominantly happens via a trial and error method [7]. Over the course of history games progressively shortened trial and error cycles going from earlier games like King's Quest which sometimes made errors apparent hours later to more current games like VVVVVV with typical trial and error cycles of about five seconds. Direct feedback proved fundamental for engaging learning cycles.

Kode Garden and Kode Studio can therefore patch games at runtime, replacing CPU code, GPU code and assets while a game is still running. Kha's runtime patching functionality is significantly faster than comparable functionality in Unreal Engine 4 which can require minutes for applying code changes. Most other game engines do not provide this functionality at all. Additionally the Kode Garden is very robust to programming errors and continues to work as normal even when the edited game ends up in an endless loop - this is in contrast to both Unreal Engine 4 and Unity where the complete editor has to be restarted in this situation.

5 Conclusion

While it will never be as popular as a general game engine, which primarily targets people who just want to make games and are not necessarily interested in the technical details, Kha has managed to build an active community around its specific target of teaching game engine development.

Kha users so far uploaded 130 h of learning material to YouTube, created more than 20 game engines running on top of Kha and often cite how much they learned via Kha as a primary motivation.

References

1. Shiraef, J.A.: An exploratory study of high performance graphics application programming interfaces (2016)
2. Kajiya, J.T., Sutherland, I.E., Cheadle, E.C.: A random-access video frame buffer. In: Proceedings of the IEEE Computer Graphics, Pattern Recognition, and Data Structures, pp. 1–6 (1975)
3. Seitz, C.: Computer graphics matrix multiplier. U.S. Patent No. 3,763,365 (1973)
4. Peachey, D.: Writing renderman shaders. In: Tony Apodaca (ed.) na. (1992)
5. Oliver, R.J.: Circular buffer for processing audio samples. U.S. Patent No. 6,044,434 (2000)
6. Apperley, T.H.: Genre and game studies: toward a critical approach to video game genres. Simul. Gaming **37**(1), 6–23 (2006)
7. Blumberg, F.C., Sokol, L.M.: Boys' and girls' use of cognitive strategy when learning to play video games. J. Gen. Psychol. **131**(2), 151–158 (2004)

Making Serious Programming Games Adaptive

Michael A. Miljanovic and Jeremy S. Bradbury[✉]

University of Ontario Institute of Technology,
2000 Simcoe St. N., Oshawa, ON L1H 7K4, Canada
{michael.miljanovic,jeremy.bradbury}@uoit.ca

Abstract. One of the challenges with Computer Science serious games is ensuring they are suitable for learners of different levels of ability and knowledge. To address this challenge, we propose a new methodology for incorporating adaptive gameplay and content into existing non-adaptive serious programming games. Our methodology includes four phases: (1) Identifying an existing game that is suitable for adaptation; (2) Modeling the gameplay tasks and the in-game assessment of learning; (3) Building the adaptation into the existing code base; (4) Evaluating the new adaptive serious game in comparison to the original game with respect to learning and engagement.

Keywords: Computer science · Education · Serious games
Adaptive methods · Machine learning · Software evolution

1 Introduction

The use of serious games is one approach that has shown effectiveness in engaging students to learn a variety of skills [11]. The potential for serious games to increase motivation and engagement among learners is particularly important for the field of Computer Science (CS), where low engagement levels give cause for concern [4]. Furthermore, the widespread interest in understanding the fundamentals of programming has led to CS being a heavily targeted field of study for serious games researchers [5].

While serious games have considerable promise, challenges still exist with respect to their design and evaluation. One of the open challenges is customizing serious games to suit learners of different levels of ability and knowledge. Existing solutions to this challenge can require substantial human effort, such as the monitoring and customization of gameplay by human experts and the creation of large, diverse problem sets. One drawback of these approaches is that they are not always practical when working with increasingly complex serious games [10]. In this work, we consider the use of adaptive serious games to make serious games suitable for learners with different skills. Adaptive serious games do not have the same drawbacks as the above mentioned approaches as they can automatically modify game elements and content to directly impact learner performance [9].

© Springer Nature Switzerland AG 2018
S. Göbel et al. (Eds.): JCSG 2018, LNCS 11243, pp. 253–259, 2018.
https://doi.org/10.1007/978-3-030-02762-9_27

The main contribution of our paper is a new methodology for incorporating adaptive gameplay and content into existing non-adaptive serious games. We have chosen to focus our methodology on CS serious games because many of the existing serious games for learning programming have widespread adoption and have empirical research to support their educational value (e.g., Code Hunt [3]). We believe modifying existing serious games that have already been adopted and evaluated is a more desirable approach than building new games from scratch.

2   Methodology

Adaptive games can be fully or semi-autonomous, allowing for game content to be included after the game's release. An autonomous serious game can promote instructive gameplay, manage the challenge of the user experience, provide scaffolding where needed, and support learners [6]. A common approach to adaptive serious games is to use Competence-based Knowledge Space Theory (CbKST) [2] in combination with a probabilistic approach. Our methodology leverages CbKST for making adaptive serious programming games from non-adaptive games and includes four key phases: identification, modelling, building and evaluation (see Fig. 1). To assist in explaining our methodology, we use the example of creating an adaptive version of Gidget [7]. Gidget is a non-adaptive serious game where players complete missions by repairing faulty programs.

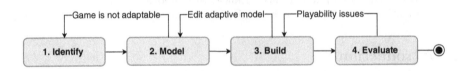

Fig. 1. An overview of our methodology for making adaptive serious games.

2.1   Identifying a Potential Adaptive Game

Both technical and learning factors should be considered when deciding if an existing serious game is an appropriate candidate for adaptive methods.

Technical Factors. In order to adapt a game, the source code will need to be publicly available and extendable. Thus, it is necessary to ensure that for third-party games, the software license for the chosen game allows for modification. The quality and robustness of the source code should be examined when identifying a serious game for adaptation as both of these factors can impact the modification of the source code. Also the playability of the game and the existence of playability studies should be considered. Gidget is an ideal choice technically because it is open source, includes documented source code, and has been evaluated indirectly with respect to playability.

Learning Factors. First, adapting the learning content of a game requires a clear understanding of the required knowledge, topics, and learning outcomes that are present in the original game [1]. Second, making informed decisions about adapting a game requires detailed knowledge about the learners who will play the game. Learners of various demographics including age groups may respond differently to in-game adaptations. Additionally, knowledge about the level of programming experience of the game's intended audience is needed in order to make good decisions on how to adjust learning content. Special consideration should also be given to adapting for learners of diverse educational backgrounds outside of CS and choosing games that are inclusive. Third, in order to properly evaluate the new adaptive serious game at the end of the process, it is best to choose an existing game that has already been evaluated with respect to learning as the existing evaluation can serve as a baseline in assessing the adaptive version. Our example, Gidget, focuses on learning debugging and has a target audience of general learners with no previous programming experience. Gidget has also been previously evaluated with respect to learning [8].

2.2   Modelling the Gameplay Tasks and Learning Assessment

Before implementing adaption into a serious game it is necessary to understand and model the gameplay tasks as well as the learning assessment (see Fig. 2).

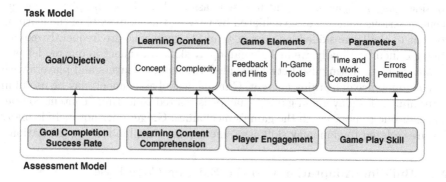

Fig. 2. Task and assessment models for adaptive games.

Task Model. A typical serious programming game includes a sequence of increasingly difficult tasks that pertain to learning content. Often, serious games are designed such that a player's success in the game is dependent on the completed and failed task objectives. Although the criteria for determining whether an objective is failed varies from game to game, failure is often accompanied by feedback or hints, as well as a reset of parameters such as time or error limits. The existing tasks in the game can be modelled and used as a template for adaptation. The most important task properties that should be included in this model are objectives, learning content, game elements, and parameters. These properties can be extracted from documentation as well as the structure and content of the game's source code. In Gidget, each level is a task with one or more objectives, each of which is completed when a given physical object on a grid is moved to a specified location. The primary learning concept in Gidget is debugging, and each level presents increasingly complex objectives, with partially incorrect code for completing those objectives. In addition to the debugging levels, newer versions of Gidget include levels that introduce concepts such as conditionals, functions, and arrays. Gidget provides substantial feedback to the player by visualizing every step of the code on the grid, and allows players to choose the number of steps to process at a given time. In order to encourage efficient programs, Gidget has an 'energy' limit that restricts the number of moves that can be taken during a level, but does not limit the gameplay time or number of errors permitted.

Assessment Model. Our model of assessment is based on CbKST and a probabilistic evaluation of the learner's competence in the learning content. The use of CbKST necessitates the inclusion of goal completion success rate and learning content comprehension in our model as predictors of a learner's competence. Since Gidget allows players to repeat a task until it is correctly solved, players must be assessed based on the efficiency of their code solutions. This includes measuring the error rate in each level, the number of lines of code in each solution, and how much energy is expended per level. The model also needs to consider player engagement and how it is assessed. Maintaining player engagement in serious games is often achieved by varying the complexity of the learning content to challenge skilled learners or to aid learners who are frequently experiencing difficulty. Finally, we include gameplay skill assessment in our model as it is important to distinguish between skilled video game players and players with high competence of learning content. Gameplay skill assessment may be useful in determining if a player's in-game behavior is related to learning content competence, or due to issues with the game's mechanics. Gidget does not include many features related to gameplay skill assessment (e.g., time limit, score tabulation).

2.3   Building Adaptation into the Existing Code Base

This phase includes using the models to plan the adaption approach, logging player behavior, initializing the gameplay, and applying the adaptation strategy.

Plan Adaptation. The task and assessment models should be used to determine which game features to adapt. Once these features are chosen, an adaptive algorithm is chosen to determine when, what, and how the tasks are adapted. Example algorithms may be rules-based approach or use machine learning, but should ultimately be probabilistic and follow the principles of CbKST. In Gidget, features for adaptation include the starting code errors, the gameplay obstacles and the energy limits. The adaptive algorithm in Gidget could involve the creation of a set of rules that use the past performance of the player to determine whether or not to adjust the features.

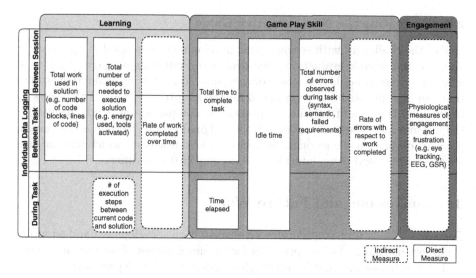

Fig. 3. Data logging for adaptation.

Data Logging. Learner-specific adaptation requires constant logging and measurement of learning data, game skill data, and engagement data (see Fig. 3). Depending on the adaptation strategy, data may be gathered for assessment during a task, between a task, or between gameplay sessions. In addition to adaptation, the data logged can be used for evaluating the gameplay experience.

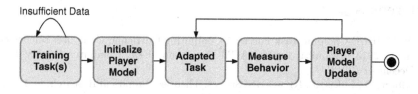

Fig. 4. Adaptive gameplay sequence.

Initialize Gameplay. An initial sequence of the game's tasks should be designated as non-adaptive 'training tasks' in order to initially assess the learner. Following training, an adaptive game should customize each task in accordance with the individual learner's data (see Fig. 4). There are several different options that a developer might consider for initializing the training portion of the game: predefined common initialization for all players, self assessment of programming skill (e.g., expert, skilled, unskilled), or game difficulty (hard, medium, easy). As Gidget is targeted towards players with no programming experience, we chose to use a common initialization of gameplay for all players.

2.4   Evaluating the New Adaptive Game

One of the challenges with serious game development in general is the need for accurate and reliable evaluation. One benefit to evaluating adaptive versions of existing serious games is that many of the games have existing evaluation studies that can be replicated and reproduced for the adaptive versions. This allows us to evaluate the benefits of the adaptation by comparing the study results for the original and adaptive versions. If the original serious game did not have a previous evaluation, we recommend following best practices, which may include questionnaires, skill tests, interviews, and controlled experiments.

3   Conclusions and Future Work

There has already been considerable investment in the development and adoption of CS serious games. As best practices for the development of new serious games evolve, it is important that we establish practices to evolve legacy serious games to leverage new ideas and methods. With this goal in mind, we have proposed a methodology for making serious games incorporate learner-based adaptation[1]. Our approach is based on the premise that an adaptive serious game will provide a better experience for learners, and improve their achievement of learning outcomes by directly adapting to their needs. The use of automatic adaptation within a serious game can provide benefits for engagement by adjusting gameplay difficulty to the learner's abilities. We are currently applying our methodology to create and release an adaptive version of Gidget.

References

1. ACM/IEEE-CS Joint Task Force on Computing Curricula: Computer science curricula 2013. Technical report, ACM Press and IEEE Computer Society Press, December (2013)
2. Albert, D., Lukas, J.: Knowledge Spaces: Theories, Empirical Research, and Applications. Psychology Press, New York (1999)
3. Bishop, J., Horspool, R.N., Xie, T., Tillmann, N., de Halleux, J.: Code hunt: experience with coding contests at scale. In: Proceedings of the ICSE 2015, vol. 2, pp. 398–407 (2015)
4. Butler, M., Sinclair, J., Morgan, M., Kalvala, S.: Comparing international indicators of student engagement for computer science. In: Proceedings of the Australasian Computer Science Week Multiconference, pp. 6:1–6:10 (2016)
5. Combéfis, S., Beresnevičius, G., Dagien, V.: Learning programming through games and contests: overview, characterisation and discussion. Olymp. Inform. **10**(1), 39–60 (2016)
6. Johnson, W.L., Vilhjálmsson, H.H., Marsella, S.: Serious games for language learning: How much game, how much AI? Artif. Intell. Educ. **125**, 306–313 (2005)

[1] This research was partially funded by the Natural Sciences and Engineering Research Council of Canada (NSERC).

7. Lee, M.J., Ko, A.J.: Investigating the role of purposeful goals on novices' engagement in a programming game. In: Proceedings of the IEEE Symposium on Visual Languages and Human-Centric Computing (VL/HCC 2012), pp. 163–166 (2012)
8. Lee, M.J., Ko, A.J.: Comparing the effectiveness of online learning approaches on CS1 learning outcomes. In: Proceedings of the 11th International Conference on Computing Education Research (ICER 2015), pp. 237–246 (2015)
9. Reichart, B., Ismailovic, D., Pagano, D., Brügge, B.: Adaptive serious games. Comput. Games Softw. Eng. **9**, 133–149 (2015)
10. Westra, J., Dignum, F., Dignum, V.: Scalable adaptive serious games using agent organizations. In: Proceedings of the 10th International Conference on Autonomous Agents and Multiagent Systems, vol. 3, pp. 1291–1292 (2011)
11. Yue, W.S., Wan, W.L.: The effectiveness of digital game for introductory programming concepts. In: Proceedings of the 10th International Conference for Internet Technology and Secured Transactions (ICITST 2015), pp. 421–425 (2015)

Serious Games for Health

The ExerCube: Participatory Design of an Immersive Fitness Game Environment

Anna Lisa Martin-Niedecken[1]([⊠]) [ID] and Elisa D. Mekler[2] [ID]

[1] Subject Area Game Design, Department of Design,
Zurich University of the Arts, Zurich, Switzerland
anna.martin@zhdk.ch
[2] HCI Research Group, Department of Psychology,
University of Basel, Basel, Switzerland

Abstract. Exergames have advanced from a trend of the entertainment industry to serious training applications. Nowadays body-centered games can be played at home, as well as in the gym, and provide an effective and motivating workout experience for the player. However, existing solutions often lack a symbiotic and user-centered design approach encompassing the three exergame design levels: the player's body (input movements), the controller (input device) and the game (story, game mechanics, dynamics, aesthetics). Consequently, existing systems exhibit weaknesses like motion sickness or a lack of audio-visual and narrative design of the physical and virtual play space. As such, the player's game experiences remain limited. Our work contributes to the sustainable establishment of fitness games as effective and attractive training tools. In this paper, we introduce the "ExerCube" and the design, evaluation, and subsequent re-design of the early stage prototype. The "ExerCube" is a fitness game setting for adults, which affords immersive gameplay experiences while engaging in a playful motor-cognitive and -coordinative functional workout. Our findings show that the preliminary "ExerCube" prototype was usable and well received by the target audience. We report insights about the target audience's preferences and identify avenues for the implementation of dual flow-based game mechanics, the optimization of the training concept and hardware, as well as for the further development of the game scenario.

Keywords: Exergame fitness training · Participatory design · Flow
"ExerCube"

1 Introduction

Virtual Reality (VR) applications and movement-based games – so-called exergames [1] – have advanced from a mere entertainment trend to serious training applications [2]. While a few years ago, exergames for the Nintendo Wii©, Sony Move© or the Microsoft Kinect© turned living rooms into playful training settings, nowadays innovative technologies have been introduced to gyms and convert the training area into virtual sports arenas: virtual training simulations (e.g., Athene Exergaming), gamified fitness training (e.g., Prama Pavigym), immersive and game-based training

© Springer Nature Switzerland AG 2018
S. Göbel et al. (Eds.): JCSG 2018, LNCS 11243, pp. 263–275, 2018.
https://doi.org/10.1007/978-3-030-02762-9_28

scenarios (e.g. Les Mills, Immersive Fitness) and exergame circuit training (e.g., Exergame Fitness) are no longer fiction, but have become reality.

The combination of trend-based training concepts, innovative input devices and game design is particularly fascination to "digital natives" and opens up new avenues for keeping fit in a motivating and attractive way. Moreover, these motor-cognitive and -coordinative training methods match or even surpass the training effects of traditional training concepts. Several sports scientific studies indicate positive effects on users' cognitive [e.g. 3] and coordinative abilities [e.g. 4].

Although these results suggest that these technologies will become increasingly established in the context of sports and training, a parallel scientific debate reveals weaknesses of the virtual training systems. Interdisciplinary human computer interaction (HCI) research and development (R&D) also deal with the analysis of existing VR and exergame concepts. Thereby, the focus is more on the multi-sensory and -modal experience and perception of specific designs, as well as on the deviation of practice-oriented approaches for the optimization of the training/gameplay experience. Buzzwords like "dual flow" [5], "embodiment" [6], "bodily interplay" [7] und "presence" [8] set a clear direction. A holistic, user-centered and symbiotic design approach on the levels of the moving body, the mediating technology and the virtual game scenario is needed to overcome current weaknesses of existing systems like motion sickness or a lack of audio-visual and narrative design of the physical and virtual play space, to fully exploit the potentials of these parallel training worlds.

The present work's contribution is two-fold: First, it serves to establish fitness games as effective and attractive training tools. Second, it addresses limitations of previous work on exergames which largely fail to consider the player experience, by explicitly putting the user experience at the forefront of the design and evaluation process. In this paper, we introduce the "ExerCube" and the design, evaluation, and subsequent re-design of the early stage prototype. Furthermore, we provide an outlook on future research and development steps towards the final "ExerCube".

2   Related Work

In recent years, researchers from a variety of disciplines and practitioners, such as trainers and therapists, have recognized the training effectiveness and motivational benefits of combining gaming and exercising. Sports science and health-related studies on commercially available and bespoke exergames confirmed the potential of these playful training technologies to increase energy expenditure [e.g. 9], positively affect the learning of sensorimotor skills [e.g. 10], coordinative abilities [e.g. 4], strength and endurance [e.g. 11] and to improve exercise program compliance [e.g. 12]. Concurrently, studies within HCI research provide insights into the effects of all three exergame design levels on players' gameplay experiences:

Body. The bodily exertion greatly influences the player's experiences and there are many ways of movement expressions and interpretations of pre-set motion sequences when playing an exergame [13]. In general, the inclusion of holistic physical activity into gameplay is found to be a positive predictor for the feeling of immersion and engagement [14]. Moreover, most of the existing, commercially available exergames for consoles lack the implementation of a proper movement scientific approved workout. Even when moving inaccurately, these games allow the player for a successful game performance and do not sufficiently correct movement mistakes. The other way around, existing game-based solutions available on the fitness market often implemented professional fitness workouts as input movements, but lack in a proper user-centered design of the interactive virtual game scenario. Hence, there is a need for better combinations of state-of-the-art designs on the level of fitness concepts, which are used as physical input to control the game and appealing virtual scenarios, which provide accurate movement feedback and instructions for the player.

Controller. During exergame play, the intermediary controller technology ideally assumes the role of mediator between the "physical" and the "virtual" game worlds [15]. However, the decisive factor is always how well an input device integrates itself into the body patterns of the moving player. Kim et al. found that an embodied interface improves user experience, energy expenditure, and intention to repeat the experience within the exergame [6]. The precision of movement recognition [16], as well as the natural integration of this recognition into the game scenario and the related movement feedback are decisive indicators for the "incorporation" of the game controller, and for the immersion into the game world [14]. Furthermore, when it comes to social exertion and bodily interplay [7] while playing an exergame together or against others, existing controller technologies are often criticized to rather limitate than "support", "enable" and "shape social" and bodily interaction between players [17]. Thus, we can identify a need for body-centered controller technologies, which serve as additional, physical playground, easily integrate into the body scheme of the player, provide a balance of guided and free movements and allow for social exertion and social play in cooperative as well as competitive settings.

Game Scenario. Considering the design of immersive, virtual scenarios for fitness game settings, there are various things, which need to be taken into account to achieve the intended effect with the player. The look and feel should appeal to the targeting group of the game and involve specific preferences for game mechanics, levels, visuals, sound and story. Thus, it is important to involve the targeting group into the design process from the very beginning [18]. Furthermore, there are various theoretical concepts and findings from game experience research, which should further serve as inspiration for an appropriate design of the virtual game design. Game experiences that are repeatedly brought up in relation to exergames are the closely related experiences of immersion and several flow variations. Csikszentmihalyi's flow theory [19] can be compared with the feeling of complete and energized focus on a particular activity, combined with a high level of enjoyment and fulfillment. An important precursor to the flow experience is the match between a person's skills and the challenges associated with a task, such as playing a game. Weibel and Wissmath define flow as a result of immersion or involvement in an activity (e.g. playing a game) [20]. Sweetser and Wyeth's "GameFlow" model determines the key elements of player enjoyment [21]. Sinclair et al. applied the flow theory to the task of playing a physically and mentally challenging exergame, calling it "dual flow" [5]. According to the dual flow concept, an optimal training/gameplay experience during exergame play requires a balance between the game-related challenge and player skills, as well as between the intensity of the required movement input and the player's fitness level. Thus, an exergame must be adjustable to suit the player's individual skill levels.

Current solutions and game experience evaluations often focus on single (e.g. body) or dual design levels (e.g. body and controller) rather than on a symbiotic combination of all dimensions (body, controller and game scenario), which take into account interdependencies and interaction effects of single dimensions on and with one another. Furthermore, they often fail a user-centered and participatory design approach, which – if implemented properly – can increase game attractiveness and effectiveness [18]. Consequently, gameplay experiences while playing existing solutions as well as insights from studies with those remain limited. Our work aims at bridging these gaps with a comprehensive approach in both, development and research, in order to make a sustainable contribution to enhancement of the attractiveness and effectiveness of these playful workout experiences.

3 Participatory Design of the "ExerCube"

In the following, we present the first design cycle of the early stage "ExerCube" prototype. For the creation of the "ExerCube", we were inspired by current workout and design trends on the fitness market, findings from HCI and games user experience research, as well as target group-specific wishes and ideas for the exergame setting which we gained through previous surveys with male and female "digital natives" at the age of around 18 – 40 years. For the design process, we further built upon our previous work with "Plunder Planet" a dynamically adaptive fitness game setting, which was designed with and for children [17, 22–24] involving a participatory and symbiotic three-stage design process at the levels of the player's body, the controller and the game. The early stage "ExerCube" was developed by an interdisciplinary team which consists of experts from the fields of sport science, game design, game research and industrial design.

3.1 Early Stage Prototype

Body Movements and Controller. On the level of body movements, we decided to design up to five challenge and complexity levels, which are based on traditional functional fitness. Functional fitness is well known for its motor-cognitive and -coordinative, as well as endurance, strength and flexibility training effects [25]. Functional fitness has been defined as emphasizing multiple muscle and joint activities, combining upper body and lower body movements, and utilizing more of the body in each movement [26]. The movement levels gradually build upon one another:

Level 1: Basic jump, squat and lateral shuffle-step with extension or flexion of the body to the upper, middle and lower section of the right and left wall of the cube
Level 2: Level 1 + lateral rotation to the middle of the right and left wall of the cube
Level 3: Level 2 + deep lunge with knee bend to the left and right side

Level 4: Level 3 + lateral rotation to the bottom of the cube
Level 5: Level 4 + burpee

For the first prototype, we implemented only the first level of the training concept. The movements were translated into a game mechanic: In the virtual game space, the player finds themselves on a track, which sets various directions, akin to a racing game track. If the track curves to the right or to the left, the player needs to move to the respective side. Additionally, the player needs to move to the upper (=uphill), middle (=at ground level) or lower (=downhill) right or left side depending on the track's changes in height. The track is looped after a pre-defined number of level sections. Towards the end of the track loop, players have to do one basic jump and squat underneath an obstacle. The player's arm movements and position are tracked with the HTC Vive system. Two cameras are positioned at the cube frame; one in front and one behind the player. While playing the player holds one Vive in each hand, which triggers an in-game feedback (particle effect) on the sidewalls of the "ExerCube", provided the player moves in close enough to the sidewall.

Hardware. We designed an open cube-like trapeze (hereafter referred to as "cube" or "ExerCube"), which serves as part of the game controller (haptic device) and as projection screen (interface). It consists of a solid wooden frame covered with stretchable, semitransparent and bouncy mash fabrics. Each of the three walls of the cube measures 2.40 m width and length, as well as 2.50 m height, whereas the projectable surface of the cube measures 1.80 m. The transition of the front to the sidewalls is slightly curved, to generate a flowing and immersive form similar to commercially available curved TV screens. The bounciness of the fabrics affords an engaging haptic experience, when touching and/or punching into the walls to trigger in-game actions. Additionally, the semitransparency of the "ExerCube" provides a lightly framed non-isolating spatial experience for the player. Three outside beamers project the game scenario onto the walls of the cube.

Game Scenario. Based on our look and feel inspirations, the first game scenario prototype takes the player into a sci-fi inspired world with a racing track, which passes through vast mountain ranges under a sparkling and atmospheric milky way (Fig. 1). For the first prototype, we experimented with very basic elements, perspectives and mechanics.

The player can either play the game in a third- or first-person perspective. The game starts in the third-person perspective and the player sees their mentor from the back. The mentor shows the movements, which the player needs to imitate in order to navigate their movements with the pre-set track in the virtual world. After the player familiarizes themselves with the movements, rules and mechanics, the mentor disappears and the player continues playing without any guidance in the first-person perspective.

Since the first design cycle focused on the basic spatial and flow experiences related to the design of the body movements, the hardware and the game scenario, we chose not to implement any sound and only few in-game events. The only virtual feedback is a visual particle effect, which shows the player whether or not they successfully performed the movement. The visual feedback would only appear, if the player reached out far enough and was close enough to the wall.

Fig. 1. Early stage "ExerCube" prototype (Source: Sphery Ltd.)

4   Evaluation

Following the first cycle of design, we conducted an early user testing. The evaluation was performed by a team of experts from the fields of sport science, psychology and game research. The aim of this testing was to evaluate our preliminary designs and gain further insights into the early stage prototype's influence on player's immersion and flow experiences, as well as identify opportunities for implementing dual flow-based game mechanics at all design levels. Furthermore, we were interested in participants' interaction and movement strategies and asked for feedback and preferences for the further development of the "ExerCube" setting.

4.1   Method

Participants and Procedure. We recruited 17 participants (8 women, 9 men), aged 15 to 43 years old (mean age = 30.88, $SD = 8.53$). Participants reported diverse game genre preferences, with strategy games (n = 13) having been most commonly mentioned, followed by sports, action and action-adventure games (n = 8 mentions each). All participants engaged in a variety of physical activities to some extent, with swimming (n = 9) and jogging (n = 9) being the most popular. More than half of the participants (n = 9) had previous experience with exergames, mostly with the Microsoft Kinect©. After providing informed consent, participants were first asked to play with the "ExerCube" for 10 min. Play sessions were video-recorded but not further analyzed for the sake of the first evaluation. However, some preliminary observations of the principal investigator have been immediately written down after each play session. After 10 min, participants were asked to complete a questionnaire consisting of several player experience measures, as well as interviewed with regards to their impressions of the "ExerCube". Interviews lasted from 10–30 min.

Measures. As the eventual aim of the "ExerCube" is to provide players with an optimally challenging experience, both with regards to gameplay and physical exertion, we employed several complementary measures of flow. First, the Flow Short State Scale [27] has already previously been employed to capture flow in sports contexts, and includes a 10-item measure for flow experience, as well as 3 items for assessing worry (7-point Likert scale, from 1 = "I do not agree at all" to 7 = "I fully agree"). Moreover, we assessed "GameFlow" via 7 items developed by Kliem and Wiemeyer [4]. This measure is based on Sweetser and Wyeth's "GameFlow" model, which specifically focuses on flow within the context of (digital) games. Moreover, we asked participants to rate their experience with regards to several other aspects, including how challenging it was to play with the "ExerCube" in terms of physical and cognitive effort, as well as whether they would consider the game fun on repeated playing.

4.2   Results

Descriptive Statistics. Overall, as listed in Table 1, participants rated the "ExerCube" as reasonably engaging and scored it moderately high on flow (M = 4.8, SD = 0.77), game flow (M = 3.86, SD = 1.07), enjoyment (M = 3.47, SD = 1.07) and motivation (M = 4.24, SD = 1.2), as well as low on worry (M = 2.37, SD = 1.45). Participants noted that while the "ExerCube" was easy to understand (M = 6.29, SD = 0.85) and to control (M = 5.41, SD = 1.58), gameplay was not sufficiently challenging, both in terms of the required cognitive (M = 3.12, SD = 0.99) and physical effort (M = 2.88, SD = 1.09).

Table 1. Descriptive statistics for all quantitative measures.

	Flow	Worry	GameFlow	Enjoyment	Control	Movements matched game	Game motivated me to move	Physical effort	Cognitive effort	Optimally challenging	Immersion	Easy to understand	Could concentrate on game without having to focus on body	Visual appeal	Game would still be fun after repeated playing	Would exercise with the game in the future
M	4.8	2.37	3.86	3.47	3.82	4.47	4.24	2.88	3.12	2.76	3.65	5.76	5.59	4.41	3.81	3.82
SD	0.77	1.45	0.94	1.07	1.24	0.87	1.2	1.09	0.99	1.03	1.17	1.15	1.5	1.46	2.04	1.78

Qualitative Evaluation. In addition to the questionnaire, we interviewed participants following a guideline and asked them to answer several questions related to their experiences with the input movements, the hardware and controller, the design of the game scenario, their motivation and their flow experience. Furthermore, the notes of the main observations of the principal investigator are discussed in relation to the results of the interviews and revealed further insights, which underline the results of the quantitative data collection. Following, we shortly summarize the main findings:

Although the first prototype was designed very rudimentary on all design levels (body, controller and game scenario), participants felt immersed and experienced the typical flow indications (e.g. loss of sense of time and space; see also Table 1). Their main memory was the futuristic and abstract look and feel of the prototype, which all of them liked very much. Some testers anticipated existing games (e.g. "Guitar Hero" or "Mario Kart") or movies (e.g. "Tron: Legacy" or "Star Wars") with it. Although all testers enjoyed the general look and feel of the prototype and the fact, that they were surrounded by a cube, they asked for more variety (e.g. story, sound, levels) and challenge (e.g. more obstacles). Participants appreciated the approach of combining fictional and natural elements in the visual design of the game and suggested to further deepen this approach.

We found that participants easily became familiar with the navigation mechanisms of the game (see also Table 1) and could effortlessly control the game without the guiding mentor. The guideline-based interviews as well as the participatory observation revealed, that the majority felt even more immersed, when the mentor disappeared. However, participants found the mentor helpful in the beginning and suggested, that the mentor should move more accurately and provide better movement instructions. Concerning the visual appearance of the mentor, participants could imagine both, a fictional and human-like avatar, as long as the locomotor system looks like a human one.

Generally, participants reported that the required input movements felt natural and intuitive. This finding could be further supported by participants' statements, which revealed that the majority oriented towards the virtual setting to coordinate their movements. There was no mismatch between the physical and virtual movements and the hardware and controller technology were implemented discreet enough. Consequently, nobody experienced motion sickness. A wish for an additional input movement was boxing.

At the end of the interview, we gave participants a quick outlook on future development plans for the "ExerCube" and asked for feedback on these ideas. Participants liked the idea of being able to play together or against others while being challenged on an individual physical and cognitive level. They also liked the idea of a racing game including a clear goal, more variations and a matching adaptive sound design.

5   Re-design of the "ExerCube" and Discussion

Based on the results of the first user testing, we re-designed the "ExerCube" prototype (Fig. 2). We further developed single design elements on the levels of body movements, hardware, controller and game scenario in order to provide all facilities for the future implementation of the dual flow.

Fig. 2. First re-design of the "ExerCube" setting (Source: Sphery Ltd.)

5.1 Second Draft Prototype

Body Movements and Controller. To increase the interaction of the player with the walls of the cube, we decided to extend our existing movement levels with some boxing elements and came up with the following:

> **Level 1:** Basic jump, squat and lateral shuffle-step with extension or flexion of the body to the upper, middle and lower section of the right and left wall of the cube
> **Level 2:** Level 1 + lateral rotation to the middle of the right and left wall of the cube with and without punch
> **Level 3:** Level 2 + deep lunge with knee bend to the left and right side
> **Level 4:** Level 3 + left and right punch
> **Level 5:** Level 4 + squad jump with punch into the front wall of the cube
> **Level 6:** Level 5 + burpee

With the first user testing we could prove the general feasibility of the basic movements. However, participants reported that it was quite easy to control the game and the physical and cognitive challenge were experienced rather low (see also Table 1). Hence, to sustainably increase the challenge and to allow for a comprehensive and holistic workout experience, we implemented all movement levels into the re-design. Generally, the idea is that every player can work out in their best suiting motor-cognitive and coordinative challenge level. The movement sequence of every level follows a random and thus not foreseeable, but movement scientific meaningful approach (including warmup, guidance to the individual peak and balancing of motor-cognitive and -coordinative stimuli).

During the testings we could observe that participants interacted rather tentative with the cube hardware. This might have been triggered by the fact that players had to hold HTC Vives in their hands while playing. Therefore, for the second stage prototype, we replaced the HTC Vives with two HTC trackers, which are attached to the player's wrists. Again, the cameras track the position of the player's arms and legs in the cube and the player is able to freely use their hands.

Hardware. The observation and feedback of participants on the rather tentative interaction with the cube hardware was also related to the missing orientation points in the lower section of the cube, which was not covered with fabrics. Thus, we re-designed the height of the walls' covered surface, which is now reaching from the cube's top to nearby the floor (Fig. 2). Furthermore, we are also experimenting with different materials (bouncy fabrics and foamed materials) to further enhance the interactive and haptic experience with the hardware. The aim is to create both, a virtual and a physical play space, which are symbiotically interconnected with each other.

Game Scenario. Based on the feedback and wishes of the participants, we also further developed the game graphics and the scenario. We came up with a virtual underwater sci-fi racing scenario (Fig. 2). The player's avatar/mentor is positioned on a hover-board, which needs to be navigated by the player following the track layout. The player and their avatar must overcome and target at obstacles, which appear in front or on the sides and try to be as fast and successful as possible to win the race. If the player is to slow, others and their avatars will overtake them. In the end, there is a leaderboard, where the high scores and winners are listed.

Again, the track layout provides information about which movement the player needs to perform next. For a maximum realistic and accurate movements of the mentor, we captured the movements of a real functional fitness trainer with the professional motion capturing system OptiTrack and implemented them into the game. Thus, the virtual mentor performs all movements accurately.

In summary, we can state the following things: Despite the rare implementation of interactive elements in the first "ExerCube" prototype, the scenario provided the illu-sion of being more interactive due to its immersive structure, graphics and perspectives. It appealed that the majority of participants felt like they were actually controlling everything in the game for at least the first couple of minutes of the test session. Only some testers realized earlier that the actual interaction possibilities with the scenario (dependency of in-game actions on input movements) were very limited. However, they still were involved in the gameplay and experienced flow. This could also be confirmed by the results of the questionnaire, which prove that participants felt immersed throughout the game session.

Despite the fact that we tested the first prototype with a very heterogeneous group of participants (gender and age), the futuristic and technological seeming game scenario was generally very well valued.

6 Future Work and Conclusion

We could show that the basic "ExerCube" setup including body movements, hardware and virtual game scenario is usable and has been well received by the targeting group. We gained insights into targeting group specific preferences and wishes in terms of the look and feel, the game mechanics and dynamics. We could identify new avenues for the implementation of dual flow-based game mechanics, for the opti-mization of the training concept and hardware as well as for the further development of the game scenario.

Based on the R&D steps we conducted so far, we will further evaluate and develop the "ExerCube". For the next testing, the "ExerCube" will feature dual flow-based game mechanics related to the player's motor-coordinative and -cognitive abilities as well as emotions. Based on the player's heart rate (measured with a heart rate sensor) and in-game performance, the game difficulty and complexity will be automatically and manually adjustable via a specifically developed trainer UI. We further implement three gradually adjustable sub-levels (low, medium, high) of each movement level to challenge the player's physical abilities and experiment with different cognitive challenge levels as well as sounds and atmospheres. The player's avatar/mentor will provide more or less feedback and instruction, depending on the player's in-game performance: If the player performs well, the mentor will automatically disappear and if the player performs poorly, the mentor will reappear and support the player with real-time instructions and visual movement feedback and corrections.

Beside the adaptive single player version, we will also offer a collaborative and a competitive multiplayer version of the "ExerCube". With the collaborative version, two players can play together in one cube or against each other in different cubes. To ensure equal opportunities for all player and athlete types to win the exergame battle, the "ExerCube" will also feature dynamic multiplayer balancing mechanics [28]. Last but not least, we are also developing a specific sound design featuring adaptive sounds, which will have an additional impact on the player's dual flow experience.

In the near future, the "ExerCube" by Sphery Ltd. will be commercially available as gym application. Beside cooperative play sessions, players can then join multiplayer battles within the same gym and across gyms in the same region or across the world. There will be further "ExerCube" game scenarios providing different training concepts (e.g. high intensity training or yoga) and specific hardware extensions.

To sum up, our work contributes towards the current trend of fitness games and exergame research in a number of ways: First, we developed a prototype, whose design and concept extend existing solutions by combining innovative approaches from related R&D fields like sport science, game experience and HCI research. Second, we present a user study and provide insights into our user-centered, iterative R&D work. We describe the re-design of the first "ExerCube" prototype and provide an outlook on future work, which shows how we further implement the user's feedback into the design and work on better, holistic game experiences. Thus, we contribute towards filling gaps in exergame design and research.

Acknowledgment. Anna Lisa Martin-Niedecken thanks Sphery Ltd., Koboldgames, Roman Jurt and Ronnie Gaensli for the excellent collaboration in developing the "ExerCube". Authors further thank Şahin Yilmaz for his support in preparing and processing the quantitative evaluation.

References

1. Oh, Y., Yang, S.: Defining exergames and exergaming. In: Proceedings of Meaningful Play, pp 1–17 (2010)
2. Wiemeyer, J., Temper, L.: Edutainment in sport and health. In: Nakatsu, R., Rauterberg, M., Ciancarini, P. (eds.) Handbook of Digital Games and Entertainment Technologies, pp. 883–908. Springer, Singapore (2017). https://doi.org/10.1007/978-981-4560-50-4_67

3. Pietrzak, E., Pullman, S., McGuire, A.: Using virtual reality and videogames for traumatic brain injury rehabilitation: a structured literature review. GAMES HEALTH Res. Dev. Clin. Appl. **3**(4), 202–214 (2014). https://doi.org/10.1089/g4h.2014.0013

4. Kliem, A., Wiemeyer, J.: Comparison of a traditional and a video game based balance training program. Int. J. Comput. Sci. Sport **9**(2), 80–91 (2010)

5. Sinclair, J., Hingston, P., Masek, M.: Considerations for the design of exergames. In: 5th International Conference on Computer Graphics and Interactive Techniques in Australia and Southeast Asia, pp 289–295. ACM, New York (2007). https://doi.org/10.1145/1321261.1321313

6. Kim, S.Y.S., Prestopnik, N., Biocca, F.A.: Body in the interactive game: how interface embodiment affects physical activity and health behavior change. Comput. Hum. Behav. **36**, 376–384 (2014). https://doi.org/10.1016/j.chb.2014.03.067

7. Mueller, F., Gibbs, M., Vetere, F., Edge, D.: Designing for bodily interplay in social exertion games. ACM Trans. Comput. Hum. Interact. (TOCHI) **24**(3), 1–48 (2017). https://doi.org/10.1145/3064938

8. Skalski, P., Tamborini, R., Shelton, A., Buncher, M., Lindmark, P.: Mapping the road to fun: Natural video game controllers, presence, and game enjoyment. New Media Soc. **13**(2), 224–242 (2011). https://doi.org/10.1177/1461444810370949

9. Murphy, E.C., Carson, L., Neal, W., Baylis, C., Donley, D., Yeater, R.: Effects of an exercise intervention using Dance Dance Revolution on endothelial function and other risk factors in overweight children. Int. J. Pediatr. Obes. **4**(4), 205–214 (2009). https://doi.org/10.3109/17477160902846187

10. Fery, Y.A., Ponserre, S.: Enhancing the control of force in putting by video game training. Ergonomics **44**(12), 1025–1037 (2001). https://doi.org/10.1080/00140130110084773

11. Sohnsmeyer, J., Gilbrich, H., Weisser, B.: Effect of a six-week-intervention with an activity-promoting video game on isometric muscle strength in elderly subjects. Int. J. Comput. Sci. Sport. (Int. Assoc. Comput. Sci. Sport.) **9**(2), 75–79 (2010)

12. Harris, K., Reid, D.: The influence of virtual reality play on children's motivation. Can. J. Occup. Ther. **72**(1), 21–29 (2005). https://doi.org/10.1177/000841740507200107

13. Bianchi-Berthouze, N.: Understanding the role of body movement in player engagement. HCI **28**(1), 40–75 (2013)

14. Pasch, M., Bianchi-Berthouze, N., van Dijk, B., Nijholt, A.: Movement-based sports video games: Investigating motivation and gaming experience. Entertain. Comput. **1**(2), 49–61 (2009). https://doi.org/10.1016/j.entcom.2009.09.004

15. Martin, A.L., Wiemeyer, J.: Technology-mediated experience of space while playing digital sports games. Int. J. Comput. Sci. Sport. (Int. Assoc. Comput. Sci. Sport.) **11**(1), 135–146 (2012)

16. Nijhar, J., Bianchi-Berthouze, N., Boguslawski, G.: Does movement recognition precision affect the player experience in exertion games? In: Camurri, A., Costa, C. (eds.) INTETAIN 2011. LNICST, vol. 78, pp. 73–82. Springer, Heidelberg (2012). https://doi.org/10.1007/978-3-642-30214-5_9

17. Martin-Niedecken, A.L.: Designing for bodily interplay: engaging with the social exertion game plunder planet. In: Proceedings of Proceedings of the 17th ACM Conference on Interaction Design and Children (IDC 2018), pp. 19–30. ACM, New York (2018). https://doi.org/10.1145/3202185.3202740

18. DeSmet, A., Thompson, D., Baranowski, T., Palmeira, A., Verloigne, M., De Bourdeaudhuij, I.: Is participatory design associated with the effectiveness of serious digital games for healthy lifestyle promotion? A meta-analysis. J. Med. Internet Res. **18**(4) (2016). https://doi.org/10.2196/jmir.4444

19. Csikszentmihalyi, M.: Flow. Harper Collins Publishers, New York (1990)

20. Weibel, D., Wissmath, B.: Immersion in computer games: the role of spatial presence and flow. Int. J. Comput. Games Technol. **2011**, 1–14 (2011). Article No. 6

21. Sweetser, P., Wyeth, P.: GameFlow: a model for evaluating player enjoyment in games. Comput. Entertain. **3**(3), 3 (2005). https://doi.org/10.1145/1077246.1077253

22. Martin-Niedecken, A.L., Götz, U.: Design and evaluation of a dynamically adaptive fitness game environment for children and young adolescents. In: Annual Symposium on Computer-Human Interaction in Play, pp. 205–212. ACM, New York (2016). https://doi.org/10.1145/2968120.2987720

23. Martin-Niedecken, A.L., Götz, U.: Go with the dual flow: evaluating the psychophysiological adaptive fitness game environment "Plunder Planet". In: Alcañiz, M., Göbel, S., Ma, M., Fradinho Oliveira, M., Baalsrud Hauge, J., Marsh, T. (eds.) JCSG 2017. LNCS, vol. 10622, pp. 32–43. Springer, Cham (2017). https://doi.org/10.1007/978-3-319-70111-0_4

24. Martin-Niedecken, A.L.: Exploring spatial experiences of children and young adolescents while playing the dual flow-based fitness game "Plunder Planet". In: Proceedings of the International Conference on Computer-Human Interaction Research and Application (CHIRA 2017), pp. 218–229 (2017). https://doi.org/10.5220/0006587702180229

25. Weiss, T., et al.: Effect of functional resistance training on muscular fitness outcomes in young adults. J. Exerc. Sci. Fit. **8**(2), 113–122 (2010)

26. Brill, P.: Exercise your independence: functional fitness for older adults. J. Aging Phys. Act. **16**, 88 (2008)

27. Rheinberg, F., Vollmeyer, R., Engeser, S.: Die Erfassung des Flow-Erlebens. In: Stiensmeier-Pelster, J., Rheinberg, F. (Hrsg.) Diagnostik von Selbstkonzept, Lernmotivation und Selbstregulation (Tests und Trends Bd. 16), pp. 261–279. Hogrefe, Göttingen (2003)

28. Altimira, D., Mueller, F., Lee, G., Clarke, J., Billinghurst, M.: Towards understanding balancing in exertion games. In: 11th Conference on Advances in Computer Entertainment Technology (ACE 2014), pp 1–10. ACM, New York (2014). https://doi.org/10.1145/2663806.2663838

Instant Measurement of the Difficulty Level of Exergames with Simple Uni-dimensional Level Goals for Cerebral Palsy Players

Mohammad Rahmani[1]($\boxtimes$) ⓘ, Blas Herrera[1] ⓘ, Oleh Kachmar[2] ⓘ,
Julián Cristiano[1] ⓘ, and Domenec Puig[1] ⓘ

[1] Department of Computer Engineering and Maths,
University of Rovira i Virgili, Tarragona, Spain
mohammad.rahmani@urv.cat
[2] International Clinic of Rehabilitation, Truskavets, Ukraine

Abstract. In this paper we propose a solution to introduce a function for difficulty degree of achieving a simple, uni-dimensional goal of a level of an exergame. This solution, takes advantage of a statistical method built upon the results of the specific cerebral palsy (CP) player under study, inspired from normal distribution. It is appropriate for CPs, since it favors a content-based approach which is formed upon each player's personal results. Using a population of 20 CP patients trying to achieve the goals of games, we arrived to an 85% correlation between number of goal achievement failures and our introduced difficulty function.

Keywords: Difficulty degree · Exergame · Cerebral palsy

1 Introduction

Cerebral palsy (CP) is a group of permanent disorders of movement and posture, causing activity limitations, which are attributed to non-progressive disturbances of developing brain [1]. It is the most common motor disorder among children, affecting approximately two children per 1000 live birth. One in five children with CP (20%) has a severe intellectual deficit and is unable to walk [2]. Many therapies and rehabilitation approaches exist to improve their quality of life. Physiotherapy is considered one of the most beneficial and effective parts of the rehabilitation process [3]. To increase the motivation of these patients, rehabilitation should be interesting, for example, through gamification. Rehabilitation computer games are gaining more attention of the scientists and health care providers for this reason [4]. They offer even bigger potential to draw player's

This work has been supported by the GABLE project funded by the European Commission under grant agreement No 732363.

attention with dynamic difficulty adjustment (DDA). If the player wins too easily, the game experience will quickly turns out to be boring and if the player is unable to achieve any success, he turns to be discouraged and frustrated [5]. Both situations are undesirable and negatively affect the rehabilitation efficiency. DDA allows the game to change the difficulty parameters based on player's performance level, staying interesting for any skill group. The main goal of DDA is to create the state of flow in the patient and keep him/her in that state for entire game session [6]. A Numerical function which denotes the *Difficulty Degree* for a particular player to approach his results closer to a given level goal of a game with its pre-determined settings, is important in designing the goals and settings of that level to keep the game exciting. By *difficulty degree*, we mean, game levels which are more difficult, entail more level repeats to accomplish.

In [7], the authors have introduced a difficulty degree from semiotics to explain the link between tension-resolution cycles and challenge with the player's enjoyment, then they introduced a statistical method to measure the difficulty degree based on the relation between abilities and difficulties. On the other hand, Glen Berseth et al., in [12] have worked on the effect of small changes in the placement of game elements that lead to significant changes in terms of the challenge experienced by the player on the path to their goal which is mostly a study of effect of modification applied to graphics of the games which is out of the scope of our subject. Another study which tries to use the level of difficulty as a scale to suggest an automatic leveling of a game, [8], focuses on a probabilistic approach, mostly based on players' losing probability for game obstacles which is also relevant to the specific game they have exemplified. As suggested by [9], the adaptation of difficulty in a competitive arm rehabilitation game based on two physiological signals results in that, it is possible to control the physiological responses of unimpaired participants in a competitive arm rehabilitation game, thus controlling their level of workload and exercise intensity. But this method entails the usage of a robotic arm while we are seeking a solution that is implementable with hardware such as balance boards to control the games. In another study, [10], using a feed forward neural network, a solution is developed to classify the players' motivation which is directly correlated with game's difficulty level, into three classes (not motivated, well motivated and overloaded) while in this paper, we assign continuous real values to difficulty level of a game. The goal of this paper, on the other hand, is to introduce a real-value function from which, not only relevant correlated values to number of failures are driven, but also the tangent of the function symbolizes a relevant growth rate in difficulty to use in automatic difficulty adjustment as a future work.

2   Methodology

Imagine a computer game, that a player can move an avatar to right and left on the bottom of a screen to hunt (drink) the falling drink from top of the screen such as that of Fig. 1 in which the player must drink exactly 10cc of syrup. The objective of such a game is to teach the player to take the exact amount of medication the doctor has prescribed. The goal is that the player must direct the avatar on screen to drink exactly $10cc$ of syrup in a game session not longer than a limited period of time. (since CP kids are reluctant to continue playing a level more than this amount of time) in which the speed of falling syrup bottles are 8 m per second and the speed of the movement of the avatar to left and right is $9\,mm/s$, in this level. So, the settings are those which are concerning the speed of the objects, or $\vec{s} = (s_1, s_2) = (8\,mm/s, 9\,mm/s)$. A *level* is an ordered pair composed of vector of setting and a goal as follows $\vec{l} = (\vec{s}, g)$ which translates to:

$$\vec{l} = ((8\,mm/s, 9\,mm/s), 10cc) \tag{1}$$

in this example. Whenever the player tries a game session with a determined level, ends up to either pass or fail the goals of the level. Consequently, he achieves a result such as r, correspondent to the goal, g. For example, 3cc which results in a failure to accomplish the goals of Eq. (1) or 10 cc which will be recorded as a success. After every accomplishment, the player may decide continue playing the same level or ask to move to a higher level. As the player continues trying, he generates more and more results such as $R = \{r_1, r_2, ..., r_n\}$ in which each of the r_is are correspondent to the goal, g, under the setting vector, $\vec{s} = (s_1, s_2, ..., s_m)$. Our goal in this paper is to introduce a solution to assign a real value to a given level such as $\vec{l} = (\vec{s}, g)$ so that the larger this value is, the more number of tries it takes the player to accomplish the goal of the level. It is important to notice that although we are planning to introduce the difficulty of a level for a given player, and a level is a composition of a goals and a vector of settings, but the difficulty function will explicitly depend on goals and implicitly on settings since the settings are included by the data driven from the results. Additionally, this value is tailored to the player and is not applicable to other players. The choice of a function that generates a degree of difficulty for a given level personalized to a specific player must be certainly confined to a series of rules derived from trivial intuition. For example, when results closer to a given goal component such as g' are favored, then

$$\lim_{g \to \pm \infty} d(g) = +\infty \tag{2}$$

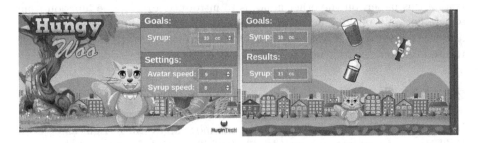

Fig. 1. Goals, results and settings of a game exemplified in Sect. 2 while the player tries to pick exactly 10 bottles (cc) of syrup

It is important to note that the difficulty function will depend on the goal, g, and not the settings or their delegates which are the results. That's why in Eq. (2) neither the settings nor the results appeared.

2.1   A Difficulty Function Inspired by Normal Distribution

A good difficulty function addresses the fact that the more the player tends to achieve various results, the more probable it is to approach the goal. Imagining the exemplified game in Sect. 2, a player who frequently drink syrup amounts very concentrated around 5cc ($\mu_1 = 5cc$) in each game session is less probable to be able to approach the goal amount which is exactly 10cc in comparison to a player with the same average of amount ($\mu_2 = 5cc$) but with values more dispersedly. We introduce Eq. (3) as a good choice for difficulty degree meter. This function is derived from the multiplicative inverse of normal distribution density function which is divided by $\sqrt{2\pi\sigma^2}$ and deducted from one. As Fig. 2 illustrates, it complies with the reluctance factor. Additionally it assigns 0 to the players whose mean of results are closer to goal value and ∞ to those far away the given goal value. In other words, in Fig. 2 it is clear that since the distance of $g^{(2)}$ from μ is greater than that of $g^{(1)}$, the values driven from the difficulty function is greater for $g^{(2)}$ than that of $g^{(1)}$.

$$d(g|\mu,\sigma) = e^{\frac{(g-\mu)^2}{2\sigma^2}} - 1 \tag{3}$$

where

$$\mu = \frac{1}{p}\sum_{k=1}^{p} r_k \quad and \quad \sigma = \sqrt{\frac{\sum_{k=1}^{p}(r_k - \mu)^2}{p}}$$

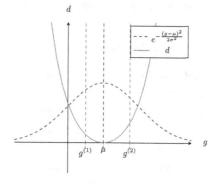

Fig. 2. Difficulty function when values closer to μ are preferred

3   Results

As a trivial bias, we expect that higher values of difficulty generated by difficulty function, result in higher number of level repeats. Eventually, the correlation

value between the difficulty value and number of failures in accomplishing the
level goals (repeating the level) must be a positive value and the closer it is to
1 the stronger is the correlation. In an experiment with kids who are suffering
from cerebral palsy, 20 patients from 9 to 15 years old (with mean of 12.1 and
standard deviation of 1.7), played a game such as the one described in Sect. 2 and
controlled by Nintendo^{TM} Wii Balance Board, as shown in Fig. 3, to achieve 10
different levels of the game while settings were kept fixed. The attendees were all
patients of International Clinic of Rehabilitation(ICR) providing rehabilitation
services to patients with Cerebral Palsy in Ukraine. The games were played on
personal computers without application of external libraries to sync the balance
board with computer. Table 1 shows the correspondent level repeats and the vector goals derived from 3000 game session tries. Using the correlation between the
driven difficulties and the level repeats by Eq. (4), we reached 85% of correlation
which shows the effectiveness of Eq. (3)

$$Corr(d, n) = \frac{cov(d, n)}{\sigma_d \sigma_n} \tag{4}$$

Fig. 3. The game exemplified in Sect. 2 being played by a CP kid with the help of a
caregiver.

Table 1. Results

Level	Level repeats	Goal	Difficulty
1	256	7cc	43
2	255	8cc	20
3	273	9cc	49
4	284	10cc	84
5	291	11cc	311
6	299	12cc	631
7	314	13cc	1005
8	316	14cc	1701
9	335	15cc	2217
10	337	16cc	4211

4   Conclusion

For CP kids, a methodology driven from the results of each patient should be favored over the similarity between them. The coefficient of multiplicative inverse of normal density function in Sect. 3, suggests an efficient way of describing players' reluctance to induce his results toward the level goals which leads us to introduced difficulty function.

References

1. Rosenbaum, P.P., et al.: The definition and classification of cerebral palsy. Dev Med Child Neurol. Suppl. **109**, 8–14 (2007)
2. Surveillance of Cerebral Palsy in Europe: Prevalence and characteristics of children with cerebral palsy in Europe. Dev. Med. Child Neurol. **44**(9), 633–40 (2002)
3. Novak, I., Mcintyre, S., Morgan, C., Campbell, L., Dark, L., Morton, N.: A systematic review of interventions for children with cerebral palsy: state of the evidence. Dev. Med. Child Neurol. **55**(10), 885–910 (2013). https://doi.org/10.1111/dmcn.12246
4. Bonnechère, B., et al.: Can serious games be incorporated with conventional treatment of children with cerebral palsy? A review. Research In Developmental Disabilities **35**(8), pp. 1899–1913. https://doi.org/10.1016/j.ridd.2014.04.016
5. Lohse, K., Shirzad, N., Verster, A., Hodges, N., Van der Loos, H.: Video games and rehabilitation. J. Neurol. Phys. Ther. **37**(4), 166–175 (2013)
6. Andrade, K. Pasqual, T. Caurin, G. Crocomo, M.: Dynamic difficulty adjustment with evolutionary algorithm in games for rehabilitation robotics. In: 2016 IEEE International Conference On Serious Games And Applications For Health (SeGAH) (2016). https://doi.org/10.1109/segah.2016.7586277
7. Aponte, M., Levieux, G., Natkin, S.: Measuring the level of difficulty in single player video games. Entertain. Comput. **2**(4), 205–2013 (2011)
8. Mourato, F., Santos.M.: Measuring Difficulty in Platform Videogames. CONFERENCE, : 4ª Conferência Nacional Interacção humano-computador. At Aveiro, Portugal (2010)
9. Darzi, A., Goršič, M., Novak, D.: Difficulty adaptation in a competitive arm rehabilitation game using real-time control of arm electromyogram and respiration. In: CONFERENCE ICORR (2017) https://doi.org/10.1109/ICORR.2017.8009356
10. Glauco, A. Caurin, P. Adriano, A. Siqueira, G. Andrade, O. Ricardo, C. Hermano, I.: Adaptive strategy for multi-user robotic rehabilitation games
11. Aponte, M., Levieux, G., Natkin, S.: Scaling the level of difficulty in single player video games. In: Natkin, S., Dupire, J. (eds.) ICEC 2009. LNCS, vol. 5709, pp. 24–35. Springer, Heidelberg (2009). https://doi.org/10.1007/978-3-642-04052-8_3
12. Berseth, G. Haworth, M. Kapadia, M. Faloutsos, P.: Characterizing and optimizing game level difficulty. In: CONFERENCE 2014, MIG, Playa Vista, California, pp. 153–160 (2014). https://doi.org/10.1145/2668084.2668100

An Application to Promote Emotional Skills in Children with Autism Spectrum Disorders

José Azevedo[1] , Vinicius Silva[2] , Filomena Soares[1,2(✉)] ,
Ana Paula Pereira[3] , and João Sena Esteves[1,2]

[1] Department of Industrial Electronics, University of Minho, Guimaraes,
Portugal
a70448@alunos.uminho.pt, {fsoares,sena}@dei.uminho.pt
[2] Algoritmi Research Centre, University of Minho, Guimaraes, Portugal
a65312@alunos.uminho.pt
[3] Research Center on Education, Institute of Education, University of Minho,
Braga, Portugal
appereira@ie.uminho.pt

Abstract. This paper presents an approach regarding the use of a serious game with a playware object to improve the development of emotional skills in children with Autism Spectrum Disorder (ASD). The playware object is an interactive way for the user to play the game. It acts as the game controller, has six buttons, each displaying an emoji with a different facial expression, and communicates wirelessly with the android device through Bluetooth. For this purpose, the six facial expressions tested are happiness, sadness, fear, anger, surprise and a neutral/normal, which were implemented in three different game activities: imitation, recognition, and storytelling. The avatars used in the game to represent these facial expressions were first validated through an on-line questionnaire (with 114 answers) with a mean success rate of 96.2%. In order to assess the usability of the game and the playware object, a test was performed with six typically developing children, with 94.4% answer accuracy. At last, the recognition activity was tested with six children with ASD during three/four sessions. Due to the small group test and the short number of sessions, the goal was to test the acceptance of the game rather than the users' improvement in the activity. It is worth referring that both the serious game and the playware object had a high level of approval from the children and they expressed their interest during the activities. With this preliminary study its intended to contribute to the development of pedagogical resources to be used by professionals and families in the support of children with ASD.

Keywords: Serious games · Playware · Autism spectrum disorder
Emotions

1 Introduction

Emotions play an essential part in our everyday social interactions as human beings, reason why being capable of identifying them is so important. According to Paul Ekman, humans have six basic emotions: happiness, anger, surprise, sadness, fear and disgust [1] – and the ability to understand and express them starts developing from birth.

© Springer Nature Switzerland AG 2018
S. Göbel et al. (Eds.): JCSG 2018, LNCS 11243, pp. 282–287, 2018.
https://doi.org/10.1007/978-3-030-02762-9_30

Children with Autism Spectrum Disorder (ASD) have difficulties to identify and replicate emotions, as well as interpreting and controlling them. Opposite to the vast majority of babies who can understand these facial expressions by 12 months of age, these individuals have impairments in developing emotional responses and only by 5–7 years of age are they able to recognize happy and sad emotions. This difficulty is present in their life even as adults [2].

The recognition of emotions improves the social relation between children with and without ASD [3–5]. Tanaka et al. [6] reinforce this position, explaining that ASD is characterized by difficulties in terms of socio emotional reciprocity and that success in social interactions goes through the ability to recognize and interpret facial emotions in social context.

Mobile applications have already proved to be a successful aid for therapists and teachers in a learning environment, by facilitating the intake of information by individuals with ASD. Many studies using serious games have already been done, exploring different purposes such as education and therapy [7].

Serious games is the term associated with games that move beyond entertainment to deliver engaging interactive media to support learning [7]. Their focus is to facilitate the learning of important topics by making the entire process more appealing and fun. This way, the user is willingly engaged in an activity that they enjoy and the assimilation of knowledge is not so much a burden but more something that happens naturally.

This work is inserted in a larger project with the purpose of using robots and serious games to improve the social life of children with ASD. This way, a playware was included in the project, which has the function of motivating the user to engage in the activities that the serious game has to offer. The goal of the work presented in this paper is to evaluate the acceptance of the developed application (serious game and playware object) by the target group.

This article is divided in five sections: Sect. 2 addresses the materials and methods utilized, serious game is presented in Sect. 3, the obtained results are discussed in Sects. 4 and 5 ends with the conclusions.

2 Materials and Methods

The serious game is divided into three different activities. The first one is the replication/imitation of emotions by the user; the second is centered on the recognition of emotions and the last activity is a story mode with fifteen different scenarios, each with its own narrative. These stories were already validated by the work developed by Costa [8]. The main resource that was utilized during the development of this project is Unity. Unity is a common game engine that supports both 2D and 3D game development. It also has a free version for students and a large online community with members that are mutually helpful.

Playware is the term attributed to the use of intelligent technology that aims at producing playful experiences through the combined use of both hardware and software [9]. Following these lines, this project integrates a peripheral that makes use of a microcontroller and six buttons (each with a different emoji) to send the user inputs to the software by Bluetooth (Fig. 1).

Fig. 1. Playware object developed to control the game

3   The Serious Game

The serious game has a simple and intuitive design. Due to its objective and target audience, the chosen language is Portuguese. The main menu allows the user to select the desired game mode or to access the options panel which has the possibility to regulate the output volume, start the Bluetooth connection with the playware object and to check the scoreboard.

The scoreboard registers the current activity that is being played, followed by the facial expression displayed, the answer provided by the user and finally how long it took the user to provide that answer, in seconds.

Furthermore, the application utilizes audio not only to tell the different narratives during story mode, but also as a positive or negative feedback depending on the user's answer, as well to explain how to play each activity.

The three game activities implemented in the serious game are as follow:

- **Imitation:** Initially, it is displayed a screen in which the user can listen to the game mode's instructions on how to play it and upon any button press the activity begins. The user is supposed to be accompanied by a therapist or a teacher which has the function to check if the children is performing the activity correctly and register which emotion he/she is displaying. It also has the task to motivating the user to participate in the activity.
- **Recognition:** As in the previous game mode, it starts with a screen which allows the user to listen to the instructions of how to play. In this case the therapist only has the role of being a motivating agent and ensuring that the user is playing correctly. The user is engaging with the playware and after seeing the emotion displayed on the screen, he/she is free to choose the button that more accurately matches it, after stating what emotion it is.
- **Storytelling:** After listening to the game mode's instructions the activity begins. For each scenario a unique narrative associated with it is played, ending with a

question that prompts the user to provide an answer. This answer is the emotion that the main character would feel in the situation that was described. The child must select the corresponding emoji face in the playware object that reflects the emotional state of the avatar.

4 Results

Several tests were performed in the elementary school with typically developing children and children with ASD. The ethical concerns associated with this type of study were previously ensured: a protocol was formed between the parts, elementary school and university, and the informed consents were signed by the parents/tutors of the children that participated in the studies.

In the following sub-sections are presented the results gathered from the different phases of testing and validation, regarding the second activity mode – recognition of emotions.

4.1 Avatars Validation

After creating the different avatars representing each of the six facial expressions there was a need to validate the suitability and relevance of those images before implementing them in the application. For this purpose, an online questionnaire was developed and presented to different groups of teenagers and professionals with experience in aiding students with ASD, with ages ranging between 17 and 58 years old. The volunteers were asked to answer 6 pairs of questions (previously validated by an specialist in the field of ASD), each pair being composed by a question where they had to label the emotion that the avatar was portraying, followed by a second question where they were asked to specify how well that emotion was being represented by the avatar, in a scale of 1 to 5.

In total, the form had 114 submissions and each image had an accuracy of over 90% regarding the emotion that it was trying to portrait. These numbers correspond to fear – 94.7%, surprise – 93%, neutral – 95.6%, happiness – 99.1%, sadness – 98.2% and anger – 99.1%.

4.2 Tests with Typically Developing Children

The next step was to test the activity with typically developing children. The target group was constituted of six children and each played once. They were asked to look at the avatars and after stating what emotion it was representing they would choose the emoji they considered to more accurately represent it (recognition game mode). The accuracy of their answers was 94.4%. These children showed no difficulty playing the game or interacting with the playware object and stated that it was enjoyable, and they would do it again.

4.3   Tests with Children with ASD

The recognition activity was performed with children with ASD. The goal was to test if the children were able to interact with the playware object in a friendly way and could understand the game activity. The success of the activity was measured in terms of response time and number of correct answers. These two indicators allow extrapolating how the child is accepting the game scenario.

The test group was composed of six children but only five ended up performing the activity for more than one session, since one of them could not concentrate in the game and did not participate at all.

From the other five subjects (referred as child S1 to S5 in the following), with ages ranging between six to ten years old, the game data was gathered regarding if the answer was correct or not and the time they took to give that answer. Table 1 displays the average response time and the percentage of correct answers obtained per session and per child.

Table 1. Data gathered from the testing with children with ASD (S – Subject; AT – Average Time; AA – Answer Accuracy)

S	Session 1		Session 2		Session 3		Session 4	
	AT (s)	AA (%)	AT (s)	AA (%)	AT (s)	AA (%)	AT (s)	AA (%)
S1	4.7	100.0	5.7	100.0	–	–	–	–
S2	11.5	83.3	5.5	100.0	5.5	100.0	–	–
S3	5.5	92.3	5.7	100.0	6.8	100.0	–	–
S4	11.4	40.0	14.0	12.5	18.5	35.7	–	–
S5	14.7	50.0	9.1	77.8	16.7	100.0	29.0	66.7

Even though our main objective during this last testing phase was to find out how engaging this application was for children with ASD, it is also possible to notice improvements in their answers during the sessions. It is worth noting that S4 was very young and showed a significant attention deficit, which led him to ignore the game and focus on the avatars on the screen. S5 demonstrated a lot of interest but still had many difficulties interpreting emotions.

Everyone interacted well with the application (except S4), performing the tasks accordingly to the instructions (later, many were able to do so even without the therapist's support) and expressed their fondness for the game.

5   Conclusions

This paper presents the application developed using a serious game and playware object to promote social interaction with children with ASD. The main goal of this study was to develop and validate an application intended to contribute to the development of pedagogical resources to be used by professionals and families in the support of children with ASD, and its impact validated in future work.

The system was first tested with typically developing children in order to evaluate the application constraints. Then, four sessions were followed with six children with ASD. The purpose of the game and the instructions on how to play it were very well assimilated and the playware object alongside the serious game revealed itself to be a very attractive and intuitive tool to interact with. The first tests with children with ASD allowed to infer that using serious games with playware object as intermediate in the interaction may be an adequate tool. In fact, children react positively, giving the answers by pressing the buttons. In general, the children improved their success rate when interacting with the game.

Future work involves further tests that are mandatory to validate if the skill (emotional behavior) was in fact acquired, with more children with ASD and a higher number of sessions, covering all the game activities. This would allow to extrapolate more accurate and reliable results regarding the use of playware objects with serious games in the intervention sessions with children with ASD.

Acknowledgements. The authors would like to express their acknowledgments to COMPETE: POCI-01-0145-FEDER-007043 and FCT – Fundação para a Ciência e Tecnologia (in Portuguese) within the Project Scope: UID/CEC/00319/2013. Vinicius Silva also thanks FCT for the PhD scholarship SFRH/BD/SFRH/BD/133314/2017. The authors thanks the teachers and students of the Elementary School of Gualtar (EB1/JI Gualtar) in Braga for the participation in the tests.

References

1. Ekman, P., et al.: Universals and cultural differences in the judgments of facial expressions of emotion. J. Pers. Soc. Psychol. **53**(4), 712–717 (1987)
2. Begeer, S., Koot, H.M., Rieffe, C., Meerum Terwogt, M., Stegge, H.: Emotional competence in children with autism: diagnostic criteria and empirical evidence. Dev. Rev. **28**(3), 342–369 (2008)
3. Kasari, C., Rotheram-Fuller, E., Locke, J., Gulsrud, A.: Making the connection: randomized controlled trial of social skills at school for children with autism spectrum disorders. J. Child Psychol. Psychiatry **53**(4), 431–439 (2012)
4. Sivaratnam, C.S., Cornish, K., Gray, K.M., Howlin, P., Rinehart, N.J.: Brief report: assessment of the social-emotional profile in children with autism spectrum disorders using a novel comic strip task. J. Autism Dev. Disord. **42**(11), 2505–2512 (2012)
5. Salomone, E., Bulgarelli, D., Thommen, E., Rossini, E.: Role of age and IQ in emotion understanding in autism spectrum disorder: implications for educational interventions. Eur. J. Spec. Needs Educ. **6257**, 1–9 (2018)
6. Tanaka, J.W., et al.: The perception and identification of facial emotions in individuals with autism spectrum disorders using the let's face it! Emotion skills battery. J. Child Psychol. Psychiatry Allied Discip. **53**(12), 1259–1267 (2012)
7. Noor, H., Shahbodin, F., Pee, N.: Serious game for autism children: review of literature. World Acad. Sci. **6**(4), 554–559 (2012)
8. Costa, S.C.C.: Affective robotics for socio-emotional development in children with autism spectrum disorders (2014)
9. Lund, H.H., Klitbo, T., Jessen, C.: Playware technology for physically activating play. Artif. Life Robot. **9**(4), 165–174 (2005)

SmartLife – Exergames and Smart Textiles to Promote Energy-Related Behaviours Among Adolescents

Jorge Doménech[1(✉)], Josué Ferri[1], Ruben Costa[2], Pedro Oliveira[2],
Antonio Grilo[2], Greet Cardon[3], Ann DeSmet[3], Ayla Schwarz[3],
Jeroen Stragier[3], Andrew Pomazanskyi[4], and Jevgenijs Danilins[4]

[1] AITEX – Asociación de Investigación de la Industria Textil,
03801 Alcoy, Alicante, Spain
jdomenech@aitex.es
[2] KB Consulting, 2804-537 Almada, Portugal
[3] Department of Movement and Sport Sciences, Ghent University,
9000 Ghent, Belgium
[4] Nurogames Gmbh, 50676 Cologne, Germany

Abstract. SmartLife aims to promote healthy living habits and avoid sedentary lifestyles in adolescents by creating a mobile game that requires lower body movement, and uses tailored feedback, based on physical activity indices measured by a smart shirt. To date, no serious games exist that tailor game play by real-time feedback on achievement of the target behaviour. This approach can improve current exergames by reaching higher levels of intensity in physical activity, which is needed to impact on health. The tailored approach also supports competence and feasibility and hence reduces drop-out and injury risks.

SmartLife combines exergame and smart textiles. Gaming experience is tailored according to feedbacks and the physical activity indices measured by the smart shirt providing the user with better game experience.

Consequently, SmartLife holds the potential to contribute to better health by exergaming. A mobile exergame has been developed in co-creation with the target group and improved in an iterative testing process.

Keywords: Smart textile · Exergame · Adolescents · Data analytics
Lifestyle · Game · Gaming · Sensor

1 Introduction

Energy-related behaviours (physical activity, sedentary behaviour) are main modifiable determinants of several non-communicable health conditions, e.g. diabetes type 2, overweight and obesity, and track into adulthood [1]. Promoting these behaviours among youngsters can have great health and societal gains. Meeting these recommendations shows a strong decline in adolescence and is especially low among adolescent girls and those of lower socio-economic status. These unhealthy lifestyles are known to hinder several areas of physical [2] and psychosocial development for youngsters, and to be associated with a lower academic achievement [3]. An

S. Göbel et al. (Eds.): JCSG 2018, LNCS 11243, pp. 288–293, 2018.
https://doi.org/10.1007/978-3-030-02762-9_31

intervention to promote energy-related behaviours among adolescents is thus indicated and may also address social inclusion. Exergames, which require movement to be played, have great yet underused potential to promote these behaviours. To fully utilise this potential, exergames need to promote moderate-to-vigorous physical activity; need to be tailored to the individual user; and need to be more engaging. SmartLife project aims to create such an exergame. This project is co-funded by the Horizon 2020 Programme of the European Commission under Grant Agreement No. 732348.

2   Introduction

SmartLife exergame is a mobile game, which requires lower body movements. The game combines with a textile with smart wearables which can be a valid method for measuring physical activity [4], and for example provide immediate feedback (e.g. heartrate, respiration, movement…) and ensures exercises are performed at a moderate-to-vigorous intensity level. The sensors send the information to the user's Smartphone and the game adapts to the physical conditions of the player in order to promote healthy living habits and avoid sedentary behaviours in adolescents in such a way as to reduce the risk of suffering cardiovascular diseases at early ages.

The game is tailored to individual user's needs, using the smart textile data, and based on available evidence and big data analysis. Furthermore, SmartLife try being highly engaging, e.g. by adding a narrative and context information, and using user input throughout the design ('participatory development'). At the end of the project will have two main outputs, the exergame for mobile phones and the development of an intelligent garment in which wearable movement sensors such as accelerometers, gyroscopes and magnetographs is integrated. These objectives are realized within the following SmartLife features.

2.1   Wearable Sensor System

A wearable sensor system has been developed and integrated into textile, for example: t-shirts, wrist bands, bands, etc.; which monitors adolescents' physical activity and sedentary behaviour by obtaining data such as movement of the user while playing the SmartLife game. These sensors integrated into textile are able to send physical activity and sedentary behaviour parameters of the player to the game and the game adapts the activities to the physical condition of the player.

The electronics include physical movement sensors, but also additional functions such as processed activity data obtained from the sensor data, this allows sending relevant information to the game already processed ir real time. This could be controlling different aspects of the game like speed, difficulty, etc. according to the physical activity.

2.2   SmartLife Exergame and Narrative

The game consists of a mobile game requiring lower body movement where the player has to move to meet the game challenges. Specific game features have been tested together with the target group. Thanks to this game, SmartLife promotes active and healthy habits among adolescents, making them run, move or jump for example. The game is synchronized with the wearable sensor system and connected to a community of players where players could share their results with other players encouraging them to improve and obtain better results (Fig. 1).

Fig. 1. First draft of the game shelter

Exciting game mechanics have been developed to engage the users that leads the player in an entertaining narrative experience. The story takes place in a post-apocalyptic world and can be played indoors and outside with a focus on mini challenges that require physical activities that are tracked by a smart textile the player must wear. In the game the user slips into the role of a human survivor in a post-apocalyptic steam punk scenario. This character lives alone in a shelter surrounded by a contaminated abandoned environment. He only can survive by maintaining the shelter's power supply and by exploring the surroundings to gain new resources from time to time. Should the character desire to explore the environment, he or she must wear a protective suit that unfortunately has a limited power, therefore forcing to return to the shelter in time. With the help of the radio set, the player gets in contact with other survivors and finds out that there is a clean decontaminated island next to the coast where other survivors are building up a new livelihood. With this good news in mind, the player must lead the survivor to the coast step by step, increasing the range of the suit durability, improving the shelter together with the help of some robots.

The SmartLife game consists of several goals that can be seen as the main drivers of the game and supporting activities to ensure longevity of the gameplay as well as a long-term engagement. The overall goals of the SmartLife Game are:

- Survive in the present!
- Get in touch and meet up with other survivors!
- Find a way to reach the coast in order to travel to the save island!

As part of interactive storytelling scenarios, a number of narration types are differentiated. These can be narrated to the level the player is currently playing on or to the activities they are performing.

Narration Related to Level - The story tells with the use of events that appear in form of pop-ups with text, illustrations and sometimes voice over dialogs. These events are triggered by the player's progress in the game that is expressed in their current level.

Narration Related to Activities - Some of the activities the player has to execute (outside, inside, daily jobs, other players) are introduced with a story snippet that is related to different situations, NPCs and places. During each activity, the player is accompanied by the navigator bot via radio set that gives status updates to the player via headset or smartphone internal speaker. Some of these updates also contain story relevant texts.

Some of the story events allow the player to influence the story by making decisions via multiple choice answers. These selections influence the progress of the story in different ways therefore ensuring non-linearity of the gameplay and increases perceived autonomy and sense of control. During the performance of the physical activities, the story experience is also related to and influenced by the intensity level of the user that is tracked by the smart textile (T-Shirt).

2.3   Game Data Analytics

Data collection, cleaning and fusion services, can use the collected data to classify physical activity. The users' physical activity can be classified in two separate ways, activity type or activity intensity. Regarding activity intensity, the main objective is to identify when the user is doing moderate to vigorous physical activity (MVPA). Since the project aims to promote physical activity and reduce sedentary behaviour, it's very important to be able to detect when the user is doing the so called MVPA. This identification is made in real-time and is directly connected with the game itself. Classifying physical activity type is the other classification method that was developed. The activity type was considered, in order to add an extra layer of activity identification and to allow a better personalized gaming experience to each user, by label them depending on the type of exercise they usually perform. This type of classification is done in an offline mode and using two different types of input, activity index (AI) and raw accelerometer data, both collected from the wearable sensor. In short, a creative model has been used in the Data Collection Module to measure the intensity and magnitude of the activities, but for detecting the activity type, a more complex data analytics model had to be developed.

A common approach to data analysis, usually requires applying machine learning algorithms to data. Among various tasks of data mining, supervised classification is suitable for activity recognition task. Classification is used to categorize data into predefined classes. In this sense, by defining a set of activities, a classification model can reveal the activity performed at the time of data collection. The data collected from the sensor is used in Data Analytics module to train a classifier for detecting six different activities: Still, Walking, Brisk Walking, Running, Up Stairs, Down Stairs. Supervised learning models, sometimes also referred as predictive models, use a set of known data samples (training data) to build a model for predicting the value of unknown occurrences. The training data is used to find relations between values in the same class and later can be applied to unknown data (testing data) to find the most similar class for it. Hence, like any other classification application, activity classification requires to train a classification model based on labelled activity data and then use the model to predict the label of unlabeled activities.

The collected data from the sensor is captured by the smartphone and used by the Data Collection Module in real-time to calculate users' MVPA. While this data is being used in real-time, it is also saved locally on the device in a SQLite database to lately serve as an input to the offline data analytics module. When measuring physical activity, the data usually includes noise in the start and in the end of the activities data that can reduce the accuracy of the model. The noise on the collected data can occur for several reasons such as the time difference between starting the data collection in the app and start doing the exercise. Another type of noise can come from the sensor itself, since if the data collection process starts mid-exercise, the first values are always off the normal expected values. Thus, before providing the activity data as training data into the model, it is necessary to **clean it**. Machine learning and statistics techniques can also be used for automatic outlier detection and removal. The objective in outlier removal is to eliminate the observations that are very different from the others and considered as polluted. These deviant observations can be detected using standard deviation.

The accelerometer sensor provides data in two modes, AI and 3-axis acceleration. While 3-axis data can provide more details about the situation of the player for detecting the physical activity, AI mode consumes less energy and can be used for longer playing sessions. Two different **training models** have been developed for recognising the activities of the players in each mode of the sensor. The first model uses machine methods such as Decision Tree to do the activity classification using AI data and the second uses deep learning methods for implementing a Neural Network to predict the activity using 3-axial data of the sensor.

After the training process, the model is ready to be used to identify the activity type that the user is performing. The activity type model is able to predict which type of exercise the user is doing, based on the similarity between the data being collected and the occurrences that had been used in the training phase. The output of the model is the activity label usually including a prediction certainty value.

References

1. Craigie, A.M., Lake, A.A., Kelly, S.A., Adamson, A.J., Mathers, J.C.: Tracking of obesity-related behaviours from childhood to adulthood: a systematic review. Maturitas **70**, 266–284 (2011)
2. Hills, A.P., King, N.A., Armstrong, T.J.: The contribution of physical activity and sedentary behaviours to the growth and development of children and adolescents: implications for overweight and obesity. Sports Med. **37**(6), 533–546 (2007)
3. Biddle, S.J.H., Asare, M.: Physical activity and mental health in children and adolescents: a review of reviews. Br. J. Sports Med. **45**, 886–895 (2011)
4. Evenson, K.R., Goto, M.M., Furberg, R.D.: Systematic review of the validity and reliability of consumer-wearable activity trackers. Int. J. Behav. Nutr. Phys. Act. **12**, 159–181 (2015)

Author Index

Printed in the United States
By Bookmasters